The
Management
of
People
in
Hotels
Restaurants
and
Clubs

DONALD E. LUNDBERG
JAMES P. ARMATAS

The Management
of People
in Hotels,
Restaurants, and Clubs

DONALD E. LUNDBERG
Professor in charge
Restaurant and Hotel Management Program
University of Massachusetts

JAMES P. ARMATAS
Consulting Psychologist
Thomas and Associates
Mission, Kansas

WM. C. BROWN COMPANY PUBLISHERS
135 SOUTH LOCUST STREET • DUBUQUE, IOWA 52003

2-17-65

003

86.00

TX 911

.L79

1964

Manufactured by WM. C. BROWN CO. INC., Dubuque, Iowa

Printed in U. S. A.

Table of Contents

Introduction

Traditionally management in business has been said to deal with the five m's -- men, materials, money, machines, and methods. By all odds the most important and most complicated of the m's is men, for they are thinking animals whose needs proliferate, whose desires change, whose morale fluctuates, whose feelings influence all behavior. The motivation of people has occupied the best minds since man emerged out of the lower animal state. All leaders of men are concerned with setting goals and motivating people to strive towards those goals. Hotel and restaurant managers are no exception. This book, then, is concerned with people management.

Why not title the book Personnel Management? The reason lies in the fact that the subject of personnel management has developed into a discipline which is aimed largely at persons who intend to work as personnel managers, few of whom are found in the hotel and restaurant business. This book is for every manager and for every supervisor. Theory is illustrated with practice, and practice is drawn from the hotel and restaurant field.

Necessarily the book is based upon an attitude towards man and human nature.

Healthy human beings want to work. They need management to help them arrive at goals and encouragement to learn techniques by which goals can be reached. People are not lazy by nature unless they have learned that it is more pleasant to avoid than to perform certain kinds of work.

Much of the work in the hotel and restaurant field is intrinsically satisfying because it brings employees into contact with other people, mostly in pleasant surroundings, and rewards are forthcoming for performing work for these people, the customers or guests. Much of the work in a hotel or restaurant is unpleasant, and it is the function of management and of wages and other benefits to overcome a natural reluctance to perform unsatisfying work.

People by nature seek out groups and attach themselves to them. Since people are social animals, there are intrinsic rewards in being part of a hotel and restaurant staff, provided the staff is fairly harmonious within itself and has no active dislike for the management.

Management has more responsibilities than do employees, performs work which may be as unpleasant as much of the work done by the employees, may have to strive harder psychically than do employees, and receives rewards for this extra effort and extra ability.

The goals of the management of a hotel or restaurant are not the same as those of the employees. It is management's job to try to bring management's and employees' goals in as close harmony as will permit maximum productivity and earnings for the hotel or restaurant. To do this requires constant sensitivity to the "human problems," the definition and redefinition of goals, the constant reaffirmation of the value of the product and the communication of enthusiasm for the goals of the hotel or restaurant.

Much of management knowledge is intuitive and grows out of the learning experience of the person as he matures. Experience in management is essential to the development of a first-class manager. At the same time, much of management can be learned from books such as this.

Greedy management or ownership can or has resulted in fortunes. Greed is associated primarily with short-term gains and is not compatible with effective management in the long run. Workers today are selective about where, how, and for whom they work. Management should expect to share the rewards of an enterprise with the employees.

Management requires capabilities far beyond those demanded by line jobs in a hotel or restaurant and so should be rewarded accordingly.

Management should be assigned certain responsibilities, and these responsibilities should not be lessened too much by employee committees or union desires. Management must manage, be given authority and be made accountable for management.

v

The management of people in any enterprise is probably the most complex and demanding aspect of that enterprise. In the hotel and restaurant business the challenge is even greater than in other businesses. People management in hotels, restaurants and clubs is more complex simply because more cultures are involved. The accents heard in a restaurant kitchen may be Spanish, French, Hungarian, or mixtures. Between 35 and 40 per cent of the restaurant employees in New York City, for example, are Puerto Rican or Negro. The management of people must necessarily take into account these national origins, their different belief systems, and their values.

Many of the employees in the hotel, restaurant and club business come from the less privileged groups, the disenfranchised, and from those who have had little opportunity for education or for the advantages in life. Their motivation level may be low simply because they have had few "winning" experiences and see little advantage in extending themselves if they never can win.

The sheer size of the industry makes it important. According to the Census of Business of 1958 there were about 29,000 hotels and over 41,000 motels with annual receipts exceeding $3 1/2 billion. The industry employed nearly 500,000 people and had a payroll exceeding $1 billion.

Commercial food sales, food eaten away from the home, accounted for an income in excess of $13 billion in 1963 and over 1 1/2 million people are engaged in this food service.

Because the industry is one of the lowest paying of all industries and because many of the jobs are semiskilled or unskilled, the turnover of employees is much higher than in most other industries. Low wages aggravate the amount of turnover and in part account for the lack of motivation among employees found in many hotels and restaurants.

On the other hand, the industry offers a way of life which to thousands of people is more rewarding than jobs found elsewhere. The industry is made up largely of relatively small establishments, which fact gives the individual opportunity for personal recognition. Most establishments offer steady year-round employment plus the benefits of at least one meal while on the job, uniforms, and other "fringes" not often found in other industries.

The opportunity to work directly with people is rewarding in itself for the thousands of service employees in the industry.

While management in the hotel, restaurant and club industry calls for a person with higher than average energy, the desire to mix with people and a willingness to tackle people problems on almost an hourly basis, the financial rewards are probably as great or greater than could be had for the same amount of ability in other fields, and there's always the opportunity to go into business for oneself.

The information, techniques and philosophy expressed in this book are those which can be used by a person with a title of personnel manager and also by any person who is managing people.

The person holding the title of personnel administrator or manager in a hotel or restaurant organization does a variety of jobs, depending upon the philosophy of the chief executive or owner, the training and philosophy of the personnel person, and the complexity of the organization. In a small hotel the personnel manager is often little more than a clerk, placing advertisements for personnel, arranging for job applicants to fill out application forms, maintaining vacation records, home telephone numbers and the like. A more appropriate title would be personnel clerk, and the salary for the position is appropriate to a clerk. In the Hot Shoppes organization the personnel department comprises some forty people.

In some large organizations the personnel administrator is really an assistant to the chief executive, whose principal function is to deal with outbreaks of labor unrest and to negotiate with union officials. His title is then more appropriately vice-president of industrial relations.

In one large restaurant organization in New York City, the personnel director spends much of his time visiting the restaurants of his competitors, enticing those employees who perform well to come with his organization.

Often the job of personnel director is not clearly defined, largely because the personnel function is not a part of the thinking or philosophy of top management. What the personnel director finally does in his day-to-day work is likely to emphasize recruitment, cursory selection and whatever else the situation requires.

In some cases he finds himself working the cafeteria counter line in an emergency or training employees if he happens to have job skills. In other organizations he may find himself as a principal advisor to the president, provided the president has confidence in him.

In short, the requirements of a personnel administrator -- regardless of whether he be in a large or small organization -- may vary from "everything to nothing."

This book provides some degree of history, philosophy, tradition, and system which may serve as a practical guideline for anyone engaged in the management of people in hotels and restaurants.

The Management Process

The management of people is a continuous process which goes on day after day, the manager or supervisor relating to the employees in a number of ways. Basic to management is planning, anticipating the future -- both the immediate and the more distant future. Planning can be formal or informal. Plans can be written down or kept in the mind. Planning precedes almost all business action, or should precede it.

In management, after planning come communication and decision-making. These three processes are involved in almost every aspect of management.

In the management wheel illustrated, planning, communicating, and decision-making are placed in the center of the wheel because they are central to and part of the other functions. Around the outside of the wheel we see that management is engaged in recruiting personnel, selecting them, training them, and appraising them. Management is also involved in setting standards and goals, in delegating responsibility, authority, and accountability, and in motivating people to accomplish the goals and standards which have been set. Finally management controls people in one or several ways.

MANAGEMENT OF MEN

Recruiting

Systematizing · · Selecting

Scheduling · · Training

PLANNING
COMMUNICATING
DECISION-MAKING

Controlling · · Appraising

Motivating · · Delegating

Goal and
Standard Setting

The Appropriate Action

Listing the functions of people management is fairly simple. Carrying them out is something else. As in most of life, experience, judgement, drive, and worthwhile goals help to determine the appropriate action to be taken in day-to-day affairs; we never can avoid values. At times a soft-spoken manager may be called upon to be hard-bitten and forceful. In case of emergency he may be required to shout to maintain the necessary control. At times he should "hand hold" with the employees; at other times apply the spur. Some employees will react to his slightest suggestion while others must be verbally hit over the head to get a reaction.

The effective manager systematizes as many of the functions of people management as he can without loading the organization down with red tape. He recognizes that system can be his great ally if it does not smother initiative.

The wise manager recognizes that there is no one best solution for most problems, especially people problems. Too often a manager reviews his decisions with the assumption that he did not pick the right one. Life is too complicated, there are too many variables playing in most situations, to be able to pick a correct solution. Inevitably, there are multiple factors bearing on a problem situation and these are changing so that what might be a good solution at a given moment may no longer be a good one a few hours later.

1

The manager who seeks certainty where there is no certainty cannot help but be disappointed with human affairs and become discouraged. Rather there are probabilities and the player in the drama of life tries to pick the best odds in his favor. To do otherwise creates anxiety, remorse, and dissatisfaction with the self.

The manager in making decisions can help himself in making better decisions if he identifies assumptions on which he is acting. For example, the manager who feels that people are generally lazy, indifferent, ungrateful, will come to different conclusions about the development and training of personnel than the manager who feels that people are generally appreciative, ambitious, and willing to work if given the proper leadership. The first manager will probably want to fire the employee who does not produce since he feels there is no hope for him anyway, while the second manager will be more apt to think of ways to motivate the employee and to find out what is troubling him if he is not producing.

Generally speaking, a decision is no better than the information on which it is based. It should be recognized, however, that seldom does anyone have all the information which applies to the solutions of a particular problem. The executive continually acts in the absence of complete information, using his past experience, his intelligence, and judgement in arriving at a decision which he thinks will be successful or adequate. Then too there is the matter of luck. Once he has arrived at the decision and has gotten as much approval and cooperation as he thinks is feasible at the moment from the people who will carry out the decision, he goes ahead and acts. Should the decision prove to be the wrong one, he spends little time in reviewing what went wrong or in self-castigation. He recognizes that everyone makes wrong decisions, even the most successful of people. He might do well to remember Mark Twain's comment on decision-making to the effect that he felt himself lucky if he were right 51 per cent of the time.

Of course, the competent manager is not a fatalist. He believes that he will profit or suffer from the results of his decisions and actions and that he can influence his destiny and the direction of the enterprise he manages. This belief in positive action and the power to change the tide of affairs marks the American businessman apart from those of several other cultures and partially accounts for the difference of industrial growth between the United States and the rest of the world.

The first step in the solution of any problem is to identify it and try to state it clearly, at least within the mind. The next step is to collect information which bears on the problem and then to frame several solutions. Most businesses are continually making decisions, changing and modifying goals, and are well-advised not to have only one plan ready to accomplish a goal but to have others which can be used in case the first plan fails.

The effective manager usually is skilled in drawing forth the ideas of his associates and of incorporating them into major policy; however, this is not always the case. There are many examples of highly successful businessmen who were autocrats of the first order, who consulted very few people in making their decisions, and couldn't care less if their associates agreed with the decisions. A decision which is the result of group thinking may not be as good as one formed in a superior mind. Since most of us don't have superior minds and can have more effective organizations if the people concerned have a voice in the decisions, we do well to learn techniques for getting interest and cooperation.

One way to get other people's viewpoints is to be willing to listen to them and to listen respectfully. This often takes more time than it is worth, especially when dealing with people who have meager imaginations and little real impact on the effective decision once it is implemented.

Most managers can get more effective results by holding regular staff meetings of department heads. Often the manager unwisely dominates the group and presents a monologue. After a time such meetings lose their effectiveness except to offer a podium from which the manager gives orders. Department heads generally are reluctant to stand up and be counted on any issue and when asked their opinion of a given subject make a ritualized reply which means practically nothing and commits them to nothing. To avoid such nonproductive experiences, the climate of such meetings must be such that the people with ideas will express them and will learn that they will be rewarded for their ideas as well as for their obedience to the ideas of the manager.

It is not effective to go around a conference table and ask each person his opinion, but it is worthwhile to try to identify those who would express themselves if encouraged. An idea, as presented, may not be valuable, but with slight modification might be of use and the manager, or whoever is leading the discussion, often can turn the idea presented in such a way that the person presenting it is enhanced. This encourages others to step forward and be counted.

There are always some people in the group who speak compulsively and for them the meeting is a form of group therapy, but their ideas often only serve to confuse the issue at hand.

In larger organizations the executive lives on a diet of compromise since leadership often rests on an amalgamation of opinion and a fusion of standards. Often compromise is the only way to secure group action and may be much more effective than a more logical idea espoused by one or a few people.

To be effective the manager must enjoy his work, for he depends to a greater degree on his job for his personal satisfactions than most employees. He does not manage simply because he loves to manage just as no man goes fishing just to fish. Management offers other rewards, bringing him into contact with people, giving him a sense of purpose, bringing him the material rewards of the society as well.

He recognizes that he gives up some, or much, of his freedom in being a manager, but it is a bargain which he has made. If it does not work out to his satisfaction in a general way, he should change jobs for something which is satisfying.

Psychological Factors Affecting Decision-Making in Hotels -- Restaurants -- Clubs

Decisions are based on past experience, judgement, and are effected by the amount of steam generated in the emotional system. Because the manager works long hours or is under undue stress, his judgement is likely to be less sharp, less focused, and his decisions less effective.

The economics of marginal utility relate to the manager's use of his own energy as well as to the use of any other resource. Fatigue lowers stress tolerance, resulting in decision-making's being a real effort.

Temper is more easily frayed, things are said which often can never be undone, and less appropriate decisions are made which, when added up, have a cumulative deleterious effect.

The manager who takes a secret pride in displaying his temper over a period of time usually finds that losing one's temper is habit forming, that one day he loses his temper with the wrong people. He becomes less discriminating as to the time and place he dares display temper, and explosive level is reached more quickly.

Some executives with low boiling points have learned to recognize the symptoms that precede the explosion and have developed techniques to avoid it. Auguste Escoffier, the famous chef, had a simple technique for avoiding temper flare-ups: he simply walked off the scene, took a turn around the block, got a new perspective, and returned better able to cope with the problem or person at hand. Not a bad technique for anyone with short fuses!

The manager who cannot control himself has a difficult time controlling others. The famous leaders of men know when to show anger and often do so for dramatic effect. In other words, a display of anger can be effective at the right moment, more so if the individual concerned has not really "lost" his temper, but has it well in hand, directing it for his own purposes.

Righteous indignation, reaction to injustice is a perfectly normal and appropriate response and without it life would undoubtedly be full of more injustice than it now is. The trick is to avoid the smoke point when all of the information about a problem is not in or to know the real intent of a person's remarks which may be taken as offensive. If the manager continually reacts with anger the people around him adjust to it, and any possible desirable effects of stimulating others to greater effort or changing a behavior are soon lost. The manager who cries wolf too often is soon accepted as being overwrought rather than righteously indignant. If he continually spoils for a fight the strong people in his organization will leave. He finds himself with a weak organization full of yes-men, chameleons who are quite ready to do as they are told, up to a point, but who have no real vitality in their personalities or strength of character to force through necessary changes.

Real anger clouds judgement to the point where precise thinking is impossible, overriding past experience, never allowing good judgement to form. The "big" manager apologizes for actions taken in anger, but a steady diet of eating crow does not build confidence in him.

Anger does not permit balanced perspective, nor the consideration of alternatives which may be important. The angry person is not likely to come up with new ideas or new possibilities.

Revenge Is Sweet and Self-Destroying

The manager of a resort hotel suddenly found himself with a revolution on his hands with the entire dining room staff ready to walk out in the middle of a full dining room. His reaction was to identify the ringleader and fire him on the spot. In this case, ownership did not back the manager and he found that he was soon on his way home. While the owners probably should have backed the manager and the manager probably felt "good inside" while doing the firing, this was not the best immediate solution. A desire for revenge on the manager's part often unites employees, but unites them against the management. "Teaching an employee a lesson" seldom affects only one employee. Every other employee is focused on the action and each weighs the significance of the action in terms of his own personal welfare. The manager has a larger class than he bargained for and he may be teaching more about himself than about the subject which he thinks he is putting across. While he is involved in such a lesson his attention is monopolized and he is likely to neglect other decision-making areas.

A continuing desire for revenge festers in the emotional system, coloring the person's attitudes toward life in general and hamstrings his power to function. A grudge eats away like acid at the innards of the person holding it, and even though he may "settle the score" he really loses in the end.

Often when something is done in anger or in revenge, guilt feelings well up and the person hastens to make amends in one form or another, frequently to the detriment of the hotel or restaurant. The manager may say yes when he should say no, compromising his responsibility. He may even go so far as to promote a person he has offended even though such a promotion is unjustified. He may hesitate to exercise critical judgement and pay penance for his personal acts.

Anxiety Lowers the Smoke Point

The condition illustrated by the military expression, "pushing the panic button," can be brought on by extended anxiety or by the build-up of tension as a result of not being able to structure a situation or to formulate a plan of attack on problems. Acute fright paralyzes mental and physical activity, can precipitate action which is unreasonable and completely unappropriate. Taking on too much responsibility triggers anxiety because the person becomes anxious about jobs which have not been done. The lack of time to complete everything to which he is committed gnaws not only at his conscience but at his stomach. The hard-driving manager is likely to take on too much, which is fair neither to himself nor to the hotel or restaurant. He has not learned to delegate or he feels that asking for an assistant is an admission that he cannot take the job in stride. In many instances he may be wise to back off, absolutely refuse to take on further commitments, or to insist upon having additional assistance. He must restrain his competitive desire to take on more than he can handle. Hard work may be satisfying, but unfinished work is seldom so.

The Need for Consistency in Decision-Making

Human beings want a predictable environment and the manager of the hotel or restaurant is in a critical position to develop or fail to develop consistency in the environment. Experiments with animals show that they can become conditioned to withstand considerable pain and inconvenience and will accept it; as long as it is predictable, they know what to expect. The animal becomes neurotic when it does not know what to expect, even though the inconvenience or pain in itself is not severe. Human beings are much the same and the capricious manager -- the fellow who cannot be predicted -- keeps everyone in a state of alarm simply because he cannot be predicted. If the manager makes decisions according to the time of the day, his own level of fatigue, or his buoyancy at the moment employees are hard pressed to figure out the timing and the conditions for approaching him. If a person gets a reprimand one day for doing something, a grin the next day for doing the same thing he becomes confused and would rather have the reprimand, if it is predictable. The old saying that "it is not the severity of the punishment, but the certainty of it which is important" has relevance to all of supervision. The fact that "you can count on old George" even though you can count on him to do the wrong thing is somehow more satisfying to his associates than if "you don't know what George will do next."

Levels of Decisions

It is useful when thinking about decision-making to differentiate between decisions according to their importance to the hotel or restaurant and the magnitude of their effect. By dividing them into three levels the management sometimes can save time by restricting itself to first- and second-level decisions.

First-level decisions can be thought of as those that are most critical for the success of the enterprise. Decisions concerning location, menu, broad personnel policy, and standards fall into this group. Second-level decisions might be thought of as operating decisions, while third-level decisions are routine decisions made by workers engaged in performing work of a routine nature. The chart on the opposite page lists some typical decisions which fall into the three classifications. In a chain operation top management ordinarily deals with the first-level decisions, while store managers or individual hotel managers are concerned with the second level.

EXAMPLES OF THREE KINDS OF DECISIONS

First-Level (broad decisions)	Second-Level (operating decisions)	Third-Level (performance decisions)
Location	Kind of detergent to buy	When to remove a hamburger from the griddle
Sanitation standards	Applicant's qualifications	How to make a soft-serve cone with a twist at the top
Menu	Inspecting deliveries	
Personnel policy	Checking ad results	How to slice an onion
Food quality standards	Whether to fill in for absent employee	How to mop a floor
Advertising and promotion policy	Number of portions to produce	When to mop a floor
Manager's role		When to call a purveyor
Rate structure		

Unconscious Factors Affecting Decisions

It is also helpful in thinking about decision-making to recognize the influence of unconscious factors. All of us make important decisions without being completely aware of the influences which directed them. The following chart illustrates how the unconscious mind interacts with the conscious mind in making a decision.

EXAMPLE OF THE DECISION-MAKING PROCESS

● The Problem: Is a particular location good for a restaurant?
● The Decision: "Yes" or "No"

CRUST OF RELUCTANCE TO RISK MAKING AN IMPORTANT DECISION

Conscious Level	Automobile traffic	Drainage features	Cost of lot
	Pedestrian traffic Size of lot	Competition	Speed zone

| Unconscious Level | Past experience with similar sites | Likes and dislikes for the neighborhood | Health of the person making the decision | How the site affects the person's picture of himself and his need for status and success |

Two Trends in Management

In modern America, the management of people has followed two trends, the Scientific Management Trend and the Human Relations Trend.

The Scientific Management Trend. This movement began almost a century ago and has had tremendous influence on management practices. The scientific management era has been credited to F. W. Taylor and Frank Gilbreth, both of whom were interested in improving the efficiency and technology of industry. Gilbreth, for example, made numerous experiments designed to reduce human exertion in the construction industry. Following these two pioneers, the scientific management movement has contributed greatly to the systematization and efficiency of American industry.

The improvements resulting from the scientific management movement are the following:

1. Elimination of waste: functionalization, work simplification, motion study, analysis of work flow, standardization, and other systematic procedures.

2. Reduction in the amount of learning required for workers to do jobs.

3. Establishment of clear-cut goals of management.

4. Creation of well-defined channels for communication, decision-making and control.

Serious problems also have been associated with the gains:

1. Pressure has been exerted on workers to produce more; workers have reacted to and resisted this movement.

2. Workers and supervisors have resented someone's showing them how "stupid" they had been.

3. Men have resented the view that their only role was to work and not to contribute anything original to their jobs or to their work.

Human Relations Trend. The second trend developed at the end of World War I as a small attempt to combat some of the problems inherent in the scientific management approach. The one most dramatic study giving impetus to a human relations trend was the famous study of the Hawthorne plant of the Western Electric Company where it was shown that morale and motivation determined how workers reacted to such concrete variables as illumination, ventilation, and fatigue factors. The Hawthorne study and studies subsequent to it showed that workers responded to scientific management principles simply by restricting production to levels which the workers felt were appropriate.

THE HUMAN RELATIONS APPROACH

Human relations is an approach which places a premium on the needs of workers. It is easy to be glib in talking about human relations, but humanistic, democratic philosophies of management are difficult to implement. Whether management admits it or not, there are three strong forces in organizations which work against the total success of human relations approaches.

1. Just as employees have their needs, one of the needs of managers is to maintain their power;

2. Companies are geared strongly toward uniformity and conformity; it is an unusual company that can break completely from such chains;

3. All companies have bureaucratic traditions that are extremely difficult to break. Some of these traditions are valuable in maintaining the organization.

Within the bounds of practicality then, "pure" human relations concepts probably never can be implemented in many organizations. Human relations principles, however, are principles toward which all organizations can strive to self-advantage. As such, effective human relations is not seen as an end in itself but as an approach.

The functions of effective human relations may be conceived of as follows:

1. To Promote Maximum Use of Employee Effort. Workers are most effective and most satisfied when they can utilize the maximum of their abilities. Specifically, this means that "assembly line" operations are not conducive to the best human efforts because human beings have the ability "to use their brains" and to become involved with diverse types of activities. From a practical point of view, of course, it is not always possible to broaden responsibilities. As much as possible, management needs to be concerned with providing employees with greater responsibilities within the scope of their interests and abilities, greater involvement in the over-all process of the organization, and a voice in decisions relative to their welfare. The rise of automation -- contrary to earlier belief -- enables management to free employees from activities that formerly required specific and undivided attention.

2. To Have Concern for the Welfare of Employees. It is true, of course, that to some extent management has been "forced" toward human relations by strong labor unions, government regulations, and labor shortages, but in fact most enlightened executives are sincere in accepting their responsibilities for promoting human welfare.

The human relations trend in American industry is inevitable -- a sign of the times. Americans in all walks of life are being allowed greater freedom and responsibility. Few youngsters experience situations in schools or homes where orders are given without some accompanying explanation.

Youngsters today expect to be involved in decision-making processes. People are motivated to work for many reasons other than the dollar.

3. <u>To Promote the Maximum of Job Satisfaction</u>. If a person "enjoys" his work, i.e., if he gains <u>intrinsic</u> satisfaction from it, he is likely to be a successful employee because he provides his own steam or motivation. The "problem" worker is the one who is interested only in a pay check so that he can hurry out to enjoy himself off of the job. He gets <u>extrinsic</u> satisfactions from his job. A major responsibility of management is to provide its employees with work they enjoy and find intrinsically satisfying. If the work is not satisfying, management has the responsibility of finding ways of making it more satisfying. This implies that management must "know" its employees and its jobs. It implies that management must recognize that people are different and that they have different interests, needs, and aspirations.

4. <u>To Select Workers Effectively</u>. If it is management's responsibility to "make" jobs more interesting and satisfying, it is also management's responsibility to "select" people for the jobs in the organization who are most likely <u>to be satisfied</u> by those particular jobs. The implication of the fore-going statement focuses a major <u>responsibility</u> on management to develop a keen understanding of the problems of recruitment, selection, interviewing, and testing.

The hotel-restaurant-club industry lives with selection problems that are complex and serious. They are problems associated with low wages, difficult working conditions, and the fact that many of the workers in hotels and restaurants are there by default -- because they could find no other jobs. One of the chapters that follows illustrates research by one of the authors aimed at describing the kind of food service industry worker who is <u>satisfied</u> in working in <u>most</u> food service industry outlets. This research exemplifies the need for all hotel-restaurant managers -- even those imbued with the most humanistic ideals -- to be <u>practical</u> and <u>realistic</u> in picking the <u>specific person</u> for a <u>specific job</u>.

5. <u>To Train and Develop</u>. Research has demonstrated that supervisors often are villains in organizations, not purposely but unknowingly. A good supervisor is the kind of person who is able to reorganize the assignments of his subordinates to a point where his subordinates will enjoy their work. It is important to remember that neither a "good personality" nor a good work record are keys to the success of supervisors. Good supervision consists of good <u>organizational</u> and <u>planning</u> functions. A good supervisor is able to maximize the abilities of his subordinates.

To be a good supervisor requires sensitivity, ability, and training. Toward the end of providing effective supervision in the organization, a major role of management is to provide training and development experiences for supervisors and managers within the organization.

6. <u>To Provide Realistic Worker Participation</u>. It is unrealistic to assume that the workers at the lower levels of the organization will ever exert much influence in the actual establishment of the over-all goals of the organization. On the other hand, it is a basic need of workers to have <u>participation</u> in the organization. Those workers who feel they are a part of the organization are more <u>effective</u> and responsible workers.

It is a recognized management responsibility to decide on <u>goals</u> or <u>ends</u>. On the other hand, it should be a management responsibility to provide as much <u>latitude as</u> is <u>possible</u> to workers to develop for themselves the <u>ways</u> that the ends of management are to be achieved.

7. <u>To Insure a Program of Mental Health</u>. It may seem strange to talk about mental health for a hotel or restaurant setting. After all, the person who "breaks down" on the job is a rarity. On the other hand, in an industry that depends on action and speed as much as the food service industry, frayed nerves, frustrations, and anxieties are the rule rather than the exception.

Rather than "chasing the horse after he is out of the barn," the food service industry needs to concentrate on <u>preventing</u> strained relationships and frustrations before they develop. It needs to concentrate on utilizing the techniques of counseling, group dynamics, and other effective human relations tools that have enabled other industries to short-circuit problems before they erupt. A trained personnel administrator or a consulting psychologist has a definite place in the progressive hotel or restaurant.

8. <u>To Promote Constructive Goals</u>. It is axiomatic that organizations want to achieve maximum gain with <u>minimum risk</u>. It is in the method of achievement that organizations often differ in their approach. An increasing trend in American society is to view work as so meaningless that it sometimes is felt that workers must be lavished with high pay and fringe benefits to make up for the sacrifice they give in their labor. The expression, "People just don't want to work today," is a common one.

Adequate pay and good fringe benefits are important of course, and without them people may be dissatisfied with their work. For hotel-restaurant managers to blame work or workers in general because they are having problems is just an excuse for their being poor managers. Regardless of exclamations to the contrary, work is just as meaningful today as it ever was in the lives of human beings. It is the manager's responsibility and role to implement the eight areas named in order to provide opportunities for employees to enjoy meaningful work experiences.

CHAPTER 2

Motivating Employees

In human affairs there are always leaders and followers -- some people who set goals and get other people to accept them and work towards them or force other people to do their wishes. Even in lower forms of animal life, wherever there is a group of animals, some emerge as leaders and others as followers. Chickens, that have only a glimmer of what might be called intelligence, develop a pecking order among themselves. A kind of social organization evolves with a dominant male at the helm.

Millions of people do the bidding of others, not because they particularly want to but because they are forced to. People, like animals, are motivated by the offer of reward or by the threat of punishment in one form or another. More important, however, the human being wants self-respect; and he goes to great efforts to achieve it, marching into the face of sure death, giving himself up as a martyr, committing hari-kari to assure that he will maintain his self-respect. "For in each of us," says Sigmund Freud, "there is a desire to be great." Or as John Dewey, the famous educator says, "We are all motivated by the desire to be important, a desire which is almost as potent in the affairs of men as is a need to survive." Men want challenge, want recognition, want to be a part of an organization which has the approval of the community and of society. Most men want to interact with other people, since humans are by nature social animals.

Using these strong "self-realization needs" and playing on fears and hostilities, political leaders have motivated masses of people into doing incredible things. Men like Julius Caesar, Napoleon, and Garibaldi have inspired common people to uncommon effort. The desire to be somebody, for self-enhancement, lies buried in everybody's mind no matter how deeply. Toussant l'Ouverture, once a slave himself, motivated thousands of ex-slaves to fever pitch in driving the French out of Haiti. Slaves, brutalized by years of monotonous and heavy labor done on a poor diet, have still risen up against their masters indicating the divine spark of discontent innate in mankind.

The motivation of people has necessarily interested the finest minds and is a part of all supervision and management. Getting people to change their values, to want something new to the point of parting with their money, giving up a comfortable habit, or exerting effort is part of salesmanship in the art of persuasion. The motivation of people -- getting them to vote for him -- is the concern of every political candidate. The motivation of others is a subject which covers a large share of social life. Little wonder motivation has been the concern of men intent upon accomplishing almost everything, good and evil; it occupied the writings of some of the better thinkers of history. One such thinker, Niccolo Machiavelli, devoted himself to drawing up a set of guidelines which he submitted to some of the rulers of Renaissance Italy. These guidelines are of interest to supervision and management today for the reason that they reflect keen insight into human nature, especially that of Machiavelli himself. His guidelines are effective in creating a strong central authority in any organization, based on a lack of ethical principle or real concern for others and a cynicism for the nobility of mankind. Here are some of his rules which have relevance for the business world:

Executives should never show irresoluteness.

Executives should operate somewhat aloof from their subordinates. The friendship relationship interferes with the efficiency of the organization and acts to limit the power of the executive.

Personal feelings should not be a basis for action, either negative or positive, and should be kept to a minimum. "Try to maintain," said Machiavelli, "a relationship which is not unfriendly, but rather the executive should think of people as pawns to be used in the best interest of the executive."

According to Machiavelli, the executive should distrust friends and be careful of gratitude displayed by them. Typical of Machiavelli's true respect for the individual was his statement that the prince, or in our terms the executive, should not be held to a promise if it no longer serves his benefit to honor it.

Over a period of time, such behavior is found out, and Marchiavelli exemplifies the truth of the statement in that he died poverty-stricken and forgotten by the princes he instructed.

It is difficult indeed to establish principles of motivation which are universally applicable, for it is quite true that persons trained in one culture respond to different cues and rewards than those in another. A Latin-American hotel employee, for example, expects a paternalistic type of management, and will often go to the manager to ask his opinion about a prospective bride or to get his blessing for a marriage. An employee in a Turkish hotel has been conditioned to respond to strong authority and more or less expects management to be autocratic even to the point of browbeating. The German employee has been raised in an atmosphere where authority goes unquestioned and responds to strong authority just as does the Negro employee who has been used to a "Don't ask questions, just do it" type of management. A Puerto Rican employee is more sensitive about his dignity than the North American and is likely to react violently if there is any question of his "manliness."

Some universals in management apparently do exist and are outlined here, as seen by the authors.

The effective manager recognizes that he has been given power, accepts it and uses it wisely. It enables people to see things as they want to see them; it gives control over others. Power is dangerous but necessary. It makes people feel they are experts when they are not, knowledgeable when ignorant, pleased with themselves when they should not be. It is also a force which moves people in organizations, gets things done, crystallizes opinions, gives control and direction in a hotel or restaurant.

The effective manager is able to take power in his stride, does not let it interfere in his judgements of events or people, does not let it turn his head, nor let it confuse issues. He demonstrates his power carefully, plays it down, holds it in reserve for emergencies then uses it with full force if necessary.

Implicit in every management-employee relation is the threat of punishment in one form or another. The effective manager from time to time is called upon to discharge people who are not performing, to make decisions which will stretch his power to the limit. He has enough confidence in himself to take the consequences of his failures.

Authority which comes with management involves implied force which can be used if necessary, even to the point of discharging the employee. Sometimes that force must be used to maintain the effectiveness of the hotel or restaurant.

The manager who must always be nice to his employees will find that the hotel or restaurant shows few human or production problems as long as no new demands are made on the operation. When challenges from competition force changes, however, very often drastic changes in behavior are called for and niceness usually will not effect those changes.

A Time for Autocracy and a Time for Democracy

Effective managers know when they should be autocratic, when democratic. Unfortunately, most people are not that flexible and tend to be fixed in the way they relate to people and in the manner of their leadership. If the business is systematized, most of its work can be carried on merely by the use of signals, signals which are cues to set into motion chains of learned behavior. This is a desirable state of affairs, but tends to make the employees automatons and offers little challenge to their creative capacities and desire to be somebody and to improve.

The amount of delegation for making decisions of course depends upon the personality of the person being assigned the responsibility and upon the total situation. Ideally, the manager gradually divests himself of responsibility by delegating it, acting as a coach so that other people can formulate plans, can carry them out effectively with only minimal assistance from the manager. Unfortunately human beings are fairly well set in their ways by the time they are of working age, and developing a sense of responsibility and a desire to undertake challenge is difficult. What actually happens is that the manager tends to surround himself with people who will respond well to him and who satisfy his personal needs in relating to others. A "strong boss" type of manager surrounds himself with employees who feel comfortable in being bossed and very often the enterprise is a great success as long as the boss makes the right decisions and is on hand to give the necessary orders. For such a person, the development of strong understudies and supervisors is particularly difficult because he finds it almost impossible to stand aside and set goals rather than to review his supervisors' decisions. Such a person is likely to think there is only one way to do a job when in actuality there are almost always several ways, and there is little difference in their merit.

Such a situation often occurs in a family-owned enterprise, one which the father has built up by force of his personality and intelligence over a period of years. He wishes the son to take over, but finds great difficulty in letting the son do so since the son is almost certain to manage in a somewhat different way than the father.

The Appropriate Amount of Delegation for Responsibility

One difficulty in deciding what should and should not be delegated comes in thinking that the number of decisions are the important factor in carrying out responsibility. This, of course, has no bearing on the importance of the responsibility. One major decision can ruin or make a tremendous impact upon the success of the hotel or restaurant, whereas most decisions carried out during the day are merely routine. What is appropriate in delegation is to sort out those decisions which will affect people in a major way and to involve those who will be so affected before the decision is made.

Decisions which will call for a considerable change in behavior are those which are most important, especially those which will set off a strong emotional reaction. Deciding on how to lead evolves into deciding when to use one type of leadership and when another.

The effective manager must be tough-minded; that is, he must see things as they really are rather than through a sentimental haze.

Here is a quote from the operating manual of the Downtowner Motor Inns, one of the rapidly growing motel chains which brings this point home, perhaps too forcefully:

"Unsatisfactory employees are a total liability. They are not only unproductive, substandard workers themselves, but they also disrupt the organization and destroy the morale of other employees.

"Take prompt, corrective action to eliminate the lazy, grumbling, frequently absent employee who shirks his responsibility.

"Don't put off until tomorrow what you know must be done today. Terminate immediately any employee whom you feel is not giving you one hundred per cent."

Depending upon the general philosophy of top management, supervisor, or middle manager who wants to move ahead, to travel somewhere, he must be willing to take the risks of the journey. In an old, stable organization, top management may be more concerned about "not rocking the boat" than anything else; and the middle manager or supervisor must be more cautious in making changes.

Management must set standards and insist -- even demand -- that they be met. This can be done pleasantly, intelligently, and at the right time; or it can be done arbitrarily, pre-emptorily and in a way to irritate anyone who is sensitive.

To maintain standards means that there is communication between management and employee and that it is a certain amount of correction to be made in employee behavior no matter how successful the communication and motivation.

Pick the time for correction. A leading hotel executive advises that the employees should be corrected in the morning, reassured in the afternoon. This means that the correction is made at a time when the employee has enough energy to withstand the injury to his ego. Every correction tends to belittle or shake the employee's confidence and self-regard, affecting some much more than others. We all welcome a teacher who shows us how to improve, but we resent a critic who tells us what is wrong with ourselves.

"Sometimes during the afternoon," says the executive, "I make it a point to look up the employee who has been corrected and say something pleasant, if it's only a comment on the weather. This reassures him that I still like him and that the correction involved nothing personal. If I fail to reassure the person or make the correction at the wrong psychological moment, the employee is likely to take his frayed ego home with him, dwelling on the criticism, blowing it up out of proportion; and the next morning he comes in bedraggled from worry which has set off a chain reaction, harmful to both the employee and to the hotel and restaurant."

A manager does those things which are good for the organization even though he recognizes that they may not be best for an individual or a group of individuals. Consequently, the manager is at the "lonely top"; he must keep himself somewhat aloof from employees so that he can look at them at least partially objectively. He does not join them as a drinking companion, except in a ritualistic way, such as at a Christmas party. He does not allow himself to become too attached to any employee since he must sit in judgement on the employee.

In new hotels or restaurants or those undergoing substantial change of policy, a certain amount of ruthlessness is necessary to effect changes. Whenever a new policy is introduced, policy which is likely to change a person's status or demand drastic change in attitude or behavior on the part of some employees, it may be necessary to replace them rather than to spend the time necessary to effect the change. Such employees are likely to feel threatened and if given an opportunity sabotage a new program.

When an employee has to be replaced, do it quickly and get him off the premises. Quite naturally his feelings are hurt by his discharge, and he is likely to vent his feelings or solicit sympathy from the other employees. Should the employee be in an important position, he can do considerable damage before being completely severed from the hotel-restaurant.

Management must be constantly oriented to costs and profits, at least in profit-making concerns. It is difficult to get supervisors cost-oriented, especially if there isn't constant pressure to reduce costs. Many hotels and restaurants go for years with only casual attention paid to costs until one day comes the reckoning.

Ambitious supervisors or managers naturally have a tendency to empire building, which has to be curbed. Many managers are quite free with spending the company's money, miserly when spending their own. J. Paul Getty, the billionaire, tells how one of his companies was losing money partly because there was little attention to costs. He deducted five dollars from the salaries of four of his top executives and waited to see what would happen. In a short time these men, who were drawing five-figure salaries, came in to him to complain. They were well informed about costs when it came to their personal lives but failed to carry their concern over to company matters.

It is quite possible to place cost control emphasis on the wrong things. Food cost can get too low; red tape can get so involved that no one bothers to replace tablecloths or to order needed equipment. In one organization it was necessary to see the president to order even a pencil.

Alert management is constantly looking for ways to invest money wisely, in new equipment which will save labor, in maintenance costs, in added facilities which will bring in more revenue. Each expenditure must be judged in the light of an over-all benefit. Sheraton Hotels, for example, have a stated policy that no investment will be made unless it will return 20 per cent a year. Ramada Inns state that their policy is no investment unless a yield of 20 per cent can be anticipated.

Management has the responsibility for identifying potential supervisors and replacements for themselves. Grooming a person to take one's job or to act as understudy builds anxiety in the incumbent. He feels he may be replaced. Many is the executive chef who guards his recipes, keeps the ingredient information in his head, assembles them in the corner where no one can see him, becomes angry if a learner peers over his shoulder.

It sometimes happens that the understudy does replace the manager so the fears are realistic; yet the manager must have the level of confidence in himself to enable him to encourage and train an understudy. Some companies make the first order of business of a manager the training of an understudy. In a restaurant where so much revolves around a manager and depends upon his health and well-being, an understudy or second in command is essential, not only for everyday relief but in case the manager becomes ill or is off the job for some other reason.

People with real management talent are rare and when one is found he should be encouraged and fed responsibility as fast as he can handle it. Otherwise he becomes restless and discouraged. Often such people are restless and nervous with a high level of anxiety and a need to improve themselves each day. They should be given plenty of work -- enough to challenge them.

Identification of the manager is not easy. Usually he is the kind of person who has taken on responsibility, has learned to initiate and persuade other people at a fairly early age. He probably has done something out of the ordinary by the time he is fourteen. He may not be a conformist; he may be a little hard to live with; he may be intolerant of those who are less agile mentally, less willing to plunge into new territory.

Anyone who does anything important takes a risk. Let the comer take risks, but shield him from taking ones which may ruin him or the company. Let him make mistakes, preferably little ones, so that he can experience the results of his decisions, learn some caution and the facts of life.

A precious asset for any manager is the ability to arouse enthusiasm for goals in others; stir a sense of excitement, a feeling that the hotel or restaurant is going some place, is moving ahead; and create the belief that each individual will gain self-satisfaction as well as material rewards as the hotel or restaurant increases its sales volume and reduces costs. Everyone wants to have the feeling that he is a part of something bigger than he is which will carry him along to a more desirable goal. The ability to stir the imagination, to quicken the pulse, to stimulate pride of accomplishment is a rare gift, an ability to be nurtured.

The manager of a new property can create pride in the newness; the manager of an old property can create pride in reputation and stability.

Management must have a demonstrated sense of purpose, the determination to win. When management loses such determination it is time that it be replaced or bow out to someone who has the kind of perseverance which can be communicated to all employees. Restaurants typically don't last more than one or two generations; the old management retires, the new ownership lacks the same kind of purpose necessary to keep it alive and prospering.

The effective manager likes his job, wants responsibility. Sad, but true, most people want just a job. Few really want responsibility. Most of us do maintenance or essentially routine work most of the time. The "manager" will extend himself when necessary, work day and night, plus weekends, if necessary. He goes beyond the call of duty, rises to the occasion. He is willing to make the sacrifices which are necessary to get the job done. This does not mean that he knocks himself out, for the wise manager paces himself to maintain his energy level and his sense of proportion.

Since much of what he must do each day on the job is frustrating, tiring, boring, or downright painful, he plans his day so that he can do some things from which he gains real pleasure. For some people this is TV viewing; others play golf, others bridge, some bird watch. Whatever it is the manager should schedule his "rewards," recognizing that he will be a more effective manager for doing so.

The speed of the boss is the speed of the gang. This statement means that in most work groups, the employees do not work any harder than the manager or supervisor. Not only is the industry of the boss reflected in the employees, but also the employees play back the boss's attitudes, his ambition, and his determination. His feelings are communicated to those around him. His optimism tends to be their optimism; his courtesy, their courtesy; his bearing, their bearing; his kindness, their kindness; his grooming, their grooming. A hotel or a restaurant is similar to a ship in that morale of the crew reflects the morale of the captain of the ship, and the attention of the captain to the details of administration and the tidiness of the ship is reflected in the ship's crew. The saying "A taut ship is a happy ship" applies also to a hotel, restaurant, and club.

People management involves goal setting, standard setting, and getting other people to accept them as their own. This is both an art and a technique, requiring intelligence, imagination, persuasive skill, self-confidence, enthusiasm, and determination. Getting others to accept goals is part salesmanship, based on an understanding of motivation, timing, and ego needs.

The other person must be convinced that he individually will be rewarded in some way for adopting a goal. The goals of the enterprise and the goals of the individual must be brought together at certain points.

Some employees must be prodded, others held back. Some people must be hit over the head and commanded while others will respond to the least suggestion. Some of the great leaders plant ideas, let them incubate in the other person's mind to come forth as his own. Other leaders are best at painting glorious futures. Hitler, for one, was able to convince millions of Germans that there were "supermen" and that they would be rewarded in accordance with their superiority. Napoleon offered millions of Frenchmen an escape from the monotony of life to "glory and country."

People are not necessarily motivated by visions of wealth and ease. Churchill offered the British "blood, sweat, and tears," in other words an opportunity for self-sacrifice to which they responded magnificently.

Management is concerned with morale and morale is closely related to how people feel about themselves. What all people want in this world is primarily self-regard. Make it possible for employees to have some self-regard every day. Self-regard comes in knowing that you are part of an ongoing, successful enterprise, that you can perform the work at hand well, that you have respect from other employees and from management. Management can be strong and firm, hold to high standards, and yet have high morale.

The employee must feel that he is a worthwhile person and be proud of being a part of the hotel or restaurant. Similarly, he must feel that the hotel or restaurant is a worthwhile enterprise that is offering valuable goods and service to the public.

Never destroy a person's self-regard. Do so and you will have an animal who will retreat or fight in one way or another. Depreciate a person and he will hate or fear you. If he is courageous he will think of ways to get back at you. The hitting back can be in the form of theft, doing as little as possible on the job, or even maltreating customers.

The effective manager looks upon employees and their problems as he would other problems, objectively, and as problems rather than as something to react to emotionally. He recognizes that there are many factors involved in relations among people and that continually trying to place the blame for human relations problems fails to solve the difficulties. He must find out what went wrong and how the total situation can be corrected. People are problems and to solve such problems they must be examined as any other complicated problem would be examined.

Emphasize rewards and goals rather than punishments and deterrents; pride in job rather than reprimands. Hold out the carrot rather than the stick.

Expect personnel problems and expect failures. Keep yourself physically fit and lead a well enough balanced life so that such problems do not become catastrophies. Every healthy person has a certain amount of tolerance for frustration, for crisis, and for pressure. An underlying current of dedication, determination, and physical strength carry people through these crises.

The manager who has a cold or a low-grade infection is seriously handicapped, has two strikes against him in meeting the day-to-day demands of supervision. People around him lose confidence in him because he lacks strength. He cannot cope with frustration, backs down easily, shows irritability quickly, and overreacts to minor problems. Sometimes he makes the mistake of complaining to his employees or looking for sympathy. A sense of humor helps.

Expect differences in dealing with women employees. Expect them to break down more quickly emotionally; expect them also to have more patience on routine jobs and to adjust better to routine than do men. Expect them to be more sensitive to criticism, to take things more personally, to expect more praise, and to be more sensitive to the moods of the boss.

Women have their antenna tuned in on the boss most of the time. They react to his underlying feelings, are better equipped to sense feelings because so much of their well-being depends on how men feel towards them, upon their goodwill.

Expect women to form cliques, to talk more on the job, and to resent a woman boss.

As a manager, expect to play a role on the job, the role of manager or supervisor, but do not try to be something that you are not for you will be found out. Everyone plays a role in life and the boss is being watched by his particular audience, the employees. Many of the great leaders in history were actors, but they were able to stage their productions so that the masses never knew what they were really like. A supervisor, being face to face with his employees day in and day out, can't get away with such performances.

As a younger supervisor dealing with older employees, expect additional problems. Expect that the older employee may resent you as a younger person, especially if you throw your weight around. The young supervisor should not be afraid to ask the opinion of the older employees, but this can be overdone.

In the many mergers of hotels and restaurants taking place today, older management people find themselves under vice-presidents or presidents who have had only a fraction of their experience. The younger manager must realize that he is on trial and should try to be completely fair and dignified. He must work harder than the employees and expect some time to elapse before he is completely accepted.

Age, however, is not as important as behavior and attitude, technical knowledge, and determination. The fact that someone has been on the job several years does not mean that he has learned something new while on the job. Experience "often means repetition of the same old thing."

The "success" impression must be maintained in every hotel, restaurant, and club. It is necessary to inspire the confidence of both employees and the public. The dress of the management personnel, the kind of cars they drive, the things they talk about, and their general approach to life are all part of the success impression and the eyes of the employees and of the patrons are focused on them, always evaluating, responding to the image created by the management, and to their underlying optimism or lack of it.

Dealing with the Emotionally Disturbed

In every hotel and restaurant are found emotionally disturbed people, including the management, for emotional stability is a balance which shifts throughout the day and throughout the year. We all have been mentally ill at one time or another, and must accept the ideas that we all are subject to stress and that anxiety and emotional stability are only a matter of degree. One study showed that only one person in four is free of mental illness symptoms when he is in his twenties, that there is a sharp rise in the number of mentally ill people when they move from their twenties into their thirties, and that another sharp rise in symptoms occurs in the fifty-year age group. In fact, in the fifties, only about one in seven people is considered by psychiatrists to be well adjusted.

Adjustment seems to correlate with sex and economic well-being. About twice as many men as women in their fifties have psychological problems. In the higher economic brackets only about one out of three is mentally well but when the low six per cent of the country's economic group was examined, according to one research group, only one person in twenty was considered mentally well. In other words there is a clear relationship between a man's economic strength and his mental health.

A common denominator in emotional disturbance is the amount of anxiety present, that feeling which is close to being fear but with no apparent source or object of fear observable. Everyone learns to handle his anxiety in his own way and the mind itself has unconscious defenses for coping with it. Some of us project our hostilities onto others. Repression is a fine mechanism for pushing out of the conscious mind thoughts which cause us anxiety. Rationalization makes it possible for us to twist the truth to our own advantage and the protection of our self-respect, and there are other similar ego defenses.

In the real world there are some natural stabilizers such as being a part of a happy family, trusting in God, being part of a church, and having hobbies or other interests which serve to compensate for frustrations experienced on the job.

The ideally healthy person has a balanced life, not devoting himself completely to his job, his family, or to any other single facet of life, but varying his interests. In the hotel and restaurant business there has been a mistaken tradition that one must bury himself in the work in order to be successful. Long hours, often spent amidst a highly charged atmosphere, have been the rule. Few people really enjoy such conditions when they are extended beyond their physical endurance. Some people in the business have turned to alcohol as a means of allaying their anxieties, only to find that excessive drinking adds problems and stress. Others turn to sex as an outlet which also often leads to personal problems and heightened anxiety.

Psychiatrists tell us that the healthy person reacts flexibly to stress and when he finds himself increasingly anxious, he knows enough to back off from what he is doing and get back to equilibrium. The healthy person understands and accepts other people as individuals and does not try to make them over into his own image. He is not unduly upset when they have different values than his own. Flexibility under stress can be built up with a happy childhood, plenty of rest and exercise, and reasonable goals.

The healthy person also has some insight into his own personality, accepts his strengths and recognizes his weaknesses, realistically perceiving what he can and cannot do, setting reasonable goals for himself.

In the last analysis the payoff for emotional equilibrium is the fact that the person can be productive and active.

Evidences of Disturbance. The first symptom of too much anxiety is a change in the usual behavior of a person. The person under stress who might be quite conservative becomes radical. The quiet person becomes talkative. The talkative person becomes overtalkative, or unnaturally quiet.

At a second level psychosomatic ailments appear -- headaches, colds, diarrhea, constipation, clammy hands, wet feet, upset stomachs, and so on. Many psychiatrists believe that most of such illnesses are really symptoms of overanxiety.

Most of us have experienced such symptoms but we don't often go into the third level of becoming disorganized to the point that our work falls off and we are unable to maintain consistent progress in getting things done. Accidents increase, absenteeism piles up. At this point the manager must step in and ask the employee what's the trouble. Sometimes a day or two off, a loan of money, or a change of work may cure the problem. This is the manager's responsibility and he cannot let the business suffer when psychological problems show their heads as they are certain to do in any business.

When the individual or oneself gets to the point where things appear to be unreal around him, he is in real trouble and there should be no time wasted in setting up an appointment with a psychiatrist. When a person lives in an unreal world he is termed a psychotic, and he is seriously ill.

The manager or supervisor is in no position to play counselor because he is not equipped by training to do so and he may only worsen the condition. Nevertheless, he should be on guard to recognize symptoms and be ready to give a helping hand if he can. He should recognize that employees bring their problems with them to the job and the place of work is not a therapy center. Many the manager of a hotel or restaurant has tried to carry a seriously maladjusted employee over a long period of time only to find that the employee is not productive, causes trouble among other employees, and takes much of the manager's time and thought.

How Much Tension Is Right? Every job calls for a certain level of tension if the job is to be done well. The speaker getting up to address an after-dinner meeting cannot do a top job unless he is keyed up. The opera singer cannot perform well unless her adrenalin is flowing freely and she is more excited than would be appropriate for ordinary living. The football player needs to be charged up to run at his maximum and throw himself at the opposition without fear. On the other hand, a seamstress with the same amount of tension would find herself sewing her fingers instead of her material.

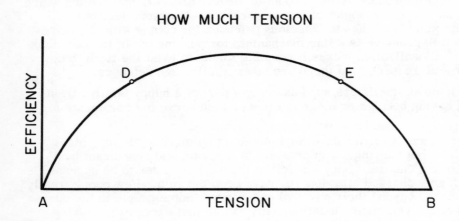

HOW MUCH TENSION

The graph illustrated on the left is one way of looking at the relationship between efficiency and tension.

As seen in the graph, efficiency is at its peak when tension is somewhere between D and E. When we get up in the morning our tension level is low and we do not really hit our stride until tension builds up to about the point of D. If, however, tension should increase beyond the point of E our efficiency begins to drop off and hypertension results in panic and absolute inefficiency, as seen at point B. We might think of ourselves as walking on a path

through a swamp. If we get off the path with either too little or too much tension, we are in deep water and in trouble as regards efficiency and mental well-being. Sometimes under stress we may be walking across a log over a stream in the sense that we have to be particularly careful not to swerve off the log into the water. Some psychiatrists have likened the problem of mental health to an escalator. Some people are going up and some people are going down all the time.

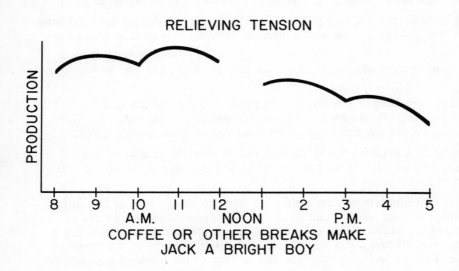

RELIEVING TENSION

COFFEE OR OTHER BREAKS MAKE JACK A BRIGHT BOY

The Use of "Breaks" To Level Off Tension. A coffee break is a useful device for leveling off tension and for breaking up the work period. As seen in the accompanying graph, tension builds up at the start of the work period until about 10 a.m. when there is a coffee break. Tension then drops down and the cycle repeats itself until the lunch period. The same process occurs again in the afternoon, with the coffee break serving as a goal gradient -- something to be looked forward to by the employee, interruption in the monotony of doing something over and over again, a real advantage in making work more pleasant, especially on monotonous jobs.

Utilizing a Knowledge of Tension and Efficiency in Getting a Job Done. To make this discussion of tension and efficiency more meaningful, think how it could be applied in the problem of putting on a banquet, one which has not been done before. The procedure can be thought of as following four steps.

STEP I -- Think the problems through and bring in those who can help. You need help in the form of ideas, information and hands, plus the imagination of others. Talk it over immediately with the supervisors or other key personnel who will be involved. Remember that you are responsible for forging the final plan, shaping it into a workable form. A strong maître d' or exceptional chef may carry the ball and should be in on the meeting. Outline the banquet proposal, ask for suggestions, let the plan set and jell. Come back to it tomorrow after people have had time to mull it over.

Ask questions, modify, change. Experience, judgement, native intelligence, and energy call the tune.

The menu has been planned, the decor theme developed. Hopefully, everyone involved -- and this is too much to ask -- knows about the plan and understands where he's going. This leads to:

STEP II -- Set the emotional stage. A new and different experience calls for a fairly high level of emotional tension in all who participate. Getting the staff keyed up to a football-playing pitch, however, is overdoing a good thing. Too much tension is as bad as too little. People wear themselves out running in place.

To avoid hypertension, guinea pig the event. Try out the menu items at home or in smaller quantities. Some changes will always be necessary and a dry run builds confidence.

Comes "show time," the cast is assembled and pitched to the performance. Expect some things to go wrong, they probably will. But anticipation prevents panic.

STEP III -- Lead off. Every group effort requires a leader, whether it be taking an enemy pillbox, initiating the mis en place or setting up a cafeteria line. Someone leads off, the rest follow. Most of us are followers and avoid leading off, especially when some new behavior is called for.

It is quite natural to fall in behind a leader. For example, the platoon leader gets the best response from his men when he says, "Follow me." Or, a cafeteria manager can exert leadership by stepping up to a salad counter and starting to arrange the salad display. If he is a real supervisor, he suggests that the salad girl help -- then he withdraws, letting her finish the job. Inertia is overcome; action is started.

At the banquet, whoever's in charge calls the starting signals, "Place the juice, lay the service plates."

Suddenly, everyone knows what the supervisor knows. Leadership is there. The group becomes aware that someone is in command. Psychologically speaking, the situation has become patterned, there is direction, and the individuals form into a group, moving toward a goal.

Once the wheels are set in motion, the supervisor turns his attention to other problems. He may wish to be around to identify the unforeseens. A well-planned banquet is like a battle. Once it has started there is little the chief can do to change the course of events. Prearranged plans and procedures take over the role of command.

Field Marshall Montgomery, for instance, slept through the first part of his important battle in North Africa.

In the case of a banquet, however, someone must have the "super" vision to spot difficulties and make changes if necessary.

STEP IV -- Correct and reward. Following any performance on stage, battlefield, or banquet the actors want evaluation. Immediately following the event, what they want most of all is reassurance and praise for things well done. As the manager, following a banquet, circulate around noticing all the good things; food, service, and otherwise.

Hold the criticism until the next morning.

People who are tired are hypersensitive to criticism; the ego is not firm enough to take it. Next morning, the post-mortem can be held and discrepancies discussed objectively.

Questions are more effective than accusations.

"Chef, what did you think of the lemon pie?" Let the chef be the first to point out that the crust was too tough or the lemon flavor too strong.

Let the head waiter come up with suggestions for improving the performance. Raise the question of whether the plates were hot enough, the salads crisp enough, the room at the right temperature.

In the morning, people are fresh and better prepared to self-evaluate.

Sometime during the day take the time, as manager, to reassure everyone of your personal interest. Stop around for a few minutes of small talk, a question about the family. Be sure to chat with those who might have guilty feelings about poor performance or those who have been criticized in the morning meeting.

The manager thinks it through, sets the emotional stage, leads off, then rewards and corrects.

A Check List for Leadership

√ Motivation: One who gets things moving and everyone moving in the same direction.

√ Enthusiasm: He gets a kick out of his job and is able to impart his enthusiasm for a project or idea to co-workers and subordinates.

√ Vitality and a high energy level.

√ Confidence and composure: He has things well in hand. He reacts well to emergencies and crises, thinks quickly, positively, and maintains his poise at all times. Enthusiasm is contagious and desirable; the excitement that accompanies trouble is also contagious, but must be controlled.

√ Tough-mindedness: A leader faces things realistically and understands that decisions must be made that may hurt people.

√ Inspirational: A leader has a sense of urgency and is skilled in stimulating people to get the job done. A leader also sets a good example in behavior and attitudes.

√ Imagination: A leader must know how to tap the energies of others in getting the job done. He has the imagination to exploit the best qualities of the young firebrand, stir the cynic and give purpose to the discouraged.

√ Integrity: A leader believes his word is important and keeps his promises.

√ Responsibility: The leader has the ability to make decisions and to act, but is also willing to take the consequences.

√ Objectivity: The leader or supervisor has super vision; he sees all sides of the problem calmly.

√ Orientation: The leader is oriented to costs and profits, not overlooking the human element. He is oriented to solving the problems. He is constantly redefining goals, reviewing objectives, setting new goals.

In relating to the employee, management should remember the following: Relating to people is more important than technical knowledge.

CHAPTER 3

Organizing People Relations

To be effective an enterprise must be organized. Personnel must know the objectives of the enterprise, the lines of communication and authority, and the manner in which their jobs are related to the organization. Each member must have an understanding of his duties, authority, responsibility, and accountability.

What is organization? It is a structure of relationships which controls a group of persons for the accomplishment of specified ends. The ends for which hotel and restaurant enterprises strive are service at a profit and maximum satisfaction for those participating. Organization is necessary to coordinate the efforts of all the personnel towards these goals. Organization, then, is a means to more effective concerted effort.

Organization proceeds through people. A purpose of organization is to get effective results with people. In order to get maximum results organization aids and encourages personnel within the organization to utilize their capacities to the full. It also partially sets the conditions for giving people maximum satisfaction in their work, and concomitantly, in life.

Through organization every activity which contributes to an enterprise is brought under a centralized direction. This avoids cross-purposes, and encourages decisions made from the point of view of advantage for the entire enterprise. Decisions which may appear advisable for certain units may be inadvisable when viewed as a part of the entire enterprise.

A separate personnel policy for the girl who operates the cigar and candy counter may increase her morale and sales. It may, however, cause enough dissatisfaction among other employees to more than offset the advantages to the whole enterprise.

Organization establishes a communication system by which a two-way flow of ideas, suggestions, and information is made possible. It also serves as a channel for complaints and grievances.

A defective organization means trouble ahead for the enterprise. Management that is not capable of identifying organization weaknesses is not capable of good management generally.

SOME PRINCIPLES OF ORGANIZATION

Delegate Certain Kinds of Authority and Responsibility to the Lowest Level Possible

Certain kinds of authority must be delegated if an organization is to be efficient. The manager of a hotel or restaurant is correct in requiring that he have a voice in all policy decisions and in long-range planning, but all too frequently the otherwise capable executive fails to delegate authority. By so doing he not only burdens himself but hamstrings his subordinates. Valuable time is wasted because all decisions must be cleared through him. He takes on work that could be done better by others. He destroys initiative in his subordinates by failing to set the conditions for decision-making in his subordinates. The restaurant manager who must make out the menu himself is doing the chef or the food production manager and himself an injustice. The manager of the hotel who insists on doing the employing is knocking the supports from under his department heads. The chef who insists upon doing the steward's job as well as his own is destroying the efficiency of at least two men. Delegating authority is one of management's most difficult jobs. It entails accepting responsibility for another's work. It means acknowledging that perhaps there are others who can also make decisions and perform efficiently besides one's self. Only the real executive is big enough to do it well.

In delegating authority and responsibility the executive recognizes that he must distinguish between delegated responsibility and authority and final responsibility and authority. In other words, the executive must delegate and deputize but he also must accept final responsibility for the actions of his subordinates. Even though a hotel manager must rely heavily upon his chef to operate the food service of the hotel -- and should -- the manager must accept <u>final</u> responsibility for the food operation as well as for the other departments in the organization.

Define the Responsibility, Authority, and Accountability
of Every Position in the Organization

Job analyses have shown that jobs are often not clearly understood. Supervisors do not know the limits of exactly what they are to do and for what they are accountable. What are the porter's duties? Does his job overlap with that of the yardman? Does the assistant steward know he is responsible for the cleanliness of the dishwashing machine and for the employment of dishwashers -- or is this the steward's job? Has the addition of a new wing made the job of wall washing too much for the present crew?

Every job should be well defined and in a definite place on the organization chart. Follow the principle: one man, one boss. Try to avoid having anyone report to more than one supervisor. Every employee from the transient dishwasher to the manager should know to whom he is responsible and for whom and what he is responsible. Job information should be written and in a form available to employees. Constructing an organization chart and performing job analyses will aid in showing where an organization is weak in these respects.

A corollary to the dictum "Define everyone's authority" is the equally important precept: "Grant authority commensurate with responsibility." A supervisor without authority is as useful as the extinct dodo bird. An assistant manager who must refer all matters to the manager for decision is nothing but a clearing station -- and has no function other than as a trainee.

Clarify and Maintain the Organizational Pattern

The nature of a hotel or restaurant business demands flexibility to meet constantly changing conditions. Since organizational structure is functional and depends upon the personalities and goals of the enterprise, it too should be flexible and easily modified. Hand in hand with flexibility, however, is the danger of misunderstanding the organizational structure.

One of the best ways to define the organizational pattern is to follow it in all personnel practices. A manager should not originate orders except through channels set up by the line organization. Orders from the manager should proceed through the assistant managers, department heads, and supervisors. Supervisors are not representatives of management unless they are given a part in the management process. Bypassing a person in the organizational setup destroys the purpose of the organization by creating confusion and undermining the status of those bypassed.

The organizational pattern is also maintained by including an abbreviated chart of it in the employee's handbook and by calling attention to a wall-sized chart at personnel meetings. Knowledge of an organizational pattern usually is implicit and grows out of the everyday relations among personnel. In a large organization the pattern commonly is not well known and misunderstanding, with contingent loss of efficiency, results.

Organize Around Functions

In order to be effective organizations must be functional. The functions of purchase and procurement, accounting and auditing, engineering and maintenance, food production, and public relations are separate divisions set up according to the purpose of the organization. It goes without saying that there should be no form of organization that does not serve a purpose. Keep organization simple. Do not set up unnecessary levels. Keep the distance between the manager and lowest employee as small as possible so that communication among all levels is kept open and efficiency is not lost by including unnecessary relay stations.

How Many Employees per Supervisor?

A British general, Sir Ian Hamilton, expressed the idea that the "average human brain finds its effective scope in handling from three to six other brains." He went on to say that there is a rule "whereby from three to six hands are shepherded by one head, each head in turn being a member of a superior group of from three to six..." In other words, there seems to be a fairly well-established limit on how many persons should report to one superior. The concept of the number of persons who can be supervised by one person is known as "the span of control." The answer, of course, depends upon the nature of the work involved. When there are six subordinates whose work interlocks, then one superior has his mind full keeping the relationships clear and the group working toward common goals.

In the hotel, restaurant, and club business a common weakness in organization places too many subordinates under each department head or supervisor. In a cafeteria, for example, there is only one "manager" on duty at a given time and he may have control over as many as 50 employees. It would be far better to establish more supervisors with someone in charge of the kitchen, someone in charge of the cafeteria line, and perhaps someone in charge of the dish machine room.

In the larger chain organizations it is quite possible for as many as ten or fifteen store managers to report directly to one area supervisor provided that it is not necessary for the store managers to interact to any degree. In fact, most chain restaurant operations are set up according to a highly stand-ardized plan and the plan is effected by the means of systems and routines which minimize the necessity for consultation in management, in the broad sense of the word.

Recently, the computer revolution has reached the hotel and restaurant field and the routines of accounting and reporting have been automated to a degree which a few years ago would have seemed fantastic. For example, Hot Shoppes has computerized the ordering of food from its warehouse and central commissary, and processes payroll and sales statistics as well as inventory control for nearly 150 locations from Dallas to New York City. Oven production schedules will be controlled according to a program which is carried out by a computer. All sales of food will be entered into the system at the point of sale, transmitted by phone directly to the computer center.

Such a program removes the necessity of the store manager's making dozens of routine decisions each day and permits him to concentrate on the other functions of people management.

The amount of supervision needed in a job depends upon the amount and kind of planning, communi-cations, and decisions required to perform the job. Managing a luxury restaurant like La Fonda del Sol in New York City is quite a different job than managing a Howard Johnson Restaurant. In a Howard Johnson Restaurant the manager has little or no responsibility for purchasing food, planning the menu, making financial decisions, decor decisions, or even decisions about methods of preparation. He has little interaction with other Howard Johnson managers. The span of control of a regional supervisor in a Howard Johnson system could be much larger than in that of a company like Restaurant Associates, the restaurants of which are mostly high style and individualized.

Similarly, a floor steward in charge of the dish machine crew could conceivably supervise as many as twenty employees without too much difficulty, whereas the executive chef might be overburdened if he had more than five or six section cooks reporting to him.

Decentralization or Centralization

A problem similar to that which is contained in the question as to the proper size of the span of control is whether or not a multi-unit operation should centralize or decentralize management. The answer hinges around the definition of management and the type of and character of operations involved. Delegation of authority, responsibility, and accountability should be determined by the reliability and effectiveness of available controls. In other words, decentralization or delegation of responsibility goes hand in hand with the institution of proper controls and, of course, with the availability of managers who have the character, judgement, and skills necessary to carry out the responsibility. Holiday Inns with its standardized advertising, menu, and operational procedures relieves the innkeeper of a wide area of responsibility and the necessity for much decision-making. Centralized accounting sets up the necessary controls so that the several hundred Holiday Inns can operate effectively as a group. Responsibility, in effect, has been decentralized, but accountability has been centralized. This is the key to delegation in all organizations.

The Futterman Hotels and the Hilton Hotels comprise many operations each with a separate charac-ter, and the property manager is called upon to accept a wide range of responsibility for maintaining the character and attractiveness of the property he manages. Again, however, accounting controls are cen-tralized and other means of holding the manager accountable are in effect so that decentralization is possible.

The Howard Johnson's organization, which has been known since its inception for being highly cen-tralized in its management control and in control of operation generally, has recently found it advanta-geous to decentralize some functions. Advertising, which has been done on a national basis by one advertising agency, is now being supplemented locally, with local agencies called in to produce the ad-vertising material. Managers who have been trained to operate by the book participate in regional semi-nars held at universities around the country. The seminars allow the managers to step back and away from their operations to be able to "see the forest from the trees." By being physically removed from their restaurants the managers get a new outlook and a new surge of enthusiasm for the job, according to

Howard Johnson top management. In the case of the Howard Johnson company, the corporation was initiated and got its form under the driving force of the personality of Howard Johnson, Sr. Under the presidency of his son the company has taken on a more liberal management tone, perhaps one which is more appropriate for a company which has reached a certain stage of maturity, when decentralization of some functions can be done more gracefully.

A Separate Personnel Department?

The first answer to the question of whether or not to delegate personnel functions is that no one in a management position can ever completely delegate the problem of personnel administration. Any executive's primary concern is people. No matter whether his technical problem is decoration, sales, or food preparation, he must work through people. Even so, the executive can delegate certain aspects of personnel administration.

A personnel department is simply an office set up to centralize personnel procedures common to all departments. It provides technical personnel services to department heads.

The question of whether or not to establish an organized personnel department depends upon the answers to three other questions:

1. Will establishing a personnel department enable the manager to devote more of his energy to planning, executing plans, and being a successful salesman and host?

2. Will establishing a personnel department assist department heads in being more effective in operating their departments?

3. Will the cost of establishing a personnel department be returned in terms of efficiency and morale?

In most hotels or restaurants having 100 or more employees the answers to these questions are in the affirmative.

WHAT "AUTHORITY" SHOULD THE PERSONNEL MANAGER HAVE?

The personnel manager should be given access to the manager or president. He must have the right to take part in determining what services are to be offered personnel, what counsel, and what controls are to be exercised. In personnel matters he is supposed to be the expert and as such should be invited to participate in top management policy which applies to personnel.

"Authority" to carry out personnel policy is another matter. Personnel managers and their assistants cannot exercise line authority in an organization; that is, they cannot give orders to department heads, supervisors, and employees. To do so would disrupt the supervisory relations and break down the organization.

If a personnel department is to succeed it must work through other management members. It does this by working with department heads and supervisors. Its authority is the authority of ideas but not the authority of command. If the personnel department should have any authority in the usual sense of the word, it is to make sure that established personnel policies are being followed. If supervisors have better ideas, their ideas should be used. If not, persuasion should be used. As a last resort an appeal to the manager is in order.

ESTABLISHING A SOUND PERSONNEL POLICY

Prerequisite to good personnel relations is a sound, growing personnel policy. Personnel policy should be written. It should be broad in scope and in the nature of a philosophy, a form of reference to which all personnel matters can be referred.

Personnel policy is dynamic and is developed out of the thinking of the thinking personnel of an organization. A first statement of policy should be formulated by building it up in the course of discussion by top executives of the organization.

A general policy should cover such topics as:

1. The objectives and moral code of the business
2. A statement of policy regarding regularity and tenure of employment
3. The company's policy regarding seniority and promotion
4. A statement of training policy

5. A statement on wage and salary structure and policy
6. The company's policy as regards employee participation and that of consultation and explanation
7. The method of grievance settlement
8. Provisions for insurance against injury, sickness, and old age
9. A statement regarding sanitation and working conditions
10. The company's thinking as regards union organization among employees.

A personnel program must rest on solid thinking and must be clear in the minds of those who direct it. For it to be effective, the top executive in the organization must take the initiative and its formulation and demonstrate that he, the president or manager, is actively concerned that the program be instituted.

If a personnel manager is named, he should report directly to the president. In a chain organization he should be named a vice-president or a director on the board of directors.

QUALIFICATIONS OF A DIRECTOR OF PERSONNEL RELATIONS

The lists of qualifications which a personnel director should possess are many and long. All lists and persons engaged in personnel work agree, however, that the personality and character of the man designated to head the personnel function should be given first consideration. He must have character. In his job he is both representative of management and advocate for the employees. He must have the courage to tell management when it is mistaken in personnel matters. He must enjoy helping and being with people. His interest in the individual is more important than his knowledge of job analysis or any other personnel technique. He must have absolute honesty and sincerity and be able to inspire confidence and recognition.

In a large organization the personnel director must be an executive. He must be ambitious and able to persuade others to his point of view without arousing antagonism. He must be able to follow through in a project. He should be able to plan and to "see the forest from the trees." He should be concerned with the long-time effects of plans and policies.

In addition the personnel director of today should have a knowledge of psychology, of the motivations and values of people. He should be research-minded, a student, and have a high degree of flexibility. A knowledge of personnel techniques would be presupposed.

ORGANIZATION OF A MOTOR INN

The organization of a motor inn without a restaurant is one of the simpler types of organization. The Downtowner Motor Inns which operated without a restaurant showed a labor cost of 18 per cent of gross sales. In the chart following can be seen the number of personnel needed for a 100- and a 150-room motor inn. Included in the chart are the wages being paid in 1963.

ORGANIZATION CHART FOR A 100- AND A 150-ROOM MOTOR INN WITHOUT FOOD AND BEVERAGE SERVICE

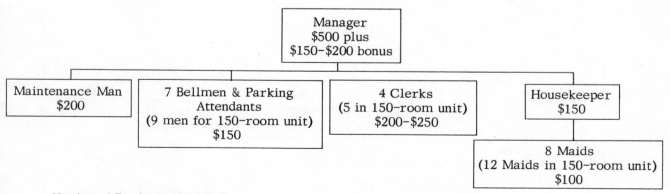

Number of Employees Required
For 100-Room and 150-Room Downtowner Motor Inn
-- Average Monthly Wage Paid --

The purpose of the preceding chart is to show that there is an optimal size of motel from the point of view of labor efficiency. The cost of labor for operating 50 additional rooms is minimal. The extra personnel needed are only two bellmen, one clerk, and four maids. In other words adding 50 rooms to a 100-room motor inn increases basic payroll costs by only about $1,150 a month. Computed on an 85 per cent room occupancy, the additional labor costs for the added 50 rooms is only 11 per cent of the gross sales.

No one has formally studied the "optimal size" motel, restaurant, or hotel, but it is fairly apparent that there are several optimal sizes depending upon the market and character of the operation. Often the addition of seats to a restaurant destroys its character or interferes with efficiency so that the owner would be better advised not to add them even though his volume of sales would suggest that he should do so. On the other hand, many motels that have 100 rooms and are doing capacity occupancies might very well add up to 50 additional rooms if market surveys indicate that they would be filled. The additional rooms would show a higher percentage of profit on the gross income than the other rooms.

In a large "luxury" hotel kitchen the personnel become highly specialized. The organization chart of such a kitchen is shown below.

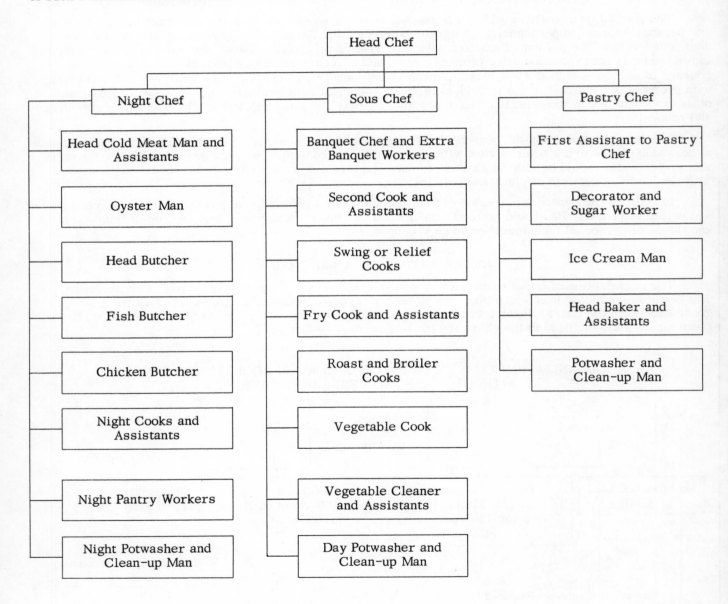

If the kitchen were manned predominately by French and other European trained personnel these titles would be changed as follows:

Head Chef -- Chef de Cuisine

Head Cold Meat Man -- Garde Manger

Swing Cook -- Tournant

Second Cook -- Saucier (sauce cook)

Other titles may also be used, but the job titles seen in the organization chart are the most common in the United States kitchens today.

A 200-bed hospital dietary department is usually headed by a chief dietitian but in the last few years in several cases by men with the title of "food service director." Where the hospital has a food teaching program for nurses or for intern dietitians, a separate division of teaching dietitians may be added. A typical organization chart of a fairly large hospital is seen below.

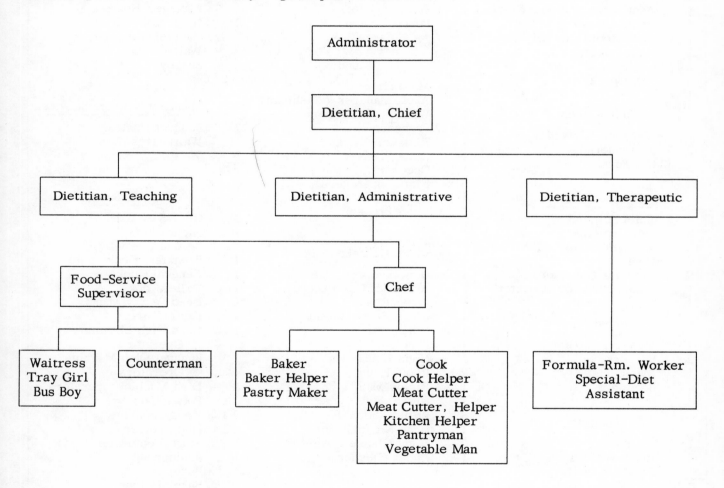

Staffing or manning tables are made to accompany organization charts. They list the number of persons on each job and the total number of personnel in each department. The staffing table for the Seminole Hotel is shown in the table on the following page. Notice that several of the jobs use 1/2 or 1/3 or 2/3 of an employee's time. It is only with such close scheduling of employees that labor cost can be held down and a profit made for the business.

Staff of Hotel Seminole
Jacksonville, Florida
(225 rooms and office bldg. Annex)

Executive Office

1	President-Manager
1	Resident Manager
2	Secretaries
4	

Front Office

1	Asst. Mgr. - Room Clerk
1	Room Clerk
1	Mail-Room Clerk
1	Night Auditor
2 1/2	Cashiers
5	PBX Operators
11 1/2	

Indian Room

1	Manager-Bartender
2	Bartenders
1/2	Bar Porter
3 1/2	

Uniformed Service

1	Chief Bellman
3	Bell Captains
15	Bellmen-Porters
2	Doormen
9	Elevator Operators
1	Annex Elevator Operator
31	

Barber Shop

1	Manager-Barber
2	Barbers
1	Manicurist
1	Bootblack
5	

Auditing

1	Auditor
1	Asst. Auditor
1	Food Controller
3	

Personnel

1	Manager
2 1/2	Timekeeper-Watchman
1	Night Officer
4 1/2	

Engineering

1	Chief Engineer
4	Engineers (Engine Room)
2	Engineers (Maintenance)
1	Fireman
1	Carpenter
1	Painter
1	Painter Helper
1	Porter-Iceman
12	

Laundry

1	Manager
1	Asst. Manager-(Washman)
1	Washman's Helper
2 1/2	Pressers
1	Finisher-Marker
1	Pants Presser
1 1/2	Checker
6	Flatwork Ironers
1	Seamstress
1	Valet Presser
18	

Housekeeping

1	Housekeeper
1	Assistant Housekeeper
1	Inspectress
1	Linen Room Attendant
1	Linen Man
1	Parlor Man
1	Night Houseman
2 1/3	Room Housemen
1	Parlor Maid
1	Night Maid
3	Relief Maids
1	Head Night Cleaner
2	Night Cleaners
1	Annex Cleaner
34 1/3	

Beverage

1	Beverage Controller
2 1/3	News-Pkg. Store Cashiers
1/2	Storeroom Porter
3 5/6	

Coffee Shop

1	Manager-Hostess
1	Hostess
2 2/3	Cashiers
13	Waitresses
4	Busboys
21 2/3	

Banquet & Room Service

1	Banquet Hostess
3	Waitresses
5	Waiters
9	

Kitchen

1	Chef-Steward
1	Night Chef
1	Second Cook
1	Breakfast Cook
1	General Cook
1	Relief Cook
1	Head Pantry Man
3	Pantry Girls
1	Head Dish Machine Operator
2	Banquet Dish Machine Operators
3	Dish Machine Operators
2	Potwashers
2 1/3	Food Checkers
1	Night Porter
1	Store Room Clerk
1	Butcher
1	Baker
1	Baker Helper
1	Cook Trainee
26 1/3	

Miscellaneous

1	Printer

Total Number of Employees: 187 2/3

June 1st, 1954

Job and Man Analysis

Basic to all personnel procedures is job analysis. Before determining what is a fair wage, the qualifications of employees, or what training is needed, we must know exactly what work is to be done. Each job must be examined and the items or tasks of work performed listed in an organization form. Job analysis is a means of taking inventory of the skills needed for a business. Each job is inventoried and the job content set down in orderly form. By using standard terminology and procedure, job analysis is done systematically and efficiently.

From a knowledge of the skills and tasks done, the next step is to determine the kind of person who can best perform the job.

PURPOSES OF JOB ANALYSIS

Job Analysis as Related to Selection and Placement

After the jobs of an organization have been broken down and written up in the form of a job description, an abbreviated form of the job description is made. The abbreviated form is known as a job specification. It is so organized that the abilities and experience needed for a job are set down in an organized form.

An employment manager usually cannot know personally all the jobs for which he must employ workers. Job specifications are the aid which makes possible his knowing what is required of the job of maid, counter girl, roast cook, sous chef, and the other more than ninety jobs to be found in the hotel and restaurant business. Job specifications are an abbreviated form of the job description, the organized, written record of the job analysis. In job specifications the requirements of the job are usually classified under such headings as mental requirements, educational requirements, physical requirements, and personality requirements. A glance at the job specification shows the employment manager the main requirements of the job. He may then proceed to determine if the applicant fits those requirements. Job descriptions are precise and enable the employer to specify exactly what position vacancy he has open.

Since particular jobs vary from establishment to establishment, each establishment must draw up its own specifications.

Job Analysis and Training

Job analysis provides supervisors and other trainers with basic information as to what is entailed in performing a job. Job analysis enables the trainer to prepare job breakdowns which are step-by-step guides to instructing. Chapter 8 shows this relationship between job analysis and training more clearly.

Job Analysis and Job Clarification

Job analysis defines jobs and lessens confusion and conflict among employees and supervisors. People need to know what is expected of them and where their responsibility begins and where it ends.

Job analysis makes it possible to draw up organization charts showing lines of authority, promotion, communication and limits of responsibility. Such charts enable the employee to see how he fits into the total picture of hotel or restaurant activity.

TERMINOLOGY USED IN JOB ANALYSIS

Some misunderstanding as regards terminology used in job analysis is common. Following are the three principal terms and their definitions.

Job analysis: a term that applies to the actual procedure of observing the job, interviewing the worker and recording the results.

Job description: the organized written form of the results of the analysis, usually done away from the job from notes taken at the job.

Job specification: more properly called a "man" specification, in that it lists the skills and personality traits needed to perform a job.

The three terms are considered to be parts of the total job-analysis procedure. In terms of the sequence of performance: job analysis (limited sense) is performed -- the job description is written from the results of the job analysis -- the job specification is drawn up, describing the kind of person needed to perform the job.

A still briefer form of write-up is the job definition. It is the most concise description of a job possible. Listed following are several job definitions of some lesser-known hotel and restaurant jobs:

GARDE MANGER; cold-meat chef; cold-meat man; cook, cold meat 2-26.16. Prepares cold meat, fish, and poultry dishes, utilizing leftover foods in such a manner as to make an appetizing and tasteful dish; prepares appetizers, relishes, and hors d'oeuvres; cooperates with employees in charge of planning menus to decide on dishes that will use greatest amount of leftover food. May prepare cold sauces, pickles, and jellies.

SOUS CHEF; chef assistant; chef, under; executive-chef assistant; supervising-chef assistant (hotel & rest.) 2-26.02. Assists the EXECUTIVE CHEF in supervising the preparation and cooking of foodstuffs; inspects food for sizes of portions and garnishing. May assist in cooking for banquets or other social functions.

HOUSE STEWARD; 2-25.12. Assumes responsibility for the maintenance (purchase) of an adequate food supply, the proper storage and issuance of food, and the efficiency of dishwashers, pantry workers, storeroom help, and all other kitchen employees except those actually engaged in cooking; cooperates with EXECUTIVE CHEF or MANGER, CATERING concerning banquet arrangements for food service, equipment, and extra employees. May be responsible for the profitable operation of the "back of the house." This job occurs typically in hotels as opposed to KITCHEN SUPERVISOR which occurs typically in restaurants or cafeterias.

BANQUET STEWARD; a STEWARD who supervises temporary banquet employees; insures that food is ready to serve when required; guards against loss and theft of banquet equipment.

STEWARD ASSISTANT; floor steward; inside steward 2-25.13. Closely supervises the activities of all employees of the kitchen, pantry, and storeroom, except those actively engaged in cooking; inspects subordinates' work to insure efficiency and cleanliness; keeps records pertaining to time and production of employees, loss of food, breakage; hires and discharges employees. May purchase foodstuffs and kitchen supplies. In establishments employing an EXECUTIVE CHEF who devotes full time to supervising kitchen employees, the STEWARD ASSISTANT may be a working supervisor.

ROUNDSMAN (1); cook, relief; cook, rounds; cook, swing; relief chef; rounds chef; swing chef; swingman; tournant. 2-26.03. An all-around cook who substitutes for and assists the BROILER COOK; FRY COOK; ROAST COOK; GARDE MANGER; and other cooks during their absences or during rush periods. May act as BREAKFAST COOK or NIGHT COOK.

SOUP COOK; potager 2-26.14. Specializes in the cooking of soups, broth, soup stocks, and bouillon. In many establishments the cooking of soups and stocks are part of the duties of SAUCE COOK, accordingly, the worker frequently acts as an assistant to the SAUCE COOK.

SAUCE COOK; saucier 2-26.12. Specializes in preparing, seasoning, and cooking of all kinds of hot sauces, stews, braised and sautéed meats, fish, poultry, soups, soup stocks, and broths. May supervise kitchen employees in the absence of the EXECUTIVE CHEF or SOUS CHEF.

THE DICTIONARY OF OCCUPATIONAL TITLES

The foregoing definitions were taken from the Dictionary of Occupational Titles published by United States Employment Service. The DOT contains job definitions of some 30,000 jobs, and is an essential tool for any personnel worker.[1]

---

[1] Dictionary of Occupational Titles, Part 1, Definitions of Titles, United States Employment Service, Washington, D. C., 1949. $2.00.

Each job is assigned a code number. The first number of the code refers to the occupational group. The groups are:

>   0 -- Professional and managerial occupations.
>   1 -- Clerical and sales occupations.
>   2 -- Service occupations.
>   3 -- Agricultural, fishery, forestry, and kindred occupations.
>   4 and 5 -- Skilled occupations.
>   6 and 7 -- Semiskilled occupations.
>   8 and 9 -- Unskilled occupations.

The first code numbers of the definitions listed, it will be noted, are 2-2's since they are all classified as personal service jobs. All jobs in the DOT are listed alphabetically for easy reference. To look up the definition of the job of hotel manager, look under manager, hotel. This reads:

MANAGER, HOTEL; general manager, hotel 0-7.13. Assumes general supervision over personnel efficiency, prorating of costs, purchase of supplies, and publicity procedures. Formulates policy on such matters as credit, personnel, rates, departmental jurisdiction, publicity, and type of trade desired.

Note that the first code number is 0, which denotes that the job is considered to be in the professional and managerial group.

STEPS TO BE TAKEN IN JOB ANALYSIS

1. Sell your department heads on the need for job analysis. Tell them of the advantages they will receive from it.

2. If a small operation, do the analysis yourself. If a large organization, delegate the job to someone who is interested. If you have a personnel man, ask him to do it.

3. Request the help of your State Employment Service. Expert advice can be had for no cost. If you do not wish to develop your own job analysis paper forms, use those supplied by the State Employment Service. Their printed forms are the:

(1) Job Analysis Schedule (for writing the observations); (2) Physical Demands Forms, and (3) Job Specifications Form.

4. Use both the questionnaire form and the personnel interview for getting the job information. One supplements the other.

5. Keep the Department Heads informed of the progress being made. Get their advice on rearranging job tasks and time schedules.

INFORMATION TO BE OBTAINED FROM A JOB ANALYSIS

The following has been provided by the Occupational Analysis Division of War Manpower Commission in "Guide for Analyzing Jobs" (Government Printing Office, Washington, D. C., Feb., 1944).

What the Worker Does

What the worker does involves the physical and mental responses that are made to the work situation. Physically the worker may transport materials, cut, bend, grind, put together, make ready, set up, tear down, insert, regulate, clean, finish, or otherwise change the position, shape, or condition of the work by the expenditure of physical effort. Mentally the worker may plan, compute, judge, direct, or otherwise govern the expenditure of his or others' physical effort by a corresponding exercise of mental effort. In a given job a worker may expend any combination of physical and mental effort required by the task.

How He Does It

How the work is done concerns the methods used by the worker to accomplish his tasks. Physically this involves the use of machinery and tools, measuring instruments and devices, and other equipment, the following of procedures and routines, and the movement of the worker himself. Mentally the methods lie chiefly in the "know how" that must be applied to the tasks. This may involve the use of calculations, formulas, the application of judgment or decision, or selection and transmittal of thought. The worker may use a single method in the accomplishment of a task or he may have at his command several alternate methods, any of which may be used with equal success.

Why He Does It

Why a worker performs his job is the purpose of the job itself and is indicative of the relationships among the tasks that comprise the total job. The "why" outlines the scope of the job and justifies the "what" and "how" of the work performed. The over-all purpose, of course, is the sum total of the purposes of all tasks. The purpose may be the conversion of material from one form to another, the maintenance of conditions under which other jobs can be performed, the catching or preventing of errors, the development of new methods or the improvement of existing methods, and so forth. Failure to explain this purpose will leave the impression that the jobs have not been reported completely, and tends to ambiguity in the description of the job.

The Skill Involved in the Doing

This part of the Job Analysis Formula brings out important information necessary to supplement the "what," "how," and "why," and to express the degree of difficulty of the work tasks involved in the job. It consists of a listing and an explanation of the basic factors which must be considered in analyzing any job. These elements bring out the manual skills, knowledges, abilities, and other characteristics required of a worker by his job, regardless of whether that job is manual, craft, professional, clerical, or other type. It may be considered a guide list to aid the analyst in obtaining and recording all the information necessary to discriminate between jobs and to establish the degree of difficulty of any job.

The specific factors or components are listed as follows:

1. Responsibility
2. Job Knowledge
3. Mental Application, including subfactors such as Initiative, Adaptability, Judgment, Mental Alertness
4. Dexterity and Accuracy
5. Experience
6. Training
7. Physical Demands
      Physical Activities
      Working Conditions and Hazards
8. Worker Characteristics

PLANNING A JOB ANALYSIS PROGRAM

In planning a job analysis program the first question is who shall perform it. It is not necessary, as some personnel people believe, that the analyst be an engineer or that he have a long course of training in the techniques of job analysis. The conduct of job analysis does require an above average general mental ability plus the ability to observe well and to express what one sees in clear and concise writing. If the analyst can do this, he need not be a college graduate. Essential qualities which formal education does not necessarily give are patience, curiosity, and the social skills necessary to question workers about their jobs. In selecting an analyst thought should also be given to the person's clerical interest and to his accuracy.

Fortunately in planning job analysis, aid can usually be secured from the State Employment Services. Most State Employment Services have specially trained job analysts whose services can be obtained free of charge. Analysts provided by the state usually act only as consultants or as trainers of persons designated by the hotel or restaurant operator to perform the actual analysis. Individual training is given the prospective analyst so that he can then conduct the analyses himself.

Aid can also be secured from some of the universities offering institutional or hotel or restaurant management courses. In the future, probably state hotel and restaurant associations will provide personnel educated to offer similar services.

In initiating job analysis it is best practice to start with but one small department. In this way errors of inexperience can be ironed out before conducting analyses in the rest of the establishment. In an establishment which is just instituting a personnel department, it is good practice to have the personnel director himself conduct the analysis. In this way he can gain firsthand knowledge of the jobs and of the organization.

Another consideration in conducting a job analysis program is its proper introduction to the workers. Anything that smacks of the efficiency expert may cause unrest among the employees. The fact that management is studying the worker's job may to the worker mean an implied criticism of the way he has been doing it. It may mean an attempt to speed him up. In any event the fact that he does not know the general purpose of job analysis is sufficient cause for resentment towards management. Where unions are present, job analysis may mean to them an attempt to steal some of their influence. If relations are at all amicable with the union, they should be informed of the proposed job analysis several days before the analysis is initiated. The union can be an aid in developing the proper attitude toward the analysis. Union or no union, the workers themselves should be informed of the purpose of analysis and how it is to be performed, with opportunity to ask questions of responsible persons. The proper introduction of job analysis programs may be just as important as the operation itself.

METHODS OF CONDUCTING JOB ANALYSIS

There are several ways of conducting a job analysis. One method is to develop a suitable questionnaire form and have the several workers doing a particular job fill it out. The procedure is then for the job analyst to assemble and compare the forms, selecting representative items from the various replies of persons working at the same job to make a job description. Proponents of this method argue that in the end the worker himself has to tell most of the tasks and responsibilities of his job. For hotel and restaurant employees, analysis by the worker should be considered only a first step. Most hotel and restaurant workers, including supervisory personnel, are not sufficiently trained in making observations, organizing materials, or in descriptive writing to perform analysis of their own jobs.

Another method of performing job analysis is to have each department head so trained that he can perform the analyses within his department. This method is advantageous in that the department head will necessarily take an active interest in the project and will be more willing to make any changes that he himself recommends as a result of his findings. Where department heads are already overloaded with work, of course this method is inadvisable.

A method which has proved workable for the hotel and restaurant is one which is a combination of those already mentioned. One man is responsible for the program, but he delegates as much responsibility as possible. All workers and supervisory personnel fill out an itemized analysis questionnaire. On page 32 is a form developed by Walter Buzby II at the Hotel Dennis, Atlantic City. The form on page 33 illustrates the job description of the personnel manager as done by J. B. Temple, President, Hotel Seminole, Jacksonville, Florida. On page 34 is the job specification of the same position. Pages 35-36 show the job description of a catering manager. This was developed by the U. S. Department of Labor.

WRITING THE JOB DESCRIPTION

Brevity and concision are the hallmarks of a well-written job description. Verbs substitute for phrases. Selecting the best words to describe an operation can delineate the job, yet eliminate paragraphs.

All of the writing should be in reply to the four key questions of analysis: what does the worker do, why does he do it, how does he do it, and what skills are involved in the doing.

Here, for example, is an illustration of the what, why, how, and skill-involved questions as applied to the job of OYSTERMAN or SHUCKER.

Work Performed:

Shucks oysters and clams (what) to the order of cooks or waiters (why): Forces oyster knife between halves of shell, and twists knife, forcing the shell open (how and skill involved); forces knife blade between oyster and bottom half of shell to sever oyster from shell (how and skill involved). The knife may be grasped in the worker's hand, or may be affixed to the workbench (how).

After the analyst has the questionnaires returned to him and has himself made the physical demands appraisal, he is ready to prepare a preliminary description of each job. It is important that he consider this description merely as a rough draft, for he must return to the personnel doing the jobs and question them carefully to learn of possible omissions. Many tasks of a job are performed only occasionally. The analyst will probably not observe them. Only through questioning the employee can he learn of these tasks. If the worker regularly performs the tasks, even though it be but once a week, it is a part of the

JOB DESCRIPTION QUESTIONNAIRE

Name of your position_____Date_____

Other Title(s)_____

How long have you held this position?_____yrs._____mons._____

How long have you worked at this hotel?_____yrs._____mons._____

Who is your supervisor?_____

What is your Age_____Height_____Weight_____Sex_____

Education: – Circle the last grade you attended.

Grade School	1	2	3	4	5	6	7	8
High School		1		2		3		4
College		1		2		3		4
Trade School		1		2		3		4

1. What time do you come to work? (If you work different shifts, state the different times you come to work.)

2. What time do you actually begin to work?

3. What do you do between the time you come to work and the time you begin to work?

4. What time are you through work for the day?

5. Is your work evenly divided during the day or are any hours particularly busy or slack? Please be definite!

6. What do you consider the most important part of your job?

7. Are there any special tasks connected with your job for which you believe a new person should be trained before he could do the work satisfactorily?

8. List any jobs that you may perform at times, which are not daily parts of your job.

9. Do you believe being able to read is important in your job? (Yes or No)

10. Do you believe being able to write is important in your job? (Yes or No)

11. Describe in detail on reverse side what you do in an average day at work. Try to remember everything. Try to account for every minute of your working day. Describe not only what you do, but how you do it, and when you do it, and why you do it. Use extra paper if you need it.

Signature_____

JOB DESCRIPTION

PERSONNEL MANAGER

Analyzes every job in the hotel, preparing job description and job specification of each one. Keeps files up to date as changes occur. Receives and interviews each person seeking employment. Has application form filled out if applicant seems suitable. If a position is open, arranges for applicant to have interview with department supervisor. Writes letter enclosing application form to each person seeking employment by mail.

On all new employees telephones or sends inquiry form to last three employers requesting confidential information. When possible secures this information before person is definitely given a job. Assists department supervisors in recruiting and securing employees. Places advertisements in newspapers and magazines. Asks present employees to recruit new employees. Phones and writes employment agencies and consults file of applications. Assists department supervisors in setting up training programs for various jobs. Prepares instruction sheet on each job where high turnover makes it advisable.

Welcomes, orients, and interviews each new employee, securing social security and income tax information. Explains vacation plan, paydays, and draw days. Asks employee to give paper notice before quitting. Fills out employee's time card escorting employee to Time-keeper's Office, where he receives time card number. Takes employee for brief friendly tour of building introducing him to fellow employees. Types earning card, Payroll Information, and Employee's Withholding Certificate (W-4 Form), turning these into Auditor.

Conducts Exit Interview of each employee separating from the hotel, checking with department supervisor to make sure keys, uniforms, etc. have been turned into supervisor. Checks final pay slip for correct number of days, initialing pay slip so Auditor will know employee has had final interview.

Assists employees with their personal problems, especially when their job performance is affected. Receives employees' grievances and reports them to Manager. Studies jobs and recommends simplifying and improving methods, hours, wages, and incentives. Encourages promotions of present employees to better jobs in the hotel.

Cooperates with Pound Hotels and Jacksonville hotels trying to place good applicants elsewhere when these hotels seek assistance. Maintains a suggestion box for employees near time clock at service entrance. Turns suggestions over to Manager.

Assists Manager in odd jobs such as operating Addressograph machine, relieving employees in emergencies, soliciting for Community Chest, etc. Cooperates and assists in planning employees' Christmas parties. Maintains First-Aid Kit for hotel employees. Completes accident reports on employees. Performs other duties as assigned by supervisor.

Uses following equipment: telephone, typewriter, and addressograph machine.

JOB SPECIFICATION

HOTEL SEMINOLE
Jacksonville, Florida

9/10/53

JOB TITLE: Personnel Manager

EMPLOYED NUMBER: 1

USUAL SEX: Female

HOURS: 8:00 a.m. to 4:30 p.m. Saturday 8:00 a.m. to 12:00 Noon
30-minute lunch period

TOTAL HOURS PER WEEK: 44 Hours

DAY OFF: Saturday afternoon and all day Sunday

VACATIONS: One week after year's service; two weeks after two years' service

USUAL RACE: White

MENTAL QUALIFICATIONS: (Routine, Medium, Great) Medium

PERSONALITY AND APPEARANCE REQUIREMENTS: Mature, neat in appearance, courteous, nice discernment of what is appropriate to do or say in dealing with people

CONTACTS: Applicants, general public, and employees

SUPERVISOR: President - Manager

AGE LIMITS: 25 - 55

SALARY:

MEALS: None

ROOM: None

OTHER EXTRAS: None

EXPERIENCE: Typing, plus general business or teaching experience

EDUCATION: High School (some college preferred)

PHYSICAL QUALIFICATIONS: Good Health, must be able to smile and always be pleasant

RESPONSIBILITY: (Light, Medium, Great) Medium

WORKING CONDITIONS: Pleasant

POSSIBLY PROMOTED FROM:

POSSIBLY PROMOTED TO:

CATERING MANAGER[2]
MAÎTRE D'HÔTEL

Hotels and Restaurants   Food Serving

Job Summary

  Supervises generally the serving of food, making arrangements for banquets, selling
  food-service, and handling complaints; may be responsible for profitable operations of the Food Serving and Food Preparation Departments; is employed usually
  in a hotel or large restaurant of the formal type.

Work Performed

  1. Supervises generally the daily service of food: Inspects work of HEAD WAITERS,
     WAITER CAPTAINS, WAITERS, WAITRESSES, BUS BOYS or GIRLS, and other
     Dining Room employees; sees that service is technically correct, efficient, and
     courteous; consults with EXECUTIVE CHEF, STEWARD, or CHEF-STEWARD
     concerning daily menus and operating problems; adjusts complaints concerning
     service or quality of food; acts as contact man between the Food Serving Depart-
     ment and the public.

  2. Makes arrangements with guests, in person or by letter, for banquets, luncheons,
     conventions, dances, and other social affairs; obtains pertinent information from
     guest, such as the number of persons expected, seating arrangements, decora-
     tions, music, and entertainers desired; attempts to analyze the requirements of
     the occasion and informs guest of suitable types of service; decides on and quotes
     prices, attempting to sell the services of the hotel; draws up contract and pro-
     cures guest's signature.

  3. Transmits necessary information to CHEF, HEAD WAITER, STEWARD, and
     other employees concerned; arranges for such details as the printing of menus,
     procurement of decorations and entertainment, table setup, and the food service
     schedule; arranges for publicity if desired.

  4. Inspects finished arrangements; may be present at time of banquet, supervising
     service and greeting guests.

  The duties performed by a CATERING MANAGER, EXECUTIVE CHEF, or STEW-
     ARD depend in great measure upon the size and organization of the hotel, policy
     of the management, and upon the individual worker's ability. In large establish-
     ments, especially in the southwestern parts of the country, the CATERING
     MANAGER may have complete charge of food preparation, food serving, beverage
     dispensation, and banquet service. In such a case he would make up and assign
     prices to articles on menus, keep cost accounts, and assume responsibility for
     making a net profit out of food preparation and service. Under such circum-
     stances, the worker might be titled "FOOD MANAGER." The FOOD MANAGER
     would either supervise and coordinate the work of a BANQUET MANAGER, CHEF,
     STEWARD, MAÎTRE D'HÔTEL (who would be directly responsible for food serv-
     ice only), and a SOCIAL DIRECTOR, or he might perform the tasks of any or all
     of these workers himself.

_____

[2]From Job Descriptions for Hotels and Restaurants, Department of Labor, U. S. Government Printing Office, 1938.

CATERING MANAGER

MAÎTRE D'HÔTEL

(Continued)

The SOCIAL DIRECTOR would have charge of social affairs, caring for guests' comfort and amusement, and arranging and promoting social functions such as luncheons, dinners, and dances.

The BANQUET MANAGER would arrange the details of banquets, providing the necessary physical equipment and employing additional workers. During the banquet, he would act as HEAD WAITER, supervising the service of food to make sure that it is correct, on time, and as ordered.

Relation to Other Jobs

Promotion from: HEAD WAITER; HEAD WAITER (ROOM SERVICE); PURCHASING AGENT; CHEF; CHEF-STEWARD.

Promotion to: HOTEL MANAGER.

Job Combination: The duties of this job may be combined with those of HOTEL MANAGER ASSISTANT, HEAD WAITER, HEAD WAITER (ROOM SERVICE), STEWARD, CHEF-STEWARD, BANQUET MANAGER, WINE STEWARD, SOCIAL DIRECTOR, or PURCHASING AGENT, or they may be included in those of HOTEL MANAGER.

Specialized Qualifications

Some establishments require graduation from a hotel training school. Many hotels employ a CATERING MANAGER who has had experience in same job in a smaller hotel, and many prefer an individual who has had European training.

Ability to meet the public, and to sell the hotel's food service; ability to speak, read, and write French, German, or Italian may be required; a practical knowledge of food preparation and purchasing may be required; knowledge of social customs and etiquette, especially in regard to banquets; knowledge of liquors may be required.

Special Information

Numbers of employees supervised and their titles.

Does worker assume responsibility for food preparation as well as service?

Type of dining rooms supervised (American or European style)?

Does worker supervise beverage department?

job and should be included in the job description. For example, a dishwasher may be required to empty a garbage can once or twice a day. It is then a part of the job of dishwashing. Perhaps some other employee should rightfully empty the garbage container. Consultation with the supervisor would subtract this task from the job description.

Reference to the job questionnaires will show the analyst variations in the same job. Follow-up study of the jobs indicated by the questionnaires may indicate areas which need drastic changes.

Forms and guide books for performing the analysis can be secured from the Superintendent of Documents, U. S. Government Printing Office, Washington, D. C. Excellent general description of jobs found in hotels and restaurants can be found in Job Descriptions for Hotels and Restaurants. This two-volume work is also obtained from the Superintendent of Documents for $2.50. While the job descriptions contained in it are not meant to be characteristic of jobs in a particular hotel or restaurant, they can be used as models for organizing and writing of the job descriptions from the job analysis data.

Data from the completed job analysis can be put into a form most useful for a given operation. This is the job specification. The specification may include wages paid, training given, hours worked, vacations, and various other details about the job which would be useful to an employment interviewer or for some other purpose. An illustration of the kind of data which might be included is seen in the form on page 38. Pages 39 and 40 show similar forms.

Training: First week on the job -- One day watching and listening; one day doing and telling why; one day under close supervision; three days working alone with checkup at unexpected intervals.

Possibility of advancement: To head houseman.

Schedule of Duties: At 8:00 a.m. report to the Linen Room in uniform for special orders and equipment stored there the night before for repair. Get clean dust cloths. Leave guest room door open (except in stormy weather). Do high dusting first; ceiling lights, draperies, cornices, Venetian blinds (if any) and window screens. Move furniture away from walls. Dust backs of each piece, also wall molding, mopboard and carpet before replacing exactly as before. Start at point farthest from the door and work with vacuum toward it, clean closet light, high rods and shelves, both lights, ventilator and high tile. Dust both sides of door and transom. Make sure the latter works easily. Report damage to furniture or fixtures at once.

Equipment: For central system. Vacuum hose and attachments; radiator brush; long-handled duster; dust cloth and stepladder.

Hazards: Only those caused by carelessness.

Duties: Vacuum 117 rooms on three floors in 12 days. This averages nine rooms a day with one corridor. This also includes washing the terrazzo, seeing that adjoining corridors are neat before leaving at 4:00 p.m. This allows for nine "check-outs" that require special cleaning or other extras during the 12 days. The man working Sunday picks up any rooms omitted or left in bad condition by guests. He also does Linen Room errands.

To prevent accidents to employees or guests, the striped black and white vacuum hose is placed in the center of the corridors with warning sign in a conspicuous spot.

Special Work: Before the maid makes the bed, vacuum mattress, spring and frame of beds in two rooms each day and help the maid turn the mattresses in two others.

JOB ANALYSIS AND WORK SIMPLIFICATION

The primary purpose of job analysis is to secure an accurate description of the jobs in an establishment. In performing job analysis, however, the analyst recognizes many situations in which operations are being performed inefficiently. Poor work scheduling and inefficient methods of work often come to the attention of the analyst during the course of the analysis. By pointing out these discrepancies and seeking better methods, the analyst becomes in effect a work-simplification man as well as a job analyst.

Job analyses performed in hotels and restaurants usually result in work simplification by eliminating unnecessary motions and tasks and by suggesting better organization of workers and of the work. The consequent savings in wages and increased production usually more than pay the cost of the job analysis program.

This means, however, that unless care is taken some employees will be abruptly thrown out of a job. It will pay the hotel or restaurant to make every effort to transfer, upgrade or otherwise find

JOB SPECIFICATION[3]

JOB TITLE: Vacuum man.

EMPLOYED NUMBER: Six.

SEX: Male.

HOURS: Eight hours daily; 8:00 a.m. to 4:00 p.m. 48 hours, weekly.

DAY OFF: Sunday except once in six weeks -- Monday.

VACATIONS: One week after one year, ten days after five years; two weeks after ten years.

NATIONALITY: Citizen or working toward it.

MENTAL QUALIFICATIONS: Average intelligence or slightly below, ability to follow directions.

PERSONALITY REQUIREMENTS: Good disposition, dependable, careful and cooperative, even-tempered.

CONTACTS: Other workers, guests, management.

TYPE OF LABOR: Unskilled.

SUPERVISOR: Inspectress.

AGE LIMITS: 30 to 60.

MARITAL STATUS: Married or single.

SALARY: $5.44 to $6.40 per day, paid weekly.

MAINTENANCE: Uniforms furnished and laundered; lunch the only meal.

EXPERIENCE: None required.

EDUCATION: Preferably grammar school. Must be able to read and write. Some mechanical ability.

PHYSICAL QUALIFICATIONS: Medium height and weight; medium working speed, good eyesight.

RESPONSIBILITY: Own work, equipment, furnishings, guest's belongings.

WORKING CONDITIONS: Pleasant

---

[3]Taken from an article by Grace H. Brigham, "Establishing Job Specifications and Merit Rating Report Systems," Hotel Management, September 1948.

HOTEL SEMINOLE

JOB TITLE: Food checker_____EMPLOYED NUMBER: 2 1/3 (part time)_____

USUAL SEX: Female_____USUAL RACE: White_____

HOURS: 6:30 a.m. to 2:00 p.m. --2:00 p.m. to 9:00 p.m. (two 30 min. meal periods for each shift.)

TOTAL HOURS PER WEEK: 36 hours_____DAY OFF: One day_____

VACATIONS: One week after year's service; two weeks after two years' service._____

MENTAL QUALIFICATIONS: (Routine, Medium, Great) Medium_____

PERSONALITY AND APPEARANCE REQUIREMENTS: Congenial_____

CONTACTS: Chef and employees_____SUPERVISOR: Chef-Steward_____

AGE LIMITS: 20-60 MEALS: Two ROOM: None OTHER EXTRAS: None_____

EXPERIENCE: Hotel food experience_____EDUCATION: Grade school and good in arith-
_____metic_____

PHYSICAL QUALIFICATIONS: Good health RESPONSIBILITY: (Light, Medium, Great)_____
_____Medium_____

WORKING CONDITIONS: Warm and noisy._____

Receives food checks from Waitresses; inspects trays for arrangement and amount of food; prices food checks on machine, returning them to Waitresses.

Receives food order for room service by phone from guest. Rings for Room Service Waiter, gives order to Waiter, gives order to Waiter on scratch pad. Writes order on room service food check, inserting room number and Waiter's name on top of stub and the food check. Prices check in machine, using Room Service Menu prices. Adds tax and gives check to Room Waiter.

Issues officer's check to Waitress, writing name of officer and Waitress number on check and top stub. As employees eat their meals, checks their names off of list on Employees' Meal Sheet. Receives party checks from banquet Waiters or Banquet Manager, checking figures for multiplication and addition, pricing in machine and adding tax.

Keeps a daily history of the number of the various meat dishes served, turning into the Chef daily. Reports to Chef any disturbance, uncleanliness, or equipment in need of repairs. Receives bread and ice cream invoices from Pantry man. Turns invoices into Chef daily.

Keeps record of Void amounts and reasons for voiding, turning into Auditor daily. Takes register reading three times a day. Makes out total food sales after each meal as follows:

DEPARTMENT	AMOUNT
Coffee Shop	_____
Room Service	_____
Parties	_____
Voids	_____

Turns total food sales with officer check and room service check stubs into Auditor. Orders supplies from Auditor's Office, and Print Shop.

HOTEL SEMINOLE

JOB TITLE: __Chief Engineer__ EMPLOYED NUMBER: __1__ USUAL SEX: __Male__

HOURS: __8:00 a.m. to 5:00 p.m. 1 hour for lunch period.__

TOTAL HOURS PER WEEK: __48 hours__ DAY OFF: __Sunday__ USUAL RACE: __White__

VACATIONS: __One week after year's service; two weeks after two years' service.__

MENTAL QUALIFICATIONS: __(Routine, Medium, Great) Medium__

PERSONALITY AND APPEARANCE REQUIREMENTS: __Congenial__ CONTACTS: __Manager and Employees__

SUPERVISOR: __Manager__ AGE LIMITS: __35 - 65__ MEALS: __One__ ROOM: __None__

OTHER EXTRAS: __Uniforms__ EXPERIENCE: __Engineering and Mechanical__

EDUCATION: __High School__ PHYSICAL QUALIFICATIONS: __Good health, walks, stands, climbs, and stoops__

RESPONSIBILITY: __(Light, Medium, Great) Great__ WORKING CONDITIONS: __Warm, noisy and dirty__

Supervises work of employees engaged in installing, operating and maintaining hotel equipment. Hires and trains new employees in engineering department. Records or logs the time that the heating system, steam, and air conditioning units are turned on and off. Calls salt and lamp bulb companies specifying delivery date for these contract items. Has fans and flues cleaned.

Orders repair parts, making out his own purchase order. If order exceeds $25.00 consults Manager's Office and has purchase order made out there. Keeps time book for engineering employees, checking with time cards on first and sixteenth. Performs general duties of an engineer. (See job description.)

Makes out "draw slips" on 12th and 27th.

Performs other duties as assigned by supervisor.

Approves all invoices for engineering items.

Uses following equipment: motors, pumps, compressors, transformers, oil cans, grease guns, hand trucks and hand tools.

employment for employees who have been displaced as a result of job analysis or work simplification. It is only by following such a policy that the cooperation of the employees can be obtained in a continuing methods improvement program. When a position is eliminated in a group operation such as dishwashing or vegetable cleaning, it may even be necessary to keep all of the members of the groups employed until one is separated on his own volition. Such a procedure is reflected in higher morale.

HOW JOB ANALYSIS RESULTED IN WORK SIMPLIFICATION
IN ONE HOTEL

An illustration of how work simplification results from job analysis was strikingly shown in a job analysis program conducted at the Hotel Radisson in Minneapolis, Minnesota (480 employees).[4]

One of the questions asked in the course of the job analysis was, "What time do you come to work and why?" No one, it seemed, knew the answer. Further analysis revealed that while in the preceding ten years offices and department stores had adjusted their opening hours from 8 to 9 or 9:30 a.m., the hotel continued to require their employees to report to work at the same time they had been reporting for the previous twenty-five years. A large majority of employees were required to be on the job at 5, 6, and 7 a.m. Since the stores and offices of the city were not open, the patrons of the hotel were not up and requiring services. The hotel employees did practically nothing productive their first two hours on duty.

The service elevator operator when asked, "Why do you come to work at 6 a.m.?" replied that he had been so instructed 15 years ago when hired. When asked what he did the first thirty minutes between 6 and 6:30, he replied, "Nothing." Further questioning disclosed that between 6:30 and 7 he took a few employees to the locker room, one-half of a flight up.

An outstanding case of inefficiency appeared in the job of steam fitter. The hotel had absolutely no need for a steam fitter. One Sunday's "work" by the "steam fitter" consisted of repacking two faucets for which he was paid $23.00. Needless to say, the job of steam fitter no longer appears in the hotel organization chart. Other examples of poor scheduling of hours were found. Job analysis enabled the management to rearrange hours and require the presence of employees only when needed. By this method the equivalent of forty-six persons were eliminated from the payroll.

Job analysis showed that maids and house detectives were duplicating each other's work in reporting on occupancy of rooms. Maids spent about 30 to 45 minutes each morning checking their sections for occupancy. House detectives made the same report every hour. Prior to the job analysis the house detective's report was filed away in the assistant manager's desk and forgotten. Under the new procedure this report reaches the room clerk four hours earlier and the 40 maids are each saved at least 30 minutes time per day. The maids now spend their first half hour doing hall cleaning, thereby eliminating the need for hall girls and some housemen.

The same analysis pointed out that although the wages of bellmen had been raised from $10.00 to $120 per month since 1938, the bellmen did little or nothing to earn this increase. They had gotten away from the responsibility of supervising the cleaning of the lobby and were "too busy" to relieve the elevator operators during their rest periods. Most of their time, it was found, was spent in delivering hotel property to customers, for a gratuity. Two night housemen spent six of their eight hours performing extra services for guests, two hours working for the hotel. By actual count the two night housemen delivered fourteen extra easy chairs, five floor lamps, six extension cords, three bridge tables and chairs, and two card tables with chairs. One guest alone asked for and received twelve extra chairs -- the house received no revenue for this service and lost the time spent by the employee. Moreover, the equipment had to be removed the next day by employees who were not working for tips.

The baggage porter, whose wages had also increased from $10.00 to $120 per month, was spending his entire day doing work wholly unproductive for the hotel. The porters who handled transportation cost the hotel $500 a month just to give and sell transportation information. A competing hotel rendered the same service for one-third this cost, while another received $150 from an employee in charge of transportation services who, after paying his rent, still made a good living.

MAN ANALYSIS AND JOB SPECIFICATIONS

Almost no scientific research has been done to define the kinds of people who do best in the hotel and restaurant field.

---

[4] Taken from an article by Byron Calhoun, "Analyzing The Job," Tavern Talk, Jan. 25, 1947.

Every restaurant and hotel manager has his own notions of what kind of personality is most successful for a food service employee. These notions vary considerably.

"I hire only high school graduates," says one cafeteria manager. "Don't use teen-agers," says a shopping center operator.

However, in the same city, a different restaurant employs teen-agers almost entirely. Another manager hires only employees who he feels have management potential. Many restaurateurs hire only persons whom they can dominate easily and who respond quickly and without question to their supervisors. Who is right?

What kind of a person makes the best food service employee? Why not investigate the personalities of hundreds of restaurant employees, separate the more successful from the less so and on the basis of the information collected construct a model, or ideal employee. The model can be used as a guide in selecting and training employees.

Necessarily the ideal or model would be described in broad terms, general enough to cover employees in such different establishments as a luxury table service restaurant and a 25¢ check-average stool operation. The model must reflect fact based on research, and be a true image of a valued food service employee. The model could be described as a picture of the personality of a successful food service employee.

Such a study has been done and a model constructed. Dr. James Armatas, working with food service employees of university and commercial cafeterias, restaurants, hospitals, and cocktail lounges, has researched the ideal employee and in the process established a model, describing his personality as related to job success.

Here are some of the facts:

Lower-level food service employees need neither great skill nor high intelligence.

Most lower-level food service employees have limited education, limited skills, and have had limited cultural opportunities.

Few people lack the intrinsic skills or capacity to do food service work, but the food service employee must have an ability to adjust himself to the personal and physical demands of food service work.

The successful food service employee is characterized by these traits:

1. Seriousness. He is task-oriented, a practical person who tends to be all business in his dealings with his fellow employees and with customers. He knows what he and other employees are supposed to do, and he works hard to accomplish what is expected of him. He plans for the future, dislikes having things happen to him by chance. He lacks color, and is not active in the social sense. He tells few jokes, does little bragging, is not apt to act on impulse.

2. Responsibility. He's the kind of person who once he finishes his own job looks for other things to do, and he knows how to perform other jobs than his own. He can fill in for absent workers.

He is sensitive to how other employees perform, and when a fellow employee "goofs off" is quick to let the supervisor know about it.

He understands the chain of command well and would not think of going over his supervisor's head, or of countermanding a supervisor's decision. He is bothered when someone does not appreciate or is not satisfied with his work and goes to that person to find out what has been done wrong.

3. Control of Anger. He keeps his anger well controlled, seldom blows off, especially towards his supervisor. Neither does he complain to his supervisor no matter how unjust an order may seem.

Basically pleasant and agreeable, he is not a bit flowery.

He goes out of his way to be helpful to his fellow workers, but can be aloof and cold towards any co-worker who violates his friendship.

His friends tend to come from among co-workers and he likes people who are like him; tending to be critical of people who are happy-go-lucky, lazy, outspoken, or irresponsible.

4. Energy. He has tremendous energy, is in action most of the time. He sets few physical limits on himself, does not hesitate to lift and move things, rarely excuses himself because of physical limitations for not doing a task. He needs little rest, does not develop physical symptoms.

5. <u>Compulsiveness</u>. He lives in a practical, concrete world, shuns theory, images, daydreams, and things that lack a "real" quality.

He is compulsive in the sense that he is keyed up and ready for action, spends little idle time, is disturbed to find jobs unfinished, and is impatient with those who spend time contemplating various ramifications of a problem, or who otherwise delay taking action.

A job description stated in precise terms of what to do and what not to do comforts him and he seeks definite instructions.

6. <u>Need for Order</u>. Being a rather rigid person, the model employee needs a sense of order about him. He himself is neat, tidy, his personal belongings are kept arranged and in place. He keeps to a schedule, usually comes early to work rather than risk being late. Before starting work he must clean and arrange things and he is careful to do the same after he has finished the task.

7. <u>Belief Systems Stereotyped</u>. His values and ideals tend to be of a stereotyped, nonreflective nature.

He holds narrow views on politics, world affairs, religion and morals. For him, goodwill does not necessarily win over evil, and personal freedom -- including his own -- should be restricted, controlled, and dictated by a higher authority.

8. <u>Conformance to the Work Situation</u>. He is sensitive to what is acceptable and nonacceptable behavior in a restaurant. If at first he does not follow the policies and practices desired by his supervisor, he quickly learns to accept and believe in such policies and procedures. There's no hesitation in doing menial tasks such as lifting, mopping, and bending, and he accepts the view that he is not capable of making important decisions.

9. <u>Truthfulness</u>. He tends to be honest and truthful about himself even though such views might hurt him. He doesn't put himself in a good light to gain favor with his supervisors or his friends.

<u>What kind of person should be hired?</u>

Using the model as described, we find that the successful food service employee is eager to conform and is a follower, not a leader. If all such conforming persons are employed, the policy of promoting from within will not work well. Consequently in employing new personnel, the vast majority of people should be selected primarily for doing the jobs that need to be done with little thought to the person's promotability. But other employees should be selected primarily for their potential as supervisors or for managers. No system of selection should be so arbitrary that people from either one of the two groups cannot be shifted over to the opposite group if their work demonstrates that such a shift is appropriate.

The ideal food service employee is not the kind of person we in American society often hold up as being most desirable, the American stereotype of the upwardly mobile citizen. He is a conscientious, highly responsible person who is eager to conform to the demands of the supervisor and of the job, in the last analysis, the kind of person upon which this great industry rests.

CHAPTER 5

Recruiting

Attracting a high type of personnel and placing them in the jobs most appropriate to their skills and personalities is a function so important that oftentimes the success of the enterprise hinges upon it. No enterprise can long survive, no matter how favored in a competitive economic system, if poor personnel and poor placement are in effect for any length of time. If one is not convinced of these statements let him examine the costs of labor turnover, the cost of dissatisfaction arising out of placing a man in a job for which he has no interest, the losses resulting from inefficiency because of the absence of requisite abilities.

Resistance to old trial-and-error methods of employment is increasing in hotels and restaurants. Hotels and restaurants are striving towards stability of employment. If a job opening is likely to develop into a career for a recruit, proper placement must be given careful attention. A mistaken placement may have years of bad effects. Organized labor is demanding more security in tenure of employment. Unions negotiate clauses which make it difficult for an employer to discharge a worker. Competitors, using expert methods of choosing employees, force the hotel or restaurant manager who has not adopted similar methods either to adopt them or be satisfied with employees found unsatisfactory by others.

There are of course many employers who pirate trained employees from neighboring hotels and restaurants. This proves satisfactory if the pirates pay a higher wage or if tips are higher.

One well-known restaurant and hotel firm sends its executives out to meals at competitors' establishments where the more desirable waiters are told, "If you think about moving, come and see us." The executive leaves his business card. Not ethical, but effective!

Recruiting can be a complex task. To take applicants as they come off the street may be disastrous because inefficient workers may result from those hired hastily. On the other hand, a similarly disastrous result may occur if "good" people are recruited without prior consideration of how such people are to be used.

Farsighted recruiting requires (1) consideration of manpower needs; (2) knowledge of the promotional ladder within an organization; (3) a prediction of future turnover rates on the basis of past experience and future growth expectations; and (4) understanding of the type of person who seems to be best suited for specific positions in the organization. This understanding comes about through research and evaluation of the performance of present employees in an organization.

Recruitment problems differ among various hotels and restaurants. Each organization -- on the basis of its experience -- must come up with certain philosophies, standards, and policies relative to its recruitment program. In standardizing policies, it is recognized that some degree of inflexibility ensues, but too much flexibility removes the value of system. The following standards and/or philosophies need to be established in developing a recruitment program.

1. The minimum skills and requirements of each of the various jobs must be spelled out prior to any actual recruitment. It is a needless waste of time, money, and energy to recruit individuals who will not be hired ultimately. For example, a large department store with a high turnover problem discovered from their research that married women stayed with them three times longer than single women. One of the conditions required of a female applicant for a position with this particular organization was that she be married. Recruiters obviously should not concentrate on high schools as a source of labor.

2. Each organization must understand and objectify the degree of potential for personal development required in new employees. An organization that develops its supervision from within exclusively may be crippling itself in the long run if it recruits individuals who do not have long-range potentials even though these individuals may have excellent qualifications for the available position. On the other hand, where potentials for growth and advancement are limited, a recruiting program that focuses on individuals with proven records of growth-seeking -- such as college students or those who leave jobs

for better positions -- is unrealistic and leads to labor dissatisfaction and turnover. The president of a chain of fast-food roadside restaurants hired twelve recent college graduates. By the fall only one of these graduates remained with the company.

3. Prior to recruitment, everyone in the hotel or restaurant who will be affected must be informed of the jobs to which new employees will probably be assigned. This procedure helps keep the organization stable in the eyes of present employees and prepares employees for the changes to come.

4. The organization must decide whether all new employees will be hired at the bottom and trained for promotion or whether new employees will be hired outside the organization at various levels and skills. It is recognized generally that an ideal is to establish a balance whereby both systems are used in order to avoid moving unqualified people up purely because of labor shortage and at the same time avoiding the lethargy that develops in organizations where people lack advancement possibilities. In chains of hotels or restaurants some positions call for skills and experience which are not developed within the chain. Therefore some recruitment for higher-level jobs from the outside is necessary.

SOURCES OF EMPLOYEES

The first step in the employment procedure is to secure a supply of desirable recruits. No matter how well the personnel function is carried out, some turnover of employees is normal and to be expected. Part-time employees are usually needed for banquets, conventions, and other heavy-volume periods.

Recruitment Through Newspapers

Hotels and restaurants usually depend upon newspaper advertisements for attracting new employees, and for some jobs newspapers are satisfactory. They are particularly useful in attracting unskilled and young people whose knowledge of employment opportunities is meager. Newspapers are a relatively poor tool for securing supervisory personnel or highly skilled workers. They should be used with caution in times of business recession, for they are likely to attract many unqualified workers, who, if refused employment, will resent the refusal. Moreover, time taken to screen the qualified from the unqualified is costly.

A different type of personnel is attracted by the various newspapers in the same labor area. One type of worker reads the sensational tabloids, another reads the conservative newspapers. The choice of the newspaper as an advertising medium should depend upon the type of job to be filled. Using newspapers most advantageously and finding which are most effective in attracting recruits requires continuing research.

"Inexperience is an asset!" says the waitress ad of one restaurant chain. Other ads ask questions such as, "Do you want to make money?" and "Do you like to meet people?" "Compare your salary as a waitress with that of the secretary next door -- you're almost sure to come out the capitalist of the pair." Ads seeking part-time waitresses might start with, "Do you want well-paying, part-time work?" Inserted in school and college papers they reach a source of recruits largely untouched.

Placing a classified ad as close as possible to the beginning of the ad section has the advantage of its immediately catching the eye of people who are scanning the classified ads. An ad for a meat cook could appear in the list as "Cook, Meat." Combination ads such as "Porters and Waitresses" do not pull as well as when the heading lists only one job, "Porters" or "Waitresses."

A tight labor market may call for a larger ad. Many position vacancies also indicate a large ad. Display ads, large ads with white space, have been effective for some hotels and restaurants; for others, the effect has been no greater than with the classified ad. Running an ad continuously is thought by some to give the implication that all is not well with the personnel policy of the company. One study, however, showed that when an ad was discontinued for a few days the number of applicants did not increase after the ad again appeared.

Older people are attracted by words such as "steady" or "permanent." A hospital dietary department might use a caption, "Do you want to be a friend of the sick?" This would attract a different type of person than the usual "Kitchen Help Wanted" ad caption.

Since the more progressive hotels and restaurants prefer to train their waitresses, the lack of experience as a waitress is no serious liability. An ad which stresses the need for good health, a pleasant appearance and speaking voice and points out that experience is not required attracts a higher type person than is likely to otherwise apply.

A run-of-the-mill advertisement will usually attract a run-of-the-mill worker. If the hotel or restaurant wants a high type of employee and has something tangible to offer, such as unusual working conditions, high pay, benefit plan, etc., these advantages can be listed in the advertisement. Listing advantages builds public relations in general.

Here are some examples of well-worded ads used by the Stouffer restaurants, one of the country's best-operated table-service restaurant chains:

WAITRESSES
18-25
to train for permanent positions as
STOUFFER GIRLS
in our new restaurant. Experience not necessary, salary while training. High school graduates preferred. Meals, uniforms provided. No Sunday work.

WAITRESSES
18-25
Train for permanent positions in dining room service. Good salary while training in attractive surroundings with pleasant public contact. High school graduates preferred. Meals and uniforms furnished. No Sunday or holiday work.

HIGH SCHOOL GRADUATES
18 to 25
Train for high-paying position in dining room service. Attractive surroundings, pleasant public contact, congenial co-workers. Experience unnecessary, salary while training. Meals, uniforms, no Sunday or holiday work.

WAITRESSES
18-25
If you are a high school graduate, like people and are interested in a position offering steady work, the best of working conditions, meals and uniforms, apply for Stouffer Girl work. Experience not necessary. Salary while training. Openings for both full-time and part-time work. High-paying positions plus meals and uniforms. No Sunday or holiday work.

STOUFFER'S
Address

HIGH SCHOOL GRADUATES
18 to 25
What do you want in your job?
HIGH WAGES
SECURITY
CONGENIAL SURROUNDINGS
CHANCE FOR ADVANCEMENT
OPPORTUNITY TO MEET THE PUBLIC
MEALS FURNISHED
INQUIRE ABOUT
STOUFFER GIRL WORK
STOUFFER'S
Address

Recruitment Through Radio Advertising

Radio advertising has been found to be effective for the procurement of extra and part-time employees, especially maids. The radio reaches women not actively seeking employment and who would not usually read a newspaper Help Wanted column. By radio they can be reminded they already have skills such as cooking and housekeeping which can be exchanged for extra money and still have time to keep up their own homes.

Employment Agencies

Public employment agencies are little used by hotel and restaurant employers except in particular localities. Often the employer finds that referrals from public agencies have not been screened, perhaps because the agency is more concerned with placing the applicant in a job than with ascertaining his qualifications for the job. Charitable employment agencies sometimes operate in a similar fashion, giving little thought to the needs of the employer. In some cities, however, the public employment services are highly satisfactory.

The state employment services are public employment agencies which have the tools to do a first-class referral job. The states must meet certain standards and cooperate with the federal government to be eligible to receive federal funds. The U.S.E.S. (United States Employment Service) acts as a clearing house of employment information, conducts research, develops employment tools, and is a non-fee referral agency for workers.

The U.S.E.S. has explored the use of tests in screening job candidates. It has developed oral trade questions for several hotel and restaurant jobs. The questions were carefully selected and standardized (tested) throughout the country on skilled craftsmen. The questions enable the interviewer to compare candidates' job information. For example, an applicant who declares long experience in bartending is compared in technical knowledge with successful, employed bartenders. The questions are especially adapted to individual administration in the interview. They are worded in the language of the worker and require concise answers centered around important trade elements. Time for administering and scoring is less than ten minutes. In some cases, the U.S.E.S. will permit employers to use the Oral Trade Tests in their own employment offices. The U.S.E.S. is also developing aptitude tests for various jobs. As yet none have been developed for use in selecting workers in hotel and restaurant jobs.

Private employment agencies sometimes provide a valuable source of recruits. Again research will show the merit of each employment agency. In the past some unscrupulous employers entered into fee-splitting agreements and other nefarious arrangements with unethical employment agencies. Needless to say, such arrangements boomerang to the employer's disadvantage and should never be considered by any self-respecting businessman.

Schools and Colleges as a Source of Recruits

Schools and colleges are excellent sources of recruits for jobs demanding special skills and supervisory abilities. Hotels and restaurants employ special recruiters to appraise and employ graduates of hotel and restaurant courses. A few months before each graduating period the recruiters personally interview the prospective graduates. This proves valuable to both the prospective graduate and the business sending the recruiter. Students are informed of the opportunities as regards available jobs, and employers have the opportunity to find those qualified to fit their particular needs. The advantage of vocational and college training will be discussed at some length in a later chapter.

Recruiting college students for summer jobs has also proved advantageous to the employer and to the student. From the employer's point of view a high type of employee is had at a relatively low wage. Students majoring in hotel and restaurant administration bring fresh ideas, and in many cases are more proficient than the regular employees, especially in auditing and other front-office jobs. Because students want a variety of work experience, they can be used to replace regular employees on vacation and they can be rotated in several jobs. Some students who have had several summers of experience have successfully managed resort operations and summer clubs during their senior year. Most resort operators find students proficient as waiters and waitresses. Hospitals have found students effective in the kitchen and business office.

Usually a systematic recruiting program is instituted by which contacts are maintained with several schools. Fraternities and sororities can provide a constant supply of recruits. Where conditions of employment and pay are desirable, college students return year after year until their college work is completed. Many later become patrons. Guest comments, such as "The most attractive people at this resort are the help," attest to the success of the idea of using students as summer employees.

Other Sources of Recruits

Numerous other sources of recruits are often overlooked. For a particular hotel or restaurant one or more of such sources may prove excellent. Some of these are foreign language newspapers, state boards of vocational education, veterans' organizations, YMCA's, YWCA's, Catholic and other denominational organizations. Some restaurants have found the best recruits in the suburbs of cities and in small country towns.

THE APPLICATION FORM

A means of securing a standard set of information about an applicant is the application form. Although the application form basically is considered as a selection tool, it is discussed in this section because it generally accompanies all initial contacts with potential employees. It can be used as a permanent personnel record and its information used in conducting research. The application form saves the interviewer time and gives him an idea of the applicant's literacy.

Questions to be included on the application form depend upon the type of work the applicant is seeking. Every item should serve a purpose. No item should be included unless the information it calls for is useful either for research purposes or for determining the applicant's eligibility for the job.

Such items as: "List all of your physical impairments"; "Have you ever been arrested?"; "Are any of your family in mental institutions?"; "Do you drink excessively?" are worthless. They will not be answered correctly and may cause the prospective employee to start his career with a falsehood. Some states restrict the type of question which may be asked in the employment procedure. At present, questions of race, religion, and political beliefs are excluded by law in several states and cities.

Application forms should be designed for a particular purpose. This means that usually a different application form is required for salaried and supervisory personnel than is needed for use in filling unskilled jobs. For supervisory and sales jobs, information may be wanted about the applicant's interests, degree of community participation, experience, financial status, level and exact type of educational background, and reasons the applicant wishes employment with the company. Such items are probably unimportant for unskilled jobs.

For purposes of filing, one of the first items on the application form should be the type of work desired by the applicant. A number of biographical and statistical items should be included if there is any reason for using such data in keeping the personnel file or in research. Some suggested items:

1. Name, birth date, social security number, and date.
2. Height, weight, and sex.
3. Address and telephone number.
4. Marital status and names of dependents.
5. Whom to notify in case of emergency.
6. Health card, if required.
7. Working papers, if a minor.
8. Hobbies.
9. Work desired.

From this data it is possible to determine something about the type of employee who will be satisfactory in a particular job. For example, in one hotel studied by the writers it was found that chambermaids were more likely to be satisfactory and remain on the job if they were between the ages of 30 and 55 and had either few or no dependents. In other hotels investigated, these facts were of no value in selecting maids.

Another section of the application form can be used to learn something of the applicant's experience and reputation. For many unskilled jobs in the hotel and restaurant, secondary or college education is undesirable unless the employer believes such candidates may soon be promoted. Questions on education for unskilled jobs need not be complete since they have little relevance. Contrariwise, for supervisory and sales positions educational items should inquire as to the specific courses taken in schooling, the place of schooling and the grades received. Previous work experience information is valuable. Items concerning place of previous employment, type of work performed, and reason for leaving can be of use if properly followed up. The use of references will be discussed later.

Through research it may be found that for certain jobs special questions are of value in predicting the applicant's success, just as age seemed to be a factor in the success of a chambermaid. Some companies have found that participation in community affairs is predictive of the kind of job performance the company desires. If so, items asking for such information can be included. Information concerning financial status, membership in clubs, number of dependents, and current living expenses are predictive for some sales jobs.

A sample application form, developed by the Educational Department of the National Restaurant Association, is shown on pages 49 and 50.

HIRING THE HANDICAPPED

Since it is true that almost all jobs require only certain faculties and skills, it is sound personnel policy to employ physically handicapped persons for certain jobs. For example, it has been found that a hearing impairment does not affect performance on such jobs as houseman and wall washer. Handicapped employees are usually more dependable and have better absenteeism and tardiness records than nonimpaired employees. A dish room crew of deaf and dumb is regularly employed by a summer hotel with excellent results.

It is unwise to employ a one-armed room clerk or a disfigured waitress. These impairments would have no effect on performance in a variety of other jobs. To show the number and variety of jobs which have been satisfactorily filled by impaired personnel, see the table illustrated on page 51. This table is the result of the experience of the Statler Hotel Company with successful placements of handicapped persons.

NOTE: This Application Form outline for nonsupervisory employees was developed by the Educational Department of the National Restaurant Association after a survey of similar forms revealed that all of them requested the basic information called for below. It is not suggested that this outline be used "as is." In practically all cases it will be advisable to include some of the additional questions that are printed on the back of the form, together with any special questions that can help determine whether the applicant qualifies for your type of operation.

Position Desired _____   Date _____

Name_____ Social Security No._____
       Last   First   Initial

Address_____ Phone No. _____

Date of Birth_____Sex_____Height_____Weight_____

Place of Birth_____No. of Dependents_____

☐ Single   ☐ Married   ☐ Divorced   ☐ Widow   ☐ Separated

Circle Highest Grade Attended in School = 1 2 3 4 5 6 7 8 9 10 11 12 College

Person to Notify in Case of Accident_____

Address_____ Phone No. _____

EXPERIENCE
(List Last Employment First)

(List Last Employment First)	Dates	Type of Job	Reason for Leaving
Firm_____	From		
Address_____			
_____	To		
Supervisor			
Firm_____	From		
Address_____			
_____	To		
Supervisor			
Firm_____	From		
Address_____			
_____	To		
Supervisor			

Signature:_____

Comments of Interviewer:_____
_____

Health:

Any defects in hearing?_____ In vision?_____ In speech?_____

List physical defects:_____

Were you ever seriously injured?_____ Give details: _____

_____

State your general physical condition:_____

_____

Date of last health examination: _____

Name and address of physician: _____

_____

Have you been attended by a physician for illness, injury or disease within the last 5 years?_____

Give details: _____

_____

Family:

List ages of dependents and relationship to you: _____

_____

Who takes care of your children while you are working?_____

What type of work does your husband or wife do?_____

Are you related to any employee of this company?_____ Who?_____

List name and address of nearest blood relative:_____

_____

Living Conditions:

How long have you lived at present address?_____ In this community?_____

Do you own home?_____ Rent home?_____ Board?_____ Live with relatives_____

How would you come to work?_____ How long does it take?_____

Interests

To what church do you belong?_____

Do you belong to a lodge?_____ Other organizations?_____

What are your hobbies?_____

Other:

Are you employed now?_____ By whom?_____

What led you to apply for work here?_____

Have you been employed here before?_____ Position: _____

Are you willing to work nights?_____ Salary desired?_____

Size uniform?_____ Right or left handed?_____ Can you type?_____

Are you a U. S. citizen?_____ Nationality: _____

Have you served in U. S. armed forces?_____ Rank?_____

Are you interested in company's group insurance plan?_____

I certify that the above facts are true to the best of my knowledge and understand that misrepresentations are sufficient cause for dismissal.

Signed: _____

FOOD AND BEVERAGE DEPARTMENTS

Assistant Steward.	Right leg stiff -- must be dragged.
Night Kitchen Runner	One eye.
Cook.	One eye.
Yardman.	One hand paralyzed.
Glass Washer.	Deaf and dumb.
Dish Washer	Fingers missing, deaf mute, crippled back, one short leg.

Pastry Cook
Vegetable Woman
Coffee Boy } . . . . Defective hearing.
Salad Woman
Bar Porter

Silver Cleaner } . . . . Deaf.
Food Runner

Silver Drier	Infantile paralysis (uses crutches).
Cashier, Cafeteria	Arthritis, deformed joints.
Hostess, Cafe Rouge	Artificial leg.
Head Room Service Waiter.	Artificial leg.
Waiter, Terrace Room	Wired shin bone.
Night Restaurant Auditor	Arm off at elbow and artificial leg.
Waiter.	One finger missing.

SERVICE DEPARTMENT

Elevator Operator (passenger) . . .	Artificial leg, one arm, short leg.
Elevator Operator (freight).	Short left leg, one arm.
Doorman.	Four fingers off left hand.
Lobby porter	Paralytic leg.

HOUSEKEEPING DEPARTMENT

Wall Washer	Deaf mute, short arm, one arm.
Houseman	Spinal disorder (hunchback), palsy.
Vacuum Man	Twisted leg.
Night Cleaner	Both feet partly amputated.
Floor Housekeeper	Defective hearing, paralyzed arm.
Chambermaid	Hunchback.

LAUNDRY DEPARTMENT

Seamstress.	Deaf and dumb.
Worker	Defective hearing.

ENGINEERING DEPARTMENT

Plumber	Short leg.
Electrician.	Short leg.
Painter.	Defective hearing.

CLERICAL WORKERS

Night Auditor.	Wooden leg.
Mail and Information Clerk.	Deformed arm.
Operator, Telephone	Deformed arm.
Clerk, Valet	One arm.

RESEARCH -- A BASIC PART OF THE EMPLOYMENT FUNCTION

To find and attract good employees and to place them in suitable jobs, management must conduct continual research. It will be found that advertising in some newspapers will result in more and better recruits than advertising in others. The location of the advertisement will make a significant difference in the number and kind of recruits attracted. Research may indicate that friends of present employees make the best employees, or that a particular employment agency can be relied upon for supplying high-quality recruits. One restaurant chain found that country girls made the best waitresses; another found that persons living more than one hour's ride from the restaurant would soon leave the job.

The employment function requires time and considerable ability on the part of those performing it. In a small business this function is by necessity delegated to the few department heads. In larger organizations, it should be centralized in a personnel department. Department heads should retain the authority for making the final selection. The personnel department does the spade work. Exploring sources of recruits and assembling suitable applicants from which the selection will be made require special training. Keeping the personnel records and the time necessary to study the relative merits of different sources of supply as well as the validity of devices used in the employment process should be delegated. The department head, freed of these duties, is able to devote himself to supervision. Department heads cannot be expected to be experts in several fields.

EVALUATION OF THE RECRUITMENT PROGRAM

The most important contribution of a personnel worker is not the discovery of employee resources but rather the evaluation of these resources. Some determination must be made of where the most satisfactory employees for each position are obtained.

To do such evaluation, a criterion of satisfactory performance must be obtained either in terms of the quantity of work performed or in quality of work performed.

EXAMPLES OF HOW TO EVALUATE RECRUITMENT SOURCES

In evaluating sources of recruitment, it is only human nature to remember the good employee who came from one source or to remember the poor employee from another source and then to generalize stereotypes of these two sources, each of which in reality may be no better or worse than the other. To discover if one source is really better than another, all of the people from each source must be evaluated. Because of the effects of stereotyping, it is always best to learn the significance of a difference between sources. These differences are expressed by comparing the average performance of workers from different sources or in terms of the proportion of differences in the performance of workers from different sources. Example One following shows how averages can be used and Example Two shows how proportions can be used.

In Example One, the total number of customers who were waited on by three groups of waitresses in their first week of employment were averaged. The groups represent the sources from which the waitresses were recruited. It was recognized that it is difficult to evaluate any one waitress with any other waitress in terms of the number of customers served, because the number of customers served on different shifts differs. Groups of waitresses can be compared because it can be assumed that the individual differences will be averaged out.

Example Two was taken from the personnel records of a hospital food service division in which the criterion, promotion during the first year, was used to differentiate successful from unsuccessful serving line recruits. Employees from two sources were thus compared in terms of the differences noted in the proportions of relatively successful employees obtained from each source.

Statistical significances of the differences can be computed for Examples One and Two by the more sophisticated personnel researcher or by those with the time and inclination to dig the methodology from statistics books. The most statistically unsophisticated, however, can quickly see that in Example One, Source 1 is by far the best source of recruits -- even though the worst worker came from that source and neither of the two best workers came from that source.

In Example Two, it is obvious that there is not much difference between Source 1 and Source 2 since the difference between proportions of 0.80 and 0.75 is slight. The implication of this finding should caution management against accepting either one of these sources to the exclusion of the other.

Comparisons of averages and proportions are but two evaluation techniques. In terms of establishing recruitment criterion measures, employees may be classified by such measures as employee turnover, accident rate, ratings of performance, absenteeism, wages earned, test scores, grades made in training courses, and other variables.

Example One

AVERAGE NUMBER OF CUSTOMERS SERVED BY WAITRESSES
RECRUITED FROM THREE DIFFERENT SOURCES

Source 1		Source 2		Source 3	
Waitress	Customers Served	Waitress	Customers Served	Waitress	Customers Served
A	490	K	316	R	531
B	263	L	385	S	290
C	654	M	473	T	386
D	732	N	911	U	940
E	556	O	522	V	622
F	755	P	460	W	341
G	692	Q	623	X	333
H	784			Y	418
I	760				
Total	5687		3690		3861
Average	631.88		527.14		482.63

Example Two

THE DIFFERENCE BETWEEN PROPORTIONS OF SERVING PERSONNEL
RECRUITED FROM DIFFERENT SOURCES
WHO WERE PROMOTED DURING THE FIRST YEAR

	Source 1	Source 2
Total Number of Employees from Each Source	30	36
Employees Promoted During First Year of Service	24	27
Proportion Promoted	0.80	0.75

CHAPTER 6

Interviewing

Selection is a procedure whereby candidates considered unacceptable are identified and screened out. Selection is based on all of the functions broadly considered thus far: job analysis, the establishment of job specifications and standards, and the recruitment of personnel from which to make the selection.

Selection involves these steps: (1) Reception of applicants, (2) Personal appraisal of the applicant, (3) Frequently vocational guidance in the sense of providing counsel to new workers who are seeking to establish careers, (4) Placement of the applicants in appropriate positions, and (5) Follow-up by periodic check of the effectiveness of the selection process and of the worker on the job.

The Role of the Interview

Aids such as the application blank, tests, and references are used in selecting employees, but no one device is more important or more widely used than the personal interview.

The interview allows two human beings to meet face to face in order to explore possibilities for employment. No other technique offers the flexibility and the depth of the interview. Unfortunately, the interview is also one of the most complex and difficult techniques to master. There is no mechanical way to interview. Interviewing requires intense concentration, intelligence, time, sensitivity, and training. There is no short cut to good interviewing, but once a person develops interviewing skills, his value to an organization is considerable.

A vast amount of information is available about interviewing and its techniques. In spite of the emphasis on it and its widespread use, the interviewing conducted in most hotels, restaurants, and clubs is a highly unreliable selection tool, research has shown.

A common mistake made by the interviewer is to proceed blindly without recognizing the barriers that exist between him and the candidate. Aside from the complex differences in personality, there are two main barriers: (1) The professional problems of the interviewer; and (2) The psychological constants found in the interview exchange.

In the professional role of an interviewer, whether he recognizes it or not, every practitioner experiences some degree of conflict concerning his competence. In truth, no one can be completely correct in his personnel judgements. This conflict may be manifested in a tendency to be overly self-conscious or to overevaluate one's skill -- either of which interferes with good interviewing. In addition, all interviewers have built-in expectations of candidates: The interviewer expects the candidate to talk, to be truthful, and to give him information which he can sink his teeth into. It is an established fact that when interviewers are thrown off guard by candidates who do not conform to these expectations, the interviewer unconsciously tends to react negatively toward the candidate basically because the interviewer feels uncomfortable.

Relative to the psychological constants in the interview, candidates for jobs are at a decided disadvantage. They find themselves "giving" and "revealing" but the interviewer is not required to give anything himself. Candidates ascribe to interviewers these characteristics: (1) Interviewers are seen as being voyeristic -- they are psychological "peeping Toms"; (2) They are autocratic individuals who tend to dominate and to control situations; (3) They are oracular; they give the impression that they are omniscient and all-knowing; and (4) They are saintly individuals who are helpful, but always in a detached "holier than thou" manner.

It is easy for the interviewer to assume any or all these roles. Such roles are traps; the degree to which he falls into the trap is the degree to which he will be a poor interviewer.

The employment interview gives the interviewer an opportunity to evaluate the applicant's appearance and manner, something of his general temperament, and the first impression he will create in meeting customers and fellow workers.

On the other hand, the interview has weaknesses and may mislead the interviewer. At best, the interview can give the interviewer only a superficial insight into the total personality of the applicant. It has little value for determining such traits as honesty, reliability, perseverance, mechanical skill, and mental ability. As a means of gaining a rough appraisal of the applicant's "first impression," his conversation facility, his physical appearance, and his skill in social participation, it surpasses any other convenient means of appraisal. It has distinct advantages and serious limitations.

The employment interview is an occasion when not only the employer but also the applicant consider each other's mutual problems and interests. The employer is not granting a privilege, nor is the applicant asking a favor. Each has something to offer -- the employer the job, and the applicant his services.

The interview is a two-way communication device, the interviewer stating the nature of the vacancy, the applicant his qualifications. In order to enable the applicant to make an intelligent decision as to whether the job is acceptable, he must be told the hours of work, the physical exertion and mental effort required, and the general benefits and disadvantages accruing from work with the company.

If the applicant appears to meet the qualifications of the job he is seeking, the other details of interest should be given. Days off, information on paydays, when and where to report for work, and the special advantages the enterprise offers to employees are all points of information. To avoid overlooking certain items, a check list form is useful. Too often the interview is a quiz session during which information passes but one way, from the applicant to the interviewer.

When communication is one-way, the interview also fails on two other points: the establishment of rapport and the promotion of goodwill towards the enterprise. The interview can be a means of establishing a cordial understanding between the applicant and the management. The conduct of the interview can assure the prospective employee of the good intentions of management, and later, if the applicant is found qualified and employed, his relations with management will have gotten off to a good start. The employment interviewer is a representative of management; his manner and behavior reflect management's attitudes to the applicant.

The other point at which the interview can fail, if the two-way communication is not maintained, is in its public relations aspects. Some of the best public relations men a hotel or restaurant has are its own employees. The employment interview is the first step in making future employees want to advertise the enterprise. Regardless of whether the interview culminates in employment, the attitude with which the applicant leaves the employment office will sooner or later be reflected in the general reputation of the hotel or restaurant. The attitudes of the unskilled applicant are not as important as are those of applicants coming from other classes of workers, but there is no excuse for the interviewing procedure's promoting anything but cordiality in the applicant. By accepting the applicant as a conversational equal, avoiding cross-examination methods, and generally encouraging two-way communication, the interview is an effective means of promoting public relations.

POINTS TO CONSIDER IN EMPLOYMENT INTERVIEWING

Before the Interview

1. Determine the goal of the interview: evaluation, information, selection?
2. Prepare an outline to guide you during the interview.
3. Schedule the interview at a time that is convenient for both you and the interviewee.
4. Inform the interviewee of the purpose and kind of interview, the papers he will need, and all other pertinent information he may need.
5. Study all pertinent information about him; take notes so that you do not forget your data.
6. Provide him plenty of time.
7. Provide ideal conditions of privacy for the interview.

During the Interview

1. Be yourself.
2. Let the interviewee settle down before beginning.
3. Be direct in your questions when possible.
4. Make your questions open-ended -- do not let him answer by a simple "yes" or "no," but ask questions that require explanations and descriptions.
5. Try to get pertinent and accurate answers to the questions you ask.
6. Give the interviewee enough time to think about a question before he answers.

7. Be a good listener, not a talker.
8. Do not interrupt the interviewee. Always let him finish what he starts if possible.
9. Make frequent use of "why?" and "how?"
10. Let him finish answering one question before you ask another.
11. Use simple language.
12. Always raise neutral questions. Do not let him know your sentiments. You want to find out about him, not how well he can discover your own biases.
13. When in doubt about what the interviewee is saying, summarize his statements. Be careful to give what you feel he has said and do not put words in his mouth.
14. Avoid taking sides on issues. Don't badger or harangue.
15. Do not hesitate to probe.
16. Be in control of an interview. You are there for a purpose. Both your time and his time are valuable.
17. At the end of the interview, give the interviewee an opportunity to ask questions.
18. Keep alert before and after the formal part of the interview. All aspects of your contact should be "evaluative" in nature.

After the Interview

1. Review and organize your notes immediately.
2. Try to answer questions you have raised to yourself about the interviewee.
3. Try to see a pattern to your analysis; try to develop an integrated picture.
4. Having summarized and evaluated your facts and attitudes, arrive at a decision.

THE TRAINING OF INTERVIEWERS

Some significant research findings have emerged in terms of what seems to be the best way to train interviewers and counselors.

1. The techniques of interviewing are not as important as his attitudes. His basic attitudes must be genuine.
2. The interviewer clarifies his attitudes toward himself, others, and his work, then he develops sound techniques.
3. The interviewer needs to experience for himself what it is like to be interviewed by someone who understands him. It is valuable for interviewers to seek constructive evaluations of their skills from others, to do role-playing with others, and to maintain a learner's approach to their work.

THE CHARACTERISTICS OF GOOD INTERVIEWERS

The criteria for deciding who makes a good interviewer or counselor are vague. At the present stage of our knowledge, the criteria adopted by the American Psychological Association seem most applicable:

1. Superior intellectual ability and judgment.
2. Originality, resourcefulness, and versatility.
3. "Fresh and insatiable" curiosity; "self-learner."
4. Interest in persons as individuals rather than as material for manipulation -- a regard for the integrity of other persons.
5. Insight into one's own personality characteristics and a sense of humor.
6. Sensitivity to the complexities of motivation.
7. Tolerance: "unarrogance."
8. Ability to adopt "constructive" attitudes; ability to establish warm and effective relationships with others.
9. Industry; methodical work habits; ability to tolerate pressure.
10. Acceptance of responsibility.
11. Tact and cooperativeness.
12. Integrity, self-control, and stability.
13. Discriminating sense of ethical values.
14. Breadth of cultural background -- "educated man."
15. An interest in psychology and understanding people.

From the foregoing description it should be obvious that the person to do interviewing should be an extremely competent person.

CONDUCTING THE EMPLOYMENT INTERVIEW

If the interview is to be successful, there are several preliminary steps to be taken. One of these is to provide pleasant physical surroundings for the interview. Well-furnished, adequately lighted waiting rooms, a supply of popular magazines, ashtrays, washrooms and toilet facilities will tend to reduce any anxiety the applicant may have and create a favorable and lasting impression. In the applicant's mind the confusion, noise, and cramped quarters of many hotel and restaurant employment offices are a reflection of the enterprise in general. The interview itself should be conducted in semiprivacy, in a room which is quiet but which has glass panels above sitting height and ready access to the waiting room. This permits cordiality but discourages intimacy.

The interviewer plans the interview and attempts to make provision for increasing the objectivity of his observations. He tries to recognize his own prejudices and discount them in his observations. For example, the interviewer because of previous unhappy experiences with red-haired persons may tend to dislike all redheads. He may favor persons of his own nationality and religion and be prejudiced against other races and religions. He may place too great an emphasis on appearance, which for certain jobs is relatively unimportant.

The interviewer knows what jobs are vacant, and he should either know what the job requirements are for the vacancy or have a complete job description at hand. He plans the type of question he will ask so as to set limits on the interview and secure only pertinent facts. Depending upon the number of applicants waiting and his other duties, the interviewer schedules his time so that applicants are kept waiting no longer than necessary.

In opening the interview it is usually well to begin casually with a friendly greeting such as, "Good morning, Miss Wells. Please make yourself comfortable." Opening questions should not be abrupt but should avoid generality. A request such as "Tell me about yourself" is likely to be answered by an intelligent applicant by "What part? Do you have a few weeks? Where shall I begin?" A better opener would be to ask something concerning the type of work the applicant is seeking. Questions which require

A well-designed personnel office of a hotel -- the personnel office of the Hotel Statler, Boston, Massachusetts. Well-lighted and appointed, this personnel office presents an efficient and pleasant atmosphere for the prospective and present employee. Privacy without intimacy provides the prerequisite for effective interviewing, counseling and other relations.

a "yes" or "no" answer should be avoided. Give the applicant a chance to express himself on a topic he knows, so he can gain confidence in himself which will be reflected in the interview.

Other ways of building the applicant's confidence are to give the appearance of being unhurried, to avoid asking leading questions and overtalking the applicant. By using simple words the interviewer can avoid embarrassing the less educated. Some don'ts for the interviewer include the dictum, "never talk down to an applicant or moralize." Avoid giving personal advice and never criticize the applicant. Do not display authority, and never argue.

Interviewing is partially an art, and as such hinges on subtleties of facial expression, bodily postures, gestures and inflections. The interviewer must realize he is playing a role, the role of the interviewer, and must act his part. Of course playing a role does not preclude honesty and sincerity, but the interviewer must remember that his very manner is an integral part of interviewing. The interviewer's mood can easily reflect itself unfavorably in his tone of voice. The question "Are you unemployed now?" may sound sarcastic, accusing, or friendly, depending on how it is expressed. Similarly, overcordiality may imply to the applicant that he is to be employed, when actually his qualifications may be unsuitable.

Interviewing requires the ability to observe carefully without the observation's being unfavorably apparent. The capable interviewer soon learns that what the applicant does not say may be more important than what he does say. A short answer to the question, "How did you like your previous employer?" may to the alert interviewer imply a positive and deep-seated dislike for the previous employer, although it is not expressed in words. The good interviewer also makes mental notes of gaps left in the applicant's account of his work experience, and he notes conflicting or incongruous statements. He does not mention such lapses.

Small bits of behavior sometimes are clues to the applicant's personality. They should be carefully verified before reaching conclusions. Obvious characteristics may exclude the applicant from certain jobs. Nervousness on the part of the applicant which would be embarrassing socially would probably be sufficient reason to exclude the applicant from positions demanding a smooth sales manner. The same behavior has little or no significance for certain skilled jobs in the house.

THE MULTIPLE INTERVIEW

To increase the validity of the interview, two or three interview sessions are often scheduled. The multiple interview gives both the interviewer and the applicant time to think the proposition over. Nervousness, untruthfulness, and other weaknesses that are not detected in the single interview often show up. Sometimes the veneer of the "personality boy" wears thin and he shows himself as he really is in the second or third interview.

Sky Chefs, Inc., a nation-wide chain of airport restaurants, tried several variations in the interview for selecting employees over the country. In Denver, a most intensive program was set up to select the 120 best qualified food service employees who could be found. "Display ads" one column by six inches were run in the classified section of the newspaper for a period of three months. Each warned that the applicant must have a pleasing appearance, personality, and a willingness to undergo a thorough screening program. Four thousand applications were received. Each applicant completed an application form of over 225 questions.

Three interviews were given to most prospects. During the first interview the personnel director explained the Sky Chefs' programs, history, and methods and asked a series of questions. If deemed satisfactory, the applicant was requested to return anywhere from one day to a week later for a second interview. The interim period was in itself a selection device, since those not really interested in working for the company failed to return for the second interview. In the second interview, even more intensive questioning was included. A third interview gave opportunity for a wise, final decision.

Mr. Mitchell, personnel director of the chain, states that the program has more than paid off in the high quality of employees procured.

THE PATTERNED INTERVIEW

In recent years the patterned interview has gained considerable acceptance as a selection instrument that has a degree of validity when properly done. Its approach is basically clinical. It is designed to measure an applicant's character traits that are important for job performance (such as his stability, industry, ability to get along with others, ability to organize, perseverance, determination, emotional maturity, and self-reliance) and his motivation. The underlying premise of the patterned interview is simply the following: The best basis for judging what a person will do in the <u>future</u> is to know what he has done in the <u>past</u>.

The patterned interview is principally a fact-finding procedure which combines information obtained from the applicant with data received from schools and previous employers. The areas of investigation generally include the following: (1) Work history; (2) Educational history; (3) Health history; (4) Family history; and (5) Social history.

The patterned interview overcomes weaknesses of an ordinary employment interview in the following ways:

1. The interviewer works from definite job specifications; he knows the qualities of the job for which he is interviewing.
2. He has a plan; his questions are predetermined.
3. He uses a series of yardsticks for interpreting and evaluating the information he obtains.

In conducting a patterned interview, the information the interviewer seeks to discover is seldom brought to light by asking the applicant a direct question. For example, it is not advantageous to ask an applicant if he is honest, if he is intelligent, if he can organize, and so on. Rather, this information is found through a discussion of his job history, his educational background, his family relationships, and his feelings on other issues.

In a patterned interview, interviewers must recognize that sound conclusions cannot be drawn from any one answer to a question. The questions which are asked should be thought of as straws in the wind. A straw is tossed into the wind and drifts to the east. Several other straws are tossed and the majority of them also drift toward the east. It is then possible to make a fair assumption that the wind is blowing from the west. The same analogy can be used in interviewing. If several questions are asked and the applicant's answers all seem to be pointing in the same general direction, then it is assumed that a pattern of behavior has been developed and that a prediction based upon it stands a good chance of being correct.

USE OF KNOCK-OUT QUESTIONS

Dr. Robert McMurry, who has had much experience using the patterned interview for selecting persons to staff hotels and restaurants, uses a series of "knock-out questions" to eliminate candidates who for some reason are not likely to perform well on the job.

For example, in selecting waitresses he asks questions which relate to the following factors:

1. Willingness to work the hours and under the conditions required by the job.
2. Acceptability of wages and benefits to the candidate.
3. Willingness to take a physical examination.
4. Time required getting to and from work -- some surveys show anyone living more than an hour from the place of work is unsuitable.
5. Length of time in the community -- to determine whether or not the candidate is a "floater."
6. Number of preschool children -- more than one makes it almost impossible for success on the job without unusual arrangements.
7. Vocational stability -- examination of the number of jobs held in the last year is a clue.

Dr. McMurry holds that to get one good waitress ten should be interviewed.

Of course, the interviewer must have clear-cut job specifications in mind before the interview begins. Here are the "specs" for a waitress as seen by Dr. McMurry:

1. Good health and physical stamina; she must be able to work long hours on her feet under conditions which call for a high-energy level.
2. Higher than average drive; the waitress position is no place for a lazy or lethargic woman.
3. Pleasant physical appearance; neatness and freedom from obvious blemishes are especially important.
4. Inherent friendliness and courtesy; these traits are the product of a lifetime of personality development, contributed to by family relations, successes and failures, and physical condition.
5. A need for money; to be successful at hard work, waitresses must be motivated by money for support of families or paying debts.
6. Self-confidence and self-reliance; a waitress must make the customer feel he is in competent hands, and impress both the customer and other personnel that she is capable of taking care of herself in any situation.

7. Relative freedom from poor habits; she will not make the grade if she overdrinks, causes friction with customers, is chronically late, or avoids side work.

Selecting Management Personnel

Thousands of dollars are sometimes well spent in executive search, thousands to find the right man to fill a single important position. As with all jobs, job descriptions and job specifications should be in hand before the search begins.

Here is an outline of a job description for a restaurant manager as drawn by McMurry:

1. In cooperation with the owner, establishes the over-all operating policies of the restaurant.
2. Is largely responsible for setting and maintaining the tone of the restaurant.
3. Continuously engages in personnel activities: hiring, firing, establishing wage rates, evaluating employee performance, and sometimes dealing with labor unions.
4. Continuously supervises employees.
5. Has final responsibility for establishing the menu, buying and preparing food.
6. Supervises the bookkeeping and accounting.
7. Often serves as a host or greeter, handling customer complaints and guest relations in general.

The patterned interview for selecting a restaurant manager probes these areas:

1. Work and military service experience
2. School and technical training
3. Early childhood and family background
4. Present family and domestic situation
5. Current financial position
6. State of health

From the patterned interview a judgement can be made regarding these points:

1. Can do the job because he has these requisites:

   a. Skills and experience
   b. Physical qualifications, including good health
   c. Availability; will work the hours, will move to a new location if necessary

2. Will do the job; has demonstrated that he possesses these traits in sufficient measure as based on:

   a. Job stability; he is not a drifter or a floater
   b. He has industry, the habit of keeping busy
   c. Skill in getting along with others
   d. Perseverance and drive; has the habit of finishing what he starts
   e. Leadership; has proved in the past that he can handle people successfully
   f. Self-reliance; is self-confident and decisive
   g. Has energy; is a self-starter and a go-getter
   h. Motivation for success; wants money, status, and power

He must have the capacity to make practical, down-to-earth evaluations of things, problems and people.

He needs a supportive home situation, a compatible wife and a home where he can go to regenerate and reintegrate himself. This can be best evaluated by visiting the home itself.

The applicant's deficiencies should be noted at least mentally, remembering that no applicant fits the position exactly.

THE EXIT INTERVIEW

A side product of the selection interview is the exit interview. Exit interviews fall into three main classifications:

1. Exit interviews with applicants
2. Exit interviews with unsuccessful workers
3. Exit interviews with workers whom you did not want to lose.

Although its value may vary considerably, the exit interview offers an excellent opportunity to increase public relations, to discover attitudes toward the organization, and to evaluate the effectiveness of various selection procedures.

The exit interview generally is a low-pressure session in which the interviewer seeks to answer specific questions he may have concerning the individual's plans, his attitudes toward the organization or the industry, and his specific criticisms and complaints relative to the organization. The exit interviewer may use the following guidelines:

1. Practice taking the applicant's point of view. Stay within his frame of reference -- you want to offer him support as well as to seek information.
2. Let him talk about the topics which interest him. Only later after he is relaxed should questions of interest to the interviewer be pursued.
3. Help him feel at ease and free to talk.
4. Provide a service to the applicant if possible in terms of answering questions, providing information, and offering constructive criticism if such is requested.
5. Be careful of offering advice. It is his life; only he can decide what he wants to do with it. If he needs professional guidance, let him seek out someone qualified to provide such guidance.
6. Do not prolong the interview.

AN EVALUATION PROCEDURE

One way to develop skill in interviewing is to "test" the skill of the interviewer by evaluating results.

A common statistical test determines how successful the interviewer is in discriminating between desirable and undesirable applicants. The process requires the analysis of numerous cases; a few individual cases cannot provide sufficient information.

APPRAISING THE INTERVIEWER'S RESULTS

John Brown, interviewer for the XYZ Restaurant-Cafeteria Chain, decided to determine his effectiveness in selecting female cashiers and checkers for a two-year period. He systematically rated each of the cashiers he had interviewed prior to employment on a five-point scale: (1) Acceptable -- excellent; (2) Acceptable -- good; (3) Acceptable -- average; (4) Acceptable -- borderline; and (5) Nonacceptable. Since the nonacceptable candidates were not hired, he was not able to determine his skill in predicting failure.

If Mr. Brown were a good interviewer, then theoretically the "best" employees should perform best on the job and the "worst" employees should perform less effectively on the job. In order to establish a criterion of performance, he asked the managers of three operations in the XYZ chain to rate all of the cashiers and checkers hired during the two-year period who had worked six months or longer. Mr. Brown presented the following instructions to each manager:

> For this study please consider as one group all of the cashiers hired by the XYZ Chain during the past two years who have worked at least six months and who are working now or did work under your direct supervision. From this group, rate each employee in terms of whether you consider her to be among the top, the upper-middle, the lower-middle, or the lower twenty-five per cent of the total group of cashiers and checkers under your supervision.

> In other words, if ten new employees who met the description worked directly under you, then you would necessarily have to assign at least two of these employees to each of the four categories. The extra two employees obviously would have to be assigned to whatever category seems appropriate; however, in the case of having two extra employees to assign, always assign one candidate to one of the two categories representing the highest rated two groups and assign the other candidate to one of the categories representing the lowest two groups. No category should ever contain more than one employee more than is contained in any other category. Use the following rating system to assign employees to categories:

> A -- top 25 per cent; B -- upper-middle 25 per cent; C -- lower-middle 25 per cent; D -- lower 25 per cent.

When Mr. Brown received the ratings from the supervisors, he made the analysis seen in the table on page 62, using his evaluation ratings prior to hiring and the ratings made by the managers at least six months after the candidate was hired. For purposes of comparison, Mr. Brown combined the workers he had evaluated as 1's and 2's and called them the "best" employees, and he combined the workers in categories 3 and 4 and called them the "worst" employees. He also combined the ratings made by supervisors into "High" and "Low" ratings. He included together all of those workers rated in the highest and upper-middle 25 per cent as high-rated workers. All of those rated lower-middle and lowest 25 per cent were grouped as the low workers.[1]

A COMPARISON OF THE AGREEMENT BETWEEN INTERVIEWER'S EVALUATION OF CASHIERS AND CHECKERS AND THE RATINGS OF MANAGERS IN THREE LOCATIONS SIX MONTHS AFTER EMPLOYMENT

Restaurant Groups	Interviewer's Category	Number of Candidates	Managers' Ratings	
			High	Low
Rest. A	1. Excellent or Good	12	42%*	58%
	2. Average or Borderline	15	53	47
Rest. B	1. Excellent or Good	18	72	18
	2. Average or Borderline	16	37	63
Rest. C	1. Excellent or Good	17	41	59
	2. Average or Borderline	22	46	54

*This number indicates the per cent of the cases in this category who were rated high by their supervisors.

From the above table it can be seen that Mr. Brown was partly successful and partly unsuccessful in predicting the future success of interviewers. His predictions for Restaurants A and C do not appear to be any better than chance. In Restaurant B, however, his predictions appear to be quite significant. Seventy-two per cent of those he rated as having the highest potential actually turned out to be the highest performing employees, and 63 per cent of the employees rated as having the lowest potential turned out to be the lowest performing employees.

It is obvious, from the table, that Mr. Brown is an interviewer with a problem. Should he forget about his interviewing altogether, should he interview only for Area B, or what?

Mr. Brown sought to discover why his evaluations seemed inconsistent. To do this, he went to the managers doing the performance ratings to discover the characteristics managers were looking at when they evaluated their employees.

To Mr. Brown's enlightenment, he discovered that true to his own job specifications, the manager in Restaurant B rated his employees in terms of their technical competence, their ability to perform their work without making mistakes, and in terms of their efficiency as workers. It did not surprise him that he and the manager of Restaurant B were in agreement because those were the areas that Mr. Brown also placed primary emphasis in his evaluation interview.

In Restaurant's A and C, Mr. Brown found that personal factors, such as ability to get along with customers, friendliness, attractiveness, and youthfulness were the factors that those managers were considering in their ratings. Technical competence did not seem to be accorded much relevance.

---

[1] It should be noted that the scaling and rating categories discussed in this problem are arbitrary and could just as easily be modified in a number of other ways. Those interested in the rationale and design of reliable rating systems are referred to: Ghiselli, E., and Brown, C., Personnel and Industrial Psychology. New York: McGraw-Hill, 1955.

Because Mr. Brown was a good personnel interviewer who <u>evaluated</u> his skill and who tried to <u>improve</u> his function, he was in a position to solve a severe selection problem. In this case, by knowing the problem all of the managers were able to re-evaluate their biases in selection. Assuming no basic shifts occurred in the manager's attitudes, Brown would know that he should use different criteria in assessing cashiers and checkers for locations A and C than he does for location B.

REFERENCES

1. Kahn, R.L., and Cannell, C.F., <u>The Dynamics of Interviewing</u>. New York: John Wiley & Sons, Inc., 1958.

2. Klephart, N.C., <u>The Employment Interview in Industry</u>. New York: McGraw-Hill, 1952.

3. McMurry, R.N., "Validating the Patterned Interview" in Fleishman, E.A., <u>Studies in Personnel and Industrial Psychology</u>. Homewood, Illinois: The Dorsey Press, Inc., 1961.

4. Rogers, C.R., <u>Client Centered Therapy</u>. Boston: Houghton Mifflin Co., 1951.

5. Tiffin, J., and McCormick, E.T., <u>Industrial Psychology</u>. (4th ed.) Englewood Cliffs, New Jersey: Prentice-Hall, 1958.

Testing

A personnel manager, learning that one of his best workers had scored very low on a test that eventually would be used in selecting future employees, nearly discharged the worker, "...the tests really opened our eyes about her. Why, she's worked here for several years, does good work, gets along well with the others. That test shows how she had us fooled!"[1]

The foregoing anecdote may sound facetious, but it is not fictitious. It is but one example of how people in responsible positions grossly misunderstand and misuse tests. Tests are extremely valuable tools of selection, but unless they are understood and used properly, are dangerous and misleading.

What Is a Test?

One way to hire good workers is to hire everyone who applies, observe them perform on the job. In time, certain people emerge as the good workers. Of course, an oversupply of poor workers would be carried to the detriment of the organization. Obviously profit-making enterprises and those interested in efficiency cannot afford such a luxury and look for methods to avoid hiring the ineffective. One such method makes use of psychological testing.

Testing is an indirect method of measurement which by definition cannot be as valid as a direct measurement. Knowing the limitations of a test, it can be seen how illogical was the reasoning of the personnel manager in the anecdote related. Tests properly used in industry are a valuable step in the selection and placement program, but they only supplement selection and placement of people.

HISTORICAL DEVELOPMENT OF TESTS

The use of tests in industry dates back to pre-World War I times with the concept of the I.Q. developed by a Frenchman, Binet. For the first time it was possible to rate individuals on a scale, high to low, on a measure called general intelligence. Following Binet, an American, Thurstone, and an Englishman, Spearman, discovered that it was possible to measure individuals not only in terms of general ability but also in terms of many specific abilities such as manual dexterity, perceptual ability, and verbal ability.

Theoretically, it was assumed at first that tests were the answer to all of the problems in industry by providing measures of the factors discovered in job analyses that were considered essential for success. Unfortunately, it was discovered that tests could not measure such intangible but essential variables as "motivation" and "personality." Some individuals, for example, score well on tests, but do not have the "desire" to work; others score poorly on tests, but compensate for their possible lack of skill by their "desire."

Up to the present, industry has not been successful in utilizing tests to measure "personality" variables except under specific research conditions. Such variables are usually investigated through an interview or through clinical tests that are interpreted by a professional psychologist who is intimately familiar with the job analysis criteria.

The tests to which industry has addressed itself successfully are paper and pencil tests measuring maximum performance.

---

[1]Lyman, H.B., Test Scores and What They Mean. Englewood Cliffs, New Jersey: Prentice-Hall, Inc., 1963.

MAXIMUM-PERFORMANCE TESTS

A maximum-performance test is a test in which each item has a "correct" answer and in which the testee is required to do as well as he can. An intelligence test is a maximum-performance test in the sense that each item has one correct response and any other response is scored as being incorrect. If two people are taking an intelligence test and one person gets more answers right than the other person, then we can say that the person with the most answers correct is the "more intelligent."

Contrast such a maximum-performance test with a test of "typical-performance" like a personality test. A typical personality test item may be the following: Do you like grouchy people? Yes No. The "correct" answer to such a question is very speculative. Also, a testee may fool himself or lie. On an intelligence test, there is no way to lie -- the person either knows the answer or he does not know it.

Because such tests as personality tests are consciously or unconsciously distorted by test takers and because the variables measured are so vague, "personality-type" tests are all but useless in employment situations -- except under specific research conditions. One such research condition involves a test called the Worker Attitude Inventory which will be described later in this chapter.

The various types of maximum-performance tests used in industry are the following:

1. Intelligence Tests: These indicate the level of problem-solving ability a person may possess. They indicate how quickly he should be expected to catch on to the intricacies of a job. They will not reveal how a man will use his intelligence in terms of judgement, creativity, and orderly thinking.

2. Aptitude Tests: These are designed to measure the probable rapidity and success an individual will achieve in a specific activity, assuming constant motivation and other factors. The tests are available in a number of areas such as mechanical, physical science, engineering, medical, etc. The most widely used general aptitude tests (i.e., measuring more than one aptitude) are the Differential Aptitude Test published by the Psychological Corporation and the General Aptitude Test Battery used by the U. S. Employment Service.

3. Achievement Tests: These are available to measure the degree of skill in specified areas such as typing, shorthand, welding, spelling, comptometer operation, etc.

BASIC ATTRIBUTES OF TESTS

All tests have four attributes which need to be considered: validity, reliability, norms, and usability.

1. Validity: This is the most important consideration in any test; i.e., whether the test is really measuring what it purports to measure. There are no set rules for deciding what is "good" validity; such decisions take time and experience. There are many guidelines and test users need to know the different ways to consider test validity.

Face Validity: This means simply that the test appears on inspection to make sense and to be valid.

Content Validity: In such validity, a check is made to see if the content of the items covers the points that seem to be essential for success on the job.

Empirical Validity: This tells how closely the test relates to some criterion (i.e., to some standard of performance, such as supervisor's ratings or production standards). It is the most important kind of validity since it sets a rigidly objective requirement on the test. As a general rule, anyone using tests in an employment situation should insist that the tests he buys be subjected to empirical validation by the publisher.

Construct Validity: This validity also requires correlation between test scores and another variable, which usually is a complex psychological variable. This type of validity is not typically found in employment situations.

2. Reliability: Reliability refers to the consistency of measurement. A test cannot be valid unless it measures something consistently; however a test can be reliable without measuring the characteristics it purports to measure.

Reliability may be evaluated statistically in either an absolute or a relative sense. For assessing absolute reliability, a measure called the standard error of measurement is used. Relative consistency provides an index of over-all dependability of scores in the form of a correlation coefficient. The main considerations to remember about reliability are listed on the following page.

a. Tests are not reliable if they are not taken under <u>standardized</u> conditions. They must be administered to all testees under the same conditions.

b. Tests are not reliable if they are not scored properly and consistently.

c. Tests usually are not reliable if the test is not administered according to the author's instructions; if testees have prior information about the test or coaching; if unfavorable physical conditions exist (e.g., poor lighting or ventilation), or if the testees experience personal illness.

d. In general, the longer a test is the more reliable it will be.

e. The more random, diverse, and heterogeneous the subjects making up a test group, the more reliable will be the correlation between the scores made by the group and a criterion measure.

3. <u>Norms</u>: Norms frequently are forgotten or overlooked in discussing tests, but the fact remains that such terms as reliability, validity, and test scores are always <u>relative</u> to those ratings made by a group of individuals on whom the test was administered previously. No test score makes sense unless the norm group relative to that score is known. For example, Joe may score at the 90th percentile on an intelligence test. The first reaction might be, "Not bad -- that's higher than 9 out of 10." A more important reaction would be, "90th percentile of what?" For example, to score higher than 90 per cent of the applicants for a pot and pan washing job may not be very good if Joe is being considered for a supervisor's job. To score higher than 90 per cent of high school graduates, on the other hand, may be very good.

As a general rule, the most relevant norms are those that come closest to representing the person with whom we are concerned. For example, if we want to know what a good score is for Joe, we should try to compare him with men who are his own age and who have his social and educational background. All organizations need to develop "local" norms for every test used. Local norms are norms collected on present employees. No norms will be more relevant for selection purposes than the norms of present employees.

4. <u>Usability</u>: This means that there are many practical considerations in testing. Because of time problems, costs, or other factors, it may be necessary to sacrifice some desirable features. It is important for test users to understand the relative merits of the tests they employ.

POSSIBLE TESTS FOR USE WITH HOTEL AND RESTAURANT WORKERS

In this section a number of the tests which lend themselves to use with hotel and restaurant workers are reviewed.

<u>Intelligence Tests</u>

Conservatively speaking, there are over one hundred paper and pencil group tests of intelligence on the market. Generally there is considerable similarity and overlap in these tests in the sense that: (1) Most of them are weighted heavily with items measuring vocabulary and arithmetic skills; and (2) Most of them depend for their validation on a correlation with older, more basic intelligence tests such as the Army Alpha or the Stanford Binet.[2]

One of the most important considerations in an intelligence test is applicability. Some tests are too verbal and too difficult for people who apply for lower-level jobs; other tests are too easy for college-level people and for those applying for management-type positions. It also should be remembered that although intelligence is one factor for success on many jobs, it is not the only factor. The most commonly used intelligence tests in industry are the following:

1. <u>The Otis Self-Administering Test of Mental Ability</u> (World Book Co., 1922): This test (several forms) contains 75 mixed items arranged in order of difficulty (arithmetic, spatial, vocabulary, sentence meaning, analogies, etc.). It may be administered as a twenty-minute or as a thirty-minute timed test. The test has good reliability. It is appropriate for use with high school students and adults. Although its validity leaves something to be desired, as is the case with all paper and pencil intelligence tests, the validation of the Otis by virtue of its long-time use is relatively good.

[2] It is interesting that the concept of "intelligence" is very difficult to define; most test constructors do not try to define it, but rather arrive at their test validation indirectly by correlating the scores subjects make on their tests with the scores made on earlier intelligence tests -- even though the earlier test constructors had the same problem of not being able to define intelligence.

The Wonderlic Personnel Test is a twelve-minute revision of the Otis. There are several forms of the Wonderlic, each containing 50 items. Because of its ease of application and administration, the Wonderlic is probably the most widely used test in industry. It is used by one well-known hotel school as an aid in selecting students for admission. Unfortunately, it frequently also is misused. It is slightly more difficult than the Otis and is best suited to adults with at least a high school background since it is highly weighted with verbal concepts. It is not at all suited to the rank and file food service applicant. The validation on the Wonderlic is surprisingly skimpy considering its general usage.

2. The Army General Classification Test (Science Research Associates, 1947): This is a civilian edition of the popular test routinely used for Selective Service during World War II. It is a 40-minute timed test consisting of three parts: vocabulary, arithmetic, and a task requiring the viewing of objects spatially. A considerable amount of research has been done with the AGCT. It is most suited to non-college groups, since it rates slightly lower in difficulty than does the Otis. The AGCT is slightly more usable with food and hotel workers than the Otis.

3. The Personnel Tests for Industry (The Psychological Corporation). The PTI consists of a series of three measures, all scored and used separately, which are designed for workers at an entry level. Good initial research and norms have been established for these tests. They include: A Verbal Test (5 minutes), An Arithmetic Test (15 minutes), and the Following Oral Directions Test (15 minutes).

APTITUDE TESTS

1. The Differential Aptitude Test Battery (The Psychological Corporation, 1947): The DAT comprises eight separate tests designed to measure eight separate abilities or aptitudes (Verbal Reasoning, Numerical Ability, Abstract Reasoning, Space Relations, Mechanical Reasoning, Clerical Speed and Accuracy, and Language Usage -- Two parts: Spelling and Sentences). The time limits set vary from six minutes to 35 minutes for each of the subtests. The total testing time is three hours and six minutes. The DAT is a well-constructed battery and the research that has gone into it thus far has been systematic and good. It has two major limitations for use in industry: (1) Its length and (2) The adult norms are not adequate since it was developed for high school use. The industrial users of the DAT should take a research approach, i.e., find out which subtests seem applicable and collect normative data.

2. Purdue Pegboard (Science Research Associates, 1943): The Purdue Pegboard is a test of arm and hand dexterity and finger dexterity. It consists of a pegboard with pins and washers. The total test administration takes less than ten minutes. The Pegboard is a widely used test. The validity on any pegboard task varies quite considerably, depending on the groups tested and the criterion measure. A few studies are reported covering food service or hotel workers.

3. Minnesota Rate of Manipulation Test (Educational Testing Bureau, 1931): This is another form board test which consists of either placing or turning disks into holes. The test takes less than five minutes. It is considered a test of manual dexterity. It has been validated on such occupational groups as butter wrappers, food packers, bank tellers, typists, and garage mechanics. Macy's department store has experimented with the Minnesota Rate of Manipulation Test for use in selecting dishwashers. Cafeteria management in a large department store is enthusiastic about the test. It is reported that persons scoring in the upper 20 per cent of all those who take the test and who have at least dull normal intelligence make the most satisfactory dishwashers. On the other hand, persons with low dexterity as measured by the test plus very low intelligence are definitely poor employment risks.

4. The Minnesota Clerical Test (Psychological Corporation, 1933, 1946): This test is an adult test to measure clerical aptitude. It has "face validity" for use in selecting bookkeepers, secretaries, cashiers, and clerks. It is a 15-minute timed test which consists of two parts, the Numbers Test and the Names Test. The Numbers Test offers two sets of numbers such as the following: 8749---8794, 4892---4892. The examinee must decide which pairs are identical. The Names Test offers two names: A. G. Smith---A.C. Smith. The examinee must decide if the names are the same. This test has been widely researched and seems to have good validity for routine clerical jobs requiring speed and accuracy.

5. Other Clerical Tests: The Psychological Corporation publishes the General Clerical Test and the O'Rourke Clerical Test, both of which are similar to the Minnesota Clerical Test. Both offer more complex reasoning items than does the Minnesota test, but neither has had widespread use, study, or validation. The O'Rourke test has been used with reported success by the Boston Statler. A validation research was conducted which showed test results to correlate highly with job performance of clerical workers.

ACHIEVEMENT TESTS

There are no specific achievement tests applicable to the hotel-restaurant-club industry, although the following tests have application in specific contexts: The Blackstone Typewriting Test, The Blackstone Stenography Test, The Seashore-Bennett Stenographic Proficiency Tests, The Elwell-Fowlkes Bookkeeping Test, and Interview Aids and Trade Questions.

Many achievement-type tests can be developed by an organization to suit its own needs. The school lunch rooms of Chicago developed such a test for selecting cooks and used it in 1950. Each applicant was required to prepare dough for a two-crust pie and to mix and serve a beef stew. Unseasoned peas, carrots and other ingredients had been cooked early in the morning by the regular school lunch employees. The applicants were given ten minutes to mix the stew, season it, and dish it up. The stew was then graded by a committee using these criteria:

1. Are the ingredients mixed in proper proportions?
2. How is the working technique?
3. Is the stew served attractively on the plate?
4. Did the candidate finish in the allotted time?
5. How does the stew taste?

The final judgement was in terms of "good," "passing," or "fair." The practical test results were weighted 50 per cent training and 50 per cent experience. The written examination was a trade test including questions on cookery, cooking equipment, personnel and human relations. The examination time to test the 200 applicants was seven hours. Those who were waiting to take the exam were shown movies on nutrition, food buying, and food preparation.

Written examinations used previously had proved unsatisfactory. Of the persons who had passed the old written exam, only one had proved satisfactory during the six-month probationary period. On the other hand, competent cooks who had worked for years were unable to pass the written exams.

INTEREST TESTS

Although not typically considered good selection tests because of their vulnerability to manipulation by the examinee, interest tests provide some measure of a person's relative interest for certain fields of endeavor. Interest tests are perhaps best used in an "intuitive" sense as a gross screening measure. For example, if a waitress does not show an interest in people, the personnel worker may want to place special emphasis in his interview deciding whether or not the applicant would have difficulty working with people.

There are three main interest tests on the market. All are untimed and take from one-half hour to one hour to administer.

1. The Strong Vocational Interest Blank (Stanford University Press, 1927 and 1938): This is one of the finest tests on the market in terms of its validation and research; unfortunately, it has limited use in most industrial situations except under skilled interpretation. It was developed primarily to compare the individual interests of college students with the interests of people successful in professional fields. The test takes about an hour to administer and must be scored by machine (Testscor, 1554 Nicollet Ave., Minneapolis 3, Minnesota, provides this service). It is applicable only to higher level, management applicants. A skilled "clinical" interviewer can make good use of the Strong in combination with the data he acquires in the interview.

2. The Kuder Preference Record (Science Research Associates, 1948): This is the most widely used test in industry, primarily because of its ease of scoring and interpretation. The test requires approximately 45 minutes to administer. Scores are obtained indicating a person's relative interests compared with a norm group in ten broad areas of activity: Outdoor, mechanical, scientific, computational, persuasive, artistic, literary, musical, social service, and clerical. It is applicable to non-professional groups.

Some research with the Kuder in defining the successful student majoring in hotel administration has been done by Dr. Gerald W. Lattin.[3] Working with hotel students at Cornell he found that the successful students tended to place high values on power, control of others, society life and personal recognition. Unsuccessful students tended to value comfort and the intellectual life. Successful students

---

[3] Factors Associated with Success in Hotel Administration, Gerald W. Lattin, Doctoral Dissertation, Cornell University, 1949.

scored higher than average in computational and persuasive interests. They scored lower than average in scientific, mechanical, and social service interests and about average in musical, clerical, artistic and literary interests.

Statler Hotels has done research in the selection of room clerks. These psychological tests are used: The Kuder Preference Record; the Wonderlic Personnel Test; and the O'Rourke Clerical Test. They find that their best room clerks score high in computational, persuasive, social service, and clerical interests. In the Wonderlic Personnel Test a cutting score of 25 is used, i.e., no one is employed who scores less than 25 on the test.

Consideration is given to the applicant's work experience and to his educational background. The most successful room clerks have had about two years of college and have taken mostly liberal arts subjects. Based on all of this information much more valid decisions can be made in hiring room clerks than are made by an interview alone.

3. The Lee-Thorpe Occupational Interest Inventory (California Test Bureau, 1943): The advantage of this test lies in its length (requires approximately 30 minutes to administer) and in its ease of taking (understandable by junior high school students). It measures six broad fields of interest. The Lee-Thorpe lacks the general acceptance and research data of the Strong and Kuder tests.

"HONESTY TESTS"

A type of personality test, the test of honesty, has not as yet found wide application in the hotel and restaurant field. Studies of the results of introducing honesty tests for use with bank and department store employees show a general tendency of employees towards petty pilfering and a marked reduction in stealing after taking the honesty tests. In one department store, for example, approximately 85 per cent of the store employees admitted to taking money or merchandise or both. In this case none of the employees were discharged. Losses from thievery dropped by 98 per cent. It has been found that persons making complete confessions usually prove better risks than do unexamined and untried persons. Hotels and restaurants with inordinate linen, food, or silver losses might well try an honesty test.

The honesty test is usually a combination of several physiological measures -- blood pressure, pulse rate, breathing, and the resistance of the skin (due to presence or absence of perspiration) to electric current. If handled by a well-trained person, the honesty test (or lie detector test) can indicate within a margin of error whether or not the subject taking the test is responding honestly to questions directed to him.

The administration of honesty tests should be made only with the consent of the majority of employees. If employees feel they are not trusted by management this feeling may be more costly than the costs of pilfering. If the personnel see that management is asking their cooperation to detect certain individuals who are harming the reputation of all employees, the detector test should accomplish its purpose.

THE FOOD SERVICE INDUSTRY BATTERY

Historically the food service industry has been handicapped by high labor turnover, unfavorable working conditions and low wages, and the generally undesirable social stigma attached to food service work. Historically, also, the food service industry has lagged behind other major industries in the utilization of effective personnel practices. Although a great need exists for the selection and the development of outstanding food service workers, food service managers and supervisors unfortunately must often pick their prospective employees from among a mass of applicants who include quite inefficient workers who already have experienced much work failure or rejection. In an industry such as the food service industry where the labor supply is high in quantity but low in quality, a systematic approach to personnel problems is essential.

The Food Service Industry Battery, available for limited use through the author, is the only battery of tests on the market which is designed for exclusive use with food service workers. It was developed on the basis of research by one of the authors of this book (James P. Armatas) to be used with food service workers at entry levels. The four tests making up the FSIB are intended to provide useful tools for employers and counselors in the areas of selection, placement, training, and promotion of food service workers.

Each of the FSIB subtests measures a main factor shown to be an important requirement for success as a food service worker.   The subtests making up the FSIB include the following:

1. The Worker Attitude Inventory (WAI), a personality measure of the degree to which a worker is willing to conform to the expectations of his superiors;

2. The Oral Instructions Test, a tape-recorded test measuring a worker's ability to follow spoken instructions;

3. The Peg Test, a pegboard measure of manual dexterity;

4. The Verbal Test, consisting of two measures of the abilities to perform arithmetic and spelling tasks related to food service work.

It is noteworthy that the factors for success in food service work -- as one could almost guess -- are not necessarily the factors measured by traditional tests of verbal intelligence.   Rather, in addition to certain unique personality characteristics, the ideal food service worker shows his intelligence in practical ways such as being able to follow spoken instructions correctly and being able to perform the applied arithmetic and spelling functions found in food service work.

In developing the Food Service Industry Battery an attempt was made to create measures which (1) are easily administered, scored, and interpreted; (2) are interesting and nontechnical for the testee; (3) minimize school-type problem situations; and (4) do not require much time from test subjects or from test administrators.

The total FSIB may be administered in less than one hour.   It is designed as a group battery to be administered to many applicants at one time.   The scoring is simplified.

Several validation studies have been run on the FSIB with food service workers in restaurants, cafeterias, cocktail lounges, hospitals, and university serving facilities.   Norms are available on the following groups: cooks, cashiers and checkers, waitresses, dishwashers and kitchen cleaning personnel, serving-line workers, and bus help.   The validation results thus far are encouraging.   The FSIB is used on a research basis by several major food service outlets throughout the country.   The pioneer organizations, including Myron Green Cafeterias Corporation, Putsch's Plaza Restaurants, Inc., and Joe Gilbert's Restaurants, Inc., were in the Kansas City area.

SELECTION OF WAITRESSES

Every restaurant operator with a service dining room has ideas, some more valid than others, about how to select waitresses.   Height, weight, hair color, number of dependents, skin color, age, and other factors are considered.   One employer asks questions he believes gets at the girl's basic adjustment, "Were you born happy?"   If the girl breaks into a smile and replies, "Yes," she usually is hired.   Other managers pick all tall girls, one selects only redheads, and so it goes.

Certainly waitresses should be selected to fit a certain clientele.   Carhops catering to family groups can be older and more mature than in drive-ins catering to teen-agers.   A resort hotel that has guests over 50 has mature married ladies of 40 and up as waitresses, but brightens up the dining room by hiring teen-age girls for passing rolls and relish -- jobs that require little responsibility as compared with the demands made on the waitress.

Eugene Laitala has done research on biographic information as related to success of waitresses. In examining the record of 2,000 waitresses who were college students and worked in summer hotels, he found significant correlation between age and size of community from which the girls came rather than between those who were college students and those who were noncollege students.

1. Girls under 18 were not successful as waitresses in one-third of the cases.

2. Girls who came from cities over 100,000 population did not work out in 40 per cent of the cases.

3. Girls over 22, those who had finished college and were looking at the waitress position as a "last fling," were problems in one-third of the cases.

4. Girls away from home for the first time were a greater problem than those who had lived on the campus.

He reasoned that girls from larger cities were not as likely to conform as those from smaller towns where social mores and customs were more stable than in the cities.

Mrs. Jean Kimball, presently assistant to the president, Jack Tar Hotels, studied waitresses in three summer resort properties and found the following questions to be significant as related to waitress selection and as described in the comments:

What has been your previous work experience?

> All persons who had no previous work experience of any kind proved unsatisfactory as waitresses. Sixty-nine per cent of those rated as outstanding by their supervisors had previous work experience which pertained to the serving of food.

What objections do you have to working broken hours -- no objections, minor objections, strong objections?

> None of the outstanding workers objected to broken work hours, but 29 per cent of the unsatisfactory had strong objections.

Are there many kinds of work you would not do because they are not good enough for you?

> Forty-three per cent of the unsatisfactory waitresses answered "yes" to this question as compared to 6 per cent of the outstanding.

Have you hesitated to accept dates because of shyness? Do you sometimes avoid social contacts for fear of doing or saying the wrong thing?

> None of the outstanding waitresses experienced these difficulties, but significant percentages of the unsatisfactory answered "yes" to both questions.

How often do you have headaches? Do you have frequent ups and downs in mood with, or sometimes without, apparent cause?

> The percentage of unsatisfactory workers reporting frequent headaches and ups and downs in mood was much larger than the percentages for the satisfactory and outstanding groups -- in fact, none of those rated as outstanding reported having frequent headaches.

Is she shy, bold, or at ease?

> Being "at ease" proved to be indicative of job success. A few shy persons were found in each rating group, but only the unsatisfactory group encompassed persons described as "bold."

HOW TO EVALUATE THE USEFULNESS OF A TEST

Theory

1. A test never gives you concrete information but only probability statements, i.e., chances are 2 to 1, 3 to 2, 3 to 1, etc., that a person will turn out as the test predicts.

2. To be of use, all that can be required of a test is that it increase our ability to predict outcome over that of using chance alone. (If a test allows us to state that a worker has a 2 to 1 chance of being successful, this is a great improvement over just taking a 50-50 chance on that person.)

Technique

There are certain required steps and conditions that must be met in evaluating a test.

1. A group on which to try out the test -- this should contain at least 20 people and the people should function on comparable jobs (treat management and worker groups separately; if the sample is large enough, treat men and women separately).

2. Test scores -- record all of the scores.

3. Ratings -- have the supervisor who knows the workers best rate all of them in terms of their over-all work performance, e.g., good, fair, poor (it is best to have the same person rate all workers; in addition, if several raters are in agreement as to the rating of each worker, you have even a better measure).

4. Table or chart results -- make a table to determine if the test can measure up to the ratings of supervisors. If it does, then you have a useful test.

5. Once you have established the test as useful and you know what kind of scores to expect, you are ready to use the test on new applicants.

6. Plan to re-evaluate the test as soon as you have hired enough new applicants who have worked long enough to be rated. (Usually after about a year.)

Examples of How to Chart Results

1. In Restaurant X it was discovered that one of the most important abilities for success as a kitchen helper and server was the ability to follow oral instructions. Each of the people currently employed was administered a test measuring this ability and 64 scores were accumulated, one for each worker. The tester ranked the scores from highest to lowest and divided the workers into three groups: those who scored in the highest 1/3, those who scored in the lowest 1/3, and those who scored in the middle 1/3. Three raters working independently put each of the workers into one of three categories of performance: low, average, or high. Once ratings were made, the raters got together and resolved their points of departure so that they were able to come up with an agreed-upon rating for each worker. The results were charted as follows:

Test Score Results	Proficiency Rating		
	Low	Average	High
Upper 1/3	18%	33%	50%
Middle 1/3	29%	36%	28%
Lowest 1/3	53%	33%	22%
Number of Workers	17	39	18

In the chart it can be seen that 50 per cent of the workers who score high on the test were rated as the highest employees, but that only 18 per cent of the workers who score high were rated as poor employees. On the other hand, 52 per cent of the workers who score low were rated low and only 22 per cent were rated high. On the basis of the results shown by the chart, this test would be very useful in the selection of food service workers. If all future applicants were required to score higher than the lowest 1/3 of workers on the test, then over 50 per cent of the worst employees would be eliminated with very little loss of good employees.

2. All 191 workers below a management level in an organization were given a test of numerical reasoning and were rated as to whether they were acceptable or nonacceptable employees. On the basis of their test scores, they were assigned to one of four groups. The results are charted following.

Test Score Results	Number of Workers	Per Cent Rated Nonacceptable
26-up	19	6
18-25	49	14
10-17	60	36
2- 9	63	73

On the basis of the numerical reasoning test, it can be seen that if all prospective applicants were required to have a score of 10 or higher, then over half of the unsuitable candidates would be eliminated.

The examples given are but two of the ways that tests can be evaluated against ratings. Until you do such evaluation, however, you never really know how good are the tests you use. Many times after you have done an evaluation you will find that the test is even a poorer predictor than just chance alone! Once you are willing to spend time and energy evaluating tests, you will find that they are a very important and worthwhile area of selection.

The more research-oriented readers will be concerned with conducting more statistically refined "validation" studies in which validity coefficients will be computed between test scores and a criterion of performance. A question frequently asked is, "How high should a validity coefficient be in order to be acceptable?" The answer to this question is variable. Tests with relatively low validity coefficients may be useful. As a general rule of thumb, it is important to do both validation studies as well as the less formal expectancy table research described in the foregoing examples. Only then is it possible for the researcher to make a relative judgement concerning the usefulness of the test.

For those interested in the statistical tools needed in working with psychological tests, see the Appendix.

SOURCES OF INFORMATION ABOUT TESTS

All of the important tests in this country are distributed by five large companies: California Test Bureau, Educational Testing Service, Psychological Corporation, Science Research Associates, and World Book Company. One hotel-restaurant battery, The Food Service Battery, is published by its author for controlled use.[4] All of these publishers are listed following. The publishers will send current catalogues on request.

California Test Bureau, 5916 Hollywood Boulevard, Los Angeles 28, California.

Educational Testing Service, 20 Nassau Street, Princeton, New Jersey.

Psychological Corporation, 304 East 45th Street, New York 17, New York.

Science Research Associates, Inc., 259 East Erie Street, Chicago 11, Illinois.

World Book Company, 313 Park Hill Avenue, Yonkers 5, New York.

REFERENCES

1. Anastasi, A., Psychological Testing. New York: Macmillan, 1954.

2. Cronbach, L.J., Essentials of Psychological Testing (second edition). New York: Harper and Brothers, 1960.

3. Boros, O.K., Mental Measurements Yearbook (fifth edition). Highland Park, N.J.: Gryphon Press, 1959.

4. Super, D., Appraising Vocational Fitness (second edition). New York: Harper and Brothers, 1961.

---

[4]For information, write Dr. James P. Armatas, 617 Jefferson Circle, Liberty, Missouri.

CHAPTER 8

Training

In the early development of the hotel and restaurant business in this country there was small need of formal techniques for training employees. The early American inn or tavern was usually operated by the owner assisted by his family and perhaps a few "servants." The proprietor learned innkeeping from his father or by a long period of informal apprenticeship. The host's wife cooked, the children and an occasional servant or apprentice were instructed by the host and his wife in housekeeping, food preparation and service.

The late nineteenth century brought many changes. The introduction of new equipment, machinery and an interest in scientific nutrition and sanitation made formal training a necessity. Large units employing tens and, in a few cases, hundreds of employees created many problems, among them the need for job training. Inn and tavern keeping changed to hotel and restaurant operation.

Until the restriction of immigration from Europe went into effect in the 1920's the training problem was not severe. Intelligent Europeans trained in the trade since childhood were anxious to come to America and take jobs as chambermaids and kitchen help. Many skilled artisans, chefs, and journeymen of many crafts took semiskilled jobs in America. Immigration laws, however, practically cut off this source of supply and left hotel and restaurant operators little choice but to train new employees.

The full effect of the immigration restriction was not immediately felt. During the thirties skilled and intelligent workers from other trades were forced by the depression to seek work in hotels and restaurants. With World War II, however, the training problem became acute. The biggest boom the hotel and restaurant business had ever experienced found it faced with a need to expand and yet losing its experienced personnel to the armed services or to high-paying war jobs. The need for employees was tremendous. Almost anyone was hired, as the saying went, "who was warm and had a pulse." Needless to say, inefficiency was great. Some of the larger hotels had to employ as many as a third more employees than previously to do the same work. The hotel and restaurant business became training conscious.

The situation, of course, was not unique to the hotel and restaurant business. The federal government appropriated $100 million to expand and speed up training in industry generally. A Training-Within-Industry service was established to set up and administer a vast job-training program. It did a remarkable service. Out of the experiences of this program have developed valuable training techniques which will be described in this chapter.

CHARACTERISTICS OF THE HOTEL AND RESTAURANT SERVICE WHICH INCREASE IMPORTANCE OF TRAINING

A large majority of jobs in hotels, restaurants, and hospitals deal directly or indirectly with the public. A flaw in a piece of machinery, or poor workmanship in a pair of shoes is not nearly so noticeable to the consumer as a piece of hair in the guest's soup or a dirty sheet on his bed. The hotel and restaurant business hinges on a face-to-face relationship with patrons. A mistake, or inefficiency of one employee, may lose a customer forever.

Waitresses, hostesses, room clerks, telephone operators deal directly with the public. Their work is under the constant scrutiny of the guests. They are inspected not by one supervisor, but by all of the public they serve. It is imperative that they know precisely what to do and how to do it. A restaurant cannot afford to place an untrained employee on the floor. The hotel cannot afford to have an untrained elevator operator or room clerk. A hospital cannot afford to have a disinterested receptionist.

Without telling employees what is expected of them or how an operation should be performed we cannot expect them to "do it our way." Byron Calhoun, a prominent hotelman, tells a story which illustrates this point in the following paragraph.

"I attended a convention in one of the southern states and went into a barber shop in one of the leading hotels, and the man who shaved me had a cigarette in his mouth. That was something I never expected to see in my life. Not only was it discourteous but I was afraid he was going to get ashes in my eyes. I decided that I would tell the man who owned the hotel that the barber was smoking while working. Anybody should know better than to do that -- a six-year-old child should know better. But I found that the manager never told the barber not to smoke. No job training at all and no instruction at all. The policy of the hotel was never explained to the barber, so he went ahead and smoked. You can't blame the barber -- you have to blame the boss."

CHARACTERISTICS OF HOTEL AND RESTAURANT EMPLOYEES
WHICH INCREASE IMPORTANCE OF TRAINING

Characteristic of a large number of hotel and restaurant employees, especially in recent years, is their tendency to float from one job to another, to have a relatively meager educational background, and to be somewhat emotionally unstable. This is not true of employees in many well-run establishments where careful selection and adequate policies prevail, but generally among hotel and restaurant employees there is a high turnover caused by these characteristics. This is especially true of certain jobs in the back of the house. In the 4,000 resort hotels in this country only a fraction of the employees can be expected to return year after year. These facts mean that a great deal of training is necessary to produce the desired level of job performance.

Many hotel and restaurant employees lack any real motivation for their work other than economic necessity. Half of the nearly 500,000 employees in hotels are women. More than half the 1.5 million employees in restaurants are women. Many regard their jobs merely as temporary positions until marriage or something better comes along. Only a small percentage look forward to making hotel or restaurant work a career. About 30 per cent of the employees in hotels are nonwhite and will never be given the opportunity to compete for the better jobs. Their incentive to learn is low. Training for them, therefore, is more difficult to conduct but nevertheless important.

Detailed instruction will be necessary. A Florida State sanitarian tells this incident which illustrates the point. A manager of a well-run restaurant was showing the state sanitary inspector and the county sanitarian his new and expensive dishwashing equipment. The equipment fairly gleamed; the water temperature of the rinse was the approved 170° to 180° and the demonstration was a success -- except for one thing. The machine operator, caught in the rush period, was stacking cups in the dish racks three deep. The bottom spray of the dish machine washed the insides of the bottom layer of cups, and the top spray washed the outside of the top layer of cups. The insides of the top two layers of cups, of course, were left uncleaned. The operator solved this by toweling the sugar out of these cups by hand.

Another and similar incident serves to show the need for not assuming that the employee knows even the basic elements of a job. A fine restaurant with all new equipment was inspected by a government sanitarian. Despite two excellent booster heaters that raised the dishwashing water to 190° at the hot water storage tank, the temperature at the dish machine was 153°, seventeen degrees less than the approved 170° to 180°. Dishwashing with 153° water had been going on for several months, with apparent satisfaction on the part of the management and the dish machine operators. No one, it seemed, had even noticed the temperature gauge on the machine, even though the 170° mark was signaled with a red arrow. The reason for the low temperature was a 250 feet run of uninsulated piping between the hot water storage tank and the dish machine.

It is a safe assumption that the average semiskilled hotel or restaurant employee is not eager for any instruction resembling the usual classroom situation. The usual employee is interested only in training that has a real, immediate objective. Theory and abstraction have little place in employee training. It is almost impossible to create interest without an immediate objective. The employee must be continually reminded of how the training will solve his problems, increase his security, make him a more valuable person.

Most useful hotel and restaurant training will involve teaching new skills that are immediately applicable. For supervisors, the skills may be how to give orders, how to reprimand, how to put over a new idea. For employees, the skill may be that of cutting steaks, making a bed, operating a PBX, or preparing a Crêpe Suzette.

ADVANTAGES OF TRAINING TO MANAGEMENT

There are a number of advantages to be gained by management from training employees. Some are tangible and can be measured directly in terms of dollars and cents. The first question the operator usually asks is, "What does it cost?" It is now commonly agreed that it pays to train employees. The cost is offset by the gains. As someone said, "It costs money to train, but it costs more not to train." Other advantages of training are intangible and cannot be measured except in a general way. A round figure for increase in efficiency as a result of training is 25 per cent. A few of the gains to be had as a result of training employees are listed following.

1. Increased Learning Rate

The learner does not have to proceed by trial and error. His rate of learning increases under instruction and he is brought to efficient performance sooner. Through an effective training program the new employee becomes adapted to the work situation faster. His emotional tensions are reduced by helping him to avoid mistakes.

Interest shown by the instructor acts as a stimulus to learning. The learner reaches full production more quickly.

2. Increased Quality of Performance

Because he is taught the correct way to do a job the learner avoids learning incorrect ways. Teaching implies imparting the best methods found through the experience of a number of persons. Only the best ways are taught.

3. Decreased Breakage and Spoilage

Most jobs involve some breakage or spoilage, be it the job of bath maid, dishwasher, or fish butcher. An untrained and inexperienced worker can cost the operation much money. A study of New York State industries showed that training reduced spoilage by 73 per cent. Training can be insurance against breakage and spoilage, and a wise management pays money for insurance.

4. Reduced Number of Accidents

In some studies in industry it has been found that accidents among untrained persons are almost three times those among trained persons. This is true particularly among employees working around dangerous machinery. In addition to the fact that untrained employees do not know how to manipulate the equipment, the nervous strain brought on by not knowing is an important cause of accidents. It would be folly to put an inexperienced worker in charge of the new ice-crushing machines, or to hand over the job of oysterman to an untrained worker. Hazards in a hotel and restaurant are of a different type than those in a general factory, and every job in a hotel or restaurant has hazards of some kind. Many jobs expose the individual to a variety of hazards not found in general industry.

5. Reduced Labor Turnover

Studies in industry have sometimes shown labor turnover among trained employees to be one-half as great as among untrained employees. Some of the reasons for making the employee more stable will be discussed later.

6. Reduced Absenteeism

A survey conducted during the war among 63 New York State plants showed a 38 per cent reduction in absenteeism among pretrained workers. An employee who does not know what he is supposed to do is a dissatisfied employee. He is more apt to find a reason to stay at home rather than appear on his job.

7. Increased Production

The most obvious reason for training is increased production. The trained waitress can handle several more tables than the untrained one. The trained chambermaid can do fifteen rooms instead of ten. The skilled painter can paint twice as many rooms as the unskilled. Much training cannot be measured directly but reflects itself to the patrons and results in increased patronage. Training given the girl elevator operator is not measurable in "increased production" but its effects are readily discernible in the "tone" of the house. Similarly it is virtually impossible to credit the presence of a gracious hostess as the reason for a certain number of regular patrons, but her importance to the business is obvious.

ADVANTAGES OF TRAINING TO THE EMPLOYEE

The trained employee is not only more valuable to the enterprise, but he is worth more to himself. What are some incentives which can be used to motivate the trainee to learn?

1. Increased Earning Power

The new employee may be trained to produce efficiently sooner. The old employee may learn more effective ways of doing his work. Increased earnings should result in both cases.

2. Prepares for Advancement

Training enables the employee to learn his own job well and also to begin to learn the next job above him. If he has the ability, training can prepare him for a supervisory position.

3. Enhances Self-Respect, Increases Feeling of Security and Economic Independence

The trained worker meets one of the ideals of our American culture. He is relatively free to make his own decisions, he can feel pride in his work, and has a relative sense of security. He is a more free individual. The electrician has a trade with which he may contribute to the success of a business. A skilled cook is the backbone of a good restaurant. Today a first-class chef may receive $10,000 annually. Training makes "workers" into self-respecting, self-reliant, participating employees.

MOST HOTEL AND RESTAURANT JOBS
REQUIRE ON-THE-JOB TRAINING

A Department of Labor Study showed that nearly all women in hotel occupations, chiefly chambermaids, elevator and telephone operators, and a few clerical workers are thirty-five years of age or older. Almost half of the women are 45 or over. Men also are a somewhat older group. In the hotel occupations, chiefly bellmen and desk clerks, considerably more than half are 35 years or older. Workers who enter an occupation at an older age usually are less motivated in learning the job than those who have selected a trade while young. More training is needed for the older group.

According to Fred Eckert, hotel consultant, 62 per cent of the total pay roll of a hotel is unskilled manual labor and semiskilled service labor, which must be trained in the hotel and instructed on the job. Of this percentage, two-thirds comprise unskilled workers, maids, waiters, waitresses, bus boys, dishwashers, housemen, porters, cleaners, yardmen, firemen. The other third are the front office clerks, cashiers, bellmen, elevator operators, telephone operators, food and bar checkers, storekeepers, watchmen, house officers, and junior supervisory department heads.

The chart on the following page illustrates a typical departmental breakdown taken from a United States Employment Service report, and this chart shows clearly that, except for a small percentage of administrative and maintenance jobs, the bulk of hotel jobs are of a service or semiskilled nature for which there is little training available outside the hotel.

INSTRUCTING THE EMPLOYEE ON THE JOB

Who Instructs?

There have been many discussions as to who should train employees. Should it be the manager or one of his assistants? Should it be the department heads or a special training officer? Should the training be given by one of the highly skilled employees already on a particular job, and, if so, should he receive extra compensation for teaching?

Like it or not, the supervisor -- the person who is in day-to-day contact with the employee -- must take the major responsibility for training. This may be formal or informal. Characteristically, in hotels and restaurants training is informal, haphazard, unsystematic. Charitably, it could be called coaching, with the employee thrown into the job, under fire almost from the moment hired. The supervisor then gives pointers, corrects and demands, until the employee performs to the supervisor's standards.

Chain organizations usually have travelling chefs, salad makers, bakers, and dining room hostesses who move from unit to unit, acting as trainers. They are most often used in opening a new restaurant or hotel, frequently acting as line supervisors until the new operation has shaken down.

DEPARTMENTAL PATTERN FOR HOTEL INDUSTRY,
INCLUDING REPRESENTATIVE JOBS

Department	Per Cent of Work Force
I. ADMINISTRATION -- Management & Control Hotel Manager Controller Front Office Manager Promotion Manager Bookkeeping-Machine-Operator	3.7
II. FRONT OFFICE -- Desk and Telephone Front Office Cashier Room Clerk Telephone Operator	10.3
III. SERVICE -- Porter, Bellboy, Elevator & Room Service Bellman Doorman Elevator Operator Head Porter House Officer	19.3
IV. HOUSEKEEPING Chambermaid Housekeeper Houseman Linen-Room Woman	26.8
V. RESTAURANT Dining Room -- 17.4% Bus Boy or Girl Hostess Waiter or Waitress Kitchen -- 16.7% Cook Dishwasher Kitchen Helper	34.1
VI. MAINTENANCE AND EQUIPMENT OPERATION, INCLUDING HEATING EQUIPMENT Carpenter Electrician Fireman Painter Plumber	5.8

Classroom instruction is rare except in a few companies that have systematic training programs for management trainees.

Realistically, final responsibility must rest with the supervisor, not with a traveling trainer or someone from the personnel department. It is the supervisor who rewards and punishes the employee, who benefits or is handicapped by training, or the lack of it. Since most hotel and restaurant jobs are semiskilled, they can and should be learned on the job. Management training and training for chefs and bakers is something else again, requiring several months to learn even when presented systematically.

SOME LEARNING PRINCIPLES

Psychologically, all learning involves the function of perception, the thought process and motivation. The instructor is concerned with all three. The following will explain some of the basic principles of learning.

Individual Differences in Learning Ability

First the trainer should know something about individual differences. He must expect that some persons will learn a great deal faster and will retain what they learn longer than others. Even in college classes where one would suppose that students are fairly well matched as regards learning ability, large individual differences are found. It is not unusual for some students to learn twice as quickly as others. Since this is true in the college population, the great differences which appear in the general population can be surmised.

Psychologists have found that fast and slow learning ability, and all degrees in between, are distributed among people according to a pattern. This pattern when plotted in the form of a curve is known as the normal distribution curve. If we could measure by a standard intelligence test the learning ability of 1,000 persons who are a representative sample of the general population, we would find they could be plotted on the normal distribution curve. We would find about 500 with about average learning ability, about 150 who were above average, and another 100 who learned much more rapidly and could solve much more difficult problems than the average person. Similarly we would find about 150 who were slower than average in learning and could not solve as difficult problems. Another 100 could be classified as feeble-minded and some of these would be found to be institutionalized. The curve would look about like the one following.

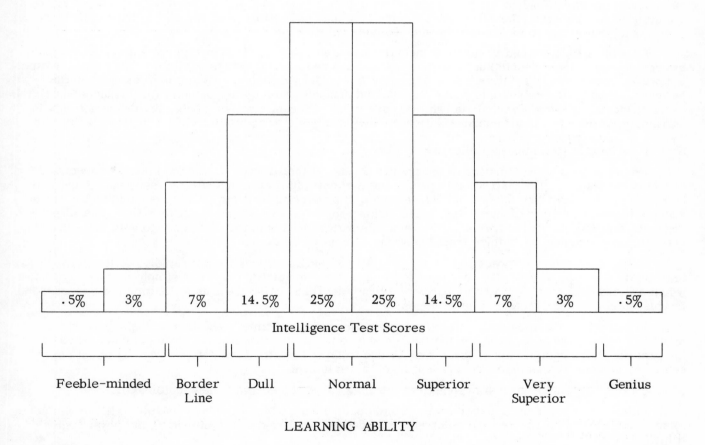

LEARNING ABILITY

Likewise results of tests of finger dexterity, personality characteristics, and mechanical aptitudes would show wide individual differences. Some learners are endowed with aptitudes and capacities for learning certain skills and types of knowledge quickly. Others have less aptitude and a few can never be taught.

The Prospective Learner Must Have Incentives for Learning

Unless the trainee is shown how training will benefit him, he is likely to have little interest in learning. Creating interest is the mark of a good teacher. Some spend one-half of the total teaching time in arousing interest, the other half in giving the subject matter. The desire to learn is brought about by a number of motivating factors: The learner's entire past experience, the way he looks at life, his values and personal adjustment, his general health. These factors determine the meaning the learning situation has for the trainee. The trainee by virtue of being alive has a desire to act. How he will act toward the learning situation will depend partly on whether the instructor can make the trainee receptive to learning and create a desire to learn.

The most characteristic thing about human behavior is the factor of internal control. To make a person work cheerfully and effectively one must connect up with these internal directive powers. This means that the teacher, supervisor or personnel director must be familiar with the energizing drives or forces that cause people to do the things they do. He must know what the motivating sources are and how to make them function. Before effort or money is expended in trying to increase human production or activity, careful consideration should be given to a proper tie-up between incentives and motives. This is particularly true with teaching. Man tends to repeat and learn those things that are accompanied by a satisfying state of affairs and tends not to repeat or learn those activities that are accompanied by an annoying situation.

It is particularly important that the social motives, such as the urge to secure those things which might build up one's ego or self-respect, like winning in competition, receiving praise, the feeling of accomplishment, avoiding censure, or obtaining security, be respected and understood by the teacher. Learning involves the whole person, his need for social participation and social approval. The instructor must be certain that he takes account of the person as well as the material or skill to be taught. In our society the physiological motives such as the urge for food, sleep, shelter, etc, are taken care of as a matter of course when jobs are available. It is the marginal effort over and above that required to "get along" that needs to be aroused in most business situations.

Careful thought should be given to incentives that will arouse these energizing influences. Money awards appeal to most people but have their limitations and are not always available. Security, at times a powerful incentive, is relatively less important in our present setup. The improvement of status, however, when judiciously employed by a respected supervisor or the opportunity for advancement on the basis of merit, or even personal recognition, are types of incentives that pay big dividends not only in learning situations but in all human relations. They are basic to high morale.

Should the Rate of Learning Be Uniform?

Having a good approximation of the trainee's general intelligence or special aptitudes needed for the learning task aids the instructor in predicting the learning time which will be required. A general knowledge of how learning takes place will also aid in predicting learning time. Learning motor skills such as those involved in dishwashing, salad making, or pastry cooking usually follows a general pattern regardless of the particular trainee. Knowing this pattern will help the instructor to anticipate learning rate and keep him and the trainee from becoming discouraged at certain times.

In the first stages of practice of a motor skill learning proceeds rather rapidly, followed by slower learning in the later steps. The fast learning is due to the acquisition of a few simple patterns, many of which are similar to or the same as patterns already learned. Also there is a minimum of boredom and fatigue which often characterize later stages.

In many jobs learning will show no increase for periods of time. The learner has reached a "plateau" and neither the instructor nor the trainee should be unduly concerned. Some plateaus serve to integrate earlier acquisitions. Others may be due to lapses of attention, fatigue, waning effects of incentives, and contentment with the present level of attainment.

On the following page is a hypothetical learning curve of learning a new motor skill.

In this case the learner experiences two plateaus during which time he is unable to better his performance. Finally he reaches the point where he cannot reach higher attainment -- his physiological limit.

Other types of learning, such as changing attitudes, memorizing, and organizing abstract materials, also proceed by patterns. The instructor will not find uniform learning ability among individuals or a uniform rate of learning within an individual. He should expect neither.

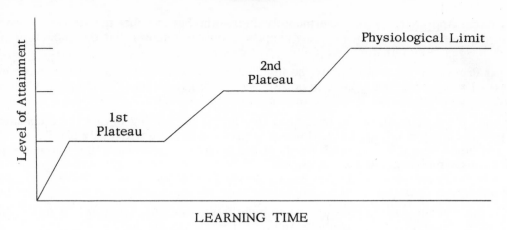

LEARNING TIME

Distributed Practice Is More Efficient than Continuous Practice

In teaching an employee a new skill, the subject matter of sanitation, or almost any type of material, the employee will learn more efficiently if his instruction is spaced through several periods rather than presented all at once. If teaching sanitation, for example, the employee will learn faster per given length of time and remember the material better if the lectures are spread out so as to be given in several periods of less than an hour each. An entire afternoon or morning in a training session is usually inefficient. It is characteristic of most learning situations that interest is difficult to sustain for any length of time. In some types of training such as that of teaching an employee to operate a machine, it is sometimes most efficient to space the training in periods as short as ten or fifteen minutes, once per day. Whether this should be done depends upon the motivation of the learner, his past experience with the skill to be learned, or with similar skills, and the complexity of the skill to be learned.

Evaluating the Employee's Progress Aids Learning

Learning proceeds more quickly when the employee is provided with a standard for indicating specifically what progress he is making. In teaching by the lecture method periodic examinations are valuable in pointing out the learner's mistakes and in stimulating his interest. In teaching motor skills approval should be given whenever any part of the skill has been mastered and the learner should be again shown just how he should continue so as to master the other parts. When the trainee is given a precise goal toward which he can work, learning is facilitated.

Step Up the Goal Gradually

Set up goals that the learner can reach quickly. In training a salad maker, for example, set the number of salads for the first day within the grasp of the new employee. Implying that Mary the new salad girl should be as expert as Joan the old employee only discourages Mary. As the new employee learns, step up the goal gradually until standard production is reached. A new maid may do well to clean 10 rooms a day the first week on the job. The next week she might be encouraged to do 12 a day and by the third week the standard of 16 a day. Setting the goals too high means that the goal is no longer a goal for the employee. A goal is a goal only as long as the employee thinks it is.

INEFFECTIVE AND EFFECTIVE MANAGEMENT TRAINING

Ineffective Training

1. <u>Gimmicks and Froth</u>: Some companies train at the level of the after-dinner speech or the booster talk. Many instructors look upon human relations training as a form of salesmanship, putting over a message. In this category come the inspirational speakers and the platitude repeaters who talk about supervisors needing to be "loyal, using good judgement," and so on. <u>These traits cannot be taught!</u>

2. <u>Bringing Others in Line</u>: This approach attempts to sell supervisors on the views of top management without giving recognition to the employee's views. Training as such is viewed as a magic cure for whatever is wrong. The "message-bearing" supervisors are expected to convey to subordinates the "party line."

3. <u>Abstract Theory</u>: Any training that does not have its primary focus on the <u>trainee's</u> own problems is not good training. Training which deals only with theories and does not get into practical situations is unrealistic.

4. <u>The Charm Approach</u>: There are those trainers who believe that the secret to supervisory success lies in making friends and influencing people. Research shows that the superficial "nice" approach actually lowers rather than raises employee morale.

5. <u>The Pat Program</u>: This is used by the instructor who follows a rigid outline from which he will not deviate. He talks <u>to</u> the group; there is no two-way communication. He frequently uses audio-visual aids like movies and slides always to prove that he has "the" answer.

The common element in all of the preceding five forms of training is that the emphasis is on generalities and praiseworthy maxims, but little help is given in dealing with daily problems. Training to be effective must begin with the expressed needs of the trainees themselves, <u>not</u> the needs recognized by the trainer or by higher management.

Conditions for Effective Training

1. The trainees must want to change. They must feel a need for training. If this need is not there, the problem is to discover why it is not there and how it might be put there.

2. The program must be geared to the needs and problems of the trainee. It is foolish to try to train people who have no interest in an area or no real reason for being interested.

3. The trainees must seek out the answers and conclusions to the problems by themselves. People learn by <u>experience</u> and <u>involvement</u>.

4. Human relations training is more effective if it is conducted in groups. Research shows that group decisions are more effective in modifying behavior than are individual approaches.

5. It is essential that the training program provide trainees opportunities to let off steam. Human relations involves feelings and emotions. Typically, behavior changes only after an emotional experience in which a person may feel quite angry or frustrated or quite fearful in the process.

6. It is important not to "strip" trainees of their old modes of operation and defense. Let the training add to but not take away from. As trainees feel more comfortable with new roles, they can be expected to change their old patterns more permanently.

7. Training should lead to <u>usable</u> skills; platitudes about "loyalty," "incisiveness," and so on are meaningless.

THE FOUR-STEP JOB INSTRUCTION METHOD

The Training Within Industry program of World War II developed through many thousands of trials an abbreviated formula for instructing. It has been adapted for training in hotels and restaurants.

JOB INSTRUCTION	HOW TO INSTRUCT

WHEN TO INSTRUCT
 	
    New crews needed
    A new employee
    Corrective measures
    Upgrading
 	
PREPARE TO INSTRUCT
 	
      Know the job yourself
        Quality, quantity and method
 	
      Break down the job
        Steps in order, key points
        Safety factors (How and Why)
 	
      Set a Schedule
        (Accuracy and Speed), date or hour to be ready.
 	
      Arrange work station
        Tools, equipment, materials and supplies.
 	
      Get everything ready
        As the worker is expected to keep it.
 	
      Approach to the learner
        Friendly, helpful, patient attitude. He wants to learn.
	Step 1. Prepare the Learner
	    Put him at ease (Break the ice).
	    State the job and find out what he knows about it.
	    Explain purpose and importance of job to get his interest.
	    Place in proper position.
	Step 2. Demonstrate the Operation
	    Show, tell, illustrate each move.
	    One step at a time.
	    Stress key points, safety factors.
	    Slowly and patiently.
	    No more than he can get at one time.
	    Repeat the demonstration.
	Step 3. Application or Try Out
	    Have him do the job. Watch for and correct errors.
	    Compliment and encourage.
	    Have him repeat operations, explaining steps and key points.
	    Question him as he goes.
	    Repeat job until you and he are both sure.
	Step 4. Follow-Up (Supervise)
	    Put him on his own, but tell him where to get help.
	    Check frequently, encourage him, invite questions.
	    Taper off coaching as he progresses.
	
	The Learner Can Perform If the Instructor Has Taught

Preparation for instructing takes a much longer time than the actual instruction. For a particular job each step must be laid out in sequence. A sample job breakdown, taken from a government publication, Establishing and Operating A Restaurant, is shown for the job of Fruit Salad Making.

FRUIT SALAD MAKING

Operation	Steps	Key Points
I. Preparing the lettuce.	1. Make lettuce cups out of head lettuce. 　a. Make single cups out of large curly leaves. 　b. Make single cups out of small curly leaves combined together. 　c. Lay aside outer flat leaves for shredding.	Be sure head lettuce is clean, crisp and not deteriorated. Be sure to shake off excess water. Cups should curl up around fruit and not lie too flat on plate.
II. Arranging fruit in lettuce cup.	1. Place heavy, firm fruit in lettuce cup to make the foundation. 2. Place less firm and smaller fruits on top of heavy fruits. 3. Place more colorful and decorative fruits on top of salad.	Keep a light touch and an artistic sense. Decide where fruit goes and put it there. Make every motion count. Remember the basic appeal of the salad is freshness, crispness, good flavor, and beauty of arrangement. Finished salad weights: Plate_____ Salad order_____. Half (or junior) order_____.
III. Marinating the salad.	1. Stir French dressing thoroughly each time you serve from it. 2. Dip out dressing and drip it over the fruit.	Use short, quick motions to blend completely the oil and seasonings. Do this only after the salad is ordered because on standing, dressing wilts the lettuce and draws juice out of fruits. Use enough dressing to season each piece of fruit but not so much that it will run off onto lettuce cup or plate.
IV. Serving Salad.	1. Serve at once to the customer or put it in the refrigerator.	Seconds in a hot kitchen affect the crispness and freshness.

In preparing job breakdowns all department heads should be asked to participate. The results should be kept in loose-leaf form and be thought of as subject to change or modification. By placing emphasis on the desirability of preparing careful job breakdowns, emphasis is at the same time placed on training and training techniques.

An excellent guide for preparing the job breakdowns appears in A Manual for Training Hospital Employees drawn up by the Cleveland Hospital Council. Sections covering housekeeping, laundry, and dietary are applicable to hotels and restaurants. A sample job breakdown taken from the Manual appears following.

WET MOPPING FLOORS

Equipment:
2 Pails
2 Wringers
2 Mops
1 Hair push brush or
1 Dust mop
Dust cloth
Supplies

IMPORTANT STEPS	KEY POINTS
Assemble equipment.	____ Listed above.
Sweep floor with hair brush or dust mop.	____ To remove surface soil.
Prepare cleaning solution and rinse water.	____ According to type of floor.
Dip mop into cleaning solution.	
Operate mop over convenient area of floor.	____ Around floor adjoining wall -- into corners first.
	Use continuous overlapping figure eight movement.
	Avoid splashing baseboard and furniture.
Return mop to cleaning solution.	
Wring mop dry -- return to floor.	____ To pick up excess moisture
Rinse dry.	____ Use clean mop partially wrung from clean water.
Return mop to rinse water.	
Wring mop dry -- return to floor.	____ Absorb all moisture.
Repeat mopping and rinsing of areas adjoining.	____ Overlap areas until entire surface is cleaned.
	Do not touch walls.
	Mop toward door.
Use damp cloth, wipe baseboards and pick up surplus moisture left in corners by mop.	
Clean and replace equipment.	

JOB INSTRUCTIONS

Job instructions are detailed lists of duties to be performed and a description of how they are to be performed. At best they are dull and dry and when turned over to an employee for his own study are not too effective as training materials. As with so many training aids, the manner of use is as important or more important than the material itself.

Pope's Cafeterias, headquartered in St. Louis, have broken down all of the jobs found in their establishment and have made up detailed job instructions which are handed to the new employee and for which the employee signs. Tests are given to the employee a few days later covering the information on the job instruction folders.

To lighten and add interest to job instructions, Tom Ham, restaurant owner of Atlanta, Georgia, produces "hand-outs" for his waitresses which make interesting reading aside from the job information contained. A sample is seen below.

---

7 WAYS TO GET A GOOD RAISE...FROM THE <u>REAL BOSS</u>

First let's get one thing straight. Who is the boss? Certainly not the tightfisted so-and-sos who pay you a few lousy bucks a week to work here. No, cousin. This may come as a shock to you, but the <u>real</u> boss is the customer. So if you are going to get a raise, honey, you better shine up to the guy who really pays you your dough. Here's how to grease him; in 7 simple steps...

1. <u>Greet Him Like You Mean It</u>

   The very first thing you do when you go up to that table, you smile and give him a cheerful "Good morning," "Good afternoon" or "Good evening." <u>We</u> are mighty glad he's come, and <u>you</u> ought to be even gladder. Remember, he's going to tip you according to how good we make him feel...so give yourself a break, and start off by making him feel welcome and at home.

2. <u>Set Him Up Right</u>

   Place mat, order form, condiments, etc. all there? All right, get him his water and silverware---and be sure you check it before you give it to him, in case the dishwasher goofed. But don't make a production of inspecting it, or you'll have everybody in the dining room looking for lipstick smudges on their cups and glasses. Be sneaky about it.

3. <u>Be Sure the Order Is Right</u>

   If he wants to fill it out, let him. But let him know you'll do it for him if he wants you to. And if he does it himself and gets it all loused up, don't make him feel like a damn fool. Chances are he's never been a waitress, even---much less a hostess. Get your order working as soon as you can.

4. <u>Bring Him Something Right Away</u>

   Sure, the steak has to be cooked. But the salad doesn't, and neither does the shrimp cocktail or the soup. Give him something to nibble on. Let him have some action---fast. It'll keep him from getting impatient. And <u>smile</u> and <u>say something</u>.

5. <u>"Make an Entrance" With the Main Course</u>

   Whether it's a 45¢ Steerburger or a $4.50 sirloin, it's what he picked from the menu, and it's darned good. So don't put it down before him apologetically. Make it a big event. He should be drooling for whatever it is. Serve it like you think it is fit to eat. And <u>smile</u> and <u>say something</u>. Remember?

6. <u>Check Back On Him</u>

   Steak cooked right? Tender? (You can replace anything but a Gambler, just by checking with the manager.) More water? More coffee? And now, dessert: Honey, don't <u>ask</u> the guy if he's going to have dessert. Ask him <u>what he'll have</u> for dessert. You'll sell ten times as many, and make your checks and tips bigger. And on every contact, <u>smile</u> and <u>say something</u>.

7. <u>Invite Him Back</u>

   Unless he turned out to be a complete so-and-so and you actually hope he chokes, tell the guy you hope he enjoyed his meal. And if you can do it without making him think you're trying to pick his pocket, tell him you enjoyed having him eat with us. This doesn't mean you have to burst into tears and tell him, between sobs, that waiting on him was the greatest experience of your life. Just make the guy feel like coming back; that's all. He might develop into the greatest call customer that ever came down the pike.

   And when he leaves, cousin, you go over to that table and pick up your tip and fold it carefully....and please go into the kitchen before you tuck it into your stocking. We do not aim to incite no riots & stampedes amongst the customers.

Probably the most valuable aspect of job instruction is that it is the result of someone in management's being forced to sit down and list everything to be done on a job. Even though the new employee may not learn much by reading the instructions, the sheet is valuable in that it can be a reference for the supervisor as a list of points to cover in training.

Most hotels and restaurants cannot afford to develop usual aids for training purposes and do not use those that are available from outside sources. Job instruction sheets constitute a minimal effort in formalizing and systematizing training. If mimeographing the sheet is too much of an effort, type a few copies and cover them in plastic, to be used whenever a new employee is hired.

Here is another example of job instructions, this set made up by J. B. Temple, presently vice-president of operations for Holiday Inns.

INSTRUCTIONS TO BELLMEN

You are one of the most important persons our guests meet when they arrive. Because service is the symbol of a good hotel, and because you give most of this service, it is essential that you do your job well. Please carry out the following instructions.

INSTRUCTIONS	REMINDERS
Report for work on time. Appear neat; hair trimmed, face and neck shaved, hands clean. Have a uniform that is clean and pressed. Wear black sox and well-polished black shoes.	Good appearance pleases guests and increases your tips!
On guest's arrival, pick up baggage from doorman and place by column in lobby. Perform doorman's duties if he is not available.	Greet guests with "Good morning, sir (or ma'am)" or "Good afternoon" or "Good evening."
When guest registers, get key from room clerk. Notice guest's name.	Call guest by name when directing him to elevator. Say, "Right this way, Mr._____."
Pick up baggage and escort guest to elevator, walking a few steps ahead.	Let guest enter elevator first so you can leave first with baggage.
Open door to room and turn on overhead lights. Place baggage on baggage rack and key on inside of door. Ask if room is satisfactory.	Let guest enter room first.
If it is, proceed as follows: Hang up guest's coat and hat if he has taken them off. Turn on bathroom light and check soap, toilet tissue, and towel supply. Check stationery supply in desk, pitcher and glasses on dresser, and laundry list and bag in closet. Tell guest about laundry and valet service. If he has any at this time, fill out laundry list and take clothes in laundry bag back down with you. Check all pockets for forgotten articles. Show guest how air conditioning and radio work. Explain that door must be locked with key. Leave promptly!	Do not carry on unnecessary conversation while doing these things unless guest asks you a question.
If room is not satisfactory, call room clerk and arrange for another room. Key will be sent up with elevator operator. Conduct guest to new room and follow usual steps.	The guest wants to be roomed quickly and efficiently and will tip well for speedy service.
	Finish filling out bellman's card and return it to bell captain.
Before going up to check out a guest, ask cashier to stamp your bellman's card "PAID" if he has paid his bill. While in his room, assist in closing bags if they are open.	Anything you find will mean a bigger tip for you and will prevent trouble later. Before you leave room, make sure that guest has all keys and that they are turned in to desk.

(continued)

INSTRUCTIONS TO BELLMEN (Continued)

INSTRUCTIONS	REMINDERS
Check for forgotten articles in bathroom, closet, and drawers, on floor, under bed. Escort guest down only after checking room.	
Keep guest's bags in lobby until he has paid his bill if he has not paid already. You must have your bellman's card stamped "PAID" by cashier before you can take baggage outside.	If guest wants baggage taken outside for a car, taxi, or limousine, deliver it to doorman. Perform doorman's duties if he is not available. Record car license number or cab number on bellman's card. Carry baggage to bus station if desired.

Here are some helpful suggestions with which you can give better service and increase your tips:

Know all the information on the "MAY WE BE OF SERVICE" sheets on the dressers.

Know the various routes out of town and distances to nearby points.

Carry the following items with you: matches or a lighter, adequate change, change tray, pencil. A pocket knife and a watch are often helpful.

Be ready to assist guests -- light cigarettes, pick up dropped articles, open doors, mail letters, etc.

Pick up wastepaper, matches, etc. in the lobby and corridors when the maid is not around.

Be careful when placing bags on baggage racks not to scrape walls or furniture.... or baggage.

Move about quietly at all times. Don't rattle things or carry on a conversation with another employee.

Call a guest by name when you can. He appreciates this personal attention.

When delivering anything to a room, ask desk for name of guest in the room, and check for mail or messages so that you can take them with you.

Be friendly and courteous -- never familiar -- with a guest, no matter how often you see him.

The following are house rules, which must be strictly adhered to:

1. You are prohibited from procuring women.
2. Deliver to a guest only whiskey or cokes purchased inside the hotel, and only when the bar and package store are open.
3. Deliver guest laundry, cleaning, and pressing to the hotel laundry only.
4. Unlock a door for a person only with an order from the front desk.
5. <u>Always</u> leave the inside door open when in a guest room.
6. Report suspicious-looking guests and any fire or smoke immediately to the bell captain or to the front desk.
7. Know how to use the fire extinguishers. Turn them upside down to use.
8. Report anything found to be wrong in a room to the proper department immediately.
9. Make only emergency outside calls, and then only through the bell captain's phone. Never use the pay phones.
10. Time stamp your bellman's card before and after going on a call.
11. Use the freight elevator for all down trips.
12. Do not come to work drunk or drink on the job, or you will be dismissed.

Included as a part of job instructions can be such information as standard portion sizes to be used. The information following was developed by the management of a roadside restaurant to be handed to new fry cooks as a part of job instructions.

PORTION SIZES AS PART OF JOB INSTRUCTIONS

Portions

1. Cooked French Fries

   a. Sandwiches   2 oz.
   b. Dinners   3 oz.
   c. Side orders   5 oz.

2. Cooked Hash Browns

   a. Dinners   4 oz.
   b. Sides   4 oz.
   c. Breakfasts   2 oz.

3. Chef's Salad

   a. Line 8" bowl with leaf lettuce, fill bowl with chopped salad;
      cut 1 slice of cold ham in strips and 1 slice of cheese,
      wedge 1/2 tomato and one boiled egg.

4. Stuffed Tomato Salad

   a. Line plate with leaf lettuce.
   b. Shredded lettuce.
   c. One tomato cut as prescribed.
   d. Fill tomato with 4 oz. tuna salad.
   e. One lemon wedge.
   f. Top with mayonnaise and cherry.
   g. Pickle.

5. Cottage Cheese Peach Salad

   a. Line plate with leaf lettuce.
   b. Shredded lettuce.
   c. Three #20 scoops cottage cheese.
   d. Two peach halves -- cut each in three wedges.
   e. Arrange in cottage cheese in prescribed manner.
   f. Top with mayonnaise and cherry.

6. Cottage Cheese and Pineapple Salad

   a. Same as Cottage Cheese and Peach Salad.
   b. Use two pineapple rings.

TRAINING SCHEDULES

To press for the accomplishment of training, some organizations regularly ask supervisors to assist their employee in terms of skills, and to check off those skills which need development. Sheraton Hotels, for example, sets up a Training Schedule, listing employees and the skills which need sharpening. One of their Training Schedule forms is shown on the following page. Notice that not only is the skill which needs polishing checked but the supervisor is asked to name the date the training will take place.

TRAINING SCHEDULE

Department TOWN ROOM

Date 6/16/58

Jobs Performed →

Name	1. Rule + Regulations	2. Town Room Uniform	3. Floor Plans	4. Table Setup	5. Menu Reading	6. Taking Orders	7. Writing Checks	8. Ordering Food	9. Pick Up	10. Serving Guests	11. Side Work	12.	Remarks
Average Training Time Hours.	2	1/2	1	4	4	2	2	2	2	4	1		
1. Mary Jones	x	x	x	x	x	x	x	x	x	x			
2. Jane Eton	6/18	x	x	x	6/19	x	x	x	6/24	x			
3. Betty Cox	x	x	x	x	x	x	6/23	x	x	x			
4. Sarah Smith	6/18	x	6/18	x	6/19	x	7/1	x	7/1				
5. Robert Gregg	x	x	6/18	-	-	-	-	-	7/1	6/25			
6. Carol Drake	6/18	6/18	6/18	6/19	6/19	6/20	6/23	6/23	6/24	6/25			
7.													
8.													
9.													

Code: x Can do the job satisfactorily.

        - Doesn't need to do the job.

        Insert the date training will be completed.

_____
Supervisor

TEST YOURSELF -- "ARE YOU A GOOD TRAINER?"

1. Do you consider preparation to be the first step in instructing an employee? Do you spend as much or more time in preparation, getting things ready as you do in actual instruction?   [Yes]   [No]

2. Do you prepare job breakdowns for what you are going to teach? Have you listed the key points around which you will build the instruction?   [Yes]   [No]

3. Do you devote any time to explaining to the employee how he will profit from learning what you have to teach?   [Yes]   [No]

4. Do you determine what the employee already knows about the job before you start training?   [Yes]   [No]

5. Do you set up a timetable showing the time you plan to use in job instruction day by day and when you expect the training to be completed?   [Yes]   [No]

6. Do you expect that there will be periods during the training during which no observable progress will be made?   [Yes]   [No]

7. Do you expect that some employees will learn two or three times as fast as others?   [Yes]   [No]

8. Do you both tell and show the employee how to do the skill involved?   [Yes]   [No]

9. When the employee performs incorrectly, do you say, "No, not that way!"   [Yes]   [No]

10. Do you give instructions so clearly that no one can misunderstand what is intended?   [Yes]   [No]

11. Do you ask the employee to try out the skill and to tell you how to do it?   [Yes]   [No]

12. Do you use praise frequently?   [Yes]   [No]

(All of the questions should be answered "yes" except number 9)

HOW TO USE VISUAL AIDS

Too often the showing of a movie or filmstrip finds part of the audience asleep when the lights go on. To be effective visual aids must be a part of a carefully planned program. Learning is not a passive affair and visual aids must be used to stimulate thinking and to impart knowledge. The instructor should get the audience to participate by pointing out things to look for in the films and by asking questions concerning key points in the film. Often a film may be most useful as a kickoff to a discussion. It is always good teaching to summarize a film after its showing and to show how it is related to problems at hand.

For teaching a particular operation the filmstrip or slide presentation are effective. One frame is shown at a time and the commentator has as much time as is needed to drive the point home. Movies are excellent devices for showing large-scale operations or for morale purposes. Orientation films which give the new employee an over-all picture of an enterprise can be effective.

Summarizing techniques of presenting instructional films, we can itemize the following steps:

1. Stimulate a readiness to learn. Pose searching questions on the film that the employee should keep in mind as he sees it. Relate the film to the past experience of the employee. Tell him the advantages the film can have for him. Give him a verbal synopsis of the film and, if possible, a written synopsis

2. Show the film.

3. Immediately start a discussion about the film. Ask for criticisms of techniques presented. "Are there better techniques?" Ask for comments as to the usefulness of the practices presented to the present situation. Ask the employees to paraphrase the important points presented. Summarize the discussion, point up key points.

4. If necessary repeat the procedure at a later date.

Among the larger hotel and restaurant companies that have developed their own employee training films are The Stouffer Company of Cleveland, Ohio; The Schrafft Company of New York City; The Fred Harvey Company of Chicago, Illinois; and Holiday Inns.

OTHER METHODS OF TRAINING

Sponsor Training

The new employee is usually confused and ill at ease. An effective way to make him feel a part of the organization is to provide a period of orientation during which he is given personal support in making adjustment to the enterprise. This is successfully accomplished, especially with girl employees, by providing a "big sister," or sponsor. The sponsor shows the new girl where the rest rooms, eating places, lounges, and locker rooms are located. She introduces the new girl to her friends and serves as an entree to the "esprit de corps" of the organization. Girls especially suited as sponsors may be so designated and given a small merit increase in wages. Sometimes sponsors may also be able to act as instructors.

The Stouffer Company makes good use of sponsor training by asking an experienced waitress to help the new one along. After preliminary training in a work dining room, the new waitress is given charge of a few tables. She gains confidence in her job by assurance from her neighbor-sponsoring waitress. Induction is gradual, emotionally satisfying and thorough.

Orientation Lectures and Tours

In larger organizations a systematic orientation program is instituted in which lectures, movies, and tours are a part. Some hotel and restaurant chains have orientation films which show the new employee the scope of the organization, its varied activities, and something of the part the employee will play in the organization. Such films when well done are an excellent means of getting the employee off to a good start. A few hotels and restaurants have set up a lecture and tour program. The Hotel Statler in Buffalo, for example, has a plan by which when a certain number of employees have been hired they are assembled and given a lecture and a tour of the building. The lecture comprises an historical background and something of the architecture of the building, a simple description of departmental organization, and a conducted tour of the building. After the tour there is an opportunity for discussion and comments. A smaller organization could combine similar orientation procedure with periodic employee meetings.

Role-Playing and Skits

A teaching method which combines fun with learning is dramatization. Three or four waitresses may put on a skit showing their way of serving a guest. The others may criticize. Sometimes the wrong way and the right way can be dramatized. An instructing chef can show how not to cut a roast, followed by the right way. The housekeeper can demonstrate the wrong way and the right way to change a bed. Humor can be used and is an effective means of driving home a point.

Dramatizing is also a good means of changing undesirable attitudes. Having various employees play the roles of others can often give them insight into their own and others' problems. Having waitresses play customers or dishwashers and vice versa will often strengthen cooperation and clear up hidden feelings of resentment.

TRAINING UNDER STRESS

A fuse blows, cutting off the electricity in the restaurant...

A key waitress calls in "sick"...

A machine grinds to a halt, a gear missing...

A salesman informs that the price of flour has gone up another cent a pound...

It's all part of the obstacle course, the test under fire, given the eighth and last week of a thorough training program. And this "obstacle course" serves to emphasize the "psychologics" which a chain -- Mister Donut -- stresses in getting top-notch franchisees.

Testing a man's mettle under the most effective simulated conditions as possible was highlighted by the Armed Services in a number of ways during World War II. And while the true test is realistic action itself, simulated situations do permit management to gauge an employee's "response" quotient....

as well as giving him enough experience so he can handle himself more effectively the next time trouble strikes.

At Mister Donut, headquartered in Westwood, Mass., "psychologics" begins right with the interview of prospective franchisees. A battery of psychological tests are given them, the aim to determine their ability to be their own boss. As an example, take this question:

When waiting in line at the movies and someone cuts in ahead of you, should you:

1. Be polite but humble and suggest there's been a mistake?

2. Be quiescent and accept the intruder?

3. Firmly tell him to get the hell out of here, etc.?

Obviously, says the company, the man who picks number 3 will be strong enough to resist salesmen trying to pressure him into paying unreasonable prices.

Prospective franchisees who enter the "Mister Donut College," under Nick Fiorentino, director of operations, go through an eight-weeks training course. The main textbook is the Mister Donut Manual of Operating Procedures. In the eighth week, students are given a store to run, and management throws the book at them. Things get progressively worse, with incident upon incident piling up. The student who not only survives but thrives on trouble is headed for instant success, the company officials say. And how students fare in this week often tips management as to the extent of guidance they will need as they take over their newly erected store.

FOOD SANITATION TRAINING

Since there is no quicker way to go out of business than to serve infected food, training employees in sanitary methods of food handling is a must in any food service operation. Illustration after illustration is available of severe illness caused by unsanitary restaurant conditions or ignorance on the part of restaurant personnel.

The Public Health Service using mobile laboratories examined 50,000 utensils from 5,400 eating places in 156 cities. Only 28 per cent were free from dangerous bacteria count. One large city showed an average count of 2,800 bacteria on spoons at eight soda fountains (the recognized limit is 100 organisms per utensil surface examined). On tumblers at the same fountains the bacteria count was 390,000 and in beer glasses at 19 barrooms the average count was 7,000,000.

Figures of the U. S. Public Health Service show 23,765 cases of food-borne disease throughout the nation in 12 months, and it is estimated that only five per cent of the diseases caused by food filth are reported. To carry this figure out, there were 475,300 cases of food-borne disease during the year.

In a study in New York City, fifty-eight cases of illness were traced to one cook who had prepared a certain dressing. The staphylococci of the dressing which had caused the illness was found in the mucous membrane of his nose. Needless to say, that restaurant lost considerable business. In another case, twelve people in the State of Washington were taken violently ill with gastroenteritis. The cause of the illness was traced to a particular restaurant kitchen. General sanitation was fair. There was no noticeable filth. The chef merely had a cut finger from which staphylococci flowed to poison the twelve guests of the restaurant. This is an illustration of personnel's not knowing proper sanitation precautions.

Lack of sanitation control results in legal claims. One restaurant chain which served over 5 million meals in one year had these claims brought against the company.

Bone in seafood cocktail	3	Glass in fruit cocktail	1
Piece of metal in food	1	Tooth broken on chicken	1
Piece of casserole found in food	1	Alleges food poisoning account of	
Chicken bone cut roof of mouth	1	fish served	1
Allergic to seafood cocktail	1	Lost filling while eating candy cane	1
Piece of glass in grapefruit	1		

Another national organization reports 49 claims on a total of 9,340,000 meals served in 1958. GLASS was the most frequent cause with 26 claims; metal resulted in 6 claims; and bones caused 5 claims. Needless to say, some claims are fraudulent. Managers should be alert to get all details involving a claim at the time the claim is made.

Because of the importance sanitary food handling has for the health of the general public, the U. S. Public Health Service has developed a Food-Sanitation Training Course which is being used by the restaurant industry. The course is divided into seven lessons, presented in three lecture periods, as follows:

1. <u>Bacteriology</u>. History, nature, growth, reproduction, shapes, and habits.

   <u>Communicable Diseases</u>. Relation of bacteria to disease; method of disease transmittal; causes of decay and fermentation.

   <u>Insect and Rodent Control</u>. Spread of disease by insects and animals; life cycle, habits of insects and animals; contamination and destruction of food.

2. <u>Sanitization of Eating Utensils</u>. Effects of various agents on bacteria; proper disinfection of utensils and equipment.

   <u>Food Handling and Public Health</u>. Food spoilage, refrigeration and preservation; relations of animal life and bacteria to food poisonings and infections.

   <u>Personal Hygiene</u>. Hand washing, rest room sanitation, uniforms, personal appearance, use of side towel.

3. <u>Detergents and Methods of Sterilization</u>. Proper use of detergents; application of steam, chlorine, etc. Lecture and demonstrations designed for those actually employed in this important phase of operation.

Food sanitation and general cleanliness are vital to restaurant success in this country. Howard Johnson's -- one of the largest chain of restaurants in the world -- owes a good part of its phenomenal appeal to highway travelers to its reputation for cleanliness. Travelers feel that at a Howard Johnson's restaurant they will get safe food served in clean surroundings. The American public grows more sanitation-minded and restaurant operators have no alternative but to reflect this sanitation consciousness.

Sanitation practices and attitudes are the result of what has been learned in the home and school. In the restaurant the manager is the key person. What he does or does not do is reflected by the employee.

Most adults in this country are generally aware of the germ theory of disease and the importance of cleanliness in food handling, but relatively few restaurant operators know food sanitation practices in detail. What follows is the kind of information which everyone in a restaurant should know. This material is part of a training manual written for Intercontinental Hotels.

YOU DON'T SEE 'EM BUT YOU FEEL 'EM

Germs are around you everywhere. They are on your hands, on your hair, on your clothes. They are also in you -- your nose, mouth, stomach, and intestinal tract.

You can't see them except under a microscope because they are about 1/25,000 of an inch long. You don't hear them or smell them. You do feel them though once they make you and our hotel guests sick.

Most germs are harmful. Germs and their smaller cousins, the viruses, cause disease and death. Some germs like those that make buttermilk and cheese are helpful, but we are not concerned with them.

What is a germ? It is a tiny, living body that moves, digests food and -- most important -- can cause disease in people, in you and in your guest. Germs, like people, come in different sizes and shapes and have their own personalities. There is the germ that poisons food, for example, the staphylococcus. He is a treacherous fellow that is almost everywhere. He's in the air, in your hair, in the dirt under your fingernails and on your hands. Once it gets into food that is neither too hot nor too cold, nor has too much acid, what happens? It grows, splits in two parts. Where there was one germ, there are soon two of them. It takes only twenty minutes of living in a nice cream pie at room temperature for the staph germ to enlarge, split and form two germs. Two germs form four and four make eight. Germs live faster lives than Hollywood stars. Within three hours one germ can start a chain reaction which results in 500 germs.

Germs are classified by shape:

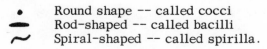

    Round shape -- called cocci
    Rod-shaped -- called bacilli
    Spiral-shaped -- called spirilla.

Viruses are even smaller than bacteria; nevertheless they cause the common cold, flu, and other serious diseases.

Seen under a microscope these germs look safe enough. But watch out. These are the killer germs that cause typhoid.

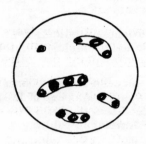

And here is another rattlesnake that is not even polite enough to give a warning rattle -- a killer that chokes little children to death -- diphtheria.

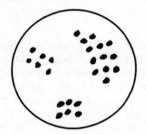

And the little weasel that we carry around with us most of the time -- the staphylo-coccus. All he needs is good food and room temperature to multiply. As he grows he gives off poison which causes diarrhea and vomiting in us and our guests.

Germs and people unfortunately like many of the same foods; for example, beef, veal, pork, poultry, and eggs. Germs like moist food, absorb it by soaking it up through their skins. As they eat, they grow, divide, and multiply. The more germs, the more dangerous the food.

The little characters that cause amoebic dysentery are tiny animals called amoeba that grow in the intestinal tracts of bigger animals, including people. They appear in the stools of those infected and often get into food which when eaten infects other people. You know the symptoms -- continuous running to the toilet and blood in the stool, leaving the victim weakened and unable to resist other diseases.

The vicious character that causes amoebic dysentery.

 Rats and mice also carry Salmonella germs in their intestinal tracts. These germs are in their droppings and on food over which the rats or mice walk.

People, you, carry germs -- many of them. We all have germs in our mouths, throats, stomachs, and intestinal tracts at all times. Not enough to make us sick, thank goodness. But enough to make others sick since they may not be able to resist our germs. The mouth which may look so clean has been called a "human cesspool." Don't let this stop you from kissing your loved ones. Who would stop anyway? Within a family the members tend to build up resistance against each other's germs.

Many people carry such deadly germs as typhoid without being sick themselves. These folks are called "carriers" and their germs can kill others who lack the same resistance.

Animals, ourselves included, can carry typhoid fever, dysentery, infantile paralysis in our intestinal tracts. By failing to wash our hands after using the toilet we may pass these germs on to others, our loved ones, and to the public in general. <u>Always wash your hands after using the toilet</u>.

Scarlet fever, septic sore throat, trench mouth, pneumonia, colds, and diphtheria are spread by discharges from the mouth and nose. Coughing without covering the mouth sprays your germs around on food, table tops, serving utensils, and directly onto other people. Picking your nose covers the fingers with germs which are later transferred to cups, saucers, foods, knives and forks.

How can you protect your health and our guests? Immobilize germs. Soap and water them to death. Isolate them and destroy them. Your hands are the instruments of protection. They can be instruments of disease. Their health, the guests' health, your own health is largely in your hands.

<u>Disease Is Always with Us</u>...

Surrounding us are all sorts of disease germs. Our problem is to prevent them from getting inside us and our guests. Luckily these germs have no legs or wings. They must be carried into the body on something. That something can be air in the case of a cold virus or tuberculosis germ; typhoid hitchhikes along in polluted water and foods, especially milk and shellfish. Amoebic dysentery can be carried by flies and is sometimes on the outside of raw vegetables. Scarlet fever and septic sore throat are caused by germs that are often in partially prepared ham, sausage, and baked custard. Trichinosis is a living worm found in pork that has not been well cooked. To be safe, cook pork until it is well done throughout.

Germs move around because we allow them to do so. They cannot walk, crawl, or fly -- only a few can swim. Without knowing it we are our own worst enemies and enemies of public health. By permitting flies, roaches, and rodents to live around our food we let them infest us and our customers. Did you know that rats and mice are responsible for one of the world's most devastating diseases, the Bubonic Plague. The fleas on rats carry the disease, bite people who then become infected. Back in the 15th century the Black Plague, as it was called, killed as many as half the people in some countries. Destroy the rats and we destroy the Plague.

Germs are like people. Some are helpful and kind. Others are sneak thieves robbing us of our vitality. Some are murderers. They are alive, they reproduce, give off wastes and, like us, must have the right temperatures and living conditions to thrive. We're bigger, but they outnumber us and can cut us down if we don't continually work at keeping them out of our bodies or destroying them with cleanliness and sanitary food practices.

Like people, different germs like different living conditions. Some like lots of air; some can do without it. Some cannot live in acids, others die in alkali. The ones that concern us like temperatures between 50° and 100° F. best. They like moisture and they do prefer their food neither alkaline nor acid, just neutral.

"Hold on! I can't carry a microscope around to look for germs." You are right. Just assume that they are around us, especially on hands; in us, especially in stomachs. Know also that other people have them and can pass them on to us if we are not on guard.

How can we tell when they are in us? Sometimes we can't. The obvious evidence is when we get sick. Food poisoning from the ever-present staphylococcus causes extreme stomach pains, nausea, and often diarrhea usually within 3 to 6 hours. Stomach upsets don't just happen.

Personal for Waitresses and Waiters...

Your wages are largely dependent upon the tips that come from good service. Good service includes your appearance and the manner in which you handle the food. Treat food with respect. Protect it and you protect the customer. The customer will appreciate it and you are giving more than food service. You are helping to safeguard his health.

Some "Do's" and "Don'ts" of Good Service:

1. Be alert in taking orders.
2. Do not stack glasses in carrying them.
3. Use ice scoop to handle ice.
4. Be sure refrigerated storage spaces are closed after using.
5. Do not fill cups too full.
6. Keep fingers away from rims of glasses and cups and out of food.
7. Replace a fallen piece of silver with a clean one.
8. Protect food -- keep it safe from exposure.
9. Do not touch eating surfaces of silver.
10. Invert cups for safe storage.
11. Pour milk at the table from original container or use an approved dispenser.
12. Never allow broken, cracked or chipped dishes or other utensils to be used.
13. Don't stack dishes of food.
14. Give prompt and courteous attention.

Personal for Kitchen Personnel...

For the bacteria that cause food poisoning, "Life begins at forty" and ends at 140 -- degrees Fahrenheit, that is. Room temperature is usually around 70 degrees. Foods that are going to be served hot need to be kept very hot -- above 130 degrees -- until they are eaten.

Foods that are going to be served cold must be cooled quickly to 40 degrees or below and kept refrigerated until time to serve them. Use shallow containers, not over four inches deep, so that the food will chill through quickly. Don't place food directly on refrigerator shelves.

Remember it is the temperature of the food that counts -- not the temperature of the refrigerator or the oven.

A good general rule to remember for serving food is: KEEP HOT FOODS VERY HOT AND COLD FOODS VERY COLD.

Many cooks believe that hot foods that are to be cooled should be cooled at room temperature before placing in a refrigerator. Nonsense! Place the food directly into the refrigerator so that the inside of the pan of food or a large piece of meat will not permit germs to grow while the food is cooling. Hot food placed directly in the refrigerator will not sour as is sometimes believed. The refrigerator cost is a little higher but it is worth money to be safe and sanitary.

THE SANITATION THERMOMETER

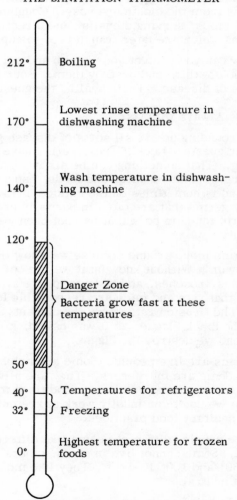

212°	Boiling
170°	Lowest rinse temperature in dishwashing machine
140°	Wash temperature in dishwashing machine
120°	
	Danger Zone Bacteria grow fast at these temperatures
50°	
40°	Temperatures for refrigerators
32°	Freezing
0°	Highest temperature for frozen foods

Keep It Hot or Keep It Cold To Prevent Bacteria from Growing.

Cover refrigerated foods to prevent them from absorbing odors.

Don't overload the refrigerator and clean it daily or as necessary.

Time...

If food ready to serve is kept longer than one hour at room temperature before it is eaten, food-poisoning bacteria may grow in it. Food prepared for large banquets is often fixed ahead of time and held until eaten. Don't give bacteria time, at room temperature, to poison food.

Some of our most popular foods are the most dangerous if left at room temperature for more than an hour. Watch out for these:

> Cream-filled or custard-filled pastries, cakes, or puddings
> Any dish made with cream sauce, cream toppings and fillings
> Bland sauces
> Poultry and fish
> Chicken and egg salads
> Dressing for poultry or meat
> Sandwiches and sandwich fillings
> Cooked salad dressings
> Casserole dishes and baked beans
> Dairy products
> Chopped meats
> Croquettes
> Hors d'oeuvres

Foods safe at toom temperature:

> Most canned goods (until they are opened)
> Raw fruits and vegetables
> Jellies and jams
> Breads, rolls, and crackers
> Candies and nuts
> Cookies and doughnuts
> Cakes with regular icing (not cream type)
> Fruit pies

Frozen food should be thawed in the refrigerator. Freezing breaks down tissues and because of it foods can be invaded by germs more readily. Foods once frozen and thawed should not be refrozen. If they cannot be eaten, storage under 40° F. is recommended.

Hash and similar preparations should be refrigerated immediately after mixing, then heated thoroughly before serving.

Croquettes, salmon cakes, corn fritters, hashes, and like preparations require complete cooking. If they are only burned on the outside, germs left alive in the warm centers will multiply rapidly.

Stir masses of food like spaghetti so cooking will be complete.

Cook pork thoroughly until it is no longer red or pink.

If cold ham is to be served, refrigerate it immediately after boiling or baking. Slice just before serving.

Don't cough, sneeze, or talk over food in preparation or while it is being served. It can be contaminated with unseen droplets of saliva.

Foods in storage and left standing in the kitchen need to be protected from contamination from flies, dust, coughs, and sneezes. Keep them covered.

Never put a tasting spoon back into the food.

Keep fingers away from mouth, lips, face, and soiled surfaces. The hands should always be washed before preparing food.

Store food off the floor.

An example of the type of quiz appropriate for such a course is one taken from the "Guide to Safe Food Service" published by the U. S. Government Printing Office.

QUIZ ONE

GERMS TAKE POTLUCK

Check either YES or NO to these questions: YES   NO

    Example: Do some germs make people sick?   ✓_____   _____

1. Do all germs cause sickness?   _____   _____

2. Are germs alive?   _____   _____

3. Can one germ produce other germs?   _____   _____

4. Do all disease germs get into the body through the nose?   _____   _____

5. Can disease germs live in food?   _____   _____

6. Has unsafe food made people sick?   _____   _____

7. If you have a sore on your finger, should you handle food?   _____   _____

8. Are there ways to fight disease germs?   _____   _____

9. Can you taste germs in a cream pie?   _____   _____

APPRENTICESHIP TRAINING

A few skilled jobs in the hotel restaurant require a relatively long and planned period of training. The jobs of chef and baker and those included in the building trades cover such a broad area that they cannot be learned in a short period. European hostelries and restaurants have traditionally trained their skilled employees by means of a long period of apprenticeship. With some outstanding exceptions few American hotels and restaurants have established systematic apprenticeships.

Rating Employee Performance

Management, alert to the growing demands for more effective personnel programs, has in some cases turned to merit rating as a method for insuring that promotions in classification and pay be placed on as fair a basis as possible. Proponents of formalized rating systems, variously called merit rating, personnel rating, and service rating, proclaim many advantages. They argue that by using "scientific" ratings management benefits by insuring a better selection of supervisors. Workers are better satisfied when they feel that their opportunities for advancement depend on an unbiased appraisal of their abilities. Employees, it is pointed out, are stimulated to higher standards when they know that they are subject to periodic rating. It is further believed that merit rating reduces grievances by promoting communication, especially when ratings are discussed between rater and ratee.

Employee rating is not without opponents. Some of the opponents have as evidence a history of unsatisfactory attempts to use personnel ratings. Some have found that merit rating has been a source of labor unrest and has increased grievances rather than diminished them. Several large industrial plants have tried and discarded well-known plans.

NOT A QUESTION OF WHETHER WE SHOULD USE THEM

The fact of the matter is that everyone who manages personnel uses a system of rating. Every military system and every business that has supervisors and workers uses ratings to determine wage payments and promotions. Two primary differences stand out in the various forms of rating: one, the degree of complexity of the rating device, and two, the degree of subjectivity on the part of the rater. The unanalyzed ratings made by the old-time boss is a rating to be sure, but is likely to be biased. An effective rating device can aid in making the judgement less biased and more reliable. Since we must appraise people, a method by which more objectivity is attained should be welcomed -- provided it is not too complicated or time-consuming.

ATTEMPTS TO MAKE RATINGS MORE RELIABLE

Several methods have been used in attempting to make ratings more precise. One method has been to rate the individual on a number of factors rather than on one over-all impression. Following this logic the number of factors that went into the rating was increased. Whereas formerly an employee may have been rated on efficiency, he may now be rated on knowledge of the job, accuracy, initiative, leadership, and personality. Some lists include as many as 28 factors.

Elaborate statistical techniques have been applied to ratings, but the application of these techniques does not improve the validity of the device. Certain factors have been weighted double the weight of others. Numbers have been assigned the factors and summed to give a supposedly accurate total appraisal. Depending on the job the ratee may be given 20 points for courtesy on the job, 20 points for neatness, 50 points for initiative, 50 for quality of work performed, and so on into any number of possible arrangements. Unfortunately these attempts have not proved too fruitful.

THE FUNDAMENTALS OF A GOOD RATING DEVICE

Basically all rating systems are alike. They provide a means of comparing one employee with another or a group of others doing a similar job. If the method aids the person doing the appraisal by making him more critical and his judgements more consistent and accurate, it is a good system. It should be simple enough to be explained to the employee -- and should not require an inordinate amount of time.

Since all rating devices are attempts to compare employees reliably, the manner in which they vary is in the way in which the employees are compared and the factors or criteria being compared.

ABSOLUTE RATING SCALES

In absolute rating scales the judge assigns an arbitrary value to the trait being rated. One judgement is made for each case involved. This may take the form of assigning a certain numerical score to a person for each trait rated. For example, if it is decided to assign a perfect score on neatness a weight of ten, the rater may judge a particular ratee as being worth a score of only seven. This type of device may be varied by placing the absolute judgement on a linear scale.

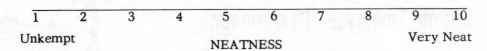

THE CHECK LIST TYPE

By the check list method the rater is given a list of traits and is asked to check those which apply to a particular employee. The check list might contain such descriptions as "always on time," "treats the customers courteously," "does not cooperate with other employees," "uses intoxicants on the job." The method has the advantage of pointing out to the employee his weak and strong points. It has the disadvantage of having to be translated into another system so that comparisons between employees can be made.

ORDER OF MERIT METHOD

This method consists of ranking the members of a group from high to low. Members are assigned positions such as 1, 2, 3, 4, and so on, according to the judgement of the rater. The objection to this is the difficulty of considering the whole group at once and yet keeping the individual in mind in a position relative to the others. It is fairly easy in a group of sixteen to pick the top two or three and the lowest two or three. Ranking the rest accurately is virtually impossible.

THE METHOD OF PAIRED COMPARISONS

By this technique each individual in a group is compared with every other individual. May is compared with Jan, with Margaret, and with Sally. The rater asks himself: "Which of these two girls is performing her job best?" Because there has been no easy way of combining the results of these comparisons, the method has the disadvantage of being cumbersome and time-consuming. It has value in that raters are not required to keep all of the ratees in mind at once. Each ratee is compared separately with every other ratee.

RECENT STATISTICAL DEVELOPMENTS

Recent investigations of rating scales which include a number of factors in the rating indicate that actually raters consider only two or three basic factors. For example, in one study it was learned that although the raters were asked to rate on twelve different factors, they were actually rating only two basic ones. In this study the two underlying factors which were common to all of the twelve were "the ability to do the present job" and "likelihood of being promoted."

INSTALLING A MERIT RATING SYSTEM

As with any new personnel program a merit rating system should be introduced only with the co-operation of those who will participate. In setting up such a plan, a "less busy" time of year should be picked and the department heads and other supervisors invited to sit in on the discussion as to what form of rating device is most suitable for the business. When the various devices have been debated and a device agreed upon, mimeographed copies of the form should be made and distributed for use.

The rating form used should be thought of as tentative, subject to change after experience with it indicates corrections. Meetings with supervisors should be held so that agreements can be reached concerning the terminology employed. It will be found that "a good employee" has many very different meanings, depending upon who is using the term. Questions as to how excellent is "excellent" and what constitutes "leadership" may arise should these terms be used in a rating form.

Employee meetings are also desirable if the rating is to accomplish the purpose of pointing out to employees areas in which they may need improving. Supervisors must understand the rating device

WAITRESS EVALUATION CHART

DATE _____

Name of Waitress _____

Name of Supervisor _____

To the Supervisor: Before asking the waitress what she can do to improve, ask yourself what you can do to help her improve.

Suggestions: Use this chart as a guide for a friendly discussion between you and your waitress. Your purpose is to set an atmosphere in which mutual problems can be approached and to change attitudes and behavior. Get the waitress to suggest changes. Let her do most of the talking.

	Needs Much Improvement	Needs Little Improvement	Is Excellent
Health and Appearance			
Is she pleasant looking: Nails, skin, teeth, clothes, posture?			
Would an improved diet help?			
Would more regularity in sleeping and other personal habits help?			
Is different make-up or clothes indicated?			
Are her vision and hearing adequate?			
Is there a possible need for glasses or a hearing aid?			
Job Attitudes			
Could she improve in her manner toward guests?			
(a) does she make guests feel important in a graceful manner? (How improve?)			
(b) does she seem to enjoy serving people? (Why or why not?)			
Could she improve her relations with her associates and superiors? (How?)			
(a) Does she feel she is 'better' than many of her associates or her supervisors? (Why?)			
Job Skills			
Does her diction or speaking voice need improvement?			
Could she improve her day-to-day knowledge of the menu?			
Does she know the most efficient ways of doing her work? (Which skills need improvement?)			
Does she know how to approach guests so that they feel they are in competent hands?			
Personal Adjustment			
Is she able to withstand the psychological pressures of the job?			
What personal problems stand in her way? (What can be done about them?)			
Is she fairly self-confident and self-sufficient? (What needs to be done to improve her confidence?)			

thoroughly in order to explain it to employees. Employees' questions may point out weaknesses in the device and needs for revision.

In hotel or restaurant operations in which the supervisors are obviously loathe to do "paper work" ratings of employees, it might be well to employ a simple "forced distribution" type of rating. The supervisor is asked to place each employee in the highest 10 per cent, the middle 65 per cent, or the lower 25 per cent. The form which might be used is shown below.

PERSONNEL RATING

Department _____ Date _____

Group I
(Highest 10 per cent)

List in this group the outstanding employees under your supervision, those who are best suited for promotion, most loyal and dependable, and those who contribute most to the efficiency of your department.

Name	Position	Name	Position

(4 lines)

Group II
(Middle 65 per cent)

List in this group the average efficient employees under your supervision, the ones who are not outstanding but can be relied upon to do their work well.

Name	Position	Name	Position

(15 lines)

Group III
(Lower 25 per cent)

List in this group the lower 25 per cent of your employees, the ones whom you feel could probably be replaced by others more efficient and responsible.

Name	Position	Name	Position

(7 lines)

USING THE CHECK LIST TYPE RATING DEVICE

The check list rating device is also a simple and easily understood device. The form below shows a check list rating device designed for use with kitchen personnel.

Different departments will require different qualities in their personnel. Check lists can be made up to fit the needs of any department. This should be done by consultation with the supervisors of the departments concerned.

PERSONNEL RATING

Department _____ Kitchen _____   Date _____

Employee _____

1. Reports for work on time.
2. Begins work promptly.
3. Turns out the required amount of work.
4. Turns out more than the required amount of work.
5. Does neat work.
6. Organizes his work well.
7. Calm and steady during rush periods.
8. Works well on his own responsibility.
9. Shows good judgement in routine application of kitchen rules.
10. Capable of assuming higher responsibilities.
11. Accepts responsibility for his own errors.
12. On lookout for short cuts and ways of bettering job.
13. Keeps self personally neat and clean.
14. Maintains cleanliness in work.
15. Courteous.
16. Self-reliant.
17. Use of intoxicants does not affect his work.
18. Does not waste materials.
19. Does not waste food.
20. Follows instructions carefully and accurately.
21. Does not allow his emotions to interfere with his work.
22. Cooperates effectively with others.
23. Keeps equipment in good working condition.
24. Capable of assuming higher responsibility during absence of superior.
25. Gives other employees recognition for good work.
26. Shows a great deal of patience.
27. Has a pleasing, friendly manner.
28. Learns new tasks quickly.
29. Takes the initiative in getting work done.
30. Is entirely honest.

Signed _____

The items included in the check list rating scale can be weighted so that certain items are given more consideration. Usually, however, it is simpler to add additional items of a similar type if the rater wishes to weight certain qualities. By giving one point for each item, the rating is simply the total of the items checked. By making all of the items statements of desirable behavior, the rater is given an opportunity to check as many as he believes appropriate rather than being required to subscribe to statements which are derogatory or unfavorable to the employees being rated.

HOW OFTEN TO RATE?

To be effective, and yet avoid being done mechanically, ratings probably should be made every six months. If ratings are made too far apart there is a danger that the rater may forget some incidents or may emphasize recent incidents too much.   Also, if the ratings are to be used as a means of pointing out deficiencies, they are more effective when administered more frequently.

Because of the time it takes to rate employees, some hotels have found it advisable to include only certain job classifications in their merit rating practice.   One hotel chain excludes all service jobs in which gratuities figure as a part of the wage and all minor positions such as the job of chambermaid. According to the general manager of the chain, persons holding jobs which are partially dependent upon gratuities in effect rate themselves by the size of their tip income.

This is no doubt partially true, but it should be pointed out that there are instances where tip employees receive large tips at the expense of the hotel in terms of guest attitude and the over-all good of the enterprise.   Such cases, of course, can be identified and usually corrected by proper supervision.

In minor jobs such as that of chambermaid, a hotel chain has instituted what amounts to an automatic merit increase based solely on experience on the job.   All maids receive a merit increase after 48 full working days on the job.   Such a system serves as an incentive to stay on the job, but it does not give extra reward to the more expert.

Since merit rating is almost invariably linked with wage payments in that "merit increases" are paid for more efficient performance, it is necessary to have a method of ready check for payroll control. This has been accomplished simply and effectively by setting standards for each grade of merit rating. In some departments it may be advisable to permit 90 per cent of the department to receive the highest pay for their classification; in others 80 per cent.   If a department head exceeds the determined standard, the excess is readily noted.

WHO SHALL DO THE RATING?

In determining who should do the rating of a particular employee, it can be agreed that the employee's immediate supervisor should be one of those individuals.   Usually the supervisor and two or three other management representatives comprise a wage or merit rating committee.   Some industrial organizations have found it advantageous to include a union representative or some other employee representative.   The wage committee as set up in one hotel organization is composed of the department head, the hotel manager, the comptroller, and the personnel manager.   All merit-rated positions that have not reached the maximum are reviewed at least twice a year.   Ten days before the meeting of the wage committee the department heads make recommendations to it.   Within that ten days' time the personnel manager prepares a report on the employee from the standpoint of punctuality, conduct, etc.   On his daily inspections of the hotel the manager makes it a point to observe the working of the employee, and the comptroller observes the extent of the payroll and whether or not the department head has a tendency to be too generous or not sufficiently generous.   The employee does not know the meeting is going to take place and that he is under observation.   On the day of the meeting the department head tells his story, there is a general discussion, the department head refrains from voting, and the three other members of the committee determine if there shall be an increase, and if so, how much.

TRAINING RATERS

As important or more important than any of the aspects of a rating program are the raters themselves.   The objectivity and hence the value of a rating program can be no better than the supervisors doing the rating.   To make a rating program effective, supervisors must be convinced of the worth of the program and understand its purposes and mechanics.

The best way to promote supervisor understanding of the present rating system is to "take them in on the act." In other words, get them to help devise the system and to change it as necessary. Frequent conferences will be necessary to keep the supervisors' support of the program. Discussion of the possible errors of rating is a painless way of instructing the supervisors in good rating.

Three errors are common:

The Halo Effect

Many of us have a tendency to judge the other man by a few of his most noticeable characteristics. A chef with a pleasing personality is more likely to be judged a competent cook than one who is obnoxious in his relation to others.   If one of our pet peeves is tardiness, an employee who is late is likely to be judged by us as something less than his true ability.   The noticeable trait colors and biases the entire judgement. We are all prone to label a man good or bad, failing to differentiate his many traits and evaluate them separately. The halo effect is a weakness most of us have in judging a person on the basis of one or two traits. It is as though the one or two traits were a halo obscuring our critical ability. The halo may be either favorable or unfavorable.

A way to avoid the halo effect is to consider each trait separately. Rate every person in one trait, then go through his list again marking each on the next trait.

The Leniency Error

Another common tendency is to want to be a good fellow and rate everyone higher than he deserves. This practice is especially prevalent in rating supervisors and department heads. Of course, this does an injustice to the superior person. By placing the best men in the same category as the mediocre, the superior person is not given the recognition rightfully his.

The Error of Central Tendency

Another failure in rating appears where the rater tends to think of everybody as being average and so rates them. He goes down the list of persons checking everyone as average or close to it. This may be a defense on the part of the rater who fails to admit that there are people in his division who are superior or who are inferior. In discussing rating it can be pointed out that in any group there usually are individuals who excel the poorest in the group in several traits by a ratio of two to one or more.

A way to reduce these errors is to analyze the ratings made by each rater. Omitting names of the rater involved, all raters can be asked to discuss the ratings made. Criticisms made by the group are likely to be accepted and to be more effective than those made by top management.

SUMMARY OF RATING EMPLOYEE'S SERVICES

A fair rating of the employee's services is essential to the success of the enterprise. If employees who display ability and proficiency are not rewarded with increases in wages or promoted to positions where their services may be best used, the business suffers. Any means which will aid the supervisor or manager in making an accurate appraisal of the employee's work is to be welcomed. If there is a device available which will help the supervisors see the employee more objectively, it should be used. Often the device itself is not as important in evaluating employees as the training which results from instruction given in the use of the device. Pooled ratings help eliminate supervisors' biases.

TECHNIQUES FOR EVALUATING THE ACCURACY OF RATINGS

Often raters agree as to the general pattern of the ratings they assign a specific ratee, but one rater may be consistently higher or lower than the other rater. This is what is known as a systematic error of the rater. By measuring the systematic error, it is possible: (1) to adjust the rating of a discrepant rater to coincide with other raters; or (2) to inform a rater that he is out of step with other raters. Another way of showing raters their deficiencies is to calculate their total errors. This technique shows how close an individual rater comes to the average.

The techniques described are not complicated, but they must be applied to an individual trait rather than to a total rating. The following steps are necessary to implement these techniques:

1. Discover the mean or average rating on that characteristic for all of the raters (designated as M).

2. Note the individual rater's ratings on the trait (designated as R).

3. The total for each rater on the trait is the following:

$$T.E. = \frac{Sum |R - M|}{N}$$

where differences (R - M) are added without sign, and N is the number of persons rated.

4. To find the systematic error on each trait:

$$S.E. = \frac{Sum(R - M)}{N}$$

where the differences are added algebraically, and N is again the number of persons rated.

Example 1 illustrates the method of measuring total and systematic errors of ratings. The total error is most suited for determining the most dependable rater.

Example 1

TOTAL AND SYSTEMATIC ERRORS OF THREE RATERS*

Data: Ratings (assumed for illustration) accorded
ten ratees on a single trait by three raters.

Ratings						Errors		
Ratees	Rater A	Rater B	Rater C	Total	Mean M_r	Rater A	Rater B	Rater C
A	7	7	4	18	6	1	1	-2
B	-6	5	7	18	6	0	-1	1
C	8	7	6	21	7	1	0	-1
D	8	8	5	21	7	1	1	-2
E	9	8	10	27	9	0	-1	1
F	4	5	3	12	4	0	1	-1
G	6	6	3	15	5	1	1	-2
H	3	4	2	9	3	0	1	-1
I	9	9	6	24	8	1	1	-2
J	5	4	3	12	4	1	0	-1

*Yoder, D., Personnel Management and Industrial Relations. New York: Prentice-Hall, 1948.

Total Errors: $\text{T.E.} = \dfrac{\Sigma |R - M_r|}{N}$

Rater A: T.E. = 6/10 = 0.60
Rater B: T.E. = 8/10 = 0.80
Rater C: T.E. = 14/10 = 1.40

Systematic Errors: $\text{S.E.} = \dfrac{\Sigma (R - M_r)}{N}$

Rater A: S.E. = 6/10 = .60
Rater B: S.E. = 4/10 = .40
Rater C: S.E. = -10/10 = -1.00

In Example 1 it can be seen that rater C is the least dependable rater -- he consistently rates higher than raters A and B. Two approaches can be used to rectify the situation: (1) All of his ratings can be lowered one scale score (as shown by his systematic error), and (2) he should be trained to correct his rater bias in future ratings.

Developing Supervisors and Junior Management

The supervisor and junior executive of the hotel and restaurant are in many ways the keys to the success or failure of the business. No matter how sound the management's plans and policies, they cannot be effective except as instrumented by the junior executive and supervisor. A chef unskilled in human relations can destroy a food business. An inept night manager of a hotel can disrupt morale and lose the hotel many guests.

In the eyes of the employee the supervisor and junior executive are management. The face-to-face relations between first-line supervision and the employees are the only realistic gauge the employees have of management. First-line supervision is the bedrock of morale. What kind of personnel should management select for supervision? What can management do to improve the standards of supervision?

We might begin by commenting on the job of supervision itself.

THE MULTIPLE JOB OF SUPERVISION

In the hotel and restaurant field the supervisor has a bigger job than in most other businesses. His job has not been functionalized as it has been in the steel industry for example, where the foreman has a few specific tasks to perform and is aided by time study men, control men, and planning and engineering departments. In the hotel and restaurant field the supervisor holds a multiple job. The executive chef of a medium-sized restaurant, for example, is responsible for the operation of the kitchen. In addition, he often does his own personnel work: hires, promotes, demotes, fires employees; arranges for vacations, rest periods, and lunch periods. As a department head much of his time is spent in conference with other junior executives and with the manager. He is his own engineering officer. If the dishwashing machine breaks down he is supposed to know something about fixing it. If there is any work simplification done, he directs it. His list of duties may be extended. He is a jack-of-all-trades and master of few.

The housekeeper of a large hotel is another example. She is responsible for accounting and purchasing of supplies, of decoration of rooms, and of upkeep and maintenance of equipment. These last duties are in addition to training new maids, scheduling their work, making daily reports and, to add a facetious note, applying first aid and comfort to the maid with a cut finger and acting as a counselor to the maid who is contemplating marriage. Training for such broad jobs cannot be done successfully in a haphazard fashion.

An illustration of but one duty of the supervisor may show something of the need for training supervisors. The illustration comes from a study made by Sanford E. Maus, hotel and restaurant consultant.[1]

> The chef in a medium-sized hotel had had frequent trouble with his fry station. He fought the problem by hiring man after man, but the station was always a source of complaints. Finally, in desperation, he manned it with two employees, but the problem remained unsolved and the cost of the station was doubled.
>
> Returning to calmer reflection, he decided that if he could not find the solution he would have to create one. So picking a likely candidate without training, he proceeded to concentrate on developing a fry cook from scratch. It took two months of concentrated effort, but it solved the problem.
>
> Once groomed, the trainee filled the station, provided satisfactory service and eliminated $1,500 of annual payroll. If your food department operation returns

---

[1] By permission, _Southern Hotel Journal_.

a departmental profit of 15 per cent of sales, the saving indicated would produce the same result as an improvement of $10,000 in sales volume.

THE SUPERVISOR A MIDDLE MAN

The supervisor in many ways is a man caught in the middle. While representing management, he also represents the employees. When top management neglects to inform the supervisor of plans and policies and fails to support him in his relations with employees, the supervisor is indeed caught in the middle. To increase his confusion the supervisor in the hotel or restaurant often has a third party to please -- the guest.

The supervisor is expected to be not only a leader but a follower. At the same time that he plans and coordinates activities, he looks to management to determine policies and originate orders. In addition, in his relations with other supervisors he is expected to act as if he were on their level of authority and responsibility. The supervisor plays a variety of roles. His position is not always clear. The supervisor is in a hazardous position from the point of view of personal stability.

THE SUPERVISOR A DEALER IN HUMAN RELATIONS

The most important aspect of the job of supervisor is that of human relations. The supervisor must be friendly and still maintain discipline. He must understand the individual and yet treat him as a member of a group. He must be able to praise people without flattery. His orders must be clear and forceful yet avoid the implication of command. He is expected to be a leader yet consider the wishes and suggestions of the employees. He appeals to ambition but avoids promises he is not certain of being able to carry out. He encourages competition but tries to build team spirit. He is expected to be firm and consistent yet flexible. He is supposed to be interested in detail, yet full of enthusiasm and ready to think in broad terms. The supervisor, in other words, is expected to be one step lower than the angels.

What are some of the traits which the supervisor should have or can learn in order to be successful? It must be admitted that some of these traits are largely the result of personality development over the course of years but most of them can be developed, at least to a degree.

1. The Ability and Attitude To Plan

Planning is the thinking that precedes the actual performance of work. It permits the avoidance of mistakes in practice by running over them in thought. It establishes goals towards which efforts can be directed.

Planning ability is not the same as intelligence. A genius according to the results of an intelligence test may be a poor planner. Planning is partially an attitude which can be acquired. It is a habit which can be encouraged in anyone.

Sound supervisory planning proceeds by definite steps. It requires the consultation and suggestions of everyone who will be affected by the plan. Sound planning welcomes modification.

An office manager sees the necessity for revising working hours. He discusses this necessity with the office employees. He discusses it with top management. He reports back to the employees and a decision is reached which is acceptable to everyone, or at least much more acceptable than if the decision were entirely his own.

Decisions which affect a major change should always be based on planning by consultation. On the other hand, day-to-day decisions which implement plans already agreed upon are properly the supervisor's. To consult in such cases is a waste of time and destroys the supervisor's rule as leader.

2. The Ability To Set an Atmosphere of Approval

An atmosphere of approval is a social climate in which there is a minimum of resentment and insecurity and a maximum of personal satisfaction. The supervisor has so arranged the human relations that each employee feels that despite his mistakes and weaknesses, the supervisor believes in him and his value to the enterprise. The housekeeper makes the maids feel as though she is a friend and always behind them. The hostess gets across the idea she is on the side of the waitresses. The service superintendent has so acted that the service clerk really believes that his services are respected and appreciated and that the superintendent believes in him as a man.

This means that the supervisor is friendly -- but not familiar. It means that the supervisor goes out of his way to do favors for the employee -- but he does not make a practice of drinking beer with him.

It means that the supervisor calls the employee by name frequently, but he does not approve of the employee's calling him by his first name. The supervisor visits the sick employee; he is interested in his experience on vacation; he is interested in his new car; he is not a "pal" in the sense of familiarity.

Some of the acts and attitudes which make for an atmosphere of approval are:

a. Recognition of each employee as an individual. Respect for his opinion. Recognition of each employee's contribution and frequent expression of that appreciation. This does not mean unwarranted flattery. It does mean an attitude of looking for and speaking about acts or traits which warrant praise.

b. Consistent, predictable behavior on the supervisor's part. The supervisor works at maintaining a stable manner of acting in supervisory relations. Employees know what to expect. They feel secure in their relationship with the supervisor.

c. Maintenance of a stable, well-defined work environment. All changes of any importance are introduced gradually and with the approval, or at least acceptance, of the employees. Wages and promotion are clearly defined. Each employee knows what he has to do to win wage increases or a promotion. Orders are planned. They are stated in a definite form. The person receiving the order is given the reason for it. The person receiving the order is encouraged. The order is followed up. Similarly other relations are planned and introduced with a minimum of confusion and anxiety.

3. The Desire and Ability for Leadership

In our culture it is tantamount to being un-American to deny a desire for leadership. Yet a minority of people have any real desire to take on responsibility, to plan, to take the blame for others' failures, to assume the guilt feelings which result from discharging or reprimanding an employee. Many other persons who have the desire for leadership do not have the ability, and no amount of education or training will equip them for leadership.

The requirements of leadership vary with different jobs. A chef need not have the same kind of leadership demanded of the hotel manager. The hostess requires a different kind of leadership ability than the sales manager. Some leadership jobs emphasize planning ability, others face-to-face relations with people. The job of hostess requires the ability to work under social pressures; in the job of sales manager this factor is not as crucial as imagination and perhaps congeniality.

Assuming the supervisor has the desire and native capacity for leadership, what traits and skills should he develop to enhance his leadership?

We have been discussing planning ability and the factor of setting an atmosphere of approval. These are requisites of leadership but were considered separately because of their separate importance. Later chapters will discuss means of creating personal satisfaction and attaining cooperation which are also factors in leadership.

a. Initiative and ideas. Leaders are distinguished by their self-starting, their desire to get things done, their willingness to take on responsibility. They have ideas which, though often mistaken, stimulate others to thinking. Leaders develop initiative in others by delegating responsibility. They encourage others to take on responsibility. They have enthusiasm.

b. Decisiveness and firmness. Once a program of action has been decided upon by the group, the leader is decisive and firm in carrying it out. This applies to work standards and discipline in general. Personnel do not want lax discipline. They admire and follow decisiveness and firmness.

c. The problem-solving attitude. The leader sees employees and events as problems to be solved. An employee who is recurrently late is a problem to be solved, not an object of scorn or of retribution. A broken-down refrigerator is something to be fixed and to be prevented from breaking down in the future. The leader does not cry over spoilt milk. He is oriented to the future.

d. The multiple-track mind. The supervisor to some extent and the executive in a large degree need to develop a multiple-track mind. Any job of importance requires that several projects be developed simultaneously. The executive must be able to switch from one thought and one project to another painlessly and efficiently, keeping all in their proper perspective.

MANAGEMENT AND COMPROMISE

Good management does not necessarily mean that the manager has the ideas -- then sells them to his staff -- lock, stock and barrel. Compromise and modification usually are needed. Often the best results are obtained when the manager's idea is amended in the light of the employee's reactions to it. The Hollywood version of the executive spending his nights dreaming up wonderful new sales and production plans at night, putting them into effect the next day happens when the executive is brilliant and forceful, but is not typical. The introduction of new ideas must always consider the already existing habits and beliefs and build on them.

Aside from the usual resistance to all major changes in behavior, new ideas and behavior must be fitted into what is already established. The manager's idea of where the new electric range should be placed will be only as good as the chef's acceptance of the idea. Probably the best location will be a joint decision growing out of consultation with the chef by the manager.

A good manager knows when to compromise, and recognizes the optimum degree of compromise. As a case in point, in a British hotel both the housekeeper and the hostess were unusually competent persons. As is often the case, some professional jealousy existed. The housekeeper, an old employee, resented the recognition of any newcomer in the organization, and, as usual, an "incident" occurred as a result.

The housekeeper's daily duties included placing the flowers in the lobby. Her aptitude for flower arranging consisted of stacking them pell-mell in the receptacle -- nothing more. The hostess, it happened, was an artist with flowers, and on seeing the disarranged flowers in the lobby, arranged them into a delightful floral ensemble, then left. Soon the housekeeper returned, and humanlike, restacked the flowers as before. Later, the hostess returned, also became perturbed, and trouble brewed.

The manager decided that one of the dissidents would have to go; however, both were competent, valuable employees. The manager talked the problem over with his assistant and secured the suggestion that the two ladies should be called in and counseled to see if they could not be brought into friendship.

The next day the assistant housekeeper was taken ill and could not report for work. The manager approached the hostess asking if she would be willing to help the housekeeper out of a jam. He spoke to the housekeeper intimating that the hostess desired to learn something about housekeeping. Could the housekeeper help? Indeed she could. The manager modified his original decision. The women became good friends and the organization was strengthened.

RELEASING HUMAN ENERGIES

Human beings have within themselves wellsprings of energy which if tapped and directed will accomplish individual growth and the satisfaction of human needs. If misdirected the energies destroy not only the person but seriously interfere with the growth of people around him.

Improving the person means releasing energies, developing enthusiasms, directing these energies to useful purposes. In other words to improve the person we increase efficiency, we promote desirable goals, and we stimulate enthusiasm. How?

First recognize that to increase personal efficiency and build enthusiasm we appeal to the person.

And what is the person? A bundle of energies, guided by instinct and learned social needs. Each person is somewhat different -- but enough like others of a similar background to be fairly predictable. To reach the person we must have some idea as to what makes him tick, what he wants today, tomorrow, and next year.

These things we know about all people, whether they be Eskimo or South Floridians: everyone needs some tension, some relaxation, frustration of a kind that is challenging but not disorganizing, to give and get love and affection, and to experience the creature comforts and satisfy at least partially the other creature urges.

Everyone, be he president of General Motors or a Georgia cracker, needs a fairly predictable environment. Everyone needs relative security: the sense that one's major needs will be satisfied.

In this country most of us have come to place high value on these ten goals -- each person ranking them according to his own experience and physical make-up:

1. Economic security consistent with the level of anxiety over prestige, status, and protection from want. (Related to class position in the culture, deprivations experienced, resistance to frustrations, level of aspiration.)

2. To know what is expected from the superior; to be able to predict within reasonable limits the behavior of the superior.

3. Rewards: To know what in the form of salary increases, promotions, commendations, etc. will be forthcoming provided we exert our best efforts. To know that punishments in all forms (loss of prestige, loss of approval, etc.) will be forthcoming if we "fail."

4. To know that associates are predictable.

5. A personal philosophy compatible with the social environment.

6. To "belong" and be accepted in our social group.

    a. Participate in decision-making and the growth of organization.

7. To belong to a family (for some this may have more liabilities than assets in stability).

8. To be "successful" in the eyes of those who count (the superiors, one's neighbors, one's associates, the community), to achieve in our own eyes.

9. To carry a favorable picture of one's self (self-esteem, self-respect).

    a. Maintain personal integrity, individuality, value as a person.

    b. To maintain consistent personal integrity in one's attitudes, beliefs, values.

    c. To at least "feel" that we are partially independent agents, that we have some share in making decisions that affect our own welfare.

    d. To experience the feeling of accomplishment.

10. To be able to express consciously our loves and hates (aggressions). To make a "reasonable" adjustment to the reality of one's culture.

To improve the person, capitalize on his constructive energies. Tie in the goals of the program with personal needs. Work can be seen as drudgery or as highly exhilarating activity. The way a person sees his work will determine his performance to a large degree. When a program is seen as a means of

1. Creating economic security
2. Gaining prestige and admiration
3. Gaining and giving love and affection
4. Performing work that is esteemed
5. Participating in sports and recreation
6. Acquiring knowledge
7. Aesthetic and spiritual development

the wellsprings of creative energy will be released.

All well and good. But how about specific do's and don'ts? Here are a few.

1. Define goals as a group. When a new kitchen range is needed get everyone in the kitchen in on the problem -- even though you already know the best buy.

If there's a bottleneck on the serving counter -- pose it as a group problem at your next meeting. We must feel close to our work team. We need to feel as though our thoughts on a common problem are important.

When there's a special dinner to be served -- ask all of the personnel involved to decide who should work, how much each can do, what to charge. Almost invariably goals set by the group are higher than those set by the supervisors. Group standards carry a lot more weight than supervisor standards.

Share decision-making with your immediate subordinates. Encourage them to do likewise with their subordinates.

2. Hold out the carrot, but be frank about wages. Let employees arrive at the idea that their work in a large degree is like that of a minister or a nurse, that their job affects the physical development and well-being of a nation.

3. Give every person a "responsible part." Delegate responsibility -- even if it's only responsibility for measuring and controlling the temperature in the rinse compartment of the dish machine.

To develop responsibility -- delegate. Expect mistakes at first. Ask people to do things. Praise results in public -- discuss discrepancies in private.

ANTICIPATE CRISES

4. You can help create a "stable" working environment by expecting crises. In the food business crises are a part of the job. Expect them, anticipate them and your adrenal glands will not be over-worked.

5. Talk progress. Point out progress. Goals that have been reached do not motivate people. It's progress toward a goal that sparks an operation.

6. Keep the goals within the range of achievement. Impossible or long-time goals don't have much pulling power for most of us. We buy houses, get married, and have babies in the absence of "long-time planning." To talk of what we should aim for next year has much less potency than what "we're gonna do tomorrow."

7. As a group, set up definite goals for each week: "to lower this week's food cost," "to paint the kitchen walls," "to overhaul the ice machine," "the target for next week is..."

8. Propagate the idea that "this operation is going to be the best in the state," "a good program with good people in it."

9. But don't be disappointed when everything is not the best. Perfectionism has no place in most supervision. Getting everything exactly right -- may be exactly wrong.

10. Improving the person improves the program. The best way to improve the person is to improve the program.

SUPERVISING WOMEN

More than half of the employees in most service occupations are women. Supervising women is much the same as supervising men but some differences stand out. Here are a few differences and some tips in working with women:

1. Women excel over men generally in hand and finger dexterity. They are ideal for such service jobs as typing, mailing, salad making, vegetable preparation, sandwich making and the like.

2. Women usually have more patience and adjust better to routine work than do men. They usually pay more attention to detail than do men.

3. Women are much more sensitive to criticism than men. In the business world women are at a disadvantage and develop defensive reactions. They take things more personally and never want to be taken for granted. Never criticise without also giving encouragement.

4. Women expect more praise -- and need it.

5. Women are more sensitive to the boss' moods. Because they are much interested in people, the moods of people around them affect them more. An upset boss almost always means an upset secretary or other women employees.

6. Women like to work together in groups and will usually produce when part of a group. They love to talk and need the opportunity to do so.

7. Be firm with women employees. Be friendly but never suggestive. Any implication of sexual interest destroys the business relationship. The rest of the girls will hate you both for it.

8. In dealing with an upset woman, give her a chance to recover her self-control; be considerate and listen to her problem, but do not give in to tears.

9. Women almost invariably prefer working for men. Help the woman supervisor and stand behind her.

10. Expect the "new girl" to have to wait some time before being accepted by the group. Women are rivals in many respects and take longer to accept each other.

TYPES OF SUPERVISORY TRAINING

Training by the Absorption or Understudy Method

The vast majority of hotel and restaurant supervisors in the past have been trained by the absorption method. The training is unsystematic and consists of the employee's picking up what information he happens upon in the course of his own work. Constructive thinking and planned presentation of the best information available is seldom encouraged.

Management Trainee Programs

Some companies and associations sponsor intern or apprentice executive training programs which appear to be successful. Careful selection of trainees plus a well-rounded systematic program of training obviates much of the failure of training by the understudy or absorption method. Periodic checks on what the apprentices have learned aids in making the program successful. Planned rotation of apprentices among the various hotel and restaurant departments gives the future executive the necessary over-all view of the organization plus a knowledge of the problems encountered in the various jobs. By planning, the program eliminates the long periods when little is learned which characterizes the absorption methods. Several hotel companies have set up trainee programs that have failed. Following are the reasons for failure:

1. The period of training is too long. Trainees are assigned manual tasks such as dishwashing, baking, and cooking for months at a stretch -- much longer than required to learn the rudiments of the job. It is not necessary for the trainee to become an expert.

2. Low pay. Trainees on some programs are paid less than the "going salary," kept on the lower rate for long periods of time. Naturally they compare their own progress with that of their peers and discover that they are underpaid.

3. Lack of authority. Trainees are often given much responsibility, little real authority, grow discouraged when objectives are not reached.

4. Lack of definite, scheduled steps upward. Trainees are given no regular salary or title, increases are unscheduled and status is ambiguous.

The most successful trainee programs are conducted on flexible time schedules for the learning of management; trainees are placed in positions of responsibility just as soon as they can handle them. Some companies will move a trainee out of the trainee status within a few weeks into supervisory or assistant manager slots.

Where there is a successful trainee program, there usually is someone near top management vitally interested in the trainees who tends to protect them and show them that the company is concerned about their progress.

Probably the most systematic management training program in the public hospitality field is that conducted by Hot Shoppes. Trainees are placed on regular jobs, but one day each week are brought into the central offices for formal discussion and classroom lectures. Something like one-half of the trainees who start the program drop out, or are asked to leave, before the training period is completed.

The John P. Thompson Company also has a systematic management training program. Graduates of hotel schools are rotated around the jobs of a cafeteria or restaurant for a period of six months before being assigned as assistant managers.

TRAINING TECHNIQUES FOR SUPERVISORS

Lectures

These allow facts to be presented in a fast, orderly manner. Because of the limited audience participation, lectures are least valuable in changing attitudes or in developing skills.

Guided Conferences

This type of conference is one in which the leader knows in advance what he wants to bring out. It lacks effectiveness because it is not directed toward the needs of the participant.

Sensitivity Training

The emphasis of such training is on helping supervisors and management trainees gain greater insight into themselves and into the reactions of others to them. This training takes place in a group. Instead of talking about what takes place outside of the group the discussion centers on what happens within the group itself. Sensitivity training helps each person understand how he actually behaves and reacts to others.

The rationale for sensitivity training is essentially the following:

1. The greatest role of the supervisor is to take <u>responsibility</u>. There is no way to teach responsibility; a person must <u>assume</u> it. What better way is there to provide a training ground for the taking of responsibility than to put people into an unstructured group where they must assume responsibility but no one tells them how!

2. People do not change from setting to setting. Basically a man's personality does not change at work or at home. Personality patterns become so ingrained it is extremely difficult to change them. People are not basically seeking to change personality patterns and as such do not respond to isolated pressures. Group pressure, on the other hand, has proven to be an effective way of modifying behavior. If through a sensitivity group a person can modify his interactions and defenses in a group, it logically follows that he will modify his behavior outside of the group, i.e., in his work role and interactions.

Research indicates that sensitivity groups are the most effective training situations available to management development. There is also a major problem: In such groups, there is no fixed agenda, no set lecture, no fixed direction; the "dynamics" of the group provides the impetus. In such groups, the discussion often gets personal and tension frequently develops. Group members frequently are uncomfortable and keep searching for someone to lead them. Because of the threat involved, sensitivity groups are best conducted by leaders of unusual skill and sophistication.

Problem-Solving Conferences

Such conferences treat specific work problems suggested by the group. The material simply is one or two incidents in a supervisor's life. The leader has no particular content objective. He seeks: (1) to help the group arrive at a practical solution to the problem presented; and (2) to help "generalize" or develop principles from the group's efforts which will aid each person in applying his solutions to future problems. If the group leader can help the group "generalize" the learning, the problem-solving conference is by far one of the most effective techniques available.

The Case Method

This technique has been popularized by the Harvard Business School. It is similar to the problem-solving conference except the case is presented by the leader rather than being suggested by the group. Needless to say, the leader of the group must possess a great deal of skill. A good leader imparts the following:

1. He seeks to have the trainees increase their observation, to ask better questions, and to look for broad ranges of problems (not "who is to blame?" but "why did it happen?").

2. He encourages the group to look for more and more implications to each solution and to avoid oversimplification of solutions.

3. He helps the student discard vague principles such as "be tactful" and urges him not only to evaluate "what" to do but "how" to do it.

4. He allows trainees to test their solutions in real situations.

Incident Process

This is a special adaptation of the Case Method in which a short incident involving the interaction of a supervisor and a worker is read to a group. Each trainee is required to ask questions of the leader in order to get all of the facts, to decide for himself what the basic problem might be, and then to exchange ideas with others in the group.

Role-Playing

In this technique, trainees are actively brought into involvement by being forced into dramatic skits involving human relations problems in which they must improvise as they go along. After the skit, the group discusses and analyzes the involvement.

A CASE STUDY

As a way of considering the complexity of management decisions relative to employees in the hotel and restaurant industry, consider the case of George Arnold.

George is the 53-year-old manager of a coffee house in the XYZ chain of coffee houses. He started working with XYZ as a kitchen helper, right out of high school 35 years ago. Over a ten-year period he worked his way up to assistant manager and then twenty years ago was made manager. The old timers in the organization recognize that George's strength always had been in his "back," his ability to work hard, his reliability. He never was creative or original; he never showed much ability to anticipate or to plan ahead; he was never too sensitive to the needs of his employees. At age 53, George is still reliable, but his energy seems to have given out. Now he seems only to go through the motions.

For the past year, Bill Baker, the assistant manager, has taken over much of George's responsibility. When difficult problems arise, the employees come to Bill. It is Bill who anticipates the need for supplies and who is concerned with personnel placement and efficiency. He is the person who prevents and resolves crises. It is common knowledge among employees that without Bill the coffee house would be in trouble.

George's name came up at a recent meeting of the top management of XYZ. One idea discussed was that George should be made to accept an early retirement, but it was felt that the financial and psychological loss would be too severe for him. Consideration was given to demoting him, but there really were no jobs available for him. Also, it was felt that such a move would affect the seniority policy of the organization and demoralize other employees. Finally, management decided to leave George in his present position. Bill's problem was discussed, but it was decided to postpone action until he expressed dissatisfaction with his situation.

The management group on the surface "solved" a problem. But did they really? Actually they brushed over two fundamental problems:

1. How much importance should management place on efficiency as against human satisfaction, and where does one draw the line?

2. Assuming that management can resolve the first problem, what are the best ways of achieving maximum efficiency and maximum human satisfaction?

In Arnold's case a number of problems were not faced. Was the company being fair to itself? to Bill Baker? to the other employees? to its long-range goals? What does a company owe its employees? Are the retirement benefits in line?

It is obvious from the case of George Arnold that "simple" management problems may be tied in with "not so simple" problems that relate to promotion policies, fringe benefits, job evaluation, recruitment philosophies, organizational structure, individual needs and motivations, and employee attitudes.

SHORT-TERM VERSUS LONG-TERM SOLUTIONS

The case of George Arnold exemplifies a common enough problem in the hotel-restaurant industry. After the initial decision had been made to leave George in his position, the managers were in fact quite satisfied with their solution to the problem. "After all," they argued, "the hotel-restaurant industry is a hard-headed, practical industry. Maybe we don't always make the best decisions, but we need to solve problems fast. Customers don't care if we have problems -- they want to be served right now." In other words, these management people were quick to admit their faults and their lack of long-range planning, but were equally fast in rationalizing their actions.

The dilemma of the hotel-restaurant executive rests in the fact that he is in an industry where short-range actions and decisions are vital. Many organizations are successful simply by the sheer force of their short-range efforts. High sales volume can hide a multitude of management sins. If an organization is blessed with a good location, if it has a good name, if it does not run into stiff competition, if its management works hard, and if it does not get too large, many organizations are successful regardless of the management philosophy inherent in their operations.

The efficient hotel-restaurant manager seeks constantly to resolve the many, diverse, conflicting problems posed to him by individuals and groups -- problems which have long-run as well as short-run aspects. The manner in which George Arnold was handled is an inefficient way of managing. To fulfill his expected role, a manager must rely on intuition, judgement, probability, experience, and knowledge. His knowledge must encompass not only the technical aspects of the work which lead to greater efficiency but also the human relations aspects of the work.

COUNSELING EMPLOYEES: THE ART OF LISTENING

Effective communication goes both ways. Giving instructions is downward communication. Listening is upward communication. Upward and downward communication go hand in hand and both are more effective if done by the same person.

Good listening is an art which properly applied becomes a general attitude. Day in and day out, the supervisor or manager who is willing to listen to the other fellow's point of view and who tries to take it into account before he takes action himself will find his role easier. The problems of making work changes and of handling supervisory problems will not be so traumatic. If in addition he has worked hard to earn the confidence of his subordinates by consistently showing them that he values their feelings and ideas, his role is more effective. If communications are blocked, situations such as the following can develop:

> The most frequent complaint was that although orders and instructions about work traveled easily enough, it was difficult to take up ordinary feelings, especially if they were critical about the job or about life in the factory. The main stumbling block in getting such feelings resolved was the reticence about communicating them upwards. The reticence was said to be due to the fact that if a person tried to express to his superior his feelings about the job, or about the superior himself, it was all too likely that the superior would argue with him and try to show him that his feelings were unreasonable and that they did not tally with the facts. Having the existence of one's feelings denied in this way only made things worse. The resentment against his superior arose for not understanding the employee and not helping him to get at what was disturbing him.[2]

A supervisor who is well accepted and is seen as a good counselor must be cautious to avoid getting involved in the personal lives of his subordinates. He should restrict himself to listening, avoid giving advice. Even when advice-giving is successful, he runs the risk of forming a dependency relationship with the subordinate. Above all, a supervisor should never play amateur psychologist with someone with a deep-seated personality problem. Besides taking up too much time, he may prevent the person from getting professional help.

THE TEACHING OF COUNSELING-LISTENING

The technique recommended is called "nondirective" because it puts the responsibility on the interviewee instead of the interviewer. It has three functions:

1. It allows the interviewer to understand what the interviewee really thinks and feels. It is thus a valuable way of getting information.

2. It allows the interviewee to release his pent-up feelings.

3. By expressing himself and having the listener reflect back his feelings, the interviewee is able to develop greater insight into his own problems.

Stages in an Interview

1. The interviewee is encouraged to release his feelings and the interviewer encourages him to release them. The interviewer accepts everything he hears regardless of how he may personally react; he does not pass judgement on the interviewee; and he needs to believe, basically, that the interviewee is capable of solving his own problems.

2. Facts are collected. Having let off steam, the interviewer can ask questions to bring out more information. He may also give information.

3. Solutions are formulated. Once the facts are assembled, the interviewee is in a position to weigh the various solutions and to pick one. The interviewer's role is to make sure the interviewee has all of the facts.

These are the three main phases of the interview, but of course the phases are not arbitrary; there may be considerable shifting throughout the interview.

---

[2]Jaques, Elliot, The Changing Culture of a Factory. London: Tavistock Publications, 1951.

By following these steps, both the interviewee and the interviewer work at: (1) clarifying the feelings so that they color the facts minimally; and (2) not jumping to conclusions before all of the facts are accumulated.

How To Counsel-Interview

Interviewing -- whether employment or counseling -- is a difficult art which can be learned best under practiced supervision. Each individual may have a different style. In general, here are a few summary points to remember:

1. Encourage the interviewee to talk. This means the interviewer must curb his natural impulses and be a <u>listener</u>. In addition to listening, he must concentrate: He must be <u>interested</u> in what the other person is saying and try to <u>understand</u>.

2. <u>Reflective Summary</u>. An effective way of encouraging others to talk is by summarizing the person's feelings, disregarding the facts. For example,

> Employee: "Yes I'm thinking of quitting. I don't seem to be getting the hang of the job. At least that's what people around here seem to think."

> Supervisor: "You feel people are sort of down on you?"

A reflective summary serves a number of purposes: (1) It shows the worker that the supervisor understands him and is fair; (2) It allows the worker to restate his attitude if he feels the supervisor did not understand; (3) It highlights what he has been saying. People often are surprised to learn what feelings were behind their words when their words are reflected back to them.

3. <u>Probe</u>. The interviewer's role is to understand. If he does not, he should feel free to ask for information by asking questions.

4. <u>Weighing Alternatives</u>. The interviewer wants to help the interviewee make a decision, but he does not want to make the decision for him. The interviewee may even make a very poor decision. The interviewer does have the responsibility of helping the interviewee make a good decision by asking questions of the interviewee when he makes a decision, such as:

> "What probably would be the effect of that?"

> "Is that the only solution?"

> "How would that help?"

Things To Avoid

1. Too much warm-up conversation.

2. Direct questions.

3. Premature judgements.

4. Arguing.

5. Advice-giving.

6. Masterminding or manipulating the interviewee.

THE "NEW" SUPERVISION

A supervisor provides as many opportunities as possible for the workers under him to make decisions for themselves. Freed from day-to-day work decisions, the supervisor can concentrate on training subordinates to be more effective workers and on planning, motivating, and communicating.

Delegation of Authority

Employees are given maximum freedom that can be handled by the employee consistent with the goals of the organization. By delegating authority, a supervisor potentially

1. frees himself to assume broader responsibilities;
2. maintains an image of fairness to his subordinates;
3. instills pride in his subordinates as they make their own decisions;
4. develops talents and skills.

Management by Objective

An "over-the-shoulder" supervisor not only gives specific assignments -- he also tells workers how results are to be obtained. This is self-defeating. Effective supervision requires that employees be given definite assignments, but the employee is not told how to do it. He is told what results are expected of him. Management by objective

1. stirs employees to work harder since they know their efforts are being measured;
2. allows each person to feel that he is his own boss;
3. makes it easier for a supervisor to maintain his objectivity;
4. allows management to see quickly which departments are having trouble;
5. provides measures for evaluation, promotion, and pay increases.

Instructing with a Minimum of Detail

Effective supervisors help their subordinates to express themselves by allowing them to work out details for themselves.

How to get things done without giving orders:

1. Set general goals and delegate authority.

2. Listen to subordinates and help them work out solutions rather than imposing solutions on them.

3. Establish routines for jobs.

4. Give information to employees, not orders -- assume employees know their own jobs.

5. Arrange jobs so that the situation, not the person, provides the order.

Use of Low Pressure

The effective supervisor assumes at the start that all men are interested in doing good work and in taking responsibility -- unless proven otherwise. Low pressure does not mean no pressure. Supervisors always have expectations of results from their subordinates.

Training

When he trains, the effective supervisor

1. explains why things are done -- both theory and practice;
2. provides opportunities for the employee to figure things out for himself -- under guidance;
3. recognizes two basic psychological laws:

   --Active learning is more effective than passive learning.
   --Feedback is an important element of learning.

To Do Work That Is Different from That of His Subordinates

The supervisor's role is not that of a "pace setter" but rather his role is to train and to motivate. Rather than taking a job into his own hands, he needs to give patient help to subordinates who are failing.

Concentration on Planning, Arranging, Systematizing

Too many supervisors see their role as "putting out fires" on a day-to-day basis. The effective supervisor spends time planning for the future, working on improving relations with other departments, setting goals, and preparing subordinates for future emergencies by his training program.

He constantly looks for programs, systems, techniques, equipment which will help routinize work, make automatic those processes, minor decisions and work detail which can be programmed. By programming the details of work, time and energy are saved for taking on fresh problems.

For example, cleaning a guest room can be programmed so that the maid is performing a series of acts tied together in a sequence which makes for efficiency. Her work is placed on a habit level so planned to make it easy, yet meet high standards of room care and cleanliness.

People are not by nature passive or resistant to organizational needs. They have become so as a result of experience in organizations.

The motivation, the potential for development, the capacity for assuming responsibility, the readiness to direct behavior toward organizational goals are all present in people. Management does not put them there. It is a responsibility of management to make it possible for people to recognize and develop these human characteristics for themselves.

The essential task of management is to arrange organizational conditions and methods of operation so that people can achieve their own goals best by directing their own efforts toward organizational objectives.

ORDER-GIVING

An important area in which supervisors need specific techniques concerns the problems of giving orders and of making reprimands. If these topics are on a training agenda, every supervisor will have ideas as to correct procedures. A well-conducted supervisory training session will usually convince supervisors that they will see these two acts in oversimplified terms. The outlines and discussion following are illustrations of ideas that will stimulate profitable discussion of giving orders and making reprimands. The results are usually apparent immediately in better supervisory relations with employees.

The Command versus the Order

In the military there is a distinction made between a command and an order. The order gives the subordinate latitude in carrying out the objective, whereas the command is a specific instruction to do something in a particular way and there is no latitude as to how it can be done. The same sort of reasoning applies to a commercial enterprise, even though there are not strong sanctions present like those found in the military. It is up to the manager to be perceptive enough to know when an order is appropriate and when a command is necessary.

Giving instructions is an art which takes into consideration the time, place, purpose, amount of change involved, and particularly the employee. New supervisors almost invariably make the mistake of giving too many orders. They demand rather than ask.

The purpose of effective instruction should be:

1. To change attitudes and behavior

   or

2. To set established habits in motion.

These purposes may appear too obvious to mention. However, instructions are also given for other reasons such as to expand the ego of the order-giver; to cover up his lack of information; or to make him feel that by merely giving an order he is accomplishing something.

When instructions are given to change attitudes and behavior, they require consultation with the employee beforehand. Discussion of proposed changes and suggestions from employees will smooth the way for final orders to start the changes. Time spent in consultation may not always pay off in better ideas -- but it usually pays off in a greater desire on the employee's part to accept the changes.

When orders are meant to set off well-established ways of doing things, time spent in discussion is often wasted.

Never use sarcasm or ridicule in giving instructions. Sarcasm, no matter how slight, immediately makes the employee feel unworthy. Then he rushes to his own defense in one way or another. This fighting back can take a number of forms, all of them bad for the business. The supervisor thus must take care that no taint of sarcasm or ridicule appears in his voice or facial expression.

Emphasize the positive. Provide incentives rather than relying on fear to get the job done. Fear takes many forms: threat of discharge, loss of the supervisor's goodwill, failure to speak on meeting, threat of no promotion, and many others. Use such motives only when other means have failed.

The instruction-giver should give the impression of self-confidence. One's bearing, tone of voice, and facial expression are important, since they build confidence in the supervisor or manager. To be firm without being overbearing, to be pleasant without appearing lackadaisical, to be friendly without appearing familiar are personality traits that often can be practiced and learned.

Do not give an order which you know will not be carried out. Each order that is not carried out makes the next one less likely to be carried out. Such orders destroy the habit of obeying supervisors' instructions.

Pick the proper time to give the order. Depending on the amount of change in regularly established habits, give the order early enough so that the employee will have time to prepare himself for doing it. An order involving a major change may require several days' discussion before being carried out. An order initiating some routine action should be given only a short time before action is expected.

Where possible avoid orders that take personnel away from jobs they have nearly finished. Breaking into a task is upsetting to nearly everyone. Asking an employee at 15 minutes before quitting time to do a job that takes 30 minutes is poor practice. The time of day should be considered. People are more likely to welcome changes during the first part of the morning and right after lunch.

Select the proper place to give the order. Depending on how much change in routine is involved in the order, call the person to the office or give it on the job. If the order involves major changes, prepare the employee for it and show him that you realize its significance. If a job is going to involve loss of face to the worker who will do it, don't embarrass him by giving the order before a group of other employees.

Managers should follow channels in giving orders. The manager who directly reprimands an employee is cutting the supports from under his supervisors.

Fit the order to the person.

Illustrations

An order to a "clinging vine" type employee: Give the order in a direct, completely self-assured manner but let the person feel that you understand him. Such a person needs to feel he is in competent hands. To him a supervisor is almost an all-wise father.

An order to a self-sufficient, "independent" employee: Give the order in a manner so that the employee is assured of his independent status. Such employees will strongly resent the "paternal" order. Even better, the "order" should be given in the form of a request for help or advice: "What's the best way to get the icebox cleaned out...do you think you have time to help Pete get it in good shape?"

An order to a woman employee who is sensitive to any thought of doing work below her dignity: "Miss Jones, I wonder if you would take charge of keeping this section of the kitchen clean?"

An order to a foreign-born employee or to a deep South colored person of meager education who expects a certain amount of authoritarianism and is upset without it: "Pete, I want you here at exactly eight o'clock, and I want all of the ice cubes out by eleven each morning. Can you do it?"

An order to an employee who needs more than the usual amount of reassurance and praise: "Miss Anxious, you seem to be exceptionally good at making hors d'oeuvres. I wonder if you could get us out 500, etc."

An order to an employee who is shy, not too intelligent, but who is strong: "Say, Jim. We've got to move all of that sugar in the storeroom. Since you're about the strongest man in the department, I wonder if you and Jake (the receiving clerk) could do the job. Jake has the dope on where it's to go."

Reprimanding

"Peterson," said the dining room manager to the new head waiter, "why did Paul Vigel quit last Sunday?" "Oh, he blew his top and quit because I jumped him for being careless and breaking a tray of dishes."

"Has he broken many dishes right along since being with us?"

"No, that's why I really lit into him. He knew better and had no excuse for it."

"Paul was a good steady man, wasn't he?"

"Oh, he wasn't as efficient as LeSeau, but he was good. I'm sorry he had to go -- but we can't stand for waiters' breaking that china, even when they're rushed."

"Peterson," said the manager, "you probably don't realize it, but this hotel has just lost an investment which it shouldn't have lost. It cost us money to hire and train Paul, and will cost us considerably more to replace him. When waiters break dishes, there are reasons -- but reasons which won't be helped by jumping on those who do it."

"Did you ever praise Paul for not breaking dishes?"

"No."

"Did you consider the effects your bawling out might have on Paul?"

"No."

Keep in mind the purposes of your reprimand: to change an attitude for better cooperation. The reprimand should be used not as punishment but as an interview during which there is mutual consideration of a problem.

Pointers in Handling a Reprimand

1. Make certain a reprimand is needed. Violations of rules are often beyond the control of the individual. Failure to meet production standards is often due to lack of training or to lack of ability. Examine yourself to see if any failure on your part may be responsible for the problem.

2. Invite the employee in question into your office or other private quarters. Any discussion of a person's weaknesses or failures always should be conducted in private. To do otherwise causes loss of confidence and resentment in the reprimanded employee, loss of your status as a respected supervisor, and resentment on the part of the other employees.

3. Begin the interview with a question. Ask the employee his interpretation of the problem at hand. His "facts" may be wrong, but they are important. Ask him, "What can we do about this?"

4. Do not argue. If you disagree with the employee's "interpretation," it will do little good to argue for your "interpretation."

5. Keep the interview aimed toward a constructive conclusion. Emphasize what should be done to change the situation. If at all possible, get the employee to suggest constructive changes. This may take time and require much listening and little talking by the supervisor.

6. Close with a statement of what has been decided. "Then you feel that it will be possible to get here on time" or "I'm glad you've told me why we haven't been getting along. Will you try to do thus and so in the future?"

7. Follow-up. Give the employee time to adjust himself to the action proposed in the interview. If positive results do not occur, repeat the procedure. Do not expect problems to be solved once and for all.

Use of Force

Force should be used only in the following instances:

1. When you are absolutely right and the employee wrong -- not in your eyes alone but in the eyes of the other employees and management.

2. When you have used all reasonable means for settlement of the problem by discussion or persuasion and the time has come when you must act for your good and for the good of the department.

TEST YOURSELF AS A SUPERVISOR

	True	False
1. Most employees will welcome a man-to-man talk with their supervisor even when their errors or faults are the subject of discussion.	_____	_____
2. Some well-qualified employees actually are not interested in being promoted.	_____	_____
3. Nonsupervisory employees often have worthwhile ideas about improving work methods.	_____	_____
4. Planning a job is more a matter of thinking, not simply a matter of jumping in and doing the job.	_____	_____
5. A poor way for a supervisor to get his men to work is through a display of authority which his job carries.	_____	_____
6. Employees should not be encouraged to keep all their grievances to themselves.	_____	_____

TEST YOURSELF AS A SUPERVISOR (Continued)

	True	False
7. If a man does an outstanding job, give him credit for it at once. Don't wait for him to repeat it.	_____	_____
8. Majority opinion is sometimes wrong.	_____	_____
9. A poor way to insure that a job will be done properly is to make two supervisors rather than just one responsible for it.	_____	_____
10. The best supervisor is not necessarily the one who has had the longest experience.	_____	_____
11. A supervisor should not emphasize the importance of a mistake which a worker has made by reminding him of it from time to time.	_____	_____
12. A man with high natural intelligence is not certain to be a success.	_____	_____
13. A supervisor's main duty is not to protect the feelings of those who work for him.	_____	_____
14. Men on higher level jobs are not entitled to take things easier than men below them.	_____	_____
15. The hardest worker is not always the one who gets ahead.	_____	_____
16. The employee who has to have things explained to him is sometimes a better man than the one who carried out the instruction without questions.	_____	_____
17. The best supervisor is not always the one who is the most popular with his employees.	_____	_____
18. Most people tend to resist changes which affect their natural way of doing things.	_____	_____
19. A good employee should sometimes express his disagreement with the orders of the man over him.	_____	_____
20. Higher pay will not always bring better workers to a company.	_____	_____
21. A common cause of employee dissatisfaction is simply the lack of individual recognition.	_____	_____
22. It is easier for a supervisor to lose the confidence of his men than to gain it.	_____	_____
23. When disciplining an employee it is often necessary to tell him things which will hurt his feelings.	_____	_____
24. Poor ability cannot always be offset by good training.	_____	_____
25. More care and caution is usually put into buying a new piece of equipment than is put into hiring a new man.	_____	_____
26. Ambition and interest will not always make up for lack of ability.	_____	_____
27. A supervisor should not avoid listening to the gripes or complaints of his men whenever possible.	_____	_____
28. In reality a good leader is not the man who knows how to push and drive others.	_____	_____
29. The best way to give instructions is not to issue a clear and direct command.	_____	_____
30. By handling more details himself, the supervisor may decrease his effectiveness as an executive.	_____	_____
31. Quiet and retiring individuals are not necessarily deep thinkers.	_____	_____
32. It is not the duty of every supervisor to make or break every man who works for him.	_____	_____

TEST YOURSELF AS A SUPERVISOR (Continued)

	True	False
33. In a progressive and producing organization of considerable size it is inevitable that some supervisors will not be able to stand the pace.	_____	_____
34. Favorable wages and hours are seldom the main factors which enter into employee satisfaction.	_____	_____
35. The average supervisor is likely to overrate the man who usually says "yes" to him.	_____	_____

You probably have realized that all of the answers to the "Test Yourself as a Supervisor" should be "true."

Of course, in some situations some of the items might be "false." This is what makes supervision and management so fascinating, makes it an art, rather than a science, makes it one of the most challenging of activities.

UNIVERSITY TRAINING

The prospective hotel or restaurant operator may learn to understand and how to modify human behavior from the study of psychology. He may learn the importance of group relationships and how to utilize these relationships from the study of sociology. He may better understand our own national economy and anticipate and partially control the economics of a business by studying economics. Engineering offers skills in kitchen layout and in time and motion study. Specialized courses in engineering may give him an understanding of the engineering department of the hotel and restaurant. Accounting skills prepare him for an immediate job in the auditing department and eventually for departmental and business management positions. College training, once a rarity to be had by but a few, is now a necessity required of the many. Most of the leading hotels and restaurants of this country are now managed by college-trained men and women.

Several hotel and restaurant periodicals were published in the twenties. Although none of them were of a highly technical nature, they tended to emphasize the desirability of pooling information and ideas, which inevitably leads to a clearer understanding of the value of institutions of higher learning. Coincidentally the magazine "Hotel Management" was first published in 1922, the year the hotel course at Cornell was founded.

In the year 1925, the first edition of Lucius Boomer's book "Hotel Management" appeared, and in the following years the editorial staff of "Restaurant Management" magazine cooperated with Yale University in a study of restaurant costs.

Beginning in 1922 colleges and universities offered four-year courses in hotel and restaurant majors leading to a bachelor of science or bachelor of arts degree. Today these universities offer four-year programs:

> Cornell University, Ithaca, New York
> Denver University, Denver, Colorado
> Florida State University, Tallahassee, Florida
> Michigan State University, East Lansing, Michigan
> Oklahoma A. & M. University, Stillwater, Oklahoma
> Pennsylvania State University, State College, Pennsylvania
> University of Massachusetts, Amherst, Massachusetts
> University of New Hampshire, Durham, New Hampshire
> Washington State University, Pullman, Washington

Several colleges offer two-year terminal courses.

Tuskegee Institute in Alabama offers a restaurant program for Negro students.

Graduate programs leading to the master of science degree are offered at Michigan State University and the University of Massachusetts.

Institutional management, a related field, is offered at about 100 colleges throughout the country. Institution management trains women as dietitians in hospitals, schools and colleges, hotels, restaurants, in-plant feeding operations, and in research.

CURRICULA OFFERINGS

College-level hotel and restaurant courses can be divided into four areas:

1. Management

2. Accounting and Control

3. Foods

4. Engineering

The emphasis on these areas varies with the school. All of the schools insist on practical training along with theory. Summer work is encouraged or required and work in the kitchens and dining rooms of the colleges is possible for most students desiring it.

DIETETIC INTERNSHIPS

The American Dietetic Association has an intern plan for training dietitians. It is a postgraduate program and provides the student who has the baccalaureate degree with training in one of three different kinds of internships: hospital, administrative, or food clinic. Most approved courses last one year. A large share of the living expenses -- lodging, meals, and professional laundry -- are provided by the institution or business offering the internship.

REFERENCES

1. Likert, R., "Patterns in Management," in Studies in Personnel and Industrial Psychology, Fleishman, E.A. Homewood, Illinois: The Dorsey Press, Inc., 1961.

2. Strauss, G. and Sayles, L.R., The Human Problems of Management. Englewood Cliffs, New Jersey: Prentice-Hall, 1960.

CHAPTER 11

Analyzing and Simplifying Work

"If you own a shaggy dog, vacuum him instead of the floors and rugs, clothes and furniture."

The foregoing advice might be changed to read: "If you manage a shaggy hotel or restaurant, analyze the operation to discover better ways of performing the work and developing systems which will make the work easier." In other words, hotel or restaurant management must step back periodically, examine the work being done to see if it can be simplified, tasks combined and/or eliminated, employees rescheduled, work batched for minimizing physical and mental effort. Every operation performed can be examined to see if it is economical to substitute equipment for manpower, machines for muscle power, electronic devices for routine mental chores.

Traditionally, hotel or restaurant keeping has been a handicraft business -- people working with their hands. Personal service has been one of its great offerings to the public. Today the service is still there but it is mechanized service. Conveyor belts running a half a block or more, carrying soiled dishwear, subveyors moving up and down through several stories, carrying food, cafeteria serving lines on wheels which can feed up to 15 people a minute, computers whirring and clicking away doing payrolls for employees hundreds of miles away, keeping food inventories, doing accounts receivable and accounts payable and keeping guest charges up to the second -- all make the hotel and restaurant business a much more efficient business than it was in the past, a business which demands a higher level of education and management sophistication.

WAITING AND CLEANING TIME EXCESSIVE IN HOTELS AND RESTAURANTS

It has been widely stated that the average kitchen employee performs productive work only 55 per cent of the time, that much of his time is spent watching food cook, waiting for something or someone. Careful research is not available to substantiate this statement, but it is apparent from gross observation of the usual kitchen that at a given moment many people cannot perform productive work. Most studies have shown that with particular pieces of equipment as much as 50 per cent of an employee's time is spent in sanitation, the term defined broadly. The cycle of business in hotels and restaurants is such that some ingenuity is required to maintain work flow in a variety of jobs: cashiers, front desk clerks, bellmen, and all waiting personnel. Most check-ins that take place in a hotel or motel occur between the hours of 4 and 8 P.M. What can the bellman do the rest of the time? Restaurant cashiers are busy during the meal periods. Can other work be assigned to them during the lull periods? Is it necessary for all of the tableware to be washed during the meal periods or can the work be spread throughout the day or over several days?

Does it pay to purchase convenience foods or even frozen meals? Will the customers accept instant mashed potatoes, dehydrated onions, the use of soup and gravy bases in sauces, and products made from bakery mixes? Some convenience foods definitely have a cost advantage, others do not. One study showed that the cost per portion of fresh potatoes came to 4 1/2 cents as compared to 2 1/2 cents for instant potatoes when the expense of labor was included. Dehydrated onions cost 10 1/4 cents a pound as compared with 18 cents a pound for fresh onions prepared by hand. The dehydrated onions were satisfactory for cooked dishes but could not be used in sandwiches.

The administration of the state mental hospitals of New York State found that it was less expensive to purchase canned, boned chicken than to have chicken purchased, cooked, and picked within the hospital kitchens.

Why not buy prepared frozen foods and do away with chefs and cooks within the establishment completely? In one of the most successful food operations in the country, Howard Johnson's, 99 per cent of the food is frozen. No one in the Howard Johnson restaurant could properly be called a cook. A certain percentage of the menu items on all Holiday Inn menus are reconstituted frozen meals made by Armour.

In general, it can be said that food processing can be done more economically using mass production methods in a factory than it can be done within a restaurant or hotel kitchen. Everyone agrees, however, that the very best food available is made from fresh food prepared to order and served to the patron at once. Truite Bleu, made from live swimming trout kept in a tank in the kitchen, tastes considerably different than frozen trout. Peas prepared from fresh peas shelled by hand generally are more tasty than canned peas. The specialty of the house usually gives the patron something a little bit different than he can get elsewhere and constitutes a part of its appeal, yet the preparation costs must be considered. Labor costs in making a pie are somewhere around 25 cents; the cost of preparing boeuf à la mode is high; the time required to prepare stuffed sole Normande is considerable and the skill required not cheap, yet they may be "right" for a particular restaurant.

Manpower costs approximately $10.00 per kilowatt hour, electric power about one cent. Hotels, restaurants, hospitals, and clubs must see to it that manpower is used only when the work requires artistry, personal service or brain power. Let machines substitute for muscles whenever and wherever possible. Human life is much too valuable even in its lowest cash terms to be used as no more than mindless mechanical power.

It is estimated that in 1850 only 26 per cent of the work energy consumed in the United States came from power-driven machines. Today the figure is 94 per cent. We employ ten times as much energy per person in the United States as the average for the rest of the world; we produce two to four times as much goods per labor-hour as the most highly industrialized nations of Europe. The larger chain operations in our field are industrializing. The little French restaurant with its four tables and its food prepared by the owner can be a thing of beauty and artistry, but not very profitable.

Wages continue upward over the years. Hours will be reduced to 40 a week or less. Maximum productivity from manpower is essential.

Labor costs in hotels, restaurants, hospitals, industrial feeding operations, and clubs are one of the biggest and most difficult to control of all costs. In commercial hotels they are 37 per cent of the gross revenue. In California restaurants labor costs are 37 per cent of the gross sales and are equal to the food costs. Clubs often run a labor cost of over 40 per cent of the gross income. Railroad dining car service runs the highest of all labor costs -- 75 per cent -- which helps to account for the loss the roads take of $1.00 to $1.50 or more per meal served. On top of these percentages the U. S. Chamber of Commerce states that hotels pay 9.4 per cent more in non-wage labor payments (meals, social security, unknown exemptions and the like). There are few operations in which alert and informed management cannot with system, controls, and good personnel techniques reduce labor costs several percentage points.

According to Harris, Kerr, Forster Accountants, 50 per cent of hotel jobs should have variable schedules. Only a small percentage actually do have them. The same firm states that only 15 per cent of the hotel repairs are emergency repairs and that 85 per cent of them can be scheduled, thus reducing maintenance men's many hours of riding up and down on service elevators for "emergency" repair jobs.

Labor cost is relative and most meaningful in terms of cost per unit of production: cost to wash a window, cost to prepare a guest room, cost per salad, cost per portion of roast beef, and so on. In food operations labor cost and food cost are two sides of the same coin. Skilled, well-paid labor may result in a higher than average labor cost but a lower than average food cost. Using frozen meals, for example, means an increase in food cost and a decrease in labor cost. Low-paid management may well cost an operation thousands of dollars of unnecessary food costs.

SCHEDULING PERSONNEL TO FIT THE WORK LOAD

Scheduling personnel to fit work load is a major factor in reducing labor costs. Harold Van Ormon, Jr., a well-known hotelman, states that up to one-third of the labor in hotels is wasted through lack of personnel scheduling. Production requirements in hotels and restaurants vary widely throughout the day, the week, and the year. Meals in a restaurant, for example, may range from 500 for a Monday evening to 25 for Sunday breakfast. Within the same day the number of dinners served may be only a fraction of the luncheons served. The number of meals vary seasonally as well as follow a weekly pattern.

Reference to the two charts on the following page points out dramatically the wide variations in sales in hotels and restaurants. In the chart "Sales in Eating and Drinking Establishments," taken from government figures, it is seen that sales in restaurants during January, February, March, and April are low compared to the rest of the year. Across the country as a whole July and August bring peak sales, then there is a gradual drop-off until November. December picks up a bit only to have January drop precipitously.

In the chart "Average Daily Occupancy in Downtowner Motor Inns," we see that Monday through Thursday in a typical successful Downtowner Motor Inn finds the house full. On Fridays the occupancy drops to 45 per cent. In many commercial hotels around the country, Saturday and Sunday occupancy falls below 40 per cent, and there are wide swings in business volume on a seasonal basis. Generally December is by far the lowest month for the hotel business, and Christmas Day finds many hotels with less than 10 per cent occupancy. Some cities have a high spring occupancy; others reach their peak in the summer. Scheduling employees to fit such variations in sales challenges management to the utmost.

SALES IN EATING AND DRINKING ESTABLISHMENTS

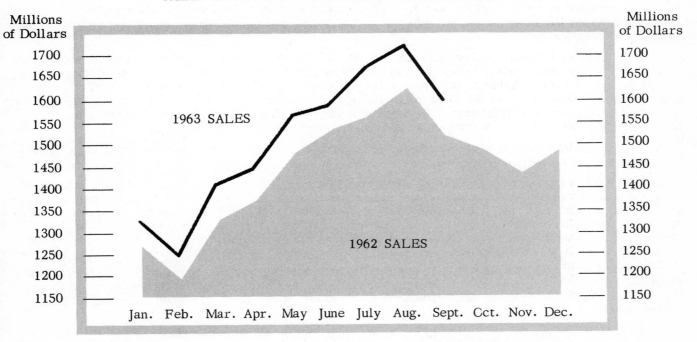

AVERAGE DAILY OCCUPANCY DOWNTOWNER MOTOR INNS

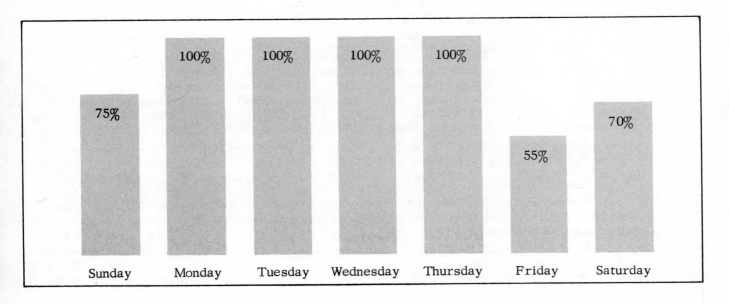

In hundreds of industrial food service operations the difference between profit and loss comes from the fact that most of the serving personnel are employed for only two hours a day, drawn from employees of the company being served who hold other regular jobs. It has been found in many restaurants that women who ordinarily would not take a full-time job are interested in working up to four hours daily. These women are a boon to the food service business.

Ideally, the number of personnel scheduled would correspond to the production turned out. Such a production curve would look like this.

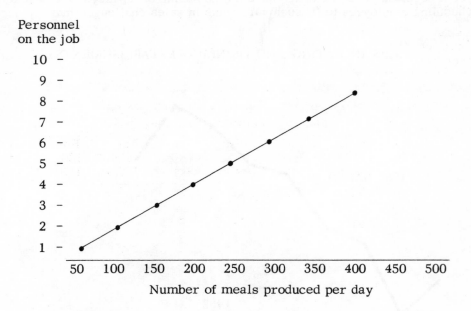

Conceivably such a curve would be achieved in an industrial feeding operation or cafeteria with a fixed volume. In most hotels it will remain an ideal only. Key personnel must be kept on regardless of the volume. Here are some scheduling practices, however, which have increased efficiency in food operation:

1. Schedule personnel on split shifts. Waiters and waitresses can be scheduled for a noon meal, for example, then be off until the dinner meal, or until a night banquet. This is especially feasible in downtown operations where personnel live close to the business and have things to do at home. In other operations split shifts are not practical.

2. Where possible schedule personnel irregularly to fit the pattern of work requirements. Some personnel may need to be scheduled to start at noon one day, morning another day, and at 4 o'clock still another day. By careful scheduling no one is overworked or inconvenienced too much -- efficiency is increased.

3. Use Part-Time Personnel. In many operations part-time employees should be used extensively. In operations where meals and functions are confined mostly to the evenings, only a core of full-time employees is needed. A large staff of full-time personnel in such instances not only creates an excessive labor cost but leads to generally slipshod operation. Keep a file of part-time help on hand. With training they can be an effective part of the work force.

4. Use of Staffing Table. Manpower can be budgeted to a large degree just as are materials or equipment. The staffing or manning table is an excellent labor cost control device and can be applied to any operation. As efficiency and equipment are introduced, the staffing table is changed. The tables show that as patrons increase the number of employees increase. Conversely, as patrons decline in number, the number of staff should decrease. Because of differences in layout, services offered, and equipment, each operation must necessarily construct a staffing table to fit its operation.

On the following page are shown two hypothetical staffing tables for a restaurant -- one for the kitchen and one for the dining room.

STAFFING TABLE FOR KITCHEN

Jobs to be Filled	For 0-49 Patrons	For 50-99 Patrons	For 100-175 Patrons	For 175-plus Patrons
Chef	1	1	1	1
Cook	1	2	3	4
Salads -- Pantry	1	2	2	3
Dishwasher	1	2	3	3
Potwasher	1	1	1	1
Cleaner	0	1	1	1
Storeroom Man	0	1	1	1
Baker	0	1	1	1

STAFFING TABLE FOR DINING ROOM
(Based on number of patrons)

Jobs to be Filled	For 0-37	For 38-58	For 59-75	For 76-95	For 96-112	For 113-129	For 130-145	For 146-166	For 167-Plus
Hostess	1	1	1	1	1	1	1	1	1
Waiter -- Waitress	2	3	4	5	6	7	8	9	10
Bus Boy	1	2	2	3	3	3	3	4	5
Bar Waitress	1	1 1/2	1 1/2	2	2	2 1/2	2 1/2	2 1/2	2 1/2

The Sales-Labor Chart

Most food service operations can afford the time to make a graph of the relationship between sales per hour and the number of man hours used each hour. Graphs are a means of breaking down a complicated subject and putting it into a form which enables management to comprehend it and to reschedule employees to fit sales volume. All that is necessary is to keep a record of the sales made each hour and to plot such sales on the curve hour by hour. The sales curve is overlaid on a work schedule graph. A hypothetical graph is illustrated.

SALES AND MAN HOURS CHART

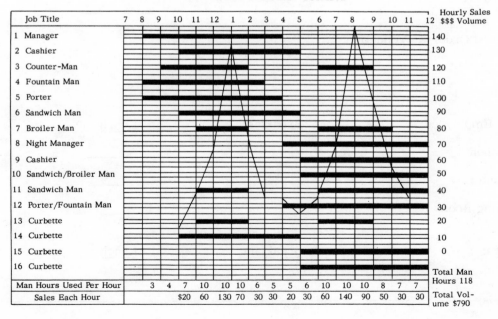

In the sales-man hour chart in the illustration it is seen that the peak sales periods are from 12:00 to 2:00 and from 6:00 to 9:00 P.M. During these rush periods 10 man hours are being used per hour, which seems appropriate. During the period from 10:00 to 11:00 in the morning only $20.00 has been taken in in sales yet seven man hours were consumed, and after 10:00 in the evening only $30.00 an hour was taken in while seven man hours each hour were used. The graph suggests that perhaps the wayside restaurant represented should close at 10:00 P.M. The manager who begins his shift at 4:00 in the afternoon could probably start at 5:00 or at 6:00 just as well. Three of the curb girls could well be off between the hours of 4:00 and 6:00. As always, there would be other factors to consider in rescheduling, but the chart is a point of departure for analysis.

Once scheduling has been revised, systems are needed to keep it in line with work requirements. The Harris, Kerr, and Forster system is an elaborate one suitable for large operations. A restaurant can use a more elementary system effectively. The "Sales and Employee Forecast" chart illustrated is one that is used in a cafeteria chain. Each cafeteria manager predicted every day what his breakfast, lunch, and dinner sales would be for the following day. The forecast was based on the sales made on a given day of the week the previous year, taking into consideration weather forecasts, unusual situations in the area which increased or decreased business, and the general trend of business -- whether it was up or down.

SALES AND EMPLOYEE FORECAST

Date _____

Weather Today: _____

Conventions in Town:

Party Business:

_____

Other Factors Affecting Sales:

Forecasted Sales in Dollars:	Breakfast	Lunch	Dinner
	_____	_____	_____

Adjusted Food Order & Production:

Number of Employees:	Breakfast	Lunch	Dinner
Kitchen	_____	_____	_____
Counter	_____	_____	_____
Dining Room	_____	_____	_____

Actual Sales:	Breakfast	Lunch	Dinner
	_____	_____	_____

A difficulty was found in getting the manager to make the forecast, since he was so involved with daily operation.

The number of employees who were used for each meal in the kitchen, on the serving table, and in the dining room was recorded. From the statistics it was soon evident that on certain days too many employees were on hand -- on other days too few. The sales income by employee was usually computed and a standard of close to $30.00 of sales per employee per day was established. In some operations the sales per employee were considerably higher and in others lower.

The chart was simple enough to be understood by the usual manager and the system which resulted required no special person such as a Food and Beverage Controller to operate it.

Standards Useful as Guides in Work Simplification

While the objective in work simplification is to achieve maximum work production with minimal effort, knowing what is possible to achieve or has been achieved in other establishments gives the analyst goals toward which he can shoot. The American Dietetic Association, for example, has published the chart following showing the number of meals produced for one man hour of effort in various kinds of food service establishments. It is seen that hotels produce the least number of meals per man hours expended while the school lunch, for apparent reasons, can produce as many as fifteen meals per man hour of effort.

MEALS PRODUCED PER MAN HOUR OF LABOR USED

Type Institution	No. of Meals
Hotels	1.25- 1.50
Restaurants	1.50- 1.87
Cafeterias	3.60- 8.75
School Lunch	5.45-15.00
College Dormitories	3.38- 9.07
Hospitals	4.76

As might be expected, productivity per employee varies tremendously with the volume of sales. In the restaurant, at least, there seems to be no point of diminishing returns as regards the amount of sales which can be produced per employee. Restaurants which have sales volumes of $100,000 per year have an employee productivity of $8,333. When the sales volume increases to $500,000 per year the productivity per employee more than doubles, climbing to $19,642. For those restaurants which do $1 million in sales -- and there are many around the country -- sales volume per employee exceeds $20,000. In a few instances in which restaurants do over $2 million per year in sales, the average productivity per employee reaches the astounding figure of $40,000. These figures were compiled from a large-scale questionnaire study conducted by Restaurant Management Magazine in 1963 and can be expected to increase as more convenience foods, more capital equipment, and more efficiency appear in the commercial restaurant.

WORK SIMPLIFICATION

Work simplification is a frame of mind and a procedure of analysis. Analysis of a job or group of jobs for the express purpose of increasing efficiency is properly called work simplification. Work simplification asks:

1. Can it be eliminated? Will the use of a wall-washing machine make it unnecessary to wash walls by hand? Will the use of a rinse injector in the dish machine eliminate time-consuming stain removal from serving trays? Will the use of a wetting agent eliminate toweling of silverware?

2. Can it be combined? Can the night clerk do food and beverage auditing? Can he act as night engineer? Can bellmen do maintenance and repair work? If the partitions are cut out of the front office, can one employee do several jobs during slow periods?

3. Are there unnecessary delays? Is service delayed by waiters piling up at the service bar? Is there a delay in getting the food from the kitchen to the pantry? Are rooms unavailable because they are not made up by the housekeeping department?

4. Is there misdirected effort? Is it necessary that each waiter serve but few covers? Can potatoes be eyed by a machine rather than by hand? Can frozen orange juice be profitably used in place of fresh oranges? Can a conveyor belt instead of muscle power be profitably used in carrying food and dishes?

5. Are skills used properly? Does your janitor use the proper stroke in mopping? Might the high school graduate working as a dish attendant be more effectively used in a higher level job? Are you using a highly paid cook to do clean-up work that can be done by a lesser paid employee?

6. Are employees doing too many unrelated tasks? Are we reducing the effectiveness of the hostess by requiring her to take phone reservations? Are we using the assistant manager as a clerk rather than as an executive? Does our chef have too many personnel duties to perform which could be done by the personnel manager? Are you spending too much time on club work on institution time?

7. Is work spread unevenly? Are the dishwashers finished and standing idle while the kitchen clean-up man never finishes? Are the housemen overworked while the maids take it easy? Does the service elevator operator get the same rest periods as the guest elevator operators?

What Is Efficiency?

An engineering definition of efficiency is simple enough:

$$\text{Efficiency} = \frac{\text{Output}}{\text{Input}}$$

In other words, efficiency is the percentage of productivity which results from the amount of effort involved. The formula can be applied to mental effort as well as physical effort and is useful in speaking about efficiency. In relating it to human effort several qualifications must be made. The human machine must rest, must be inspired, must have goals, must think highly of itself to be creative, must rest periodically, and can be thrown out of alignment easily.

It has been said that the mind is not used to more than 10 per cent of efficiency. In physical terms perhaps this is true, and any effort or technique which will increase the efficiency of the mind should probably be considered. Philosophers and religious leaders have struggled with the problem of increasing human mental efficiency over the centuries and much of what they advise is useful in the business world. The Greek emphasis on a balanced life is sound for most people, although we find men like Elsworth Statler, one of the authentic geniuses in the hotel field, whose interest and energies were focused on the hotel business in a way which would be considered "unbalanced" by some standards. He was able to get along on three or four hours' sleep a night, which helped.

Caesar Ritz was a perfectionist in a field in which perfection is dangerous. In times of stress he would add to his stress by insisting upon perfection and paid the penalty by spending the last years of his life as a psychotic.

Most of us must balance rest with activity and "reward" activities outside of business hours with the frustrations usually found on the job, must follow a cycle of activity which is unique to the individual for maximum performance. We need rest pauses and should encourage "coffee breaks" or their equivalents in establishing work schedules for employees. We need to gain satisfactions off the job such as bridge playing, golf, tennis, and travel in order to reintegrate the ego after the frazzling experiences on most jobs. Whatever is said about human efficiency must be stated in terms of the individual psyche, at least to some extent -- but there are wide areas where efficiency can be increased.

Rest Before You Get Tired

Since the hotel and restaurant business can be a stress business, management must be sensitive to cues which indicate that stresses are piling up. The tired person cannot handle new problems or new ideas with equanimity or enthusiasm. Avoid letting situations develop to the point where this is necessary. Conferences usually should be scheduled in the morning when people are fresh. Tough problems should be tackled when the person is at his peak. For most people this is in the morning, but some people don't really get wound up until late in the day.

When the individual organism begins to lose its alacrity in response, it's time to rest and replenish. This can be done by a change of work, a change of pace, a change of focus. Do not build up a debt of energy by overworking. Recovery time varies with the individual, goes down with age. The person who works himself to the bone is maltreating not only himself but the business as well, for his decisions will be less effective and his relations with other people, guests and employees, less than optimal. A fifty- or sixty-hour week is fine for someone who has a variety of challenges, is highly motivated, can move in and out of an environment at will. The executive who is conducting business at a cocktail party is not really working in the sense of the paid manager who is "on the floor" in the restaurant or in the hotel lobby. Many studies show that for most routine jobs forty or forty-two hours a week are about maximal for maintaining efficiency. Hours worked beyond this level mean a fast drop-off in productivity. When exhaustion appears, extreme frustration comes easily and frequently, sometimes leading to panic.

Where possible, establish work schedules which reflect optimal efficiency in management and among employees. Avoid those schedules which make for exhaustion, the dull-eyed counter girl, the crying waitress, the irritable manager.

Techniques for Personal Efficiency

There are dozens of techniques which can be helpful in increasing one's personal efficiency. The notebook in the pocket to keep a record of appointments, things to do, ideas to investigate can keep the mind uncluttered for absorbing new information and attacking new problems.

Bucking things which can be done by other people on down the line frees the manager for considering problems and making decisions which are appropriate for a manager. A good secretary is like a right arm, can often do the routine things better than the manager, and if she has a talent will welcome being given routine responsibilities beyond typing and filing. Personal efficiency extends to dress, housing, transportation. If efficiency is a primary objective -- and it should not always be -- the manager will live close to the operation, avoiding hours of commuting to and from work. He would probably wear clothes made of synthetics, such as mixtures of nylon or dacron and wool, and would probably drive a compact car. It is quite possible to travel around the world with nothing but a brief case for carrying all the clothes that are needed and, from an efficiency viewpoint, hauling around an extra ton of steel in a big automobile is heresy. Some of the most successful executives in the hotel and restaurant business have 10' x 15' offices, do much of their dictating on portable machines, telephone rather than write, and have developed an "efficient" pattern of life without really planning to do so. As with most things in life, values soon become involved in considerations of efficiency. The manager of the resort which caters to the upper class probably needs to drive an expensive car to maintain his status in the eyes of his guests. One resort manager has 150 sport coats, each of them costing in excess of $100. For him the sport coats may be necessary.

Specialization of Function

In heavy industry the attempt has been made to specialize every job so that each employee does only a limited number of tasks and makes few decisions. The employee on the assembly line epitomizes this viewpoint, perhaps putting a few nuts and bolts on a part of a piece of equipment as it passes by him. Productivity is increased and for some employees such work is probably satisfactory. One of the appeals of the hotel and restaurant business is that there are few such specialized jobs to perform: employees are able to start and complete a task such as greeting a guest and rooming him, taking an order and serving a meal and collecting for it. This is one of the several appeals that the hotel and restaurant field has for employees and it should not be destroyed. There are many jobs, however, which can be more highly specialized than they are at present. Many jobs, especially in the kitchen, have too much time wasted in the "make-ready and the put-away" phases of the task, too little time devoted to the production phase. For example, the time to make five apple pies is almost as great as the time to make 25 apple pies because of the make-ready and the put-away aspects of the job. Why not make 25 pies or 50 pies, if they can be frozen and used later.

Why should each cook go to the storeroom to get the ingredients for his recipe, return to the kitchen and make up the recipe? Why not have the storeroom man assemble all ingredients for recipes, assemble the pans to be used for the recipe, and wheel them to the cook? This is done in many establishments and is worth considering in even relatively small operations. The storeroom man who does the receiving, sorting, and issuing can also do the recipe assembling, and he may be called upon to be a kitchen utility man or even a cook if the operation is small. By using the storeroom assembly method or "ingredient room" assembly method, as it is called in some hospitals, desirable specialization of function is achieved.

Batching Work

In doing almost any work there is a warm-up period required of the worker before he hits his stride. He is able to maintain his stride for varying lengths of time, then there is a fall-off in quality or quantity. When a worker is required to shift from task to task a natural loss of efficiency is experienced. The secretary who is typing a letter and must answer the phone loses the continuity and rhythm in her typing. The manager who is calling a series of purveyors for quotations loses efficiency when he is interrupted by the appearance of a cook or someone else. Every task can be "batched" to make a unit which can be performed efficiently by a person. What constitutes an optimal batch size varies with the individual, but there are guidelines. Some jobs need to be divided and made more specialized; others need to be enlarged to hold worker interest, create a sense of responsibility and anticipation, and avoid monotony. What is monotonous to one person is challenging to another.

One employee can prepare all the potatoes and do all of the baking for several operations more efficiently than several employees in different locations can ready the same amount in smaller quantities. "Batching" accounts for desirability of situating much of the preparation and cooking of food in the central commissary if the operations being served are not too large. Centralized commissary preparation is not an advantage when it serves food service units which are large enough to be individually efficient. Commissary operation is advantageous when it serves a number of smaller operations, each of a size not efficient in itself. It would make no sense to prepare food centrally and deliver it to a restaurant which has $1 million in sales and is large enough to prepare its own food on a production basis.

"Batching" is a practice which can be applied to almost any work to be done; for example, the manager who must plan an employee schedule, order food for the next day, dictate letters in answer to the current day's mail is usually well advised to schedule his own time so that each of these tasks is done as a unit rather than interspersing such efforts throughout the day. He would try to do all of his dictation in the morning to get his secretary started; he might do all of his food purchasing after 6:00 in the evening when his purveyors would be less busy and could take his calls; and he could make up the employee schedule in the afternoon as a break following the noon rush period.

THE FLOW PROCESS CHART

To detect discrepancies such as those suggested on pages 131 and 132, special tools have been devised. One of the best known of these tools is the process chart, a means of identifying each step in a process or activity. Five symbols, standardized by practice, are used as signs for (1) operations; (2) transportation; (3) storage; (4) inspection; (5) delay. In analyzing the flow of food through a kitchen to the guest or for any other work process, the symbols serve as a simple recording device. The Otis-type flow chart is illustrated on the following page.

The process of getting a fruited gelatin dessert from a pantry to a guest might proceed as follows:

O   T   I   S   D   Dessert chilled at pantry.

O   T   I   S   D   Waitress places maraschino cherry in dessert.

O   T   I   S   D   Waitress carries dessert to food checker.

O   T   I   S   D   Delay caused by crowding at the food checker's station.

O   T   I   S   D   Dessert checked for portion by food checker.

O   T   I   S   D   Waitress carries dessert to guest.

The "flowing" of the dessert from the pantry to guest can in this way be followed in a systematic way and a more satisfactory analysis made.

To clarify this problem of the movement of the dessert from the pantry to the guest, a diagram of the process can be made showing the routes followed and the number of steps taken between key points. For example, we might find by plotting the route over which the dessert is taken that our diagram or work process chart resembles the one illustrated at the right.

In this case the diagram suggests that either the food checker be moved or that the doors between the kitchen and dining room be moved.

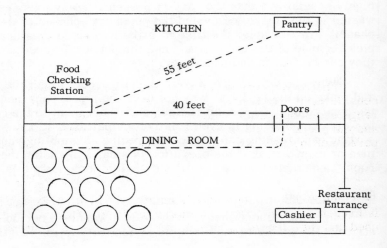

```
+-------------------------------------------------------------------------------+
|                         FLOW PROCESS CHART                                    |
|                            (Otis Type)                                        |
|                                                                               |
| O -- An operation: frying, warming, carving, boning, totaling a check, etc.   |
| T -- Transportation: carrying a tray, moving dirty dishes, trucking dirty linen, lifting a pot, etc. |
| I -- Inspection: a food checker inspecting portions, a floor housekeeper checking a room for readi- |
|      ness, a storekeeper weighing in fresh food, etc.                         |
| S -- Storage: linen in a closet, food in bins, glasses in a rack, meat in a refrigerator, etc. |
| D -- Delay: a bottleneck caused by crowding at the service bar, a waiting period for clean glasses, |
|      etc.                                                                      |
```

Travel in feet	Time in seconds	Symbol	Description
		O T I S D	
		O T I S D	
		O T I S D	
		O T I S D	
		O T I S D	
		O T I S D	
		O T I S D	
		O T I S D	
		O T I S D	
		O T I S D	
		O T I S D	
		O T I S D	
		O T I S D	

Totals

Summary:

O
T
I
S
D

The recommendation for making such changes of course would be dependent on other factors not considered in the diagram on the preceding page. The flow of food from other kitchen stations such as the range and soup station would need to be considered. The heat conditions at the present checking station and the proposed one would also make a difference in our decision. Similarly costs and the way the personnel involved will respond to the change would play important parts in the problems.

TIME AND MOTION STUDY

Time and motion study is an attempt to simplify work and reduce effort. A job or series of tasks is broken down into the elementary motions performed by the worker. By carefully analyzing the motions used and the time spent in making the motions, it is often possible to eliminate motions, to substitute more economic motions, and to rearrange the sequence of motions so that the work is simplified or made easier to perform.

Some principles on which such study is made include:

1. Both hands should begin motions simultaneously. This increases rhythm and eliminates loss of time due to overlapping motions.

2. Both hands should complete motions simultaneously.

3. Both hands should not be idle at the same instant.

4. Work should be so arranged that the arms will move in opposite and symmetrical directions. This gives the worker balance, which he lacks when both arms move in the same direction.

5. The fundamental motions of a task should be limited to as few as possible.

6. The motions made should be within the radius of the worker, thus they should not unduly fatigue him. This precludes reaching in any direction so far as to necessitate bending the trunk.

7. The hands should be relieved of work which can be done by the feet, provided there is other work for the hands to do at the same time.

8. The faster motions should be taught first.

9. Sequences of motions should be arranged to build a rhythm and to use curved-line motions rather than straight-line movements.

10. The uses of the different parts of the body should be restricted to as few as possible.

It is apparent that the principles listed above will apply most readily to jobs which are repetitive and include only a small number of tasks.

NECESSITY FOR CONSIDERING FEELINGS AND INDIVIDUAL DIFFERENCES

Job changes inevitably include changes in human relations. The human relations changes are usually more important than the job changes. The supervisor who gets an idea which will reduce by half the movements for a particular task can by introducing the change in a wrong way actually decrease the efficiency of the operation. The feelings of the employee or employees who are involved must be considered as well as the "facts" of the job change. Employees who are invited to participate in work simplification and are consulted when job changes occur are likely to accept the change and make it work. Job changes thrust on the workers from above arouse anxieties and resentment. Later chapters will discuss more fully the means and implications of gaining employee support for new ideas.

Individual differences must also be considered in a work simplification program. There is no one "best" way of performing a task. People vary widely in their temperaments and abilities. One person may enjoy a highly repetitive job and for him the job is efficiently set up. Another needs change and challenge. A repetitive job may need to be broken up and the worker given more responsibility. For him the job is inefficiently set up.

FURTHER ILLUSTRATIONS OF WORK SIMPLIFICATION

To illustrate the effectiveness of work simplification studies and to give an idea of the number of jobs to which work simplification can be applied, a summary of fifteen case studies conducted by Sanford E. Maus, of Harris, Kerr, Forster and Company, appears following.[1]

CASE ONE

Situation: A small dish pantry was staffed for years on the basis of service for three meals a day. Later when the morning meal was eliminated management neglected to change the work schedule.

Results of analysis: A bar graph was drawn up which plotted the work schedule and rated the amount of work done by periods throughout the day.

Photographs illustrating work simplification appear on pages 137, 138, and 139.

---

[1]With permission of the author and of the Southern Hotel Journal.

Thinking ahead to prevent unnecessary work. The potato sack can be tied to the drain line of the vegetable peeler. The sack collects the starch and small peelings which eventually clog the sewer drain line.

Time and effort are saved by letting the butter on the bread pick up the sandwich spread material. Otherwise, the chopped egg or other filling must be placed on the sandwich bit by bit.

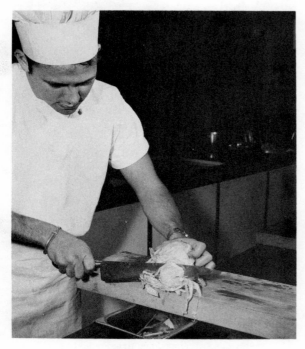

Letting gravity work for the cook. The sliced lettuce falls directly into the pan rather than having to be collected and lifted into it.

Gravity drops the sliced potatoes into a waiting can.

These oranges peel readily and the peels come
off in large pieces because the oranges were
parboiled enough to loosen the skins, not
enough to cook the orange.

Onions cause no tears if scalding water is poured
over them. They can be quartered quickly
when the top and root are first sliced off.

Cole slaw is quickly "assembled" when needed
if the ingredients are prepared ahead of time.
Final assembly must be done just before
serving to have a crisp product.

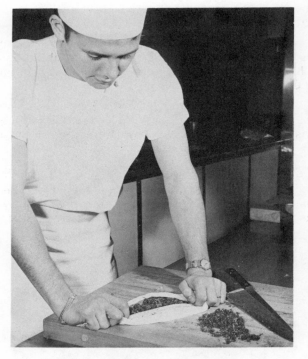

Parsley can be crisped and dried quickly by
rolling it in cheesecloth, placing it under
running water, then ringing it out while still
in the cheesecloth. Excellent for French
frying.

Why use one French knife to chop onions when two
will double the cutting action?

CASE TWO

Situation: A study of a vegetable preparation section of a hotel restaurant showed that 35 per cent of the time was spent in peeling potatoes. The potatoes were peeled rapidly but the eyeing operation could not keep pace with the peeling machine.

Results of analysis: A special table was designed for the eyeing operation which permitted the women doing the work to be seated. The table was provided with pans, one in front of each worker to catch the trimmings, and a hole made in the table through which eyed potatoes could be easily dropped into G.I. cans.

The workers were delighted. Seating the women saved 14 per cent energy expenditure. Productions went up 30 per cent with less resulting fatigue. When one vegatable woman resigned it was not necessary to replace her. Savings totaled $950 a year. The table cost $50.00 to build.

CASE THREE

Situation: A hotel formerly peeled its potatoes by machine. When the machine wore out, however, it was not replaced. Potatoes were again peeled by hand. Data from both the hand and machine operations were compared as to cost of peeling and eyeing 100 pounds of identical grade potatoes.

Results of comparison:

	Cost When Hand Peeled	Cost When Machine Peeled
Number of workers used	3	1
Average daily wage rate per worker	$7.00	$7.00
Time of operation (minutes)	22	22
Total man-minutes	66	19
Waste in peeling per 100 lbs.	26	28
Cost per 100 pounds	$ .963	$ .273

Since hand peeling cost more than three and one-half times as much as mechanical peeling, no time was wasted in the purchase of another mechanical potato peeler.

CASE FOUR

Situation: A certain hotel served an average of 500 room service breakfasts from about 7:00 to 11:00 A.M. However, most of the soiled dishes did not reach the dishwashing station until about 10 o'clock. In the dining room the bulk of the service took place from 8:30 to 9:30. The complete dishwashing crew reported for work at 7:00.

At night, after the dining room closed, only the dance room remained open. It closed about 2:00 in the morning; a complete dishwashing crew remained until 2:00 o'clock.

Results of analysis: Employees were not needed on the morning shift until 9:00 A.M. On the night shift only one of the two personnel was required between 9:00 P.M. and 2:00 A.M. One-third of the employees were not needed. When these were eliminated $10,000 of payroll was saved per year.

CASE FIVE

Situation: The accounting procedure of a large hotel required that restaurant checks be totaled twice by the dining room cashier and again by the night revenue controller.

Results of analysis: Accounting procedure was changed so that the restaurant cashier totaled checks once except in instances where a page of the restaurant control report failed to balance. The position of night revenue control was eliminated by incorporating it in day revenue control. Fifteen hundred dollars in salaries were saved per year.

CASE SIX

Situation: A new municipal regulation required that a fire watch be maintained at all public functions in hotels of a particular city. The regulation was sprung on the management of a particular hotel in the midst of a public function. Casting about for someone to fill the watch a plumber who had not gone home was pressed into service. The plumber continued the job of fire watch at time-and-a-half wages. No one thought to hire less expensive labor.

Results of analysis: Another employee was hired to do the job at a savings of $750 per year in payroll costs.

CASE SEVEN

Situation: In a particular hotel, outside contractors had previously been engaged to paint a block of rooms. Now painters on the hotel staff do the same job.

Results of analysis: The hotel's staff required twice as many man hours to paint a given area as did the crew of the outside contractor. Although the hotel painters received considerably less wages per hour, the total cost of painting was almost as great using hotel painters as it was to engage the outside contractor. Including the fact that the hotel painters took longer and consequently reduced revenue by keeping rooms unrentable, the outside contractor may have been more economical. It was concluded that poor supervision and training accounted for the inefficiency of the hotel painters.

A simple form (illustrated on the following page) was devised which could be used for aiding supervision of all maintenance employees.

The form permits the supervisor to appraise the industriousness of the employee and to spot soldiering on the job. For example, if an employee takes an hour and a half to replace a washer in a faucet, probably one of three things is wrong. The employee is loafing; he is incompetent; or the whole faucet needs replacing.

CASE EIGHT

Situation: In one hotel each maid's daily quota of rooms to be cleaned was 16. A check on the maids' performance showed an average of about 13 rooms cleaned per day. Extra payments had to be made for rooms cleaned above 13.

```
┌────────────────────────────────────────────────────────────────────┐
│                                                                      │
│                          X Y Z  HOTEL                                │
│                          JOB  TICKET                                 │
│                                                                      │
│                                                    19_____       │
│        _____                                       │
│        Name of Employee                            Date              │
│                                                    _____   │
│        _____                                       │
│        Time No.                                    Location          │
│                                                    _____   │
│        _____                                       │
│        Time Job Commenced                 Time Job Concluded         │
│                                                                      │
│        Describe nature of job briefly: _____    │
│                                                                      │
│        _____ │
│                                                                      │
└────────────────────────────────────────────────────────────────────┘
```

Results of analysis: A study showed that 20 per cent of the maids' working time was spent in getting linen from the linen room. This was caused by a linen shortage which did not allow a proper stocking of the floor linen closets. A par system of stocking linen and other supplies was installed for floor closets. The maids were then able to report to their floors and to work uninterrupted. Maids were able to do their quota of 16 rooms and were saved considerable exasperation. Extra rooms payments were eliminated. Guests' complaints subsided. Wear and tear on the service elevator was reduced and the hotel saved 10 per cent of the housekeeping payroll.

CASE NINE

Situation: It was believed necessary in a certain hotel to employ three bellboys during the morning watch. One spent 1-1/2 hours of the morning in picking up the mail at the post office and doing duties other than bellhopping.

Results of analysis: It was found that the man who relieved the elevator operator had a lull of almost two hours at approximately mail time. He was assigned the job of picking up the mail and doing the other extra tasks of the third bellboy. The third bellboy was not needed and $600 was saved in payroll costs per year.

CASE TEN

Situation: With a problem of morning and evening rush hours, management of a medium-sized hotel considered it necessary to schedule three passenger elevators at practically all times except during the midnight shift.

Results of analysis: By computing the relationship between passenger traffic demands and potential round trips per hour, it was determined that two elevators could handle the passenger traffic. However, it was necessary at times in the evening periods to detain "up" cars two to four seconds at the ground floor to avoid dispatching sparsely filled elevators. This delay was unimportant to passengers already loaded and saved considerable waiting time on the part of guests coming into the lobby. By eliminating one car, $2,500 in operators' salaries was saved without impairing guest service.

CASE ELEVEN

Situation: Management of a hotel which has two entrances stationed a doorman at the main entrance and believed it necessary to station a doorman at the other entrance (an annex entrance) at least part time.

Result of analysis: An analysis showed that room guest traffic was negligible at the annex entrance and that the entrance was used mainly by male luncheon guests. The part-time service of a doorman at the annex entrance appeared to do more harm than good, since in the guests' minds it was inconsistent service. Doorman service at this entrance was discontinued with a saving of about $400 per year.

CASE TWELVE

Situation: Service elevators in a hotel could not meet traffic demands at the relief and meal periods of the operators and it was found necessary to employ a relief operator.

Results of analysis: Department heads were aided in scheduling their staff to eliminate unnecessary travel. The cars could then be shut down alternately for short periods to provide for relief time for elevator operators during lull periods. Tremendous waste of time of the staff in waiting for elevators was substantially eliminated. The relief operator saving was $720 per year.

CASE THIRTEEN

The front office of a hotel appeared to be overstaffed and yet had difficulty in getting the work done.

Results of analysis: Analysis of the jobs of room clerk and cashier showed a large portion of time lost through poor work planning. It was found that too often the room clerk and cashier wished to occupy the same space at the same time. By rearranging the front office and moving the assistant manager and reservation clerk from a second-floor office to a space in the lobby near the front office, $50.00 a week in salaries was eliminated. The reservation clerk or the assistant manager was available to cover relief and help in periods of unusual activity. Moreover, the reservation clerk could perform additional duties such as typing of front office accounts and rack supplies.

CASE FOURTEEN

Situation: In one dining room it was found that the average production per waiter fell three covers below that which reasonably could be expected.

Results of analysis: Each waiter was given an additional day off per week. As a result each waiter could do more covers per day and his average daily earnings were higher. The hotel saved $800 per year. Its service did not suffer and the waiters earned approximately the same in five days as they formerly did in six.

CASE FIFTEEN

Situation: A restaurant maintained a staff of five bus boys. It appeared that only four were needed.

Results of analysis: It was found true that four boys could handle all bus boy tasks. When one boy left the remaining crew readily absorbed his work. Management saved $900 per year.

CASE SIXTEEN

Situation: Management of a certain hotel was very payroll conscious. It kept the hotel staff at a minimum. However, an analysis of the kitchen payroll showed excessive overtime.

Results of analysis: It was found that the present employees could not complete all the work required in normal working hours. Two employees were hired to reduce the tremendous pressure on the minimum staff. This eliminated most of the overtime payments with a reduction in aggregate salary expense.

CHAPTER 12

The Harris, Kerr, Forster Payroll Cost Control System[1]

The firm of Harris, Kerr, Forster and Company, accounting specialists, has developed a labor cost control system which has proved effective in many hotels, clubs, and other institutions. It is called a Payroll Pre-Control System since emphasis is placed on the forecasting and budgeting of labor requirements. Through the generosity of this firm their system is presented here in abbreviated form.

The purpose of the system is to achieve maximum utilization of manpower through planning, coordination and control of personnel. The system involves setting work standards, forecasting volume of business and matching labor requirements with the business volume. It is a "cycle of control" since it begins with planning, then compares forecasted results with actual results and finally arranges for corrective action. Since at least 50 per cent of the jobs in the average hotel require variable scheduling of personnel, much of the savings that result from precontrol come from scheduling employees to fit the actual work loads. The determination of production standards for each job also accounts for increased personnel efficiency.

ELEMENTS OF THE LABOR PRE-CONTROL SYSTEM

The pre-control system has six major elements:

1. The determination of work performance standards for each job classification within a particular establishment. These standards are expressed in terms of the "physical" unit rather than "dollar" units. Examples are: number of occupied rooms per employee, number of food covers served per restaurant employee, number of laundry pieces processed per laundry employee, number of rooms cleaned per maid. The physical unit does not change as does the dollar unit and is more reliable as a unit of measurement and control. Work standards are determined through job analysis, analysis of past performance, and comparison with established standards of employee productivity for various jobs. Any change in the job itself, of course, necessitates a review of the job standard.

   The job standards are assembled in table form and show the personnel requirements by job and job group for the various normal volumes of work in a particular department. The tables are called: "Range Tables of Staffing Guides at Varying Volume Levels."

2. The consideration of each job as a unit. Every job is assigned a number which represents it alone and a particular work schedule and a particular work area or station. Each employee is assigned a job number and no employee can be placed on the regular payroll unless a management approved job number is open. All jobs are classified and grouped in each department according to their degree of variability in work volume. Jobs such as chambermaids, waiters, waitresses, warewashers, and elevator operators which experience much variation in work load are termed "prime variables" and given special attention.

3. A regular system of forecasting work loads by a forecasting committee. Work loads are forecast in three stages:

   a. By months for a year in advance.

   b. Regular weekly forecasts for the coming week.

   c. Regular daily refinements and modifications of the weekly estimates for three days in advance.

---

[1] With permission of Harris, Kerr, Forster & Company.

4. A formal system of accurate daily reporting of payroll by each department head. The report is a record of the number of full-time employees by job classification. It does not include dollars of payroll since, again, all the standards are expressed in terms of physical units rather than money.

5. A formal system of control for the hiring and use of extra employees and overtime work. Department heads must request all overtime or extra labor before the labor is hired. The requisition itself, once approved by management, serves as authority for the payroll department to make the necessary wage payments.

6. A regular review of the results of the over-all system. A daily report is made by each department head of all time worked in terms of equivalent full-time employees and by job classification or group. A summary report is then compiled at the end of each payroll week. This is sent to the general manager and all department heads. It shows the number of employees over or under the standard number of employees set for each department and for the hotel as a whole.

The weekly report constitutes an evaluation of the results of the over-all system: the number of personnel days over or under the standards set as a result of the forecasts.

The pre-control payroll system sets job standards, forecasts the number of man days that will be needed, then reviews to see how many man days were used over or under the forecasted needs.

On the following pages we see the system as it operates through its paper forms. Study the forms and the comments on each. If necessary, go back to the six elements of the over-all plan.

1. Here is the weekly report which goes to the general manager and to each department head. It is the summary sheet showing the results of the pre-control plan for each department. For example, it is seen that Front Office used exactly the number of man days as forecasted, while Housekeeping used 1.4 man days more than was budgeted. Based on this report remedial action can be taken to bring the man days used in line with the forecasted man days.

HOTEL ____Y____

SUMMARY OF DEPARTMENTAL PAYROLL COMPARISON REPORTS

FOR WEEK ENDED __June 14__

Department	Average Number of Employees on Duty		Difference Under-[Over]		Equivalent Payroll Cost
	Actual	Standard	Employees	Percentage of Standard	
Front Office	5.5	5.5	-		
Housekeeping	22.1	20.7	[1.4]		
Front Service	14.6	15.1	.5		
Food Preparation	27.0	25.5	[1.5]		
Steward	25.0	26	1.		
Food Storeroom	2.5	2.5	-		
Food Service Dining Room	10.2	10.2	-		
Room Service	5.5	5.5	-		
Coffee Shop	12.9	12.4	[.5]		
Banquets	20.2	18.7	[1.5]		
Total Food Service	48.8	46.8	[2.]		
Beverage Preparation	7.2	7.2	-		
Lounge Service	7.6	7.2	[.4]		
Telephone	4.7	4.7	-		
All others	47.5	47.5	-		
Totals	212.5	208.7	[3.8]		

VOLUME STATISTICS

Total Sales	$40,200.00
Occupied Rooms	2,632
Food Covers Served	10,210
Beverage Sales	$ 6,600.00

2. This is a job number control list. Each job has an assigned number which represents a specific work area or station and a definite work schedule. All personnel are assigned a job number which represents their station and work schedule. Only jobs that have numbers can be filled.

HOTEL ___Y___

JOB NUMBER CONTROL LIST

STEWARD

Job or Clock Card Number	Job Classification	Work Area or Station	Work Schedule
220	Warewasher	Coffee Shop	7:00 A.M. - 4:00 P.M.
221	Warewasher	Coffee Shop	11:00 A.M. - 8:00 P.M.
222	Warewasher	Coffee Shop	4:30 P.M. - 1:30 A.M.
223	Warewasher, Relief	Coffee Shop	Variable
224	Open		
225	Open		
226	Warewasher	Main Kitchen	9:00 A.M. - 6:00 P.M.
227 thru 229	Warewashers	Main Kitchen	11:00 A.M. - 8:00 P.M.
230 thru 232	Warewashers	Main Kitchen	12:00 Noon - 9:00 P.M.
233 thru 236	Warewasher	Main Kitchen	1:00 P.M. - 10:00 P.M.
237 thru 242	Warewashers	Main Kitchen	3:00 P.M. - 12:00 Mid.
243 thru 250	Warewashers	Main Kitchen	6:00 P.M. - 3:00 A.M.
251 and 252	Warewashers, Relief	Main Kitchen	Variable
253 and 254	Open		
255 and 256	Kitchen Cleaners		5:00 P.M. - 2:00 A.M.
257	Kitchen Cleaner		12:00 Mid. - 9:00 A.M.
258	Kitchen Cleaner, Relief		Variable
259	Open		
260	Potwasher	Main Kitchen	7:00 A.M. - 4:00 P.M.
261	Potwasher	Main Kitchen	1:00 P.M. - 10:00 P.M.
262	Potwasher	Pastry Shop	12:00 Noon - 9:00 P.M.
263	Potwasher, Relief		Variable
264	Food Runner	Coffee Shop	6:00 A.M. - 3:00 P.M.
265	Food Runner	Coffee Shop	2:30 P.M. - 11:00 P.M.
266	Runner	Main Kitchen	6:00 A.M. - 3:00 P.M.
267	Open		
268	Iceman		6:00 A.M. - 3:00 P.M.
269	Iceman		3:00 P.M. - 12:00 Mid.
270	Open		
271	Yardman		6:00 A.M. - 3:00 P.M.
272	Yardman		3:00 P.M. - 12:00 Mid.
273	Open		
274	Silver Burnisher		7:00 A.M. - 4:00 P.M.
275	Open		
276	Kitchen Steward		6:00 A.M. - 3:00 P.M.
277	Kitchen Steward		3:00 P.M. - 12:00 Mid.
278	Kitchen Steward, Banquets and Relief		Variable
279	Open		

3. This form is used by department heads for making all job changes. It goes to the payroll department for use in maintaining job number control. Use of the form assures that all job changes are made within the staffing tables as set up in the Job Number Control list.

HOTEL __Y__

WAGE AND/OR POSITION CHANGE

EMPLOYEE'S NAME____John Smith____   EFFECTIVE DATE OF CHANGE __6/15__

The records of the foregoing named employee should be changed as follows:

	From	To	Remarks
Position	Warewasher	Kitchen Steward	
Work Area	Main Kitchen	Banquets and Relief	
Work Schedule	9:00 A.M. – 6:00 P.M.	3:00 P.M. – 12:00 Mid.	
Department	Steward	Same	
Job Number	226	278	
Rate	$7.80	$8.50	
Meals	2	2	

Changed:

Clock Card_____ Earnings Record_____ Contract Card _____ Addressograph Plate _____

Approved by:

Department Head___S. Steward___   Auditor _____A.L.M.___   Manager_____T.C.____

4. The Room Occupancy Forecast is usually made by the front office manager and presented to the committee that makes the weekly forecast. The form is prepared in duplicate, one copy going to the individual responsible for forecasting the number of covers to be served in the restaurant, the second going to the Weekly Forecast Committee.

The Weekly Forecast Committee makes the Occupancy Forecast based on their additional facts. The adjusted forecast then goes to the Payroll Control Office to be used in setting up the Weekly Volume Forecast and Payroll Budget.

HOTEL ____Y____

WEEKLY ROOM OCCUPANCY FORECAST

for period ending ____June 14____

	Sun.	Mon.	Tues.	Wed.	Thurs.	Fri.	Sat.	Total For Week
Permanent	108	108	108	108	108	108	108	756
Conventions A	85	142	142	142	12	–	–	523
B				60	60	60	60	240
C					36	36		72
Total Conventions	85	142	142	202	108	96	60	835
Transients with Reservations	33	85	108	110	122	81	21	560
Transients without Reservations	18	30	45	9	40	56	50	248
Other (Employees, etc.)	8	8	8	11	11	11	8	65
Total Estimated Occupancy	252	373	411	440	389	352	247	2464
Rooms Out of Order	5	5	5	–	–	–	3	18
Rooms Vacant	183	65	24		51	88	190	598
Total Rooms Available	440	440	440	440	440	440	440	3080
Occupancy Percentage	57.2%	84.7%	93.4%	100.0%	88.5%	80.0%	56.1%	80.0%
Guest Count	300	450	500	525	470	425	300	2970

COMMENTS

5. The daily and weekly Food Cover Forecast is similar to the Room Occupancy Forecast in that it is the first approximation of the business that is expected and is made by the department head, in this case usually the Food Controller.

The Food Cover Forecast then goes to the Weekly Forecast Committee and is adjusted by them. The adjusted forecast is sent to the Payroll Controller and posted to the Volume Forecast and Payroll Budget. Delivery of the Daily Forecast is made by the Superintendent of Service to all department heads by a specified time each day.

As with the Room Occupancy Forecast the forecasted volume of business is used as a basis for determining the number of employees needed.

HOTEL _____Y_____

DAILY AND WEEKLY FOOD COVER FORECAST

FOR PERIOD ENDING   June 14

	Date	8	9	10	11	12	13	14	Total for Week
	Day	Sun.	Mon.	Tues.	Wed.	Thurs.	Fri.	Sat.	
Dining Room									
Luncheon			180	200	225	190	175	110	1080
Dinner		400	120	150	175	160	135	290	1430
Total		400	300	350	400	350	310	400	2510
Room Service									
Breakfast		60	35	50	50	65	40	20	320
Luncheon		5	10	10	20	15	10	25	95
Dinner		20	35	45	40	50	35	45	270
Total		85	80	105	110	130	85	90	685
Banquets									
Breakfast		–	–	–	30	–	–	–	30
Luncheon		–	50	85	210	80	25	115	565
Dinner		–	250	120	60	170	40	630	1270
Total		–	300	205	300	250	65	745	1865
Coffee Shop									
Breakfast		140	220	275	290	290	250	200	1665
Luncheon		–	290	300	300	285	260	290	1725
Dinner		270	110	175	190	165	150	120	1180
Total		410	620	750	780	740	660	610	4570
TOTAL FOOD COVERS		895	1300	1410	1590	1470	1120	1845	9630

6. The Volume Forecast is the summary of the Room Forecast and all of the Food Forecasts. It is made up from the Room and Food Cover Forecasts by the Payroll Control Office. The Beverage Revenue Forecast is made as a percentage of the Food Cover Forecast. The percentage used is based on past experience.

This summary sheet goes to all operating department heads as an aid in determining their personnel requirements.

The Superintendent of Service sees to it that the Volume Forecasts are distributed to the department heads.

HOTEL _____Y_____

VOLUME FORECAST

FOR PERIOD FROM _June 8_ THRU _June 14_

	Date	8	9	10	11	12	13	14	Total for Week
	Day	Sun.	Mon.	Tues.	Wed.	Thurs.	Fri.	Sat.	
Rooms Forecast									
Occupied Rooms		252	373	411	440	389	352	247	2464
Occupancy Percentage		57.2%	84.7%	93.4%	100.0%	88.5%	80.0%	56.1%	80.0%
Guest Count		300	450	500	525	470	425	300	2970
Arrivals (Rooms)		136	121	70	64	90	20	35	536
Departures (Rooms)		53	–	32	35	141	57	140	458
Food Cover Forecast									
Dining Room									
Luncheon		–	180	200	225	190	175	150	1080
Dinner		400	120	150	175	160	135	290	1430
Total		400	300	350	400	350	310	400	2510
Room Service									
Breakfast		60	35	50	50	65	40	20	320
Luncheon		5	10	10	20	15	10	25	95
Dinner		20	35	45	40	50	35	45	270
Total		85	80	105	110	130	85	90	685
Banquets									
Breakfast		–	–	–	30	–	–	–	30
Luncheon		–	50	85	210	80	25	115	565
Dinner		–	250	120	60	170	40	630	1270
Total		–	300	205	300	250	65	745	1865
Coffee Shop									
Breakfast		140	220	275	290	290	250	200	1665
Luncheon		–	290	300	300	285	260	290	1725
Dinner		270	110	175	190	165	150	120	1180
Total		410	620	750	780	740	660	610	4570
TOTAL FOOD COVERS		895	1300	1410	1590	1470	1120	1845	9630
Beverage Revenue Forecast									
Bar A		$ –	$325	$ 460	$475	$400	$400	$ 720	$2780
Bar B		220	430	550	500	425	530	1065	$3720
Total Beverage Forecast		$220	$755	$1010	$975	$825	$930	$1785	$6500

7. These Range Tables give estimates of the number of personnel who will be needed at varying volumes of work. The tables are used as guides in budgeting the number of personnel needed and also to evaluate performance results.

Since every hotel has a different layout and type of service, the Range Table must be made for the individual hotel. Work standards are developed from an analysis of past performance and reference to an established standard of employee productivity. Each department has its own Range Table.

HOTEL ___Y___

TENTATIVE RANGE TABLES OF STAFFING GUIDES AT VARYING VOLUME LEVELS

STEWARD

Normal Volume Range of Total Weekly Food Covers

Job Classification or Group	Hours In Work Week	Upper Limit ←	10,000 Employees		9,600 Employees		9,200 Employees		→ Lower Limit
			On Staff	On Duty	On Staff	On Duty	On Staff	On Duty	
Warewashers	40		21.2	15.1	20.2	14.5	19.2	13.7	
All Other									
Kitchen Cleaners	40		2.0	1.4	2.0	1.4	2.0	1.4	
Potwashers	40		3.0	2.1	3.0	2.1	3.0	2.1	
Food Runners	40		1.7	1.2	1.5	1.0	1.5	1.0	
Icemen	40		1.5	1.0	1.5	1.0	1.5	1.0	
Yardmen	40		2.4	2.1	2.4	2.1	2.4	2.1	
Silver Burnisher	40		1.0	.7	1.0	.7	1.0	.7	
Kitchen Stewards	40		3.0	2.1	3.0	2.1	3.0	2.1	
Total All Other			14.6	10.6	14.4	10.4	14.4	10.4	
TOTAL STEWARDS			35.8	25.7	34.6	24.9	33.6	24.1	

8. This form is used by department heads in planning for their day-to-day requirements of personnel and also by the Payroll Controller in measuring and evaluating daily production.

These tables are developed from the Range Tables to show daily averages and, of course, must be prepared for the individual department.

HOTEL ___Y___

SCHEDULE OF STAFFING GUIDES AND DAILY OUTPUT STANDARDS

STEWARD

Normal Volume Range of Total Food Covers		Warewashers		All Other		Total	
Weekly	Daily Average	Employees On Duty	Output	Employees On Duty	Output	Employees On Duty	Output
9,600	1,371	14.5	94.5	10.4	131.8	24.9	55.0
10,000	1,430	15.1	94.7	10.6	134.9	25.7	55.6

9. The Volume Forecast and Payroll Budget form is a further step in payroll planning for the coming week. It is made by the Payroll Control Office for the department heads and shows the number of covers anticipated for each day of the week and the number of personnel required to service the particular volume of business. It is made up for each department.

HOTEL _____Y_____

VOLUME FORECAST AND PAYROLL BUDGET

FOR WEEK OF ___June 8___

STEWARD

Food Cover Forecast for Week

	Sun.	Mon.	Tues.	Wed.	Thurs.	Fri.	Sat.	Total for Week
Main Kitchen								
Regular Covers	485	380	455	510	480	395	490	3195
Banquet Covers	–	300	205	300	250	65	745	1865
Total Main Kitchen	485	680	660	810	730	460	1235	5060
Coffee Shop Covers	410	620	750	780	740	660	610	4570
Total Food Covers	895	1300	1410	1590	1470	1120	1845	9630
Warewashers On Duty	9.5	13.8	14.9	16.8	15.6	11.9	19.5	14.6

Payroll Budget For Week

Job Classification	Planned Staff
Warewashers	14.6
All Others	110.7
Total Staff	25.3

10. The Daily Room Occupancy Forecast is used by the department heads in planning for the day-to-day personnel needs. It is an adjusted forecast made every day for three days in advance. It is delivered to the department heads by a specified time daily.

HOTEL _____Y_____
DAILY ROOM OCCUPANCY FORECAST

	Date	June 9	June 10	June 11	June 12
	Day	Today	Tuesday	Wednesday	Thursday
Previous Night's Count		263	393	435	440
Reservations		155	49	66	82
Arrivals Without Reservations		38	15	–	18
Employees and Other		–	–	3	–
Estimated Departures		63	22	64	140
Total Estimated Occupancy		393	435	440	400
Occupancy Percentage		89.3%	98.8%	100.0%	90.9%
Guest Count		484	525	525	480

COMMENTS

11. A Daily Personnel Report is a record of all time worked in terms of man days. It is filled out by the individual department head and sent to the Payroll Control Office. The department head posts the actual time worked in all job categories for each day. Notice that time worked is expressed in terms of man days broken down into regular, overtime, and extra-employment.

HOTEL ___ Y ___

STEWARD

DAILY PERSONNEL REPORT

DAY __ Monday __   DATE __ June 9 __   SIGNED __ A. Steward __
                                                                        Department Head

Job Classification or Group	Equivalent Full-Time Employees (Compute to Nearest 1/8th)				Absent with Pay	Temporary Assignment	
	Regular	Overtime	Extra	Total		Time	Job
Warewashers							
Coffee Shop	3			3			
Main Kitchen	7	5/8	2	9-5/8		1	Kitchen Cleaner
Total Warewashers	10	5/8	2	12-5/8			
All Other							
Kitchen Cleaners	2			2	1		Vacation
Potwashers	2			2			
Food Runners	1			1			
Icemen	1	3/8		1-3/8			
Yardmen	2			2			
Silver Burnisher	1			1			
Kitchen Stewards	2			2			
Total All Other	11	3/8		11-3/8			
TOTAL STAFF ON DUTY	21	1	2	24			
TOTAL EMPLOYEES OFF DUTY	9						
TOTAL STAFF	30						

12. The Extra Personnel Requisition form serves as a control on extra labor requirements and encourages planning for such labor. Before any extra employees can be hired this form must go to the manager for approval. The approved form is returned to the department head and is his authority for hiring the extra labor.

HOTEL ____Y____

EXTRA PERSONNEL REQUISITION

Department_ Steward_

DATE EXTRA LABOR REQUIRED _ June 9_   Signed _____
                                                                          Department Head

| Extra Labor Requested | | Number of Employees | | |
Job Classification	Function or Room Assignment	Requested	Approved	Remarks
Warewashers	F.N.O.W. -- Blue Room	3	2	
	(250 expected)			

Date Approved _ June 9_   Signed ____ A. Manager ____
                                                         Manager or Representative

13. The Requisition for Overtime Authorization is similar in purpose to the Extra Personnel Requisition: it encourages planning and is a control in that the manager must approve overtime work in advance.

HOTEL ___Y___

REQUISITION FOR OVERTIME AUTHORIZATION

Department _____Steward_____

Time Card Number ___268___   Name of Employee __John - Iceman__

Job Title ___Iceman___   Date Overtime Worked __6/6/52__

State Reason in Detail for Overtime ___Ice machine broke down. Engineer estimates it will take___

___about 2 hours to repair.___

No. of Overtime Hours Required ___1-1/2___   Signed ___A Steward___

                                                Approved __A. Representative__
                                                          Manager or Representative

---

Began Overtime Work at ___3:00 P.M.___   Finished Overtime Work at ___6:00 P.M.___

Total Overtime Hours Worked ___3___   Overtime Hourly Wage Rate ___$1.34___

Total Overtime Wages ___$4.02___

                                                Signed ___A. Steward___
                                                          Department Head

14. This summary form is a compilation of the actual volume worked the preceding day. It is made by the Auditor's Office. It is a breakdown by job classification or group showing the number of employees for each grouping and also the number of guests, food covers, beverage revenue and total revenue for the hotel. It is used by the Payroll Control Office as an over-all picture of the labor results as compared with the production for a particular day.

HOTEL _____Y_____

AUDITOR'S DAILY VOLUME STATISTICS REPORT

DAY __Monday__   Date ___6/9___

Occupied Rooms

Permanent	108
Transient	268
Employees	8

Total Occupied Rooms   384

Guest Count   492

Food Covers

Dining Room	295
Room Service	76
Banquets	332
Coffee Shop	657

Total Food Covers   1, 360

Beverage Revenue

Lounge Bar	$ 340.00
All Other	419.00

Total Beverage Revenue $ 759.00

Total Hotel Revenue $ 5, 125.00

Please deliver to Payroll Controller by 12:00 noon

15. The Production Analysis form is a daily record of units of output by job classification or group which shows the number of employees who were used to perform a particular volume of work. The number of employees is divided into the total volume of work for each classification and the result is the output per employee, an excellent performance measurement by department.

HOTEL ___Y___

PRODUCTION ANALYSIS

FOR THE WEEK ENDED ___June 14___

Classification	Sunday			Monday			Tuesday			etc.
	Empl.	Vol.	Output	Empl.	Vol.	Output	Empl.	Vol.	Output	
Food Preparation										
Chefs and Cooks	10.7	880	82.2	12.2	1360	111.4	12.5	1465	117.2	
Pantry	6.0	880	146.6	7.1	1360	191.5	7.3	1465	200.6	
All Others	5.2	880	169.2	6.5	1360	209.2	6.5	1465	225.3	
Total	21.9	880	40.1	25.8	1360	52.7	26.3	1465	55.7	
Steward										
Warewashers	10.5	880	83.8	11.6	1360	117.2	13.4	1465	109.3	
All Others	8.3	880	106.0	11.4	1360	119.2	12.0	1465	122.0	
Total	18.8	880	46.8	23.0	1360	59.1	25.4	1465	57.6	

The operation of the Pre-Cost Control System can be traced through the use of the forms on the preceding pages. It is seen that the system utilizes three agencies: the department heads who make the first forecast; the forecasting committee that adjusts and refines the forecast; and the Payroll Controller who coordinates the system and prepares the operating results for analysis and remedial action by general management and the department heads. The system is "pre-controlled" in that the number of personnel who will be needed is predicted ahead of actual utilization.

The prediction proceeds by four steps:

1. A business forecast for the ensuing week is made by the department head.

2. This forecast is adjusted by the forecasting committee.

3. Based on the business forecast and using productivity standards for the various jobs, the number of personnel needed is predicted.

4. After the forecasted period is over, the actual number of personnel used is compared with the amount that was budgeted.

Control of extra labor or overtime labor is achieved by requiring that prior approval be received from management for their employment. The total process is a continuous one, review and adjustment being built into the system. Work standards change as new methods, equipment, and layout are introduced. Labor usage is tied directly to work volume. All in all the system represents a marked advance in management in the hospitality field. While the system would not be used in its entirety in a small operation, the principles are applicable to any hospitality or institutional operation be it a private club of 100 members, a 50-bed hospital, or a 1,000-room hotel.

CHAPTER 13

Defining and Measuring Morale

Morale is the complex of feelings which accompany and influence an act. The morale of a dish-washer or a manager is dependent upon such factors as his philosophy of life and the basic energy he has available for confronting the problems of his job. It is also dependent upon the level of his ambition at the moment, and, in general, his attitudes toward his work, his supervisors, and the working conditions.

The level of morale is a valve which controls enthusiasm and creative capacity. In addition to determining what act will occur, it is an important factor in how efficiently that act will be performed.

Maintenance of morale is a management responsibility. Management cannot "blame" employees who have poor morale, nor can management reasonably expect morale to take care of itself. Manage-ment, if it is to be management, must have means for analyzing morale and for taking steps to keep it at a high level. This is a continuing process, one which is never completed.

It cannot be assumed, of course, that management will be able to correct attitudes which are deep-seated in certain of their personnel. The range of attitudes which affect morale and which can be affected by management has limits. It is within these limits that management's responsibilities lie. Management can do little that will change attitudes of pervasive suspicion which have been a part of a personality for years. On the other hand, quality of first-line supervision, which has been found to affect morale more than any other factor in work, can be controlled by management. Probably management's first function is that of arranging psychological and material conditions so that personnel can secure personal satisfaction which leads to efficient production.

CHARACTERIZING MORALE

High morale can be characterized as a condition evidenced in:

1. Efficient output.

2. Genuine cooperation because of a desire to work together.

3. Interest in the work.

4. Satisfaction from the work.

5. A feeling of "belonging" to the organization.

6. A feeling of security and faith in the future of the business, that the organization is worthwhile, is progressing, and will reward the individuals.

7. Respect for other employees of the same and lower classification level as well as respect for management.

8. Low turnover.

Conversely, indications which may be symptomatic of low morale are:

1. An unusual number of disciplinary problems and grievances.

2. Low output, featherbedding or slowing down.

3. Unusually high absenteeism and tardiness rates.

4. Lack of interest and inefficiency.

5. High sickness rates.

6. Evidences of fatigue without apparent cause.

7. High turnover, bickering and internal fighting.

Effective management integrates the "scientific management" needs of the organization on the one hand with the "human relations" needs of the individual on the other hand. This philosophy, to be sure, arises in part from an "humanitarian" bias; however, in strictly hardheaded, dollars' and cents' terms, it also makes sense. Organizations that cannot meet the needs of the individuals cannot in the long run hope to compete successfully. The reason such organizations cannot succeed is simply the fact that the effect of poor morale, poor attitudes, and lack of cooperation on the part of employees is like an insidious disease that gradually and consistently saps the strength and vigor of any organization.

THE NEEDS OF WORKERS

It can be assumed that man is a wanting animal who strives constantly to satisfy his needs. His needs are hierarchical in nature and can be described as follows:

1. Physiological and Safety Needs: These are man's most basic and necessary needs. When bread is not available, man lives for bread alone. When he is tired, he needs sleep more than anything else. When his physiological needs are satisfied, they no longer are important to him. These needs help man exist, but they do not motivate him except on a primitive level.

   The next highest order of needs is safety needs such as the need for protection against danger, threat, and deprivation. Man is dependent and he fears threat to himself. He therefore is motivated to protect himself. On the job, threats of firing employees, discrimination, and recrimination are powerful motivators. He will work hard to protect himself from such threats, especially if he is not certain of finding another job quickly.

2. Social Needs: Once a man's physiological needs are satisfied and he does not fear for his physical welfare, his social needs take over as motivators of his behavior. He seeks the giving and receiving of friendships, acceptance, belonging, and love. Man intuitively seeks "groups." Management knows of these needs; frequently, however, management tries to discourage groups and to dictate against their formation.

3. Ego Needs: At the highest level are the egoistic needs which do not emerge as motivators until the lower needs are satisfied. They fall into two kinds:

   a. Needs relative to one's self-esteem -- needs for self-respect, confidence, independence, achievement, competence, and knowledge.

   b. Needs relative to one's reputation -- needs for status, recognition, appreciation, and respect from others.

   Man's egoistic needs rarely are completely satisfied. Man constantly seeks their fulfillment. They are what drive him toward individuality, creativity, responsibility, and self-fulfillment.

The paradox of industrial organizations lies in the fact that while material goods are produced in torrents few opportunities are offered for the satisfaction of egoist needs. Mass production, for example, gives little heed to human motivation. Yet a common complaint of management is, "Why aren't people more productive? We pay good wages, provide good working conditions, have excellent fringe benefits, and still they only put forth minimum effort." The problem of course lies in a need for organizations to provide outlets not only for the satisfaction of the physiological and safety needs, but also satisfaction of the higher-level needs.

WHAT ARE THE MOTIVATORS FOR WORK

Important research studies in the area of motivation[1] have enabled us to redefine objectives in providing benefits and opportunities to workers. It is unrealistic to talk about the things that bring satisfactions to workers in the same breath as we talk about the things that bring dissatisfactions to workers. It is true that workers who are satisfied with their jobs are not dissatisfied with them. The reverse is not true, however: Just because a worker is not dissatisfied does not mean that he is satisfied.

The things that lead to satisfaction or dissatisfaction are quite different. Dissatisfaction arises when a worker's physical, physiological, and safety needs are not met -- that is, he is dissatisfied if his working conditions are not good, if he lacks job security, if his pay is low, if company policies are unfair,

---

[1]Herzberg, F., Mausner, B., and Snyderman, B., The Motivation To Work. New York: John Wiley & Sons, 1959.

or if the work is too difficult or hazardous. Having these conditions improved, however, will not make him happy, but only relieve him of his dissatisfaction. It is interesting that the factors making for dissatisfaction are the factors that relate to the "tangibles" that organizations offer their employees, e.g., pay and "fringe benefits." Pay and fringe benefits are vital, but they are not the whole story. In organizations with high-powered incentive wage systems, for example, management has often equated satisfaction with money and has been rudely awakened.

Satisfactions are of a more "intangible" nature. They come about from allowing individuals to maximize their highest needs for sociability and ego attainment. A person is satisfied if he experiences achievement and the possibility of growth in a company, if he has the feeling that his ideas are worthwhile, if he feels that he is allowed to realize his creative potentials, and if he feels that he is a vital, self-expressive part of the organization. Satisfactions do not just happen. They are the gradual result of a long-term emphasis on human relations in organizations.

MEASURING MORALE

Many a manager of a hotel or restaurant has gone for years assuming he knows how the employees feel about their jobs and about management. Then one day he is rudely awakened by the threat of a strike, by an inordinately high labor turnover, an unusual number of absentees, or by a pile-up of grievances. Should not a manager be aware of the sentiment of his organization as well as the food costs, the percentage figures of room occupancy, or the efficiency of a new boiler? The way his employees feel about their jobs is probably more important to the success of the enterprise than are the cost figures. In fact, cost figures are in a large part a reflection of how the employees feel about both their jobs and management. How can the manager or personnel director keep his finger on the pulse of morale?

The job of personnel is one of continuing research. The manager or his representative, the personnel director, must keep a variety of indices to the ebb and flow of a personnel program. The more obvious forms of dissatisfaction are manifested by overt expressions of hostility such as the strike. If the personnel man watches the more subtle indices, he has the information to correct poor morale before it reaches a danger point.

LABOR TURNOVER AS AN INDICATION OF MORALE

One of the best indicators of a good or bad personnel program is the labor turnover rate. As defined by the United States Department of Labor it is either the percentage of total employees hired in a month or the percentage of total employees leaving in a month. Whichever percentage is smaller is the turnover rate, in this case called the "net turnover rate."

In figuring the net turnover rate the following data must be secured:

1. The number of employees at the beginning of the month.

2. The number of employees at the end of the month.

3. The number of quits (termination of employment initiated by employee).

4. The number of discharges (termination of employment at the will of the employer, with prejudice to the employee because of some fault on the part of the employee).

5. The number of layoffs (termination of employee at the will of the employer without prejudice to the employee).

6. The number of total separations (found by adding 3, 4 and 5).

7. The number of accessions.

To illustrate the computation of the net turnover rate, consider a restaurant which averages 100 employees for a particular month. Suppose 10 persons were hired, 10 quit, 2 were discharged, none laid off. The rates would be as follows:

Accession rate	$\frac{10}{100}$ Or 10%	Layoff rate	0
Quit rate	$\frac{10}{100}$ Or 10%	Discharge rate	$\frac{2}{100}$ Or 2%

The total separation would then be 12% and the accession rate 10%. Since the accession rate is smaller it is the net turnover rate, or 10%.

Monthly turnover rates are not corrected for the number of days in the month. This can be accomplished by computing what are called "equivalent annual rates." This computation merely takes into account the different number of days in a month in reaching an annual rate. Thus for a month of 30 days the factor is 12.17; for a month of 31 days, 11.77; for 28 days, 13.04; for 29 days, 12.62.

Using the monthly turnover rate of the restaurant in the illustration, we would find that if this rate continued our annual turnover rate would be over 120 per cent. This is not at all uncommon in the hotel and restaurant business.

Turnover is costly in dollars and cents. Robert F. Brydle of Statler Hotels, vice-president then of personnel, stated that in 1951 his organization had a turnover of 127 per cent. The cost ranged from $50.00 to $150.00, or $162,000 for the chain. The cost of replacing a salesman is figured to be between two and three thousand dollars; the cost of executive search and hiring may run several times as much.

The costs of turnover are sometimes overlooked. Some of the costs are hidden. To itemize just a few may emphasize the importance of labor turnover from a dollar and cents' point of view.

Recruitment costs -- newspaper and other advertising costs.

Induction costs -- clerical help, interviewer's time, time of department head, stationery, costs of checking references, physical examination.

Training costs -- time of trainer, cost of training materials, supervisor's time.

Production losses -- losses involved while new employee learns to perform efficiently. Losses entailed by other employees in having to work with or teach new employee. Loss of patronage because of poor service. Loss of production between decision to quit and actually quitting.

Breakage costs -- breakage of dishes, breakage of equipment due to lack of skill.

Accident costs -- higher accident rates of unskilled employees reflected in direct or indirect workmen's compensation insurance cost.

Over-all costs -- breakdown of social organization which is relected in over-all loss of morale and efficiency.

Total turnover costs run from a minimum of about $5.00 for a reinducted kitchen helper to several thousands for a top executive.

High turnover rates in themselves do not necessarily mean a deficient personnel program. First of all rates must be considered relative to the hotel and restaurant business. Turnover rates are notoriously high in this field, although where careful attention is given to the personnel program annual rates come down to 10 or 15 per cent.

Turnover rates must be viewed in the perspective of the locale and of general business and world conditions. Turnover rate is much higher during and following a period of war. One would also expect a higher turnover rate in a metropolitan district than in a smaller city or town. World conditions are reflected in turnover rates. The confusion and restlessness of the Chinese coolie probably has elements of the unrest of the waiter or the reservation clerk in New Jersey. Nevertheless, the labor turnover rate when qualified in the light of these other factors is an index of morale. When there is a spurt in the labor turnover rate of a particular department, it is time for the personnel man to look into the supervision, wage rates, and other conditions of employment in that department. Likewise, when turnover jumps for the entire organization it is time to investigate.

A certain amount of turnover, say 12 to 20 per cent a year with a minimum of 5 per cent, is to be expected. Marriage, retirement, quits by employees to continue their education, sickness, or other reasons are a part of the dynamics of a healthy organization. In order to make the turnover rates more meaningful as indications of unrest, the rates should be further refined. Unavoidable separations should be listed separately from avoidable separations. Where the business is a fast-expanding one, it is probably better to keep the separation rates apart from the accession rate.

Keeping a special monthly labor turnover report tends to point up the problem to both the manager and department heads.

Turnover of personnel often occurs in but a few jobs: These jobs turn over time and again while the majority of jobs remain stable. In the Hotel Texas, Fort Worth, for example, it was found that 26 per cent of the jobs accounted for 90 per cent of the turnover. Identifying these jobs and working on them can sharply reduce turnover.

Turnover usually occurs in the first few weeks of employment. One chain found that 75 per cent of their turnover took place among employees who had been working less than six months in their hotels. If the employee could be made productive and satisfied within that period the likelihood of a good stable employee was greatly increased.

One way of drawing attention to the turnover is to compile a monthly Labor Turnover Report as illustrated below. This is sent to department heads and serves to point up the problem for both the department head and management.

LABOR TURNOVER REPORT
HOTEL SEMINOLE, JACKSONVILLE, FLA.

For the month of July, 1954

Department	No. of Employees	No. Hired This Month	Percentage
Coffee Shop	21 2/3	14	64.6*
Laundry	18	4	22.2
Personnel	4 1/2	1	22.2
Uniformed Service	31	6	19.3
Kitchen	26 1/3	3	11.3
Housekeeping	34 1/3	3	8.7
Front Office	12 1/2	1	8.0
Barber Shop	4	0	0
Banquet	9	0	0
Auditing	3	0	0
Indian Room	3 1/2	0	0
Engineering	12	0	0
Executive	4	0	0
Beverage	3 5/6	0	0
Printing	1	0	0
TOTAL	189 2/3	32	16.8

Labor turnover is expensive to the hotel, as new employees are inefficient until they learn to perform their duties. Untrained employees cannot give good service to the guests. We must try to keep our employees.

Jerome B. Temple
President

*NOTE: Unusually high percentage of Coffee Shop caused by transfer of Coffee Shop Manager, and subsequent loss of several waitresses.

ABSENTEEISM AS A MEASURE OF MORALE

As is true with labor turnover, a certain amount of absenteeism is to be expected. It is estimated that about seven million persons are ill in any given day in the United States. Some of those seven million will be your employees. The common cold probably keeps more persons from work than any other malady. It is just about as common in California as it is in New York State. It knows few geographical or personal barriers. However, in the fast-growing study of psychosomatic medicine it is being proved that a large proportion of our ills, including the common cold, is caused by the psychology of the person involved. Persons who are tense and fearful are more prone to be susceptible to colds and other diseases than are those who are relaxed and well adjusted.

Many cases of absenteeism because of sickness can now be traced directly to the morale of the place of work. In other words, sickness can be the result of a poor supervisor, poor placement, or of any of a number of other phases of a personnel program.

It was noted in the army during the war that when the work lacked interest for the soldier, or when other conditions were unfavorable, there was a marked tendency for absenteeism and sickness to occur. Similarly a room clerk who is annoyed with his supervisor is much more likely to find it necessary to stay in bed because of a headache or to take a driver's test, or to do other "important business" than if his relations with his supervisors are pleasant. Absenteeism can be an index to personnel relations.

The manager or the personnel director can often spot departments which need particular attention by keeping records of absenteeism by departments. For example, in a large metropolitan hotel it was found that whereas the absenteeism rate for all employees averaged but four per cent per day, the house-keeping department had a consistently high absenteeism rate of about ten per cent. The personnel man-ager knew that he should pay particular attention to the personnel problems of the housekeeping depart-ment.

It will be discovered that even with the best efforts absenteeism will be regularly higher in some departments than others. By keeping graphs of the number of absentees, a rough base rate can be es-tablished. Although it will change with the conditions of the labor market, it does serve as a standard on which to formulate one's thinking concerning whether or not a certain absenteeism rate is high or low.

Absenteeism rates also may be expected to follow a weekly pattern. Depending upon the weekly work schedule and the day on which pay day falls, a characteristic curve of absenteeism throughout the week is established. Other factors such as weather conditions, the effect of convention business, epi-demics, and the caliber of supervision will influence the curve without necessarily changing its basic shape.

It is an interesting piece of research for the person responsible for coordinating personnel to keep graphs of absenteeism on which are also recorded weather conditions, conventions, pay days, and local events of unusual character. It can be expected that absenteeism climbs on cloudy or cold days, that it climbs following pay day and that following the annual employees' dance a large number of persons can be expected to be sick with "colds." Such indications are helpful in formulating a program for reducing absenteeism.

The graph on the following page is the actual record of absenteeism plotted for the month of March in a large Eastern hotel. The effect of unfavorable weather and the occurrence of pay days on the ab-senteeism rates are particularly noticeable.

The hotel from which this data was taken was able by means of a systematic program to reduce absenteeism from a rate of 6 per cent to one of 2 per cent in a period of twelve months.

The program and its results are outlined below.[2]

Steps Taken

1. Required submission of daily reports to Personnel Department.

2. Departments and/or Personnel Department contacted all absentees.

3. Department Heads interviewed all absentees.

4. Personnel Department Interviewed all chronic absentees and those out for three or more con-secutive days.

5. Personnel Department revised orientation talks for new employees to place greater emphasis on regular attendance and prompt reporting of illness, etc.

---

[2] Courtesy C. G. Thurston, Hilton Hotels Company.

MARCH

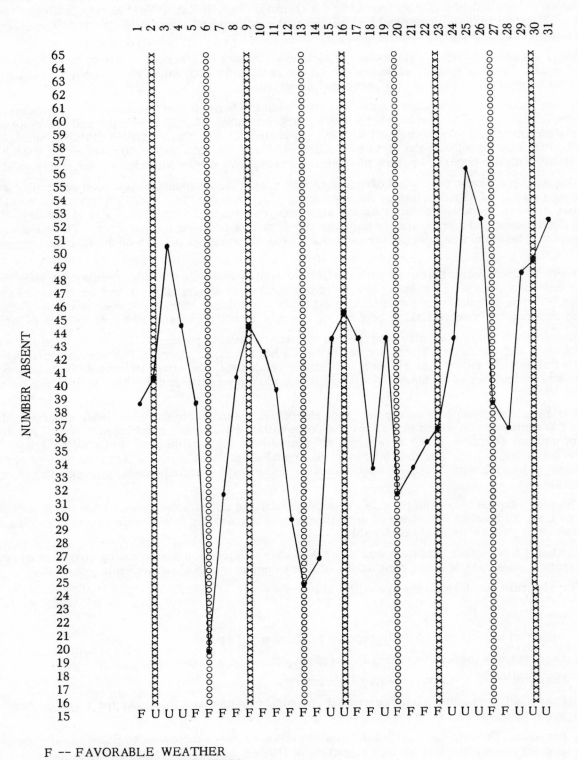

F -- FAVORABLE WEATHER
U -- UNFAVORABLE WEATHER
x -- SUNDAY
o -- PAY DAY

Courtesy C. G. Thurston

166

Results

1. Realization of ill effects of absenteeism on their department by department heads.

2. Greater interest in regular attendance by employees due to emphasis placed through personal interview by department head and/or Personnel Department regarding attendance.

3. Reduction of absentee rate from six per cent to two per cent in twelve months.

4. Reduction in overtime payment due to absence.

ACCIDENTS AS AN INDEX TO MORALE

Psychiatrists and psychologists have shown that many persons are accident prone. In other words some persons have so many more accidents than others that there is good reason to believe that factors other than chance are at work. It is believed that many accidents are caused by personality maladjustments, and that psychological conditions of work may precipitate accidents. A poor supervisor may so upset his employees that they neglect ordinary safety precautions. Some psychiatrists believe that persons sometimes injure themselves when they are wishing to injure someone they resent. The chapter on accident prevention will say more concerning accident proneness.

THE EXIT INTERVIEW AS A BAROMETER OF MORALE

In addition to saving many good employees for the organization, the interview conducted at the time an employee is being separated is an excellent means for gauging morale. At this time the employee usually feels he has nothing to lose so why not tell the company what is wrong with it. Often he is under emotional stress and will give information which he would not otherwise give. Much of what he says may be biased, but the skillful interviewer takes this into account. Exit interviews may point to areas which need immediate attention or may point up needs for a long-term reorientation of personnel relations.

The interviewer does not argue with or evaluate the employee's statements, as the employee may resent the slightest suggestion of criticism. He remains an interested, uncritical listener. He is doing a skilled job, one which requires definite techniques. The interviewer's opinions should be saved for later investigation.

Regardless of whether the employee is right or wrong, whether he is leaving for reasons which have nothing to do with the hotel or restaurant, whether to the organization he is worth saving, it is good public relations to show the employee that you are interested in him and value his suggestions or criticisms. The exit interview is a must in any personnel program.

An exit interview form is illustrated on the following page. This was developed by J. B. Temple, vice-president, Holiday Inns.

POLLING EMPLOYEE OPINION

Conducting a morale survey among employees has at least two purposes. The more obvious purpose is to get a picture of the level of morale for management. Another purpose, more subtle in the way in which it is achieved, is that of making the employees feel that management is interested in them and their opinions about the operation of the hotel or restaurant. The morale survey is probably the most direct method of securing information about morale. If carefully conducted it can be highly valuable. If injudiciously conducted it may not serve its purpose -- or it may backfire. Interpretation of the survey is just as important as the manner in which it is conducted.

Morale surveys do not give anything more than indications of trends. The results therefore should not be interpreted literally or strictly. It may be found that of 500 employees 30 to 50 are dissatisfied with almost everything the morale schedule mentions. This is no cause for alarm. One anticipates a certain amount of dissidence. Opinion questionnaires, the usual type of schedule used in a morale survey, seek to tap attitudes. Attitudes are based on emotion and consequently are rather ill-defined and change somewhat from day to day.

This is not a criticism of the attempt to measure attitudes since emotions, attitudes, and feelings determine the way we all see things. The physical working conditions of a kitchen may be ideal but to the vegetable preparation man who cannot stand the sight of the vegetable chef, the conditions may be terrible. The morale survey attempts to get at these feelings.

"EXIT INTERVIEW"

Date _____

Name _____ S.S. No. _____

Address _____ Time Card No. _____

Last Day Worked (or to work) _____ Time Card No. _____

REASON FOR SEPARATION (check)

QUIT

( ) Has another job

( ) Work unsuitable

( ) Family reasons

( ) To return to school

( ) To return to self-employment

( ) Leaving city

( ) To get another job

( ) Unknown

( ) Pay

LAID OFF

( ) Lack of work, dismissed

( ) Incompetence

( ) Attendance

( ) Intemperance

( ) Discipline

( ) Misconduct

( ) Sick

( ) Continued absence

Statement of Employee

Statement of Superior

Remarks

Following is a form which can be used in measuring employee attitudes regarding job satisfaction. As is seen, the schedule deals with over-all job satisfaction: satisfaction with training, with supervisors, with employee services, interest in the job, and so on. The schedule can be cut down or supplemented to fit the individual establishment.

HOW DO YOU FEEL ABOUT YOUR JOB?

Following you will find a number of statements which represent opinions frequently expressed by hotel and restaurant employees. You are asked to express agreement or disagreement with each statement of opinion by circling one of the five numbers which precedes it. The following key shows the meaning of each number.

2 STRONG AGREEMENT with the statement; agreement without reservation.

1 MODERATE AGREEMENT.

0 UNDECIDED; no definite opinion upon the issue involved.

-1 MODERATE DISAGREEMENT.

-2 STRONG DISAGREEMENT; complete rejection of the proposition which is stated.

THERE ARE NO RIGHT OR WRONG ANSWERS. This is not a test of information, but only an expression of your opinion about debatable issues.

PLEASE DO NOT SIGN YOUR NAME. We are not interested in the opinions of specific individuals, but only in those of the group as a whole. You therefore may express yourself frankly and without reservation.

Just one thing more: Read each statement carefully, but do not spend time debating it. RESPOND ON THE BASIS OF YOUR FIRST IMPRESSION.

2 1 0 -1 -2 I feel that I really accomplish something in my job.

2 1 0 -1 -2 My associations with other employees are satisfactory.

2 1 0 -1 -2 I am seldom overworked.

2 1 0 -1 -2 There is little monotony connected with my job.

2 1 0 -1 -2 There is little danger of injury in my job.

2 1 0 -1 -2 I receive about as much training on the job as I need.

2 1 0 -1 -2 My job is very monotonous.

- - - - - - - - - - - - - - - - - -

2 1 0 -1 -2 My supervisor never bawls me out in front of others.

2 1 0 -1 -2 My supervisors do not try to impress me with their superiority.

2 1 0 -1 -2 I can usually find out how I stand with my supervisors.

2 1 0 -1 -2 The management sincerely wants to know what employees think about the way things are done.

2 1 0 -1 -2 Most supervisors are as courteous as you could wish.

2 1 0 -1 -2 Most supervisors are careful to consider the employee's suggestions.

2 1 0 -1 -2 Supervisors for whom I work usually make the correct decisions.

2 1 0 -1 -2 I feel as though I am really a part of the organization here.

2 1 0 -1 -2 The management appreciates my work.

2 1 0 -1 -2 My supervisors keep their promises to employees.

2 1 0 -1 -2 The management here treats its employees better than do managements in most other hotels and restaurants.

- - - - - - - - - - - - - - - - - -

2	1	0	-1	-2	If he tries, an employee can get ahead.
2	1	0	-1	-2	The promotion policy here is fair as it takes experience into account.
2	1	0	-1	-2	Politics play little part in promotions here.

_ _ _ _ _ _ _ _ _ _ _ _ _ _ _ _ _ _ -

2	1	0	-1	-2	There are enough recreational facilities here for the employees.
2	1	0	-1	-2	Satisfactory eating places for employees are provided.
2	1	0	-1	-2	Suitable places for meeting and relaxing are provided employees.
2	1	0	-1	-2	My living conditions are about as good as can be expected.
2	1	0	-1	-2	The food served employees is below average in quality or preparation.

_ _ _ _ _ _ _ _ _ _ _ _ _ _ _ _ _ _ _

2	1	0	-1	-2	Comparatively speaking, I am paid about as well as I can expect.
2	1	0	-1	-2	On the whole, the plan for pay increases is fair.
2	1	0	-1	-2	I can feel reasonably sure of holding my job as long as I do good work.

_ _ _ _ _ _ _ _ _ _ _ _ _ _ _ _ _ _

2	1	0	-1	-2	One of man's greatest satisfactions is his work.
2	1	0	-1	-2	If I had it to do over again and were not under economic pressure, I would still work in the hotel and restaurant business.
2	1	0	-1	-2	If I had it to do over again I would still work in this establishment.

In asking employees to fill out such a questionnaire the first time a survey is made, some suspicion on the part of employees may be met. It is a good policy to introduce the idea of the survey several days in advance either personally or via the house organ. Union representatives will usually aid in selling the idea if approached properly. Making it clear that the survey is a group project, that management is interested in knowing employees' reactions to their jobs, and in assuring anonymity by having no names signed to the schedules, will help assure the success of the project.

If management is confident and entirely above board it will post the results of the survey or publish them in the house organ. Periodic surveys will keep management informed of marked changes in morale.

Factors Affecting Morale

Hotel and restaurant work provides many employees with personal satisfactions found in few other industries. The fact that the hotel and restaurant is often a center of community affairs and good fellowship is reflected among employees. The ebb and flow of people, the excitement of meeting and working with new persons, and the absence of routine specialization in most hotel and restaurant jobs can lead to a warmth of living which makes for personal satisfaction and efficiency. Together with its advantages, hotel and restaurant work offers disadvantages, at least some of them peculiar to the industry: long and irregular hours, low pay, unusual demands, and low social status.

The hotel and restaurant industry offers a rare challenge to the manager with appropriate skills and talent to exploit the positive aspects of the work environment and to compensate for the negative aspects for the benefit of the enterprise.

In the previous chapter, we described a unique phenomenon relative to the morale and motivations of workers: the fact that managers must be concerned with providing not only an environment that leads to "satisfactions" for workers (i.e., opportunities for growth, responsibility, and self-expression), but also an environment that minimizes the "dissatisfactions" of workers (i.e., adequate pay, good working conditions, and progressive fringe benefits). This chapter considers some of the techniques which have been used for eliminating personal dissatisfactions which impair efficiency on the job.

JOB TITLES AND THEIR EFFECTS UPON MORALE

The title of the job may in itself be a stimulus of interest. One means of identifying people in our culture is by the job they do and by the title of the job. It is only natural that workers tend to identify themselves with their jobs and to feel elevated or depressed by the manner in which the job is regarded by others. Waiters sometimes have feelings of inferiority because they are "servants" though they may earn more than their "patrons." No one wants to be the garbage man, and it is the unwise personnel man who labels any job "garbage man." Few women, regardless of their status in our society, like to be called maids. "Line hostess" is a more preferable term than "counter girl." Some hotels title bellmen "service clerks." Setting up appropriate job titles can have decided advantages.

An illustration of this is an incident which happened in a leading airport restaurant chain. By eliminating all "dishwashers" the turnover rate in those who washed the dishes fell sharply and there was less trouble in recruitment for the job. The new title, "plane equipment sterilizer," was just as appropriate as dishwasher and much more desirable a title. Other restaurants have changed "dishwashing" to "machine operating," thus bolstering the ego of those who did the work. "Machine operator" is actually a better description of the job, since machinery has been introduced, than is dishwasher. No one wants to be known as a "dishwasher"; "machine operator" is more democratic and dignified and descriptive of the work performed.

The largest restaurant chain in this country discourages the use of any terms which have taken on connotations of "inferiority." Persons who work at the less desirable jobs are classified as floormen and utility men. Counter girls are classified as sales girls. Although there is no job of hostess as the term is usually taken to mean, some girls are given the title. Where manual jobs are not made into semi-skilled or skilled jobs as has been done in most dishwashing jobs, changing the job title to one with more favorable connotations may not appear entirely ethical. Since a job title change harms no one, the writer sees no reason for not making changes which result in making people more satisfied with their jobs. Using euphemisms is an old English custom which reduces tension in a great many areas, including many outside of industry.

Another incident of the same type took place in the Hotel Radisson in Minneapolis. Instead of placing the usual small advertisement in the classified ad section -- chambermaids wanted -- the management showed a picture of a neat, well-dressed woman and asked for floor housekeepers, a dignified calling at $138.50 per month. The Radisson had no scarcity of first-rate applicants.

Similarly, one hotel had difficulty in keeping an employee on the job of garbage burner. The difficulty was fast removed when the garbage burner became an incinerator superintendent.

THE USE OF REST PERIODS

Many experiments have been conducted on the value of rest periods. Where work is of a continuous, unchanging kind, rest periods have been shown to increase efficiency, interest, and in most cases, overall production. Moreover, it is argued with some justification that whether or not there is a scheduled rest period, workers will take them anyway. If rest periods are scheduled, the employee is not required to break a written or unwritten rule. Because of the service nature of most hotel and restaurant work, the rush and slack periods, and in many places absence of close supervision, rest periods are not necessary for many jobs. Places such as the laundry, the clerical and accounting offices could well profit by scheduling rest periods. Rest periods for chambermaids are especially desirable. Their job is a lonely one, with few contacts with people and fewer associations with the other employees. Rest periods give a needed pause for conversation and social intercourse. The 10 to 15 minutes lost in the morning at 10:00 and the afternoon at 3:00 is more than compensated for in a reduction of monotony and increased interest in the work.

NIGHT WORK

It is generally agreed that night work has harmful physiological effects and undesirable social consequences. Most studies in industry generally have shown less production per hour for night work, more accidents and lower morale for night work than for day work. Night work disrupts family living, deprives the individual of the evening recreation hours, and reduces his participation in community life. Some personnel find continued difficulty in adjusting their eating and sleeping rhythm to night work.

Particular concern has been expressed over night work for women. This goes back to the first half of the nineteenth century when the abuses growing out of the factory system were rampant. The moral implications of night work for women still concerns the leaders of reform and some state regulations make the employer responsible for getting the female night employee safely to her home after work. Constitutionality of state regulation of night work was upheld by the United States Supreme Court in 1924.

How do hotel and restaurant night workers feel about night employment? An extensive survey covering hotels and restaurants in Connecticut, Indiana, and Atlanta, Georgia, showed some interesting results.[1] A preponderance of the women found night work acceptable. Some made a deliberate choice of night work either because they "liked" a night shift, or because it was the most convenient time, or the only time they could work. Some of the reasons given for liking night work are listed:

> A woman whose husband traveled a great deal liked night work because if occupied her evenings which would otherwise be lonely.

> Another woman enjoyed sleeping late in the morning.

> A hostess in a cocktail lounge enjoyed the afternoon shopping time available.

> Some service employees stated that tips during night work were considerably higher than in day employment.

> One worker felt that night work was inevitable since in her family there were not enough beds for all to sleep at one time.

Those who disliked night work did so for a variety of reasons among them the following:

> Difficulty in getting enough sleep.

> Irregularity of meals.

> Fear of inconvenience of late return to homes.

> Interference with social activities.

---

[1] "Night Work for Women in Hotels and Restaurants," U. S. Department of Labor, 1949.

Among men interviewed more than two-fifths would rather have had day work and were on the night shift chiefly because they could find no other work. None of the employees liked working on the rotating or split shifts because of the continual readjustment necessary in rearranging eating and sleeping schedules. Less than one-fourth of those studied were on the rotating shift plan.

Since the hotel and restaurant business often requires night work the question of whether or not to have it is academic. However, it should be kept at a minimum. Numerous industrial studies show it to be less productive per man hour and therefore more costly than similar day work.

CHANGE OF WORK

Where jobs are deadly routine it often helps to arrange for a change of jobs periodically. Sometimes the arrangement is official, sometimes the employees themselves arrange for trading jobs. This tends to break the monotony and to refresh interest.

In laundry jobs it is often possible to shift on jobs every two or three hours. The deadly office job of filing can be lightened by having girls agree to take it on in rotation of two or three days at a time. Many jobs in the kitchen can be shifted.

In addition to maintaining interest, shifting jobs creates a reserve of trained personnel who in emergency can take on jobs other than their regularly assigned ones.

A SOUND PROMOTION POLICY

One of the marks of a growing, progressive operation is an adequate promotion policy. Most ambitious men, particularly younger ones, are more concerned with opportunities for advancement than they are with present wages and conditions of work. Assurance of promotion is one of the most potent incentives for ambitious personnel. The effects of a policy of promotion based on ability can be seen not only in increased executive ability but as an electrical influence throughout the enterprise.

Often undue weight is placed on seniority and "experience" in the promotion policy. Some old-line managers believe that no one can possibly exercise proper supervisory control without ten or fifteen years of experience on the job under supervision. This is a costly and mistaken idea. Studies have shown that there is such a thing as too much experience. A competent individual who in the job of steward has been at his job for ten years has probably ceased to grow five years previous. The extra five years may serve only to dull his ambition and crystallize routine habits of thinking. Too much experience is just as bad for the organization in many cases as too little. When a job takes on an entirely routine nature for a man, it stymies flexibility. One of the most progressive and fastest-growing chain of hotels in the country publicizes the fact that the vast majority of its executives are under the age of forty.

PROMOTION NEED NOT BE TO A SUPERVISORY POSITION

Obviously all employees are not capable of being supervisors and executives. Promotion, however, can still be offered them as an incentive, for promotion is whatever the individual receiving it believes it to be. For most employees an increase in wages is a promotion. For others a transfer to a more desirable working environment is a promotion. As discussed previously, changing the title of the job is considered by many to be a promotion. If the change is one desired by the employee it is a promotion; if it is not desired, it is a demotion. The Jack Tar Hotel of Galveston has this promotion policy which is unusual in the hotel and restaurant business: "It is the policy of the management to advance a man every six months, or to give him more money for the same job, or let him go. In this manner a progressive system is set up which keeps the organization on its toes, and in addition, serves as a training ground for employees in other hotels of this system. It is felt that if a person does not demonstrate that he is able to advance to another job, or is not meriting an increase in pay for the job he is doing, there is no permanent place for him in the organization, and the sooner he is separated, the better for both the employee and the hotel. In general, a person who has successfully completed two years' service in the hotel should be able to go on to a more important position elsewhere in the chain of which the Jack Tar is a part. This is an operation where no attempt is made to keep a 'permanent' crew, regardless of how valuable he may be to the organization."

TRANSFERRING EMPLOYEES AS A MORALE DEVICE

The importance of placing the employee in the job for which he is best suited was brought out in the chapter on selection and placement. Even though we use the best selection and placement techniques available, there will be many employees placed in the wrong positions. Techniques of placement are, at best, tools which can aid proper placement. Such techniques cannot measure the subtle personality characteristics of the supervisor and the employee which must be taken into account if good job relations are to be obtained.

Unconscious prejudices, insignificant quirks of personality, unforeseen emergencies may seriously upset the equilibrium between supervisor and employee. If the difficulties cannot be remedied by counseling or other means, it may be well to transfer the employee to another department. The stress and excitement which press on the chef, cooks, and other employees of a kitchen may set off an emotional explosion which cannot be explained on rational grounds. Wounded vanity or a thrust at one's ego is often enough to set up a condition which is better settled by a transfer. To fire the employee is unfair to him and tends to lower the security of the remaining employees.

Transfers must be carefully arranged and caution taken that offense to either party be kept at a minimum. Transferring every employee who requests it without careful investigation and planning will undermine the supervisor and create dissension and lack of discipline. When a transfer appears advisable, the supervisor for whom the employee is working should be consulted and if possible his permission for a transfer obtained. The supervisor in the department to which the transfer is to be made must also be consulted. If he objects, the transfer to that department must be deferred until consent is given, or transfer to a different department considered.

Of course, there are a few employees who for emotional reasons or lack of ability cannot fit into the hotel or restaurant at any point. Management must be prepared to discharge them.

INTERGROUP COMPETITION

It is said that competition is the spice of life. American business maintains that competition is responsible for the remarkable progress of business. Such statements are at best half truths. Competition can be a stimulus and it can result in discouragement, frustration, and lack of cooperation. Repeated failure under the best competitive conditions may destroy interest and initiative rather than stimulate them.

Interdepartmental rivalry for accident prevention, efficiency and production and other objectives, if conducted properly, can aid in maintaining interest and morale. Certain psychological principles, however, should be observed.

Everyone participating should be permitted to win occasionally. This can be accomplished by having a weaker group compete with its own previous record. No one likes to be a continual loser, no matter how good a sport he may be. Give everyone the opportunity to win occasionally.

Competition between groups or individuals of unequal ability serves no purpose other than to dishearten the loser. It does not stimulate the winner. Because of poor competition the winner may be encouraged to perform at a lower standard than that of which he is capable. This has been observed time and again in classrooms where levels of ability are not segregated.

In our society it may be that we put too much stress on individual accomplishment, too little on group accomplishment. Experiments have shown that individuals in our culture usually compete more vigorously when working for themselves than for a group. One of the personnel man's jobs is to encourage accomplishment for the enterprise. Cooperation is sometimes more valuable than competition. One famous philosopher puts it succinctly "Competition with the self, cooperation with the group."

INCENTIVES TO REDUCE COSTS

Incentives to reduce costs not only save the operation money but also raise morale. Everyone likes a contest if it is stimulating and fair. Incentives can be set up in the form of competing with past records. The dish pantry is a good place to start. It is at the soiled dish and loading table that 75 per cent of the breakage and chipping occurs. Breakage costs average between .5 and 1 per cent of the gross revenue in most commercial food operations. This may appear small but where there is a $50,000 a month volume, the breakage may add up to more than $500 a month.

To reduce breakage costs consider these ideas:

1. Set up a display of china showing the cost per item. When employees see that some of the plates may cost as much as $1.75 each they are more careful.

2. Place one man in charge of the dish pantry. Give him the feeling of responsibility for reducing breakage costs.

3. Install duckboards on the floors around the dish machine. They will reduce slipping on wet floors.

4. Install a neoprene mat near the loading end of the dish machine. If dishes are dropped, chance of breakage is reduced.

5. Give special attention to the night operation of the dish pantry. Studies have shown that these operations are likely to be more careless than day operations.

6. Have the bus boys and waitresses presoak the dishes in appropriate racks. Do not bus glasses and dishes together.

7. Use plastic-coated racks and conveyors to reduce chipping and scratching of the glasses and dishes.

8. Install an overhead rack above the soiled dish table for cups, glasses, creamers, and the like.

9. Around coffee urns where high breakage occurs use lowerators for cup and saucer storage.

Research has shown that dishwashing costs break down into these percentages: labor, 70 per cent; indirect costs 11 1/2 per cent; dish breakage and replacement 11 1/2 per cent; hot water and detergents 7 per cent. Any or all of these costs can be reduced through an incentive plan. Here is a plan that was used by a large Midwestern hotel.

The cost of the breakage was computed over a six-month period and found to be about $4,800, or approximately $200 per week. Some of the loss was believed to have been caused by a poor physical set-up and inadequate supervision and training. Most of it, however, was due to a high turnover of low-paid, rather poor-caliber personnel.

Corrective measures entailed three changes: (1) closer supervision and more thorough job instruction of the dishwashers; (2) a planned change in the physical setup; and (3) the introduction of an incentive system, whereby dish and glass washers were urged to compete with their previous breakage records. As an incentive they were paid a percentage of the savings resulting from reduction in breakage. In this way both management and employees would share in the increased efficiency. The plan was put into operation with the effects shown in the following table.

Cost of Weekly Breakage	Weekly Payroll of dish & glass washers	Incentive Pay	Savings to the hotel
$200.00	$200.00	$ .00	$ .00
175.00	208.00	8.00	17.00
150.00	218.00	18.00	32.00
125.00	230.00	30.00	45.00
100.00	244.00	44.00	56.00
75.00	260.00	60.00	65.00
50.00	278.00	78.00	72.00

Additional savings to the hotel were made because the turnover rates were materially reduced. Finally breakage costs were established at about $90 per week.

Some difficulties were encountered in administering the plan. Dividing the incentive money equally among the employees did not work because some of the employees were far superior to others. Arguments, sometimes violent, were precipitated among the dishwashers over the operation of the plan and the speed of the department was reduced because of the extra caution taken in washing the dishes. Most of the difficulties probably could have been eliminated had a management-employee committee been designated to administer the plan.

Other hotels and restaurants have established similar breakage reduction plans successfully. One successful plan pays employees 60 per cent of the savings occurring. Where management is not prepared to continue the incentive payments and uses the plan just to set up a lower breakage figure as a standard, the plans will result only in ill will.

Sky Chefs, a large chain of restaurants, uses an incentive plan for reducing all controllable operating costs. The latter include food, salaries, ice, laundry, linens, uniforms, paper and guest supplies, cleaning expenses and supplies, utilities, removal of waste, medical examinations, china, glassware, silver, and kitchen utensil replacements and maintenance.

A study showed that their business would "break even" when controllable costs totaled less than 85 per cent of sales. Eighty-five per cent therefore was the standard for measuring employee efficiency. The following incentives were offered:

1. A monthly bonus of five dollars to each employee of the restaurant or plane meal kitchen who showed the largest decrease in controllable operating cost percentage over the unit's lowest previous month. This bonus was for the purpose of encouraging individual and group efforts to reduce costs.

2. A monthly bonus of three dollars to all the employees in each unit which showed a 5 per cent or larger decrease in controllable operating costs over the unit's lowest previous month. This was a means of recognizing group effort when a unit showed a substantial decrease but not the best in the system.

3. A monthly bonus of three dollars to every employee in each unit which maintained monthly controllable costs between 80 per cent and 85 per cent (below the break-even level).

4. A monthly bonus of five dollars to every employee of each unit which maintained controllable operating costs below 80 per cent (a level of reasonable profit).

Employees guilty of absenteeism were not eligible since they detracted from the group's efficiency. Controllable cost percentages of all units and bonus winners were posted on bulletin boards of all units.

The incentive plan was later modified. The standard was changed from the chain-wise uniform one to a standard for each unit. A contemplated change was to make the rewards directly proportional to group efficiency by offering a dollar for each percentage point of reduction below standard.

As with most such plans, it was learned that employees participate only when they understand the value and purpose of the plan. Meetings were held to help employees understand company problems and thus to gain their cooperation. Evidence of the results of the meetings was reflected in a question asked by a high school boy while opening a crate of oranges. He asked, "What effect will these spoiled oranges have on our food costs this month?"

Several restaurants have increased the interest of waitresses in their work and improved the quality of work by sponsoring a monthly contest in which prizes are given to those who receive the most compliments on service. The compliments must be made through a hostess or cashier. Prizes of $50.00, $25.00, and $10.00 are given to the three winners. Incentive plans can be set up in any department. By paying a $10.00 or $15.00 bonus to bartenders who surpass their previous gross of $50.00, the sales figures jump markedly. By paying a percentage of the reduction in food costs to kitchen employees, food costs have been cut as much as 15 per cent. The contests more than pay for themselves in increased patronage. Waitresses formerly disinterested in spots on the silverware and glasses take the dishwasher to task. Salad arrangement and attractiveness of food become incentives.

INCENTIVES FOR ATTENDANCE AND PUNCTUALITY

Characteristically hotel and restaurant managements have depended upon disciplinary measures to keep attendance at a high level and tardiness at a minimum. Because discipline often has unpredictable and undesirable results, some managements have set up positive incentives for insuring attendance and reducing tardiness.

In jobs with high turnover it usually pays to give a bonus at the end of a month. Figuring the price of turnover at least $20.00, a bonus of a few dollars builds stability at low cost. The amount of the bonus is not as important as the idea. A successful housekeeper in a Mississippi hotel has increased both stability and good workmanship by giving a $5.00 monthly bonus to housemen and maids. Maids are started at $12.00 a week. If they prove satisfactory the wages are increased to $13.00 a week. A bonus of $5.00 is paid each month that the maid or houseman is never absent or late and when the room inspection reports show "excellent."

The Harding Restaurant Company gives employees merit points for continuous service, punctuality, and attendance. The merit points can be exchanged for a wide variety of nationally known products at wholesale prices.

COMPETITION AMONG CHAMBERMAIDS

A job which many managers stoutly maintain can never be placed on an incentive basis is that of chambermaid. Some managers report that they have tried incentive plans with maids and that the plans have failed. Maids, it is averred, can work only under strict supervision; they will work only so fast. This does not appear to be true since the quota of rooms a maid is assigned to clean varies from ten to twenty-five in different hotels and in different parts of the country.

Byron Calhoun, formerly manager of the Radisson in Minneapolis, stated that in the course of their job analysis study they also investigated the potential working speed of maids. The investigation was conducted by announcing on a Sunday that maids would leave as soon as their rooms were completed. All of the maids were finished and left by one o'clock. The Lincolnshire Hotel of Boston has practically no turnover among maids. One of the reasons for the low turnover can be explained in that they are permitted to "keep their own hours" as long as their work is completed so as to fit the hotel schedule. Some of the maids come in at 9:00 and leave at 4:00, others take longer. The arrangement allows for individual differences in initiative and skill and places responsibility on the employee.

Several hotels pay twenty-five to forty cents for each room done above quota. Some maids regularly do twenty-five rooms a day under such a plan. Many hotels hold contests in which the maid doing the best job of cleaning is given a prize or a day off. Such plans undoubtedly stimulate interest and morale when conducted fairly and the prizes "distributed" so that everyone has an opportunity to win once in a while.

Many of the smaller motels schedule maids to work in teams of two. Beds are made by both maids working together. Two maids can make beds faster working together than can two working singly. After the beds are finished, one maid does the bathrooms while the other finishes the rooms. If one gets finished before the other, she helps the slow one.

In other operations a team of two maids works together on stripping and making beds. They go from room to room stripping linen and then repeat, making them up.

Many hotel maids come from underprivileged classes. It has been shown that underprivileged workers do not have the same values as do, for example, workers from the lower middle class. Perhaps incentive plans will not work with this class of worker. Such workers who have never really shared in the "opportunity for all" motif of American life are naturally suspicious of any plans which tend to speed them up and of management's motives behind such plans. Careful introduction and follow-up would be necessary to allay such suspicions.

Competition of maids between floors has several advantages. It tends to promote cooperation and friendly relations between maids on each "team." It also adds a new factor of interest to the work. In some cases it might be advisable to permit maids who so desire to work in pairs instead of the customary lone wolf style. While it is true that many maids, perhaps a majority, prefer to work alone, others would take more interest in the job and do better work were they teamed with another maid. It would be expected that two maids working together could accomplish more than two working separately. Two persons making a bed together or moving heavy furniture can usually do more than working individually. Each could be trained to check the other's work as well and reduce inspection costs.

Opposed to such a plan it can be argued that two women working together are likely to spend too much time in conversation, to develop animosities, or to overlook parts of their job. It would be worthwhile for a personnel director to try the plan out on one floor only and to record the results. Maids requesting the arrangement should be permitted their choice of companions, care being taken that two aggressive, persuasive persons not be paired.

A variation of the team plan has been used successfully in the Jack Tar Hotel Court of Galveston, Texas. Twice a year the housekeeping department conducts a maid's contest, the purpose of which is to stimulate interest in doing a better job. The plan is unique in that each maid is assigned a sponsor, either a member of the front office staff or of the manager's office. The sponsor and the maid work as a team and both members of the winning teams, the staff man and the maid, are rewarded if their team wins the contest. Managers from outside properties of the chain operating the court hotel are the judges. According to the manager, this teamwork stimulates activity so that a maid learns more about hotel housekeeping in this way than in any other.

OTHER TYPES OF INCENTIVES

A large number of unique methods for stimulating interest have been used successfully. Most of them have not been publicized. In order to remove the stigma of the term "waiter" some restaurants call them salesmen and build their service around a "sales" plan. By guaranteeing "salesmen" a ten per cent service charge they have removed the necessity of "gratuities" and all that the term implies. A manager of a candy manufacturing concern caught the interest of his dishwashers by equipping them with instruments for taking bacteria count. The dishwashers then became quasi-technicians and their morale went up accordingly. The same manager has an unusual scheme for keeping his kitchen immaculate. He has had painted a white line three to six inches wide around each piece of kitchen equipment. The idea is to keep the white line spotless. In so doing the rest of the kitchen is kept clean. This manager avers that if he cannot spend two or three days a week fishing he is "no good as a manager."

A simple and readily understandable incentive plan which equates bonus payments with the room count was used in an Atlantic City Hotel. Bonuses were divided into four classifications: A, B, C, and D. The bonus classification which applied was dependent upon the room occupancy above a standard figure. All employees of the hotel were covered by the plan. When the room count went a certain figure above the set standard, all employees received a small bonus payment. The bonus payment increased as more rooms were sold. Employees had ready access to the room count record.

Since there was a direct connection between room count and wages, there was a great deal of interest in keeping room occupancy high -- which was advantageous to all concerned.

Service teams in dining rooms are effective. At Wohl's restaurant in St. Louis, waiters, bus boys, and cart boys work as teams. One bus boy works with two waiters. Bus boys remove soiled dishes to either of two wheeled carts. The carts which have removable shelves and hold soiled dishes and silver from 40 tables are moved by two other employees, cart boys. As each is filled, it is rolled to the dish pantry where the full shelves are exchanged for empty ones. Waiters are kept free for taking orders and delivering food. Bus boys set up the tables, clear and wipe them.

Showing employees how they will profit by using better methods and enlisting their cooperation is just as important as the method itself. We are all motivated to a large degree by self-interest. When we can be shown how we stand to share in the rewards of increased efficiency, we are more likely to want to participate. In one large hotel a particular elevator operator refused to fix her hair in an upsweep style which had been decided by management as neater and more attractive. Despite threats of her supervisor, the girl persisted. Her refusal had become a personal issue. She wanted her rights. Probably if she had first been consulted on the idea she would have agreed, but it was a plan "handed down" from above. The personnel manager, a woman, solved the problem when one day riding in the girl's elevator she casually remarked: "Have you ever thought of trying your hair in an upsweep? Your features are just right for an upsweep." The next day the hair was in upsweep style -- a compliment settled the question of hair style.

The same personnel manager had difficulty in getting the elevator operators to post their numbers in the elevators. Soon after explaining that they would more likely receive letters of commendation from guests if the guests knew how to identify the operator, the elevator numbers were in evidence.

USING COLOR IN THE WORK SITUATION

It is something of a shock to visit the "back of the house" of some of our luxury hotels and restaurants. Leaving guest territory and walking through the portal to worker territory is like stepping into another world. In place of the atmosphere of friendliness and comfort and cheer, one meets the dingy, ill-lighted, overcrowded "working quarters." Does this make for employee satisfaction and interest in the job?

Hotels and restaurants are careful to call in design specialists, color experts, and interior decorators to develop the most pleasant arrangements for the guests. Some take the experts into the back of the house. Those who do are more than repaid, for employees have the same senses as the guests. It costs little more to paint the walls of a laundry in pastel shades than in an uncompromising gray. Color used in industry improves housekeeping: employees take greater pride in keeping newly-painted areas clean. With color contrast and light backgrounds there is less possibility of neglect of corners and obscure places. Equipment is more likely to be returned to its proper place. Contrasting wall colors are reported as useful in relieving monotony and tension of employees and in affording relaxation from tasks which require a high degree of concentration. Contrasting wall colors are also used to reduce problems related to temperature conditions. Some colors are psychologically warm; others cool. One hotel found an interesting response to the use of warm colors in its paint. Soft rose tints were substituted for the oyster white walls of a recreation room which was rarely used. Employees apparently had considered the room cold and unpleasant because the introduction of color was followed by an immediate increase in the room's use. Employees began to express appreciation for the room's additional "warmth" although no additional heat was supplied, nor were other changes made to improve the appearance of the room. Color also may be used to minimize undesirable room proportions.

In order to reduce tension and eye fatigue, especially designed colors may be used to differentiate critical and noncritical parts of machinery. Light paint on machinery serves as an effective background against which dripping grease can be readily detected. Lubrication points are emphasized by the use of special color. Painting emergency equipment red speeds up location of the equipment when needed. Caution strips around dangerous machinery reduce accidents.

Kitchens should be painted in whites or other "cool" tints. In addition to boosting morale "cool" colors reveal soil and dirt. Semi-gloss or gloss enamel makes cleaning easy. Employees are just as proud of a kitchen which is a showplace as is management.

OTHER PHYSICAL FACTORS IN THE WORK AREA

Badly-lighted, poorly ventilated upholstery shops do not turn out first-class repairs. Worn-out tools save no one money. Outmoded equipment does not reduce costs. Poor working conditions do not promote loyalty. Layout planning is just as important to the restaurant, the laundry, the kitchen, and the other working spaces as it is in the industrial manufacturing plant. Some kitchens are so ill-planned that the employees expend most of their energy in overcoming the results of the planning, or lack of it. Where waiters and waitresses must climb stairs between the kitchen and dining room, efficiency naturally decreases. The Hotel Statler in Buffalo, New York, and the Hotel Shoreham in Washington, D. C., have recently installed escalators to overcome the arrangement -- and with excellent results.

According to the management of the Shoreham, the escalator for food handlers has saved many man hours per day, resulting in a marked saving in breakage, and is the biggest morale builder in the hotel's history.[2] During the war, because of shortage of waiters the Shoreham attempted to hire waitresses, but the girls refused to carry the trays weighing twenty to twenty-five pounds up the stairs. Installing the escalator saved much energy and makes for more alert employees.

Often simple routing plans save many man hours of labor. One prominent chain of restaurants has found that by having waitresses sort their dirty dishes into appropriately arranged racks, trays of dirty dishes do not pile up at the dishwashing counter, nor do the waitresses have to stand in line to dispose of their dirty dishes on the counter. The old system of merely heaping trays full of dirty dishes onto the counter and waiting for the dishwashers to sort and remove them led to congestion and confusion.

New equipment may often change a job from a monotonous, laborious task to one requiring skill, and hence to pride in accomplishment. By installing a machine which cuts 50-pound cakes of ice into cubes and transports the cubes by conveyor belt to storage, one well-known hotel reduced the number of men needed from three to one. The one man now remaining, with the aid of hoists and other machinery, is able to make and cube all the ice required. His job is one requiring a knowledge of machinery and one of responsibility. It is no longer a simple muscle and brawn operation. Machinery and planning have increased his efficiency threefold. He can be paid a much higher wage and can feel a sense of accomplishment.

Included in pleasant working conditions are the employees' cafeteria and its management. Just as much attention should be given the employees' restaurant as to the guests' restaurant. It is not necessary that the food be Lobster Newburg and steak, but it should be of high quality and sufficient quantity. Its preparation should be under the direction of the chef. Planning the serving of the food is important. At one large hotel, employees were allowed thirty minutes for lunch. A checkup by the personnel manager revealed that many of the employees were standing in line waiting to be served for thirty minutes. By handing employees time checks while in line and picking them up when the employee emerged from the cafeteria it was found that the total time to eat in some cases ran to one hour and a half. The employees were not benefiting from the time lost. They were just as dissatisfied as was management when it learned of the situation.

This situation was not of recent origin. It had been going on for a number of years. After the meal hours were staggered for various departments, employees were able to eat without wasting time. True, some had to break their habit of eating at twelve and change to eleven, but this was no great problem.

In the investigation of the employees' cafeteria it was also learned that all the chambermaids ate lunch at the same time. This left no maid on the floors in case she were needed. By planning, it was possible to arrange that there was at least one maid on; the result was a smoother-running organization.

---

[2] Taken from "The Hotel Industry," May, 1947, p. 33.

NUMBER OF WORKING HOURS AND EFFICIENCY

In 1850 the average employee worked 60 hours per week. By 1920 this had dropped to 50, and in 1941, to 40. However, during the war some employees in certain key industries worked as many as 80 hours per week. Now the nation's average is back to 40 hours or less per week. The hotel and restaurant industry has an average which is considerably higher, probably 48 or more. Many hotel and restaurant employees regularly work more than 50 hours per week. Do such long working hours make for efficiency; are they the best way to spend the labor dollar?

Extensive studies conducted by the government during the past war revealed some remarkable facts. Where some industries were working seven days per week, a reduction to six days actually increased production. In one instance a reduction to five days did not decrease production. The studies showed that there is no optimal number of hours for all jobs. Depending upon the amount of physical exertion and other factors, the number of hours which gives maximum efficiency varies from job to job. The optimal number of hours for most jobs varies between 40 and 50. For a few jobs, it drops to 30 and sometimes less. To be sure, over-all productivity may be more by working 55 hours rather than 45, but productivity per hour will be significantly less.

Hours worked beyond high efficiency levels are usually costly to management. Overtime wages are seldom profitable to an enterprise. The average employee who does not have adequate time from his work for change, rest, recreation and relaxation does not have high interest in his work.

Sometimes management has superstitions about hours of work, believing that employees must stay on the job regardless of whether the work is complete. Most dishwashing jobs are placed on an eight-hour day basis. Since there are few restaurants which maintain a schedule by which there are always dirty dishes to be washed, there are sometimes long periods when the dishwashers have nothing to do. This is especially true when banquets do not begin at the time planned. Dishwashers, or more correctly "machine operators," may stand around for several hours. This is not conducive to morale. "Old line" management may declare that there is always something to be done. This smacks of the regimented "made work" to be found in the armed services which is so distasteful. Waiters work split shifts with no ill effects. Why not permit machine operators to leave when their work is completed? By having such an incentive, interest in work and in new ways of doing things is brought about. Everyone gains.

In recent years many notions about the proper number of working hours for hotel and restaurant employees have been changed. The job of bellman, for example, has traditionally been one of long hours, six days a week. In the Hotel Roosevelt of New York City bellman hours were reduced to forty per week. Surprisingly enough, the bellmen who depend almost entirely upon tips for their income made as much in five days as they formerly did in six. They were fresher and could handle more patrons in a given time. Being more alert they gave better service and received higher tips. A reoriented outlook concerning hours of work and productivity in the hotel and restaurant business is indicated.

VACATIONS

Vacations with pay for employees are an investment by management in the health and morale of the employee. Vacations can give the employee a new lease on life. Change of scenery, change of interests, travel, rest and relaxation are no longer considered a gift from a benevolent employer. Vacations with pay are part of our democratic way of life. In cold dollars and cents they are an investment which pays off in production and efficiency.

A typical plan of more progressive hotels and restaurants is that by which employees are granted one week's vacation after one year's service and two weeks' vacation after three years' service. A few managements give three weeks' vacation after ten years of service. The trend is to increase the number of days of vacation.

Some restaurants shut down their complete operation and all employees go on vacation together. Often remodeling or extensive maintenance work may be scheduled during this period. Most hotels and restaurants try to plan their vacation schedule so that vacations are spaced throughout the summer months. Some take on additional summer employees to fill in for regular employees who are vacationing. College students are often used to replace vacationers.

By publicizing vacation trips in the house organ, their value to morale is enhanced. Often the management may aid employees in making their plans for vacations. Some provide summer camps for employees or secure special rates for them at the seashore. Hotel or motel chains can give their vacationing employees reduced rates, especially at resort hotels during the off-season. A genuine interest by management in vacations is an excellent index of management's sincerity in dealing with employees.

ADVANTAGES OF HOMOGENEITY IN THE WORK GROUP

It is common sense to believe that personnel working together should be of similar backgrounds and beliefs. This is not necessarily true, however, as has been shown in many organizations where Negroes work very well with whites. However, where it is possible to have homogeneity of racial and social groups there is less likelihood of interpersonal friction.

Prior to the restricted immigration laws of the twenties it was common for all employees in a particular department to be recent immigrants of the same European origin. Today this is not true. Some hotels and restaurants have all Negroes or all Puerto Ricans working in particular departments. One hotel employs male Puerto Ricans as chambermaids. They have been highly satisfactory. A resort hotel employs Chinese as kitchen employees and finds them unusually clean, industrious and generally capable workers. Such employees constitute an ingroup and have to depend on each other more than those who are adapted to our culture. Because of this and because of common interests and backgrounds their interpersonal relations are usually harmonious and they are an efficient working group.

ASSURING THE EMPLOYEE OF REGULAR EMPLOYMENT

Several studies of employees' attitudes indicate that security in employment ranks above wages received, opportunity for advancement, working conditions, and other aspects of employment. Several large industrial companies have demonstrated the value of guaranteeing employment by showing an increase in production and employee stability. According to the recent comprehensive Guaranteed Wages, Report to the President by the Advisory Board, a guaranteed wage plan "will beyond question reduce labor turnover." This cuts training and hiring costs and workmen's compensation and other employee injury costs. In addition to cutting labor turnover, the report continues, "guarantees will tend to lift productivity because of the buoyant effects of a greater degree of individual economic security."

Surprisingly, the hotel and restaurant business which, generally speaking, offers one of the most stable employment records in business, makes little moment of this fact and fails to use it as an inducement in securing and keeping employees. Most of the larger hotels have an "old timer's club" it is true, but they do not publicize the regularity of employment offered, nor do they give assurance to the employee that, provided his services are satisfactory, he will be guaranteed employment.

For a person to be an efficient and enthusiastic employee requires a sense of security. A complete sense of security is probably impossible in our culture and may not be desirable, but there is a minimum sense of security which the hotel and restaurant business can usually give their employees by merely publicizing what is already true.

Another means of reducing fear of unemployment is to set up measures which assure the employee that he will not be fired without just cause. If the employee is insured against the whimsy, personal feelings and caprice of his department head, he is a more stable worker. The Biltmore Hotel of Los Angeles, California, provides a control which insures job security. No employee can be discharged, not even by the president, managing director, or manager of the hotel, if the board of directors disagrees. The board of directors consists of five members elected annually from the working personnel by a general election of employees. When an employee receives notice that his services are no longer required and feels that his dismissal is not justified, he may present his case to the board of directors for their decision. A special meeting of the board is called, and a thorough investigation made. The employee may appear before the board, present any evidence he wishes, and summon any witnesses he may feel will strengthen his case. Likewise the head of the department concerned is requested to appear and present any evidence and witness he may desire to justify his action.

SHARING PROFITS WITH EMPLOYEES

Profit-sharing plans have been given considerable publicity the last few years. Some exponents of profit-sharing plans urge their adoption for all employees as a new cure-all for labor and economic troubles. Actually profit-sharing plans have a considerable history. Several plans were in effect in the United States, France, and England in the last century. The plans have had a variety of success and failure. Sharing profits with employees is a basically sound idea. The administration of profit sharing, however, often has weaknesses which result in failure of the plan.

Holiday Inns, the largest public accommodations company in the hospitality field, has a combined employee profit-sharing and savings retirement plan. The Company contributes an amount equal to 5 per cent of its net profit, may contribute more, but not in excess of 50 per cent of the total wages paid to participating employees. Half of the total amount contributed by the company is paid to the employees on the basis of wages and number of years employed. The other half is placed in a savings fund and any amount placed into the savings account by the employee is matched by the company, up to $1,000 per person each year.

The amount saved by the employee plus interest can be withdrawn at any time. The amount contributed by the company accrues to the employee on a prorated basis according to the number of years he is with the company. After working eight years his vested interest is 100 per cent and he can withdraw the total amount contributed by the company as well as by himself, whenever he wishes. To explain the plan, Holiday Inns has published a cartoon booklet which is a running conversation about the plan between an employee and her friend.

Profit-sharing programs are not numerous in the hotel and restaurant field, and where they exist, are not well known. Descriptions of successful plans are suggestive as to the form such a plan may take.

THE GREENFIELD-MILLS PROFIT-SHARING PLAN

A profit-sharing plan marked by its simplicity and by the large share of profits awarded employees is that of the Greenfield-Mills Restaurant Company. The gross amount distributed to "co-workers" equals one-half of the net profits, after six per cent net return annually on the capital investment is deducted. Profits are computed quarterly and are computed by management after payment or accrual in full of all costs of operation including wages, salaries, depreciation, assessments, and all taxes have been deducted. Each "co-worker's" share is based entirely on the wage or salary received by him. Employees are eligible for half-participation in the plan after completing a full quarter beginning the first of January, April, or October. All "co-workers" who have completed five consecutive quarters are full participants in the plan.

A DEFERRED-DISTRIBUTION PLAN

Plans setting aside certain profits to be distributed later in the form of retirement pay are growing in popularity. Two advantages of this kind of plan stand out. First, if the plan is approved by the Bureau of Internal Revenue, the employer may deduct his contributions from his current taxable income. Secondly, the employee is not taxed until his share is made available to him, at which time his income is usually in a lower tax income bracket.

The Drake Hotel of Chicago, Illinois, put a profit-sharing plan into effect in 1946 which represents the deferred-distribution type of plan. Each year the company owning the Drake Hotel contributes ten per cent of its net earnings to a trust. All employees who have five years of continuous service participate in the trust on a "unit system basis." In the "unit system," participants receive one unit credit for each year of continuous employment at the Drake Hotel and also one unit for each $100 of wages received. The trust is administered by five trustees, two chosen from employees, two from management, and the fifth from the bank handling the funds. The participant receives his share under any of the following conditions:

1. When a male participant reaches sixty-five (65);

2. When a female participant reaches sixty (60);

3. When a participant is relieved because of mental or physical disability;

4. When a participant dies:

5. When a participant severs his employment with the company.

The money may be distributed to the participant or his beneficiaries in a lump sum, in installments over a period not to exceed ten years, by the purchase of an annuity, or in such other manner the trustee believes will best provide for the participant or his beneficiaries. Employees discharged for insubordination, gross inefficiency, or dishonesty, or who commit a crime forfeit their interest in the trust. Those who voluntarily quit before ten years of employment forfeit a percentage of their share in the trust. The percentage forfeited is distributed among remaining members of the trust.[3]

USING A BONUS PLAN TO INCREASE EMPLOYEE STABILITY

Profit-sharing or bonus plans properly administered reduce employee turnover and absenteeism. Making the amount of bonus directly dependent upon attendance rewards employees for good attendance.

---

[3] From a booklet, "Drake Hotel Employees' Profit-Sharing Trust," Drake Hotel, Chicago.

Rather than penalizing employees who do not conform to the establishment's rules, it provides positive motivations for doing so.

Mawby Incorporated, a restaurant in Cleveland Heights, Ohio, has demonstrated the effectiveness of relating bonus payments to the attendance record. Their plan places a premium on dependability and loyalty. Of their 25 employees, 20 have been with the company at least one year, 15 at least three years, and 10 at least five years.

The highlights of the plan are as follows:

1. The company has a sound wage plan which is entirely distinct from the bonus plan. Employees receive wages which are equal to or exceed those paid by competing food service establishments.

2. The company has a history of sound personnel relations with its employees. Merit increases are paid for efficient work. In addition the company provides each employee with a paid-up $1,000 life insurance policy.

3. Provided that they have no unauthorized absences, employees are paid an annual Christmas bonus. In their first year kitchen men receive 4 per cent of their annual wage, girls 6 per cent and cooks 8 per cent. This increases with each year's service at the rate of 2 per cent of the annual wage until a maximum is reached. The maximum for kitchen men is $250 per year; for the girls $350; and for the cooks $600. Two and one-half per cent of the bonus is deducted for each day of unauthorized absence. Absences on Monday and Saturday reduce the bonus payment at the rate of 5 per cent for each day. A total of 20 per cent is deducted for a lost week without a written statement from either their doctor or the company's doctor.

4. Two vacations yearly are granted to all employees with six months' service. One is given the last week of July, the other between Christmas Day and New Year's Day. A condition of receiving payment for the Holiday Week vacation is the completion of two weeks' work with no time lost following New Year's Day.

An interesting side light on the Mawby plan is the fact that the company has had excellent success in employing men in their sixties. At the time of this writing two men who have passed the seventy mark are employed. The company finds the older employees to be as efficient as the younger employees and far more dependable. In addition they possess a strong sense of loyalty to the organization.

Other facts are witness to the success of the plan. In seven years only one employee lost his holiday vacation pay because of failure to work the full two weeks following the vacation. In 1948, a total of $6,500 was distributed as profits to the employees. The business has had unusual success and the stability among the employees is indeed remarkable.

A PROFIT-SHARING PLAN THAT STIMULATES EFFICIENCY

A New York City chain of restaurants, Prexy's, has a profit-sharing plan which turns twenty-five per cent of the firm's earnings back to employees. The Prexy plan divides profits on the basis of length of service and wages earned.

All employees participate in the plan after six months' service. One point is awarded for every six months' service plus one point for every hundred dollars of wages earned. Profit-sharing meetings are held twice a month. Employee representatives elected by popular vote of each store's employees attend the meetings.

The profit-sharing plan has resulted in numerous employee suggestions to eliminate tasks. Employees who work at tasks no longer found necessary are transferred to other jobs. A dishwasher originated the idea for a special cup rack, a dish rack with a false bottom which keeps cups raised slightly above the edge of the rack for easy removal. The racks located under the counters are filled with used cups by the waitress. Cups may be empty or partially filled. Bus boys remove the loaded racks to the dishwashing room. An empty cup rack is placed over the filled one and turning both over places the cup upside down, ready to be washed in the dish machine. Breakage and time are saved.

Another employee suggested that the menu items be sandblasted on the backs of the mirrors facing the counter. The idea saved many hours of cleaning the large metal scrolls previously hung over the mirrors.

The management feels that employees offer suggestions because they know that greater profits will be realized, profits in which they share. They also expect their suggestions to add more business, more and better positions.

Several restaurants have found profit sharing particularly successful when limited to key personnel. There is less question that a manager, a chef, a bartender, a steward will leave his job or lose interest in it when he has a personal direct interest in the profits of the enterprise. The plan must be geared to operating results to be effective. One company that paid all department heads a flat percentage of salaries as a bonus got no results at all.

Making the employee's returns from his work at least partially dependent upon his efforts and production is common sense. In the past, however, employers have felt that employees should be paid only a certain standard wage, and all profits above this wage rightly belong to the entrepeneur. In the days of rapidly expanding industry this conception worked in many cases and provided the entrepreneur with a fortune. Short cuts and a high degree of efficiency which can be acquired only by the wholehearted participation of the employee were not so important. Today the hotel and restaurant industry is a well-established business. Its success will depend increasingly on management's ability to meet competition. In the hotel and restaurant business, more than in most businesses, the wholehearted interest and co-operation of the personnel are of the utmost importance in meeting competition. Profit sharing, if properly administered, not as a gift but as a fair return for work done, has shown itself to be one means of increasing personal satisfaction, efficiency, and the economic status of the enterprise.

INSURANCE AND PENSION PLANS

A few years ago insurance and pension plans were a rarity in the hotel and restaurant business. Today, scarcely a well-known hotel or restaurant does not have some form of insurance plan for its employees, and in the larger organizations pension plans which supplement that provided by the federal government.

Pension and insurance plans help to reduce the feeling of insecurity which most of us have in our culture. Security plans enable us to do a better job. Making a more emotionally stable employee, as well as one who is less likely to leave his job, is one of management's jobs.

One of the better type of retirement pension and insurance plans is that established in 1943 by the Pick Hotels Corporation. The purpose of this plan, according to a brochure issued to employees, is threefold.

1. To provide an assured life income for participants after they have completed their working years and are ready for retirement;

2. To make provision for their families and other dependents in the event of death prior to retirement age, and;

3. To furnish a further incentive to remain with Pick Hotels Corporation for many years, and do all possible to insure the success of its operations. By so doing, employees will contribute not only to their own future success, but to that of their co-workers, as well.

The Pick Hotels' retirement pension plan supplements Social Security by paying a pension of 3/4 of 1 per cent of the wage above $100 per month for each year of service. Thus, if an employee retires with twenty years of service and a wage of $250 a month, his pension is 20 × 3/4 × $150 (the amount over $100) or $22.50. This sum is in addition to his Social Security payments. Under the plan the minimum pension is $10.00 per month at normal retirement age.

The Pick Plan is unusual in that it is a combination pension, insurance and savings plan. Retirement benefits are insured. Life insurance premiums are paid by the company if the employee can pass the insurance company's examination. The plan has a savings provision by which some benefits are paid the employee if he is discharged or leaves before retirement age.

Provided the employee has had two or more years' service and is not discharged because of dishonesty, he receives a "cash value" for his share in the fund as shown in the table on the following page.

Many insurance and pension plans provide that the employee must contribute a share, usually one-half, to the cost of maintaining them.

Some companies make their pension plan an integral part of a profit-sharing plan. For example, Schraffts sets aside 10 per cent of profits before computing taxes to provide for retirement benefits for employees. Witness to the effectiveness of this plan and the high caliber of their personnel relations generally is the fact that of about 7,000 employees over 2,500 have been with the firm five years or more.

The Lamar Hotel of Houston has an outstanding pension trust plan. All employees including maids and other service personnel are eligible after they have completed five years of service. The employees

Years of Participation in Plan	Employee Entitled to	Years of Participation in Plan	Employee Entitled to
Less than 2 years	Nothing	9 to 10 years	45%
2 to 3 years	10%	10 to 11 years	50%
3 to 4 years	15%	11 to 12 years	60%
4 to 5 years	20%	12 to 13 years	70%
5 to 6 years	25%	13 to 14 years	80%
6 to 7 years	30%	14 to 15 years	90%
7 to 8 years	35%	15 or more years	100%
8 to 9 years	40%		

contribute between a minimum of 1 per cent and 5 per cent of their compensation: 1 per cent for wages under $1,500; 5 per cent for salaries in excess of $6,600 a year. The plan is designed to supplement rather than substitute for Old Age and Survivor's Insurance (Social Security). No one receives more than $400, including Social Security benefits.

The trustee responsible for the operation of the pension trust buys life insurance policies of $1,000 for each $10.00 of monthly life income prescribed in the plan. The insurance is ordinary life which can be converted to a retirement income endowment. In case of total and permanent disability the employee is vested with 100 per cent of all the values accumulated to his account. If he should be called into the military service the hotel makes both its own contribution and the employee's contribution for as long as he is in the service.

The National Press Club of Washington, D. C., has a retirement plan which provides that all of the payments are made by the club for employees who earn less than $3,800 a year. All employees are eligible who have completed one year of continuous service.

Affiliated National Hotels, a Southern chain, has a retirement plan for all employees except those covered by a collective bargaining agreement. In other words, the plan does not include any union employees.

HEALTH AND ACCIDENT INSURANCE FOR EMPLOYEES

Prior to World War I there were few plans which made systematic preparation for the care of sick or injured employees. Usually an injured employee received no compensation. Sometimes, however, the company was sued for an inordinate sum as accident compensation and required to pay it. In such cases the company often faced bankruptcy. Whatever the sum collected the employee received only a small share, most of the money going for court costs and lawyer's fees.

Today there are state and federal laws which protect both the employer and employee. Insurance plans provide for definite payment of compensation in case of injury, and a recent trend is to include insurance protection against sickness. The employee is relieved of undue anxiety concerning possible sickness or accident. Consequently, his efficiency is greater. In hospitalization and sickness protection plans the employee's health is protected and maintained. Periodic physical examinations spot potential illness and enable the physician to check the growth of disease.

CREDIT UNIONS AS THEY AFFECT MORALE

Credit unions can serve as one of the many "security measures" which reflect themselves in higher employee morale and efficiency. More important, credit unions can keep employees out of the hands of loan sharks. By providing a relatively convenient and low-cost type of credit, the credit union removes many expressed or implicit fears from the minds of workers. Faced with the possibility of an emergency need for money, many employees do not possess the frame of mind necessary for interest in their work and the self-confidence necessary for many hotel and restaurant jobs.

True, an employee who needs medical or other emergency bills can turn to the personal loan services; but often once he has met these gentlemen, their acquaintance is difficult to lose. Loan sharks

THE GRAND HOTEL

Date _____ Dept. _____

In column I, indicate the importance to you of each factor by using numbers from 1–10. Place a 1 after your first choice, a 2 after your second choice, etc.

Indicate by a check (√) in one of the next five columns, under Section II, your opinion as to the operation of each factor in your department.

Indicate by a check (√) in one of the last three columns of Section III your opinion as to changes.

Factors	I — Rate of Importance	II — Where I work, these factors are working:					III — Where I work these factors are:		
		Poor	Fair	Aver.	Good	Excel.	Getting worse	Not changing either way	Improving
Encouragement to offer suggestions									
A fair hearing on grievances									
Credit for suggestions									
Satisfactory future									
Immediate supervisor's knowledge of whether work is good or not									
Pay increases when deserved									
Recognition of good work (exclusive of pay)									
Friendly and helpful criticism									
Promotion of persons best qualified									
Knowledge of standing with executives									

Undoubtedly many hotels and restaurants are still conducted in ways similar to those described. They may be highly successful financially. Nevertheless they are out ot tune with the times and could be more successful if thought were given to plans which get at basic factors of motivation.

Some techniques of management which could have been successful twenty years ago are now outmoded and will result in resentment and lowered efficiency. Consider but one job in the hotel and restaurant field. Waiters today do not wish to feel like servants; neither do they wish to be treated as children by employers. Waiters in our large cities often earn more money than the patrons they serve. A wellknown psychiatrist to the contrary, the best waiters are not morons, nor do they wish to be dominated either by their patrons or by management. In some cities they are strongly unionized. If they are made to feel like a separate group, outside the enterprise, they are at odds with management and not a cooperating part of the business. It has been said that some hotel service workers do not wish to be made a part of management, that they are too low in intelligence and too lacking in education. Chambermaids have been held up as members of such a group. Yet in hotels that have carefully selected maids and have made a sincere effort to make them feel an integral part of the enterprise, the maids have responded with efficiency and loyalty. Let us examine some more effective techniques for securing cooperation.

MULTIPLE MANAGEMENT

A plan which is considered within the law because it is entirely a function of management is that known as multiple management. Started by the president of McCormick Spice Company in 1932, the plan has been adapted to the need of more than 500 other companies throughout the United States, the British Empire, and South America. Recently multiple management was instituted in one of our largest hotel chains, The Sheraton Corporation of America, and one of our most progressive restaurant chains, The Hot Shoppes, Incorporated.

OBJECTIVES OF MULTIPLE MANAGEMENT

Multiple management is an attempt to apply democracy to business by making the employee feel that he is close to management and has a voice through representation and participation. This results in not one manager but several. If properly coordinated and formulated the ideas of many persons are better than those of a few. The plan also provides a method by which prospective executives can be selected and tried. Communication between all levels of management and workers is increased and competition among supervisors is enhanced. The plan as developed by McCormick provides not only for executive action based on the participation and ideas of many but also for security of employment and profit sharing. Many of the other adaptations do not consider security of employment and profit sharing in their plans.

HOW MULTIPLE MANAGEMENT WORKS

Central to the plan is a Junior Board of Directors appointed originally by top management. Once appointed, the Junior Board has a procedure for replacing itself. Membership is of two types: regular and associate. At regular intervals members rate each other and the top-ranking members become a membership committee. The membership committee determines which of the regular members will be dropped. The new regular board then determines which of the associate members will be replaced. Under the McCormick plan rating is done on the basis of six characteristics:

1. Human Relations
2. Vision
3. Initiative
4. Judgement
5. Cooperativeness
6. Poise.

The Junior Board meets periodically and makes suggestions to top management. Success of the plan is evidenced by the fact that of over 2,000 ideas submitted to the Senior Board by the Junior Board at McCormick Spice, only six were rejected. In the Sheraton plan over 95 per cent of the Junior Board's suggestions were accepted.

Other boards may be established along the same lines for other divisions. McCormick Spice Company has a Factory Board, a Sales Board, and a Consumer Board. Probably just as important to the overall success of the plan are the monthly meetings held for all employees. The board chairman of the group presides and sees to it that everybody gets to know what is going on in the department and in the business as a whole. Rank and file participation is thus encouraged. Suggestions formerly discarded now reach top management. Employees have a ready channel for the transmission of their ideas and a board which can sift and reformulate the ideas. A bus boy with an idea to improve efficiency will have no timidity in explaining his idea to a member of the restaurant board whereas he would be more than hesitant to take it to the general manager.

Another advantage of the plan is that it sets machinery in motion whereby executive talent is actively sought and developed. The McCormick people believe that about one in ten employees is of the creative or thinking type. They are the people who should be eligible for Board membership. The Junior Boards do not have the authority to make final decisions -- that is the prerogative of the Senior Board. However, they gain experience in formulating ideas. Boards usually follow parliamentary procedure in meetings. They may use standing committees to investigate problems and follow through recommendations. They often have permanent committees on safety, efficiency, or housekeeping. By providing such experience Junior Boards prepare men for the Senior Board membership.

Under the Sheraton Corporation plan four of the members of the Senior Board are permanent; the other six are general managers. The plan provides that eventually all general managers will be elected to the Board. A general manager in attendance at multiple management meetings receives $50.00 and expenses. In the Sheraton chain each hotel sets up a Junior Board, usually consisting of eight employees, selected from various departments. Each member receives from $3.00 to $5.00 per meeting.

MULTIPLE MANAGEMENT IN A RESTAURANT CHAIN

The Hot Shoppes, Incorporated, of Washington, D. C., a large restaurant and motor inn corporation, has installed a multiple management plan and finds it highly successful. Eighteen men in their early thirties of potential executive capacity were selected from the organization to form the Junior Board. They represented all departments of the business -- the restaurants, store managers, commissary production department, procurement department, and the personnel and finance departments. The Junior Board was given authority by President J. W. Marriott to investigate and make recommendations on any subject they considered vital to the business. The only restriction placed on their recommendations was that they must be the result of unanimous opinion among the twelve voting members of the Junior Board.

Under the Hot Shoppe multiple management plan the highest-rated members of the regular Junior Board are elected chairman and secretary for a six months' term. The next three highest-rated regular members along with the chairman and secretary constitute the executive committee of the Board. The Junior Board formulated its own by-laws defining the Board's purpose, the place and time of meetings, the officers' duties, and the procedure for rotating membership and making recommendations to the Senior Board of Directors. Meetings were scheduled for every other Wednesday at 5:30 in the afternoon. Following dinner together a meeting is held which usually lasts from two to two-and-a-half hours.

The Junior Board of Hot Shoppes has already made a number of valuable recommendations. Typical of such recommendations and the manner in which they were conceived are two described by Ben E. Lewis of Hot Shoppes.

1. There are any number of laundries whose annual sales volume is substantially less than the total annual laundry costs for our restaurants. Recognizing this as an area where substantial savings might be made, members of the Junior Board conducted an extensive survey to determine the relative merits of operating our own laundry or continuing to have it done by outside firms. Comparative cost figures were carefully worked up, and procedural details thoroughly investigated over a period of several months. All findings indicated we could profitably set up and operate our own laundry. This was recommended to the Senior Board and approved, and at present we are proceeding along the lines of making a change-over.

2. The location of our Commissary and business offices is about 3 1/2 miles from the center of town. This is true also of our Employment Office. It was felt by the members of the Junior Board that we would enhance our recruiting of personnel if we had a downtown location for an employment office. It was decided to run an experiment for a period of a month to determine the relative merits of having a downtown location. A suitable place was obtained, and ads were placed in the paper   Our experience showed that our recruiting would be greatly enhanced, both from the standpoint of quantity and quality of applicants. Based on this survey, a recommendation was made by the Junior Board to move the Employment Office downtown. It was approved, and we are now in the process of acquiring a suitable downtown location.

One of the biggest advantages of multiple management has been found to be the manner in which it increases cooperation and enterprise. People who take part in decisions are much more likely to be enthusiastic in implementing and carrying out the decisions. People who are encouraged to take on responsibility develop responsibility and learn to understand democratic procedures and to understand the value of group participation.

Those interested in learning the plan in detail may write McCormick Spice Co., Baltimore 2, Maryland, or may purchase the book Multiple Management from Jacobs Press, Charleston, S. C. A slide film can also be had on loan from the McCormick Spice Company.

Comment Cards

Perhaps the simplest yet one of the most effective devices for gaining the continuous interest of employees in the effect thay make on customers is the comment card. The cards are placed on each table and in each guest room in the hope the guest reacts to the service by completing the card.

In the case of a restaurant the completed card is handed to the manager, cashier, or dropped into a box located near the exit. The hotel guest leaves the completed form on his desk where he found it, or at the front desk.

Guest comments are read at employee meetings. Employees receiving favorable comments are praised publicly; those receiving adverse comments talked to privately.

The owner of a Miami chain of table service restaurants believes the comment cards to be his most effective personnel control device. He states that he can keep his finger on the pulse of management in each restaurant merely by reading the cards. He keeps the key to the card collection boxes, and collects the cards weekly.

In a business where it is difficult to keep employees continuously concerned with service, the comment cards act as a device to exert pressure for service awareness.

---

the **MCL** real cafeterias

- the SHERMAN
  sherman drive & 38th

- the RIPPLE
  2121 east 62nd st.

- the ARLINGTON
  arlington & 10th

Do we meet your high standards and respected requirements?

Your suggestions are appreciated. Do you have any ideas to help prevent our human errors and omissions?

Please indicate with check (√) marks and drop in suggestion box near the door.

SERVICE
☐ EXCELLENT
☐ GOOD
☐ FAIR
☐ POOR

FOOD
☐ EXCELLENT
☐ GOOD
☐ FAIR
☐ POOR

_____ Time of day _____ Date

Remarks and Suggestions: _____

_____

Signature and Address: (Optional)

_____

Thanks and please come in again, soon!

the **MCL** real cafeterias

ROOM _____

Because ... we want to be perfect in your eyes, please tell us how we rate with you.

	Excellent	Average	Not satisfactory-- comment
ROOMS			
ROOM CLERK			
GARAGE			
DOORMAN			
CONCIERGE			
BELLMAN			
ROOM SERVICE			
PHONE SERVICE			
VALET--LAUNDRY SERVICE			
MAID SERVICE			
GOURMET ROOM			
PINK KITCHEN			
CLOAKROOM			
SWIMMING POOL			

THE SUGGESTION SYSTEM

The suggestion system is usually thought of as a method for securing ideas that may prove beneficial to the organization. It can be more than this; it can be a device for securing employee participation and cooperation.

The history of the formal use of a suggestion system in hotels and restaurants is one of excellent results and dismal failures. Some hotels have found the suggestion plan valuable not only from the cash value of the ideas presented but in the long-term benefits resulting from employee participation.

Much of the failure of suggestion systems in the hotel and restaurant industry can be traced to the manner and spirit in which they are conducted. If management considers the suggestion system merely as a cheap means of securing ideas for increased efficiency, the plan is likely to fail. If it is looked upon as one way to secure the worker's interest and participation and a way to share with the employees the rewards of increased efficiency, the suggestion system has a chance to be successful. No suggestion system is any better than the effort put into it by management.

Payments for ideas accepted in hotels and restaurants generally are made in a lump sum -- usually $5.00 to $15.00. If you were an employee would you submit a $1,000 idea for a possible reward of $10.00? Probably not. Successful suggestion systems usually pay a generous proportion of the savings resulting from the suggestion. In industry, the per cent paid is as much as 50 per cent of the savings: Many suggestions are paid for even though they may not have an immediate value to the organization. Employees are thus encouraged to do constructive thinking about their jobs and about the company.

In order that the suggestion system be effective, management must give evidence that it feels the system is worthwhile. All suggestions, accepted or not, should be answered -- usually within two weeks. Reasons for their acceptance or rejection should be given in writing or by personal interview. Award winners should receive publicity. Repeat winners can be pictured in the house magazine.

An excellent way to explain why suggestions are not used is to have a Suggestion Corner in the employees' magazine. Employees see the reasons why their suggestions were not accepted in print -- which eases the disappointment. The suggestions published serve to stimulate others and to show what type is considered useful by management or the suggestion committee. An excerpt from the "Suggestion Corner" of Staff Stuff, the Hotel Henry Hudson employees' magazine, will serve to illustrate the value of using the employees' magazine to explain why suggestions were not used:

We offer the following explanations on the suggestions submitted this month:

Suggestion #113:   Refers to improving Cafeteria food. A committee of food employees are having regular bi-weekly meetings on the subject.

Suggestion #37:   To tip the large fan in the lobby parallel with the ceiling. The Engineering Department claims that this procedure would cause too much wear and tear on the fan bearings for operating costs.

Suggestion #38:   To have all silver coins washed before being given out in change. The cost of operating such a system, with the coins passing through a number of hands, and the initial cost of machinery to accomplish this would be too costly for the amount of publicity obtained from it.

Suggestion #91:   To put drapes or curtains in the Whiffenpoof Room. Because of the high cost of flame-proofing draperies, and the fact that this must be done twice a year in any room where liquor is sold, is the reason why we have no draperies in the Whiffenpoof Room. However, we are getting bids on storm windows to try to shut out the cold during the winter.

Suggestion #86:   Put a juke box in the Recreation Room. This was voted on some time ago, by the employees committee, and it was decided at that time that the majority of the employees would object to it, as they like to listen to the baseball games on the radio.

Suggestion #114:   To give the breakfast guest a cup of coffee before he orders his breakfast. Because we serve breakfast only in the Cafeteria, this would not be feasible at this time.

In addition to the actual value of the suggestions offered, management secures added cooperation from the employees. To enhance the feeling of participation at least one employee, not a representative of management, should sit in on the committee which accepts or rejects suggestions and determines their value to the hotel or restaurant. Employees should be rotated so that participation can be extended. Perhaps the employee is not qualified to judge the value of a suggestion. His presence, however, assures the rank and file of a voice; in particular it makes that employee sitting in the committee feel a part of management.

Attesting to the enterprise of the management of the Buffalo Statler and to the effectiveness of the booklet, the employees of the Buffalo Statler turned in 75 suggestions the first month the system was installed. Within a few months one employee alone handed in 20 suggestions. Participation in the plan is abetted by selecting those who were previous winners to serve on the committee charged with executing the system. The personnel director is chairman. The other management members are the executive assistant manager and a department head.

Typical of ideas suggested was that which recommended installing a clock in the employees' locker room -- a simple idea and a useful one which no one had thought of before. Using everyone's intelligence is good business and is a means of stimulating employee participation and efficiency.

The form on which the suggestion is written is often an aid in stimulating suggestions and can help the employee clarify his ideas for presentation. The form on the following page is an example of a suggestion blank.

Sheraton Hotels has an active suggestion system also. Here are a few of their prize-winning suggestions made by employees:

> Rags and dust cloths should be cut with pinking shears to prevent raveling.

> Each maid be equipped with a leather belt with straps and snaps to avoid losing their keys.

> Copies of the graphs showing increases and decreases in waste, sales, operation, etc. be hung in each department so employees as well as Department Heads "will know their good work or shortcomings."

> Napkins be collected when tables are cleared after functions to prevent loss.

> White or light-colored matches and match covers, instead of black to avoid discoloration of table linen during laundering process when matches are included in wash by mistake.

> Printed instructions including a map, on small cards for departing guests, who are unfamiliar with the shortest and best driving routes from the hotel out of the city; this would be a time-saver for the hotel as well as the guest, because it would eliminate the need for verbal instructions from hotel personnel.

> Suggestions on the back of Bellmen's Front and Last cards that will serve as "duty reminders" with questions such as, "Did you leave Room slip with guest and duplicate at the Mail Desk?"

EMPLOYEE MEETINGS

A personnel procedure closely related to the conference is the employee meeting. Both the conference and the employee meeting are designed to gain the participation of employees. Both aim at gaining information and ideas from employees and both are unusually effective at changing attitudes and gaining acceptance of new ideas.

Customarily the conference is thought of as being held primarily for supervisory and executive personnel, while employee meetings are held for nonsupervisory employees. In this light, the conference deals with policy matters of a higher level in the organization than does the employee meeting. Because of this, we would expect some differences in the method of procedure used in the conference and the employee meeting.

When the problem for discussion is centered in a particular department or division, the department head or supervisor should lead the discussion. Being the recognized leader by virtue of his position, it is important that he should assume the responsibility for the employee meeting. To do otherwise might endanger his position in management. After the meetings have become an established procedure in the minds of the employees, employees who have leadership potential can be given the opportunity of leading the meetings without endangering the supervisor's position.

Since most supervisors are not prepared to lead an employees' meeting in a manner that realizes the purposes of the meeting, training is necessary. Probably the most important skill to be learned is that of drawing ideas and the expression of emotion from the employees. Supervisors schooled in the

THE INN OF THE SEVEN HAPPINESSES

Proposal For Improvement

I believe my proposal will:

☐ Eliminate unnecessary steps	☐ Eliminate other unnecessary work
☐ Improve the cleanliness of this hotel	☐ Save time
☐ Improve safety conditions	☐ Reduce waste
☐ Improve working conditions	☐ Attract more guests
	☐ Improve service

Present Method	Proposed Method

Author's name _____

Department _____

Date _____

For Office Use

Date Received _____

Action taken _____

Amount paid _____

Date Paid _____

No. 594

- -

(Tear off this stub and keep as a record of your suggestion.)

No. 594

Date _____

hard-boiled approach of motivating employees have the greatest amount of <u>unlearning</u> to do. Supervisors who are flexible and skilled in gaining support by consultation have the least to learn. Understanding that the "fear approach to motivating employees is a liability in the employee meeting" is fundamental. Learning that the acceptance of ideas hinges largely on the ego involvement of the participants is also important. Accepting the fact that group expression of resentment is necessary and healthy for the development of morale is a further prerequisite.

HOLDING EMPLOYEES' MEETINGS

Old-fashioned institution managers believed that they had all the answers and had only to plan and give orders to make their enterprise successful. Modern management knows that such beliefs were wrong on two counts. First, no manager has all the answers and second, we now know that giving orders is only a part of motivating people to do anything. To motivate employees requires that they be made to feel a real part of the organization and that the interests of the enterprise are their interests.

One means of tapping employees' ideas and interests is to hold periodic employees' meetings.

WHAT CAN BE GAINED FROM HOLDING EMPLOYEE MEETINGS?

Depending upon how they are conducted and upon the caliber of the over-all employer-employee relations program, employee meetings can have a number of values.

1. A Means of Putting Across Changes

It is one thing to have ideas, another thing to implement them. The manager or the supervisor may be the most intelligent, the most highly educated, and the most experienced person in his organization, and yet his "good" ideas may fail to achieve what is desired because the ideas are not accepted. One reason for failure is that the ideas are "theirs" and not those of the people expected to carry them out.

Ask yourself which of these two ideas you would be more likely to accept:

a. "From now on you will turn in a report on every ounce of cooking fat you use!"

b. "We have a problem of keeping track of the cost of cooking fat. Can I get your ideas as to how we can remedy the situation?"

Perhaps some people trained in a Nazi or other dictatorship-type of culture would prefer the first. Most Americans will go along quicker with the second approach. The superior-inferior relationship is almost always resented. When ideas are presented in the context of such a relationship enthusiasm for them is almost invariably certain to suffer.

Asking people's opinions is a subtle form of compliment which all enjoy. Dishwashers and assistant managers, janitors, and food supervisors all react alike in this regard.

When ideas are presented in employees' meetings "for your criticism and suggestions," the ideas are likely to be accepted. Many times the manager or supervisor's idea emerged from an employee meeting in practically the same form as it would have been detailed by the manager or supervisor in private. So much the better. The value of the idea is multiplied because now it has employee interest and is well on the way to action.

2. A Means of Getting the Best from Employees

Every manager or supervisor should realize that one of his primary functions is to utilize others' abilities and enthusiasm. Managing means working through other people, drawing upon their skills, their experience, and their ideas. The employee meeting can be a device for drawing out and utilizing the talents of many.

The employee meeting led by a competent supervisor can stimulate critical thinking and new ideas. It can enlarge the individual's perspective and aid him in realizing his job as a part of the department. He is helped to see his problems as they are related to that of the department and the total organization. In a hospital, for example, the over-all goal of making the patient well is often lost sight of by the maintenance man or the vegetable girl. The porter in a hotel often forgets the main purpose of the hotel -- service at a profit and personal enjoyment in the doing. The employee meeting can reorient and restructure the goals for everyone concerned.

On the following page is an excerpt from an employee meeting held in a Midwestern hotel. It illustrates how the employee meeting can enlarge the participant's perspective.

At a regular kitchen meeting a wall washer, whose assignment included the kitchen area, was sitting in on the meeting.

Steward: Now, does anyone have any gripes?...(Pause, followed by some laughter)

Wall washer: Yes, I have one. Why can't the food runners be a little more careful in the way they knock their trucks up against the walls?

A young food runner, half in earnest, half kiddingly: If we did that, you wouldn't have anything to do. (Laughter)

Wall washer: Anything to do, why I can't keep up with the upstairs rooms I've got, let alone keep the kitchen clean.

Runner: Oh, I thought when you left here.......

Steward: Yes, Jonesy (the wall washer) does the kitchen and also a lot of rooms upstairs.

Runner: Okay, we'll be more careful with the trucks.

(Other runners nod in agreement)

In a discussion in which many competent people participate, ideas are forged which stand the test of practicality. Every idea which concerns a department as a whole should be subjected to the bombardment and modification of discussion. In addition to gaining acceptance of changes, discussion subtracts un-workable parts and implements the desirable parts.

Following is an illustration of how it pays to use everyone's ideas. The scene took place in a cafe-teria's employee meeting.

Supervisor: We've got a bottleneck in getting clean trays. We haven't got room in our present set-up for another tray-wiper, and we've got to have the trays dry. They come out of the dishwashing room plenty fast. Has anyone got any ideas?

(Long pause)

How about you, Mrs. Small (the tray-wiper)?

Mrs. Small: I'm going as fast as I can already.

(Another pause)

Mrs. Katsch (a counter girl): I worked at the Longbow last year and the lady who wiped the trays there has a system of wiping with both hands at once, which was supposed to be a lot faster.

Mrs. Small: You can't wipe with both hands. You've got to pick them up and turn them over with one hand.

Mrs. Katsch: Yes, but the wiper there had a sponge in each hand and wiped the top of one in one job and the bottom of another in the other pile at the same time.

Mrs. Small: I don't think it will work.

Supervisor: Maybe Mrs. Katsch will demonstrate after our meeting and see what Mrs. Small thinks of it. Would you be willing to give it a try, Mrs. Small?

Mrs. Small: Why yes, we can try it anyway.

Later the new method was installed and increased the number of trays wiped by more than one-third at no increase in energy expenditure.

3. A Means of Building a Cooperating Work Team

Cooperation comes from the attitude to cooperate and experience in cooperation. The employee meeting can help to build both. The face-to-face relations which result when people sit together in a meeting are an emotional experience which ties an aggregate of people together into a group of people en-joying the experience of association. Through competent leadership the group takes on common goals and solves common problems. A discussion of proposed kitchen layout with kitchen personnel is not only a means of solving the layout problem but is a means of drawing the group together. A discussion among chambermaids of the best way to clean a room is not only a training session but also a period of tighten-ing the emotional bonds which are so necessary for teamwork.

Employee meetings can give experience in give and take. Chambermaids who work all day alone have little practice in cooperation. The storeroom clerks are practically isolated. While kitchen personnel interact at a high rate, they often do so under stressful conditions which may destroy cooperation. Employee meetings can bring people together in a relaxed, friendly, problem-solving atmosphere. They provide a workshop in which to learn to work together.

4. A Means of Releasing Tensions and Resolving Personal Problems

Frustrations are inevitable on any job. The employee meeting provides a means of relieving part of the day-to-day job frustration. Here is an illustration of how it has worked in a waitress meeting:

Hostess: Well, that about winds up the discussion of today's menu. Is there anything further we should talk about?

(Pause)

Waitress: Is there anything we can do about that Beau Brummel who makes a pass at me every day at 12:15?

(Laughter)

Another waitress: Stop swinging your hips.

(More laughter)

First waitress: But I don't swing my hips.

Another waitress: Then you should try.

(More laughter)

Hostess: What can you do to politely discourage mashers?

Voice: Send them to me!

Hostess: How would it be if I always manage to seat the gentleman, and I know who you mean, at Charlotte's table.

First waitress: Fine, he really gives me a bad time.

Hostess: We'll try it anyway, and if he bothers anyone else I'll talk with him, and if need be, talk with Mr. Carlile (the manager).

5. How To Make an Employee Meeting Worthless

The success of an employee meeting hinges on the skill of the leader. Many well-meaning, intelligent people fail as leaders in an employee meeting because they overlook the needs of the participants. Here is a verbatim record of one such failure:

Mr. Manager: Well, let's get this thing going. I have another meeting after this one. (He sat down.) We're spending a lot of money to make this place over and to improve the service to the customers. So far as I can see, our efforts have been positively wasted. We ask for your cooperation and what do we get? Nothing! This has got to stop. All of you are making good money here and you seem to think, 'Why should I worry about the customers?' Things have got to change around here. This hotel is not going to be run for the employee's benefit any more. It is a place of business and it's going to be run that way. If any of you don't like it, get out! We don't want you here! etc., etc., etc.

PLANNING EMPLOYEE MEETINGS

There are two schools of thought on planning employee meetings. The first subscribes to a carefully planned meeting. The other subscribes to an informal, regularly scheduled, but nonstructured meeting. The rationale of the nonstructured meeting is that it is more democratic and provides more opportunity for employees to accept responsibility. Of course, a nonstructured, unplanned meeting may have periods of "dragging." On the other hand, such dragging may be advantageous in the sense that the members of the meeting become embarrassed and uncomfortable, are subtly "forced" to become involved with the meeting. Either the planned or the unplanned meeting can be effective, provided the leadership truly makes it an "employees' meeting" and not an "employer's meeting."

The most successful meetings are often those which are carefully planned and so conducted as to give the impression of casualness, flexible enough to develop ideas or discuss problems as they arise.

The advocates of a carefully planned meeting adhere to the guidelines shown on the following page.

1. Meetings should be called only when there is a definite need for them. Do not hold meetings "to be holding meetings."

2. Have definitely in mind what you wish to accomplish in the meeting.

3. Prepare an outline or agenda for the meeting.

4. Schedule the meetings at least a day in advance. Arrange for a quiet, well-ventilated room in which to hold the meetings.

5. Schedule the meeting during a lull in working hours. Avoid the first and last hours of the day for holding the meeting.

6. When possible, include employee representatives in the planning of the meeting.

The supervisor can gain employee participation by:

1. Presenting the problem and asking for opinions. The problem may be of any nature which affects the employees and which is within the supervisor's compass of responsibility. It may be merely the introduction of a new cooking range, a proposed change in working hours, the problem of courtesy, the problem of breakage, or of work simplification. When discussion touches upon areas of responsibility which are not the supervisor's, he should make this clear.

2. Refrain from giving answers himself, even though he has the answers.

3. Asking pertinent questions and giving illustrations which are related to the discussion.

4. Suggesting alternative solutions to the problem presented -- but only if none are forthcoming from the employees.

5. Making certain there is no personal embarrassment to an individual by:

   a. Making efforts to save face by "covering up" obviously mistaken ideas and rephrasing them in more suitable form.

   b. Avoiding humor which may be at some individual's expense.

6. Allowing everyone his "fair say" even at the risk of creating uncomfortableness in the group by allowing an unwise or overly emotional person to monopolize time.

7. Making use of the "reversible why," that is, when questions are directed to the supervisor, he throws them back to either the questioner or to some other discussant.

8. Assuring the employees that their suggestions will be followed up. When suggestions concern policies which are not the supervisor's responsibility, he should make it clear just what he will do to bring the ideas to the attention of his superior. He should make no promises as to what reception his supervisors will give the suggestions.

9. Keeping the meetings short and to the point. As someone has said, "The human capacity for maintaining contact between the rump and a hard-bottomed chair is definitely limited." The supervisor should announce at the beginning of the meeting the time the meeting will end, and stick to his decision as nearly as possible. An hour is a reasonable time for most meetings.

Follow-up:

Report back to the employees the progress being made on the ideas growing out of the meetings. Also report on failures to follow through on ideas and explain why.

SHOULD EMPLOYEES BE PAID FOR ATTENDANCE?

The answer to this question is that some incentive to attend -- and to learn -- must be given. If the meetings can be made so interesting that employees will attend on their own time, well and good. Usually meetings can be scheduled during slack periods. Bishop-Stoddard Cafeterias sometimes give a door prize of $10.00, which adds attendance incentive.

Where possible, schedule meetings in the morning when energy for learning is highest. Avoid the period following lunch.

Some hotels have found it profitable to schedule a dinner meeting, the training period immediately following.

UTILIZING THE GRIEVANCE PROCEDURE IN COORDINATION

One way to remove employee dissatisfaction and to promote harmony within an organization is by the use of grievance procedure. Alert management does not wait for trade unionism to press for a systematic settlement of grievances. It provides for an orderly hearing and settlement of grievances in its personnel policy.

Some managements seem to believe that the statement of a grievance is an indication of poor management. One manager when questioned about grievances declared, "We don't encourage 'em." On the contrary, where there are no stated grievances you can be sure there are plenty of unstated ones. Even though unstated, unsettled grievances appear inconsequential, they have a tendency to build up until an explosive point is reached. Poor work or high turnover results.

Where stated or unstated grievances accumulate in one department, it is of course a danger signal which means an investigation is needed. Often the supervisor is at fault, or the cause may be the lack of information or of misunderstanding. Whatever the cause of a grievance, there should be an orderly procedure known to all for settling it. Life in any organization is a dynamic process. It requires continual adaptation and changing attitudes by all participants. Differences of opinion are a benefit to any organization and should be anticipated. However, as in society generally, differences of opinion must be solved by definite rules of procedure and in an orderly fashion. The grievance procedure sets up the pattern for such settlement. Where there are no differences of opinion, there is resentment and stagnation. Management's function is to coordinate the differences to the benefit of the enterprise.

The manner in which complaints or grievances are handled is a large factor in successful settlement. Supervisors who deal directly with employees are in the best position to keep complaints from growing into grievances, grievances into resentment, loss of efficiency or retaliation. It has been found that the employer-employee relationship which is the keystone to all others is that which exists between employees and first-line supervisors. Supervisors should be educated to an awareness of the significance of grievances and how best to settle them. A pattern which has been found particularly helpful in settling complaints and grievances runs as follows:

Give the Employee Full Opportunity To Tell the Story. Keep an open mind. Do not interrupt. Do not argue. Be friendly and understanding. Get all the facts and opinions.

Restate the Complaint in Your Own Words. Make sure you have the story.

Get the Employee's Opinions as to How the Matter Can Be Taken Care Of. Explain any policies involved. If his suggestions are reasonable and satisfactory, accept them for consideration.

Review Any Other Pertinent Facts and Discuss the Situation with Immediate Superior.

After Careful Consideration of the Facts and Possible Solutions, Take Appropriate Action Which Will Bring About Mutual Satisfaction.

STEPS IN A GRIEVANCE PROCEDURE

Where grievances cannot be settled between the supervisor and employee, provision should be made for further consideration. Hotel and restaurant contracts usually make arrangements for settling disputes arising over interpretation of collective bargaining contracts but have not gone far in setting up plans for settling grievances of employees which are not related to the provisions of the contract. A recent survey indicated that less than one-half of the respondents had established machinery for handling grievances.

Where grievance procedures are a regular part of the personnel policy and are being utilized to coordinate the goals of all concerned, they are usually set up on a four-step basis. The first step, where the vast bulk of grievances are settled, is that comprising an appeal by the employee or by his union representative to the first-line supervisor. If conditions are such that there is no satisfactory settlement, the grievance goes to step two, the next level of supervision, the departmental supervisor. The third step may be between top management and the union representative and the fourth an appeal to an impartial umpire hired by terms of the contract to settle disagreements arising over interpretation or application of the contract. Some grievances can be settled only by collective bargaining.

Whether or not a grievance has any basis in objective conditions, it is always real to the person having it. Often the stated cause of a grievance may not have any logical connection to the complaint. An employee may complain that he cannot stand the work in a kitchen because of a draft caused by an open window. To satisfy him the window is closed and now the grievance changes to "it is too hot in this kitchen." An interview with the employee may disclose the real cause of his complaint to be his feeling against a certain loud-mouthed cook who works next to him. Since the stated cause of the grievance does not correlate with the facts, should management disregard such complaints? Obviously not. The fancied grievance about the draft is just as real to the employee as though it were fact. Management, as management, attempts to make all conditions correct for optimal efficiency. If the grievance were disregarded, management would be falling down on its job. Stated grievances give management opportunity to eliminate conditions which impair morale and production.

The mere expression of a grievance to a sympathetic listener may settle it. The real causes of many grievances are injured feelings, a lack of friendship, a need to confide in someone. Supervisors who understand such feelings can, by attentive listening and a genuine expression of interest in the employee's stated problem, often solve the unstated problem. Where real deficiencies exist in the work situation, pay rates, or personal relationships, the grievance procedure is a valuable means of calling attention to them so that they can be corrected.

Of course, if employees do not know and understand the grievance procedure, it is of no value. Real or imagined injustices are permitted to simmer and finally erupt. The employee feels he is subject to the whims of his supervisor and has no appeal. His feeling of security, which is necessary for job satisfaction and best job performance, is seriously impaired.

A policy which permits any employee to appeal to top management for a review of his case in the event the employee's supervisor or department head places his job in jeopardy is one calculated to increase employee security and the all-important feeling of belonging. Some chain operations provide a system of appeals by which an employee in a branch house may appeal to the home office for a review of a grievance. This would appear to be an excellent policy as long as it is handled so as not to undermine the supervisor's or branch manager's leadership.

DIAGRAM OF GRIEVANCE PROCEDURE

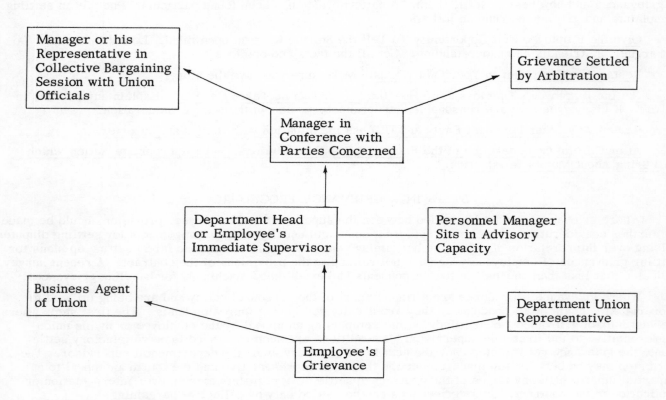

Grievance procedure was not as necessary fifty years ago as today. Employees expected arbitrary decisions from management. Today there is a new and progressive spirit which has the spirit of democracy about it. Management is management by virtue of its ability to get employees to work efficiently for a common goal -- service at a profit and enjoyment while serving. It is management's responsibility to know and to set into operation techniques which will increase employee cooperation and participation.

UTILIZING EMPLOYEE LEADERSHIP

In addition to formal leadership in a business as represented by organization charts, supervisory personnel and management personnel, there are always informal employee groupings which center around and are led by certain employees. The alert supervisor and the manager is aware of this informal group structuring and utilizes it to the advantage of the enterprise.

William F. Whyte in his book, Human Relations in the Restaurant Industry,[1] has shown clearly how groups of waitresses, kitchen employees, and other restaurant employees form definite social structures. Cliques of waitresses centered around one or two waitresses have their own structure and leadership. In the kitchen every employee has a rank in the minds of the other employees depending upon the job and personality of the individual. Informal social structures are necessary to carry out any enterprise. Everyone in the enterprise must have some knowledge as to his relative position in regard to the others. He must know to whom he may originate orders and from whom he should expect to receive them. Without these informal patterns the individual is lost. He does not know what to expect; the situation is unpredictable.

Wise management does not attempt to break down the informal social structure. It makes use of it for the efficiency and well-being of organization. Recognizing who is the leader in a kitchen or what chambermaid most influences the thinking of the others, or who in the front office is the informal leader is part of management's job in coordinating management and employee for maximum efficiency. Working through informal leadership is like oiling a machine. If the machine is never oiled, it finally breaks down.

A case illustrating the results of failing to recognize informal group leadership recently occurred in the kitchen of a Texas hotel. One of the members of the dishwashing crew was the acknowledged leader. The fact that all of the crew were Mexicans seemed to increase the feeling of being an in-group and enhanced the importance of the informal leader.

A new supervisor took it upon himself to break up the clique led by one José by firing him. Morale among the remaining dishwashers fell apart almost immediately. The obvious dollar and cents cost of this disintegration became painfully apparent when one evening the crew "allowed" over $300 worth of china breakage. In this case, the management rehired José over the head of the supervisor. The alternative would have been to replace the entire crew. As it was the supervisor lost face and effectiveness.

Recognizing leaders among employees and securing their participation means a much lighter burden for formal management. Anyone interested in personnel management should read Whyte's book. A sociological approach to the problem of management, it is invaluable in understanding the importance of group dynamics in an organization.

PROVIDING OPPORTUNITIES FOR SATISFACTION THROUGH THE JOB

Some individuals receive intrinsic satisfactions from their work, i.e., it is "like play" and there is nothing in the world they would like to do better. Other individuals get extrinsic satisfactions from their work, i.e., they receive money for it which then provides a means for them to receive satisfaction away from the job through such things as recreation, hobbies, reading, and socializing. The ideal situation is to have an organization in which all workers are intrinsically satisfied. Needless to say, the problems of motivation would be minimal with such an organization.

There is no one-to-one way of providing opportunities for workers to experience intrinsic satisfactions on the job. Each job situation is somewhat different as are the needs of each individual. Realizing these restrictions, the following guidelines can be used:

1. Redesign the job where possible to increase intrinsic satisfactions through such things as job enlargement, job rotation, understanding of how the work is coming along, and more involvement with the whole project. For example, many cafeteria operators rotate counter-serving personnel from station to station, changing each meal. One university operator rotates even the cashier's job. (Since the cashier is critical in moving a cafeteria line and in cash control, rotating this job is not recommended in the usual cafeteria. Cashiers require special talents had only by a small percentage of the general population. The meat-carving station is another job which cannot be rotated easily because of special skill requirements.)

---

[1]Whyte, W. F., Human Relations in the Restaurant Industry. New York: McGraw-Hill, 1948.

In some Howard Johnson restaurants soda fountain personnel are trained to be "interchangeable," a practice which gives management flexibility in staffing as well as adds employee interest.

2. Greater opportunity can be provided for social satisfactions on the job. For example, employee friendships can be encouraged and opportunities provided for working together as a team. When members of the group participate together in solving work problems, they become more involved with the job itself and their productivity increases.

   Management should be careful, however, about forming work teams, expecially where no formal supervisor is assigned to the group. Maid teams for cleaning guest rooms are seldom used for the reason the maids are likely to become too "sociable."

3. The style of leadership by management should give employees a feeling of accomplishment in their work and the confidence to make decisions on their own as much as possible. The supervisor should try to conceive of his job as a means of helping subordinates rather than as a means of pushing them.

4. Each work group should have at least two "veterans" who can wheel the group when under the fire of high-volume sales. A soda fountain or a cafeteria line must have two or more old hands who know by habit what to do, giving confidence and stability to the group.

   Green department heads spell exasperation for a manager no matter how competent he is. Their lack of experience and know-how is reflected at once in the work being done and in employee morale.

MANAGEMENT REDEFINED

Management today is fast becoming leadership. The emphasis is shifting from motivating employees by fear in the form of threats or punishments to an emphasis on offering positive incentives and upon changing basic attitudes. Leadership makes an appeal to the constructive capacities of the individual. While the leader today is not the same feared and respected manager of twenty-five years ago, his power in terms of results in production and morale is greatly increased.

Check yourself on the following items to see in what category you fall.

The Autocratic Manager

1. Thinks that because of his training and experience he has all of the answers.

2. Feels indispensable.

3. Cannot bear to let any controls out of his hands.

4. Is tied to routine jobs.

5. Feels "responsible" for personal lives of "subordinates."

6. Reacts to subordinate ideas:

   a. by assuming that a suggestion implies a criticism.

   b. kills suggestions that do not strike him as perfect with a withering or sarcastic remark.

   c. while seeming to reject it, restates it as his own, giving no credit to the originator of the idea.

The Leader

1. Realizes the potential power in all levels of individuals.

2. Recognizes that he is but one of many important contributors.

3. Knows how to delegate authority.

4. Frees himself from routine details in order to tackle the problem of group motivation.

5. Assumes everyone has a right to his own life.

6. Is quick to recognize and praise others' ideas.

The Autocratic Manager	The Leader
7. Expects hero worship from sub-ordinates.	7. Wishes to be respected as a capable person as he respects others.
8. Is greedy for publicity.	8. Pushes others to the foreground so that they can experience success.
9. Gives few opportunities for leadership to others.	9. Gives as many opportunities for leadership to others as possible.
10. Believes that men are best motivated by fear.	10. Believes that men are best motivated by self-respect and accomplishment.
11. Says "I," "I," "I."	11. Says "We."
12. Says "Go."	12. Says "Let's Go."

Lao-Tse centuries ago had the answer when he said:

> A leader is best
> When people barely know that he exists.
>
> Not so good when people obey and acclaim him,
>
> Worst when they despise him.
>
> Fail to honor people,
> They fail to honor you.
>
> But of a good leader, who talks little
> When his work is done, his aim fulfilled,
> They will say, "We did this ourselves."

From brief of speech "Good Human Relations in Industry Pays Off" by Harry G. Easmann, Potomac Electric Power Co., Washington, D. C.

Fire and Accident Prevention

Fire protection and accident prevention programs have one thing in common: both require the active interest of top management to be effective. Fire protection and accident prevention are functions of management, reflecting management alertness and its relation to employees. Both involve human life, misery, and high costs if neglected. Over a period of years more than 600 people have died in hotel fires. Some 12,000 fires occur in hotels and motels each year.

Accidents are costly; over the period 1952 to 1963 annual premiums paid for workmen's compensation have doubled in many states. The average rate for restaurant employees during 1952 was 74 cents per $100 of payroll; in 1963 it was $1.12 for the same amount. Weekly compensation benefits have been increased by state legislatures. Medical and hospital costs have gone up and court awards made for settlement of injuries have skyrocketed.

FIRE PREVENTION AND THE GUEST

Cigarette smoking, particularly smoking in bed, is the number-one cause of hotel and motel fires. In Texas, for example, the Board of Insurance Commissioners reported that 74 per cent of the hotel fires are caused by careless disposal of cigarettes and matches. The cigarette falls on the carpet or bedding and a fire starts. How to prevent such habits? The answer is not in posting the guest with "No Smoking!" signs for we do not change habits fixed over a period of years by the use of signs.

Fireproofing as much of the room furnishings as possible helps. The placing of ash trays in swivels that permit the trays to swing close to the stretched-out smoker helps. One motel with two parallel lines of sleeping units introduced swiveled ash trays in one line of units and left the other line as before. During the succeeding year several fires occurred in the units without the swiveled ash trays, none in the other units.

Another preventive method is to make the guest pay. The city of Houston, Texas, has passed an ordinance which makes it a misdemeanor for guests to cause a hotel fire through carelessness. Guilty guests pay not only the fire damage to the hotel but also a fine to the city. Detroit, Michigan, has a similar ordinance.

NOTIFYING GUESTS OF FIRE

State laws require that the innkeeper exercise "reasonable and ordinary care in the safety of his guests." The hotel is responsible for notifying his guests immediately of any danger. A fire in a Wichita Falls, Texas, hotel started at 4:20 A.M. and by 4:30 was beyond control. Employees tried to extinguish the blaze but failed to notify the guests by telephone or otherwise. Several people died and the hotel was held liable because of the 10-minute delay in warning guests. A guest of a western hotel charges that he detected smoke and told the desk clerk. Nothing was done and about two hours later the guest awoke in a smoke-filled room. Getting no response on the telephone he tried to take the elevator but it was not running. Escaping by means of a rope fire escape, the rope parted.

The hotel proprietor was held liable in the amount of $6,500 for failing to notify all guests and do all in his power to save them from danger.

The American Hotel Association issued this fire prevention bulletin.

FOR SUMMER HOTELS

*1. Make sure that "No Smoking" regulations are enforced. Modern practice is to confine smoking to a special "safe-smoking area" supplied with plenty of ash trays or sandpails for the disposal of smoking materials. State and municipal laws must, of course, be considered here.

*2. Store painters' supplies in an outlying building or other safe storage space. Keep everything including drop cloths in this area except for immediate requirements. Make sure that rags and oily waste are put in tight, metal containers and removed at the end of each day.

*3. Do not leave unattended salamanders in a building at any time.

*4. Provide fire extinguishers and a fire watch for operations involving cutting or welding equipment. (See also the item on cutting and welding following.)

*5. Maintain good housekeeping conditions. Do not allow combustible trash to accumulate; rather, remove it daily and burn it in a safe location.

6. Clear excessive underbrush around principal buildings and make sure that grass and weeds are close-cut. A well-groomed space of 100 to 300 feet is advisable depending on the amount of combustible undergrowth and dry grass beyond the clearing space.

7. Make certain that your employees know how to turn in an alarm to your local fire department and understand the need for immediate action in the event of fire.

8. Check to see that water has been turned on hose standpipes or other fire protective equipment and that extinguishers have been recharged.

9. Arrange storage outdoors or in a small outlying building for any large quantities of furnishings, plumbing, fixtures, etc. that are delivered in combustible wrappings or light crating.

10. Provide watchmen at night and other times when the premises are unattended.

11. Notify your insurance carrier of any structural alterations made.

12. To ensure the safest means of heating your buildings, use your own heating plant or portable Underwriters' Laboratories listed oil-fired units. If salamanders must be used, place them on a solid, noncombustible footing away from woodwork or tarpaulins. Coke or coal are the safest fuels for salamanders.

13. Use only flame-proofed tarpaulins.

14. Check electrical circuits to make sure they are properly fused and that frayed lamp and appliance cords have been replaced.

15. Make certain that light arrester and lightning-rod wire grounds are in good condition.

The first five items have been starred because they demand checks, preferably daily; the others should be examined once or twice during the season.

Cutting and Welding

Since cutting and welding are important methods for severing or joining piping and structural steel, they are frequently used in hotel maintenance. Both present hazards although oxyacetylene equipment is more dangerous in welding than either gas or electrical equipment.

Here are the precautions you should take before and during such operations:

1. Sweep clean and wet down the surrounding floor.

2. Relocate combustible storage 30 to 40 feet away and use asbestos or flame-proof tarpaulins to protect any that cannot be moved.

3. Provide extinguishing equipment such as hose lines, extinguishers, or water pails at the scene of operations.

4. Keep the area under watch for at least a half hour after the work is completed. It is necessary to extend this care to any location on floors above or below where metal globules may go. (When a piece of pipe or a steel building member is cut, small globules of molten metal are thrown out in a heavy shower resembling rain. The globules may bounce and roll for as far as 30 to 40 feet from the actual cutting operations; sometimes they get through pipe holes or cracks to the floor below. They can easily start smoldering fires that burst into flame when no one is present.)

5. Appoint someone from your own staff to designate areas where cutting or welding can be done. It is unwise to give outside workmen unlimited choice in this matter.

6. Make sure that at least one helper is available to use extinguishing equipment if necessary. A small fire may not be visible to the cutting-equipment operator while he is wearing dark glasses.

Ash Trays

A good supply of ash trays is a mark of a considerate host. It is also a cheap investment in fire protection. According to fire statistics, about 40 per cent of all hotel fires are due to careless smoking. Desirable though legislation is, with fines for offenders, it still does not remove the element of human carelessness; two or three ash trays in the room will remind the guest that a dresser top is a poor place for a burning cigarette.

Avoiding Spontaneous Ignition

Spontaneous ignition can be easily avoided if you observe these simple safety rules:

1. Use cans with tight, self-closing covers for the storage of materials that may heat spontaneously. (Garbage cans with tight lids may also be used for this purpose.)

2. Empty the cans at the end of the day.

3. Make sure that all waste and sweepings are burned in a well-arranged incinerator, trucked away, or otherwise safely removed.

Materials in common use that heat spontaneously include: (1) vegetable oils such as linseed, cottonseed, coconut, palm, olive, peanut, and soybean; (2) animal oils including lard and tallow; (3) certain solids including soft coal. All forms of fermenting or decaying organic matter (e.g., hay or silage) produce some heat although temperatures seldom become high enough for ignition.

Properly stored, these materials are harmless. Take linseed oil, for example. It will not heat spontaneously in a bottle because of the small surface exposed. If thinly spread fibre-waste is soaked with linseed oil, the exposed surface area is greatly increased and oxidation takes place. However, the thinly spread waste affords no insulation and the heat is dissipated rapidly enough so that ignition is unlikely. Now take the same oil-soaked waste and wad it up in a ball. Oxidation proceeds at the same rate, but the outer layers of the ball provide insulation so that heat is not so readily lost from the center. The heat at the center of the wad rises, and the chances that it will rise high enough to ignite the wadding are increased. If the whole package is placed in a warm place, look out!

Foam Rubber Products

In recent years foam rubber has been used more and more as filling for upholstered chairs, sofas, pillows, mattresses, and seating equipment. If may vary considerably in its composition, but foam rubber is as about as easy to ignite as feathers, cotton stuffing, hair, etc. When it is covered with a combustible textile as it usually is in mattresses, pillows, and chairs, the ignition hazard becomes that of textile covering; rapid surface burning of the foam rubber will then result. When foam rubber materials are taken from a laundry drying tumbler and placed in a hamper where they are effectively insulated by other materials, spontaneous heating can result in ignition. Once ignited, foam rubber or foam latex is rapid burning under most conditions.

Foam rubber releases almost as much heat when it is burned as gasoline. It burns rapidly and gives off dense clouds of heavy smoke. Thus the storage of large piles of foam rubber pillows or mattresses presents a serious fire hazard. The danger is not so much from spontaneous ignition under normal storage conditions, but in the intense burning rate and rapid flame spread once the material has been ignited from any source. Storage of large quantity of foam rubber requires automatic protection engineered to meet these conditions.

How Are Your Fuses?

Fuses are the safety valves of electrical circuits. Their purpose, of course, is to shut an electrical circuit when it becomes overloaded. Heat in or around a fuse box indicates that circuits are overloaded and fuses with too high a rating are used. If the circuits are seriously overloaded, the fuse box itself may be warm to the touch. If the wiring is overloaded, the temperature of the wire rises and this can be detected at the fuse box.

If a fuse blows out, it does not solve the problem to replace it with a fuse rated too high or by placing a coin behind a plug fuse. That only increases the chances that the safety equipment will be unable to function properly. Fuses with a "time-lag" have been available in recent years. These fuses permit the overload to continue for an interval. With the starting of a motor the "time-lag" fuse permits a momentary overload; but the fuse will "blow" if the overload persists. Call your electrician for advice if fuses of the proper rating cannot be used without continued interruptions of service. These interruptions serve as warnings of overloaded circuits that may cause fires.

A FIRE PROTECTION PROGRAM

A complete fire protection program is more than fire prevention in the usual sense of the word. It is more than a set of rules of what not to do, of where to store inflammables, and the upkeep of fire extinguishers. The best fire prevention program sometimes fails. It is at such a time that the need for a more complete program is glaringly evident.

Training in ways of combating fires is a necessity. The training should not be perfunctory or sporadic. It must be continuous, instilled by regular drills. Every key person in the organization must know the particular duty assigned to him. The training must be such that in case of fire, a trained fire brigade is already on the scene.

WHO SHOULD BE RESPONSIBLE FOR FIRE TRAINING?

Since every hotel and nearly every large restaurant is a fairly well-contained unit, usually within a single building with its own power, light, and heat supply, and a close-knit type of organization, the logical man to head the fire protection program is the manager of the business. Just as aboard a ship all responsibilities center under the office of one individual, the captain of the ship, so it is in a hotel or restaurant. If a fire occurs, the manager or his representative is responsible. As aboard a ship, however, no one individual can perform all the duties for which the captain is responsible. The manager who attempts directly to control the training, hiring, firing, and other jobs rightly performed by the personnel manager or his assistants is a jack-of-all-trades, master of none. In the large manufacturing establishment the responsibility for fire prevention is usually delegated to a safety department. The hotel and restaurant do not have such a specialized department. Department heads cannot coordinate fire protection activities. There is but one department which cuts across all department lines, and that is the personnel department. All phases of training which affect all employees should be under the direct control of the personnel manager. Next to the manager of the enterprise he has the broadest view of activities affecting the entire organization. Where there is no personnel department, the chief engineer should be responsible for the fire prevention program.

TRAINING FOR FIRE FIGHTING

During the period preceding World War II, the U. S. Navy believed its fire fighting program to be adequate. The war soon dispelled such notions. More ships were lost as a result of fires than from any other reason. Drastic steps were taken. Almost every man in the seagoing Navy was required to spend an intensive period of training during which he was literally sent into the flames to extinguish roaring oil and gasoline fires. Aboard ship continuous drills made his knowledge of fire fighting equipment a workable, active knowledge. In the case of actual fire his reactions could be predicted. He acted automatically. He knew his fire station, he knew his piece of equipment and, more importantly, he had been so conditioned that he was not panic-stricken. Ship losses due to fires were greatly reduced. The Navy training program followed well-known learning principles, namely learning by doing, and learning by repetition. Fire drills were repeated until the individual acted automatically. He had learned the manner in which to act so thoroughly that associational thinking was unnecessary.

Some factories dealing with dangerous inflammables have several fires every day. No one gets particularly excited, and no one becomes frightened. The fires are quickly extinguished by highly trained fire teams. The hotels and restaurants can so train their personnel that, given proper equipment, fires will offer no danger.

TRAINING FIRE BRIGADES

The Drake Hotel of Chicago has introduced a plan of fire protection patterned after the Navy plan. In the plan all key personnel are assigned fire stations. All stations and the names of personnel assigned to the stations are posted. Monthly fire drills are held.

Keeping the fire bill (roster of personnel and their duties in case of fire) effectively manned at all times is a continuous job on the part of the director of the fire program. Employee turnover and changes in shifts necessitate rearrangement in the fire organization. Often the fire organization is least effective at night, when serious danger is most likely to develop.

Working closely with the director of the fire protection program is the chief engineer. The engineer's responsibility is to see that the fire fighting equipment is in working order. Too often fires have become uncontrollable because of faulty equipment or lack of an adequate water supply.

Telephone operators are also key personnel in any fire protection program. Because they are in control of communication, they should receive special instruction. Kent W. Francis, staff representative, hotel services of the National Safety Council, recommends the following instructions to telephone operators:

1. Notification of municipal fire department.

2. House officers to be notified, and in what order.

3. Procedure for warning guests.

4. Wires to be kept open for emergency use only.

Of course, periodic drill is essential if the personnel are to learn their duties. Instruction in the use of the fire fighting equipment is also necessary. Instruction can be reinforced by periodic demonstration lectures. Every possible emergency should be investigated and the steps to be taken gone over in drill. Leaving matters to a "general understanding" is not enough. When the emergency arises "general understanding" becomes general confusion.

Every employee should be so trained that in case of fire his first act will be to do one of two things. If the fire is small he will fight it himself. If it is of any size he will immediately notify the hotel switchboard and the municipal fire department. Immediate and swift action is imperative. The first few moments of a fire determine whether it can be extinguished without damage or whether loss of property and perhaps life will result.

Employees will respond enthusiastically to fire brigade training if it is properly presented to them. As in all other joint practices, employees must feel that it is their program. Induce people, do not force them. When employees understand the importance of fire prevention and gain an ego reward from participation in prevention programs, the program is likely to be a success.

The patrons of the hotel and restaurant are probably more of a hazard in case of fire than are flames, smoke, and other attendant dangers. Reports of panic-stricken guests leaping to their deaths and killing one another only serve to emphasize the need for careful planning. Key personnel must be trained to direct the flow of patrons to the proper exits. Such personnel must be schooled in the proper course of action for any of the possible emergencies which may arise. Should the front exits be blocked, they must know of other routes, or direct the making of exits.

CODE BELL SYSTEM FOR LOCATING FIRE

The Hotel Cosmopolitan, Denver, has a coded alarm system for dispatching employees to the scene of the fire immediately. Bells and alarms have been installed at strategic points throughout the hotel: manager's office, assistant manager's desk and in his apartment, linen room, engineer's office, and in the halls and public spaces. Fires are reported to the telephone operator who, by referring to a chart, rings the bells identifying the fire's location.

The code is derived so that the fire location is quickly identified. For example, 3 short bells followed by 4 long bells means that a blaze has started in section 3 of the fourth floor.

AUTOMATIC SPRINKLER SYSTEM IN THE HOTEL AND RESTAURANT

One of the best methods of controlling fire by mechanical means is by the installation of automatic water sprinkling systems. Fusible units are installed in the systems in locations to be protected. These are so constructed as to release automatically and distribute a shower of water when heated to a predetermined temperature. The system can be installed in such a manner that the sprinkler heads and piping can be concealed or camouflaged so as to be scarcely noticeable.

H. Edward Bilkey, insurance consultant to the American Hotel Association, has prepared a pamphlet which includes several statistics proving the effectiveness of the automatic sprinkler system.[2] A study of fires in hotels and apartments for the period 1897-1946 showed that where automatic sprinklers were installed they were 98.2 per cent satisfactory. Of 227 fires in hotels during the period studied, only 5 were not controlled by the sprinkler system. More importantly, not one life was lost in these fires.

Bilkey points out that the National Automatic Sprinkler and Fire Control Association of New York City will make a survey of the cost of installation without cost or obligation. Reduction of insurance rates

---

[2] Bilkey, H. W., "Automatic Sprinkler Systems as Applied to Hotels," American Hotel and Motel Association, New York.

may make possible the amortization of equipment over a relatively short period of years. The chart below shows how much installations of sprinklers have reduced rates in several hotels.

RATE BENEFITS ENJOYED BY SOME SPRINKLERED HOTELS

Name	When Built Sprinklers Installed	Construction	Fire Insurance Rate		Experience Since Sprinkler Installation
			Before Sprinkler Installation	After Sprinkler Installation	
Hotel Ruffner Charleston, W. Virginia	Sixty years old	Brick and wood	$3.12	$1.04	Three fires extinguished
Hotel Wyoming Orlando, Florida	Sprinklers Installed 1927		4.00	.55	One fire controlled by one sprinkler head
The Caroline Pinehurst, N. Carolina	100% sprinklered	Frame	2.54	.65	Several fires extinguished
New Crosby Beaumont, Texas	100% sprinklered	Brick with wood beams and joists	1.861	.58	Three fires extinguished
Cloister Hotel and service group Sea Island, Ga.	Sprinklers Installed 1930	Stucco on frame	3.25	.55	Six fires extinguished
Hotel Woodruff Watertown, New York	Sprinklered thruout except 2 dining rooms and lobby	Brick and concrete	1.47	.64	A number of fires extinguished

GOOD HOUSEKEEPING

Good housekeeping prevents fires. In modern fire-resisting structures there is still the danger of fires from accumulated inflammable materials in non-fire-resistant storage places or other rooms. Adequate storage of inflammables, precautions in the use of the incinerator, rapid disposal of refuse are a part of good housekeeping. In guest rooms where a primary cause of fires is carelessness in smoking, a good supply of ash trays handy to the bed smoker is good housekeeping. One way of insuring good housekeeping is by means of the Periodic Inspection Check List. Department heads with the manager and/or the personnel director should make biweekly or monthly inspections. Each inspection is recorded on a special form; defects are noted. Part of the check list supplied by the National Safety Council appears below.

(√) indicates satisfactory		(x) indicates unsatisfactory	
KITCHENS		**STEWARDS**	
Floors and stairs	( )	Floors	( )
Power-driven equip.	( )	Hand trucks	( )
Ranges	( )	Hand tools	( )
Utensils	( )	Storage of materials	( )
Dishes	( )	Others	( )
Glassware	( )		
Knives, cleaver, etc.	( )		
Light	( )		
Doors	( )		
Steam tables	( )	**SERVICE DEPT.**	
Housekeeping	( )	Floors	( )
Others	( )	Elevators	( )

Of course perfunctory inspection is not sufficient. Follow-up of all defects is usually delegated to particular persons. In addition to reducing fire hazards, a periodic inspection program improves working conditions and raises morale.

ACCIDENT PREVENTION

Employers are constantly seeking to gain further information concerning the causes and prevention of accidents. In the larger cities employers form associations for the purpose of developing and disseminating safety information. In New York City the Greater New York Safety Council is a clearing house for such information and actively sponsors safety training conferences. A national organization, The National Safety Council is the best known and perhaps the most active of all safety organizations. Founded in 1913 as a nonprofit coordinating institution, it collects and publishes accident statistics of all types. It also provides films, posters, and works with the American Hotel Association. It furnishes lecturers for the various topics concerning safety.

The National Safety Council now offers a complete accident and fire prevention service to hotels. According to the Council, its members have 30 per cent to 40 per cent fewer accidents than nonmembers. Among its services:

1. Industrial hygiene and technical materials including Hotel Accident Prevention Manual, Bibliography of Safety and Health, data sheets, safe practices manual, Industrial Supervisor magazine, and technical releases.

2. Education and training materials including posters, safety instruction cards, safe worker magazine, "Broken Glass," bus boy cards, and a quantity of the Safety Register, a 20-page employee booklet in fundamentals of safety.

3. Accident analysis and records including the accident analysis chart and the Inspection Check List.

4. An opportunity for consultation services, participation in the largest lending library on safety in the world and participation in nation-wide safety contests.

5. Safety calendars, posters, and hotel room and guest literature to promote public relations by assuring the guest of an active safety and fire prevention program.

COMPARATIVE ACCIDENT RATES

Is the hotel or restaurant a safe place to work? The hotel and restaurant business has a higher rate of disabling injuries than the steel industry. In fact these are the statistics for disabling injuries per million man hours worked in representative industries:

Hotels and Restaurants	14.17
Machinery	13.32
Rubber	12.94
Chemical	10.06
Cement	7.89
Steel	7.57

Danger is everywhere depending upon the care with which people work and live. People fall on perfectly flat surfaces. They cut their fingers wrapping packages. Bruises are incurred by walking into walls in broad daylight. Danger is very much a function of people.

KINDS OF HOTEL ACCIDENTS

Heading the list in number and cost of all accidents in hotels and motels in Florida are strains due to lifting or handling materials. The Florida Department of Industrial Safety tabulated 410 such accidents occurring in Florida hotels and motels in the year 1952. Their cost was $58,720.58.

Typical of these accidents were the following actual cases:

A housekeeper was lifting wet linen from a washing machine when her foot slipped on a wet floor. The resulting back strain cost $2,770 in medical and hospital expenses plus workmen's compensation.

A maintenance man was lifting a cement flower pot when he felt a severe pain in his back. He had ruptured the intervertebral disk, which necessitated an operation. The cost was $8,000 including workmen's compensation.

A PBX operator received a lumbar strain from doing nothing more than lifting a guest-card file case. The total expense was $2,499.82.

Hernias and back strains are commonplace in any work which involves lifting. Many times a history of strains is present and the current accident has only precipitated what has gone before. Where medical examinations are not given during the employment procedure, employees can come on the job with already existing hernias and back ailments, later claim that an accident on the job was the cause. No one can disprove their claims.

When lifting, keep the back as straight as possible and make use of the leg muscles.

The next largest cause of hotel and motel accidents as found by the Florida Department of Industrial Safety was from slipping on a level area. Total cost for these accidents in 1952 was $38,054.59.

Illustrative of such cases was the one involving an office clerk who, tripping over her own feet, fell and struck an object and broke her arm. The medical and compensation expense for this little accident was $4,465.

A dining room captain slipped while walking into the kitchen and struck the back of his head with a resulting cerebral concussion. Cost of the accident was $750. This amount covers the workmen's compensation expense.

A maid slipped on a waxed floor, fell and broke her wrist which involved a total expense of $742.49.

A waitress received a permanent partial disability by falling while carrying a glass pitcher. Her left hand was severely lacerated. The cost of this accident was $5,013.40 for medical expense and workmen's compensation.

A maid broke her toe when she stepped on a dog's foot. The dog jerked suddenly, she struck the toe against the bed. The total cost of the accident was $1,221.85.

To avoid such accidents see to it that rugs or mats that are wrinkled or have upturned edges or that have been rolled up are not left lying so as to present a tripping hazard. Keep all floors dry and if you have large waxed floor areas use a nonskid wax.

Falls from one level to another were the third most important kind of accidents in Florida in 1952. Falls from stairs or steps occurred 130 times and cost $25,420.21. Falls from ladders were even more costly, $28,658.97.

Here are two examples:

1. A repairman was working on top of the ceiling of a room when he fell through and landed on a concrete floor. The fractured ankle which resulted ran the workmen's compensation and medical expense up to $4,207.

2. A houseman was painting standing on an eight-foot scaffold. The telephone rang, he lost his balance, fell and broke his wrist. The medical and compensation costs were $1,250.

Use safety ladders and keep people who become dizzy while working on ladders from doing that kind of work. Spend time in getting ready to work and making a safe place in which to work. Never use boxes, chairs, and other makeshifts in place of ladders.

Many accidents fall into strange categories. For example, there was the case of the dignified assistant manager whose sense of propriety and chivalry was offended when the muscular swimming instructor passed a few remarks to the waitress. The assistant manager remonstrated with the swimming instructor. Result, a possible concussion for the assistant manager and a total cost of $3,313.

Accidents strike in many forms. Who would guess that a can of trash could cost $1,835.07. One can did which contained mango peels and seeds which caused a mango rash on the face, neck, and arms of the maid who was carrying it.

The housekeeper did nothing more than open a door when a heavy gale was blowing outside. She was jerked off her feet and thrown to the ground. Injuries to her back cost a total of $4,720.

A case which could happen to anyone using a power mower occurred to a gentleman who tried to clear the choked reel while the motor was still running. His hand and fingers were severely lacerated to the tune of $600.

According to a report of the New York State Department of Labor the two greatest accident sources in a restaurant are broken glass and burns. The report on the following page explains.

"The most frequent accident source in a restaurant is broken glass, which slashes like a razor if handled carelessly. The best preventative of such mishaps is constant alertness."

Waiters and waitresses are frequently cautioned against putting broken drinking glasses and crockery among soiled dishes. Dishwashers must often work so rapidly that they cannot examine each piece carefully before handling. Kitchen personnel must be particularly careful to guard against burns -- the second greatest hazard in a restaurant.

Other common accident hazards in restaurants lie in improper lifting resulting in hernias and strained backs, collisions in cramped quarters, and finger pinching.

In a study of 1,561 accidents to hotel employees conducted by the Liberty Mutual Insurance Company, percentages of accident by cause were listed for the various departments in a hotel. The percent-breakdown by departments is shown in the chart on the following page.

Since accidents to guests and to the public are also a reflection of personnel training and alertness, it might be well to examine a chart which lists the cause of accidents to the guests and the public. Such a chart is shown on page 214. It was drawn up by the Liberty Mutual Insurance Company from data on 393 guest and public accidents in 18 major hotels over a 15-month period. It will be noted that slips and falls and defective equipment account for about 60 per cent of all the accidents.

From the foregoing discussion and presentation of accident figures it is apparent that the hotel and restaurant industry is nonhazardous by reputation only. That the restaurant industry can be a hazardous field is borne out in the accident figures of the State of Pennsylvania. In one year that state had a total of 3,000 lost-time injuries and 14 fatalities in its eating and drinking places. These figures are about two and a half times that of the frequency in industry in general and more than four times those in the steel industry. The fact that restaurant accident insurance rates in the states of Illinois, Pennsylvania, and New York are 70 per cent to 80 per cent as great as that for machine shops is another evidence of the danger that can exist in the restaurant business.

ACCIDENT PREVENTION IN A CAFETERIA CHAIN

Illustrative of what can be done to reduce accidents is the experience of Morrison Cafeterias, a large company with headquarters in Mobile, Alabama. In 1954 the company shifted their insurance coverage to self-insurance, instituting an accident-prevention program. Managers and supervisors were brought to the home office in groups up to 10 for two to three days of instruction.

A course to check on safety practices is conducted by a safety committee within each cafeteria, in addition to routine analysis of monthly reports of accidents which have occurred. Accident reports are made in triplicate: one copy is kept in the cafeteria, one in the central office, and one with the state board or state commission.

Morrison routinely incorporates built-in safety to their stores as they are constructed or remodelled. Base areas under a dish machine are depressed, for example, so that water will not seep out onto the working area. Areas in front of ice machines are recessed and nonslip grids installed so that employees will not slip while removing ice from the machine. The emphasis on accident prevention and the fact that the company is a self-insurer has reduced their workmen compensation insurance cost by more than 50 per cent.

ACCIDENT CONTROL BY A TRADE GROUP

In 1955 the New York State Hotel Association formed a safety trade group. Their objective is accident prevention as well as the improvement of claims handling. Periodic inspections by a safety engineer and safety organizations within the member hotels and motels, together with contesting unjustifiable claims and malingering, have resulted in savings of about 25 per cent in costs. Where a hotel is found negligent and developing a bad accident trend, it has been asked to resign.

GAS HEATER SAFETY IN MOTOR HOTELS

Each year many lives are lost in motels from carbon monoxide poisoning, the result of improper venting of gas heating equipment. In one year Florida alone had 12 deaths caused by carbon monoxide poisoning. Some of these were undoubtedly suicides, but some were not. One motel operator who had two guests die because of his ignorance of gas appliances cried, "Please, please, don't let this awful thing happen to anyone else."

ACCIDENTS
TO EMPLOYEES

% BREAKDOWN BY DEPARTMENTS

	% OF ALL REPORTS	HOUSEKEEPING	ENGINEERING	FOOD	SERVICE	ALL-OTHERS
MISC. BUMPS & CUTS — Striking Objects, Nails & Splinters, Dropping Objects, Pinched Between Objects, Falling Material, Door Pinches & Bumps	28.0	35.6	13.8	33.0	12.4	5.2
SLIPS & FALLS	15.6	32.4	10.7	42.6	9.8	4.5
HANDLING MATERIAL STRAINS	12.9	28.4	16.4	40.2	11.0	4.0
BURNS FROM HOT SUBSTANCES	7.4	20.0	27.0	51.3	1.7	
FLYING OBJECTS IN EYES	7.1	23.4	27.0	27.0	18.0	4.6
GLASS & CHINA	7.0	25.5	4.5	68.2		1.8
HAND IMPLEMENTS	4.7	9.6	12.3	75.5	1.3	1.3
OPERATION OF ELEVATOR	3.8	3.4	6.8	6.8	83.0	
RAZOR BLADES	1.7	96.3			3.7	
MACHINERY	1.5	46.1	7.8	46.1		
ALL OTHERS	10.3	27.9	11.2	35.4	8.1	17.4
TOTAL ACCIDENTS REPORTED BY DEPT'S.		454	227	616	186	78
% OF TOTAL ACCIDENTS REPORTED		29.1%	14.5%	39.5%	11.9%	5%

ACCIDENTS

TO GUESTS AND THE PUBLIC

CAUSE		%	SLIPS & FALLS AGENCIES		
SLIPS & FALLS		47.4	PUBLIC ROOM FLOORS		29.6
DEFECTIVE EQUIPMENT		13.2	STAIRS & STEPS		25.3
FOOD Foreign Substances Illness Spilled		10.4 2.0 1.8	SIDEWALK ENTRANCES		10.7
			ROOMS		8.6
STRUCK By DOORS		4.1	DOORS—ENTRANCE		4.8
STRIKING STATIONARY OBJECTS		3.8	ELEVATORS		3.2
			ALL OTHER		17.8
ELEVATOR DOORS & GATES		3.5	AGENCIES OF DEFECTIVE EQUIPMENT		%
			GLASS & CHINA		34.6
FALLING OBJECTS		2.6	FURNITURE		21.2
			BURNS FROM ELECTRICAL APPLIANCES		15.4
			PLUMBING FIXTURES		9.6
MISCELLANEOUS		11.2	ALL OTHER		19.2

214

Space heaters that use gas as fuel in rooms for sleeping are safe only under specific conditions. If for some reason the burning gas is extinguished the gas may continue to flow and soon poisons the occupants of the room. To guard against this all gas heaters must have 100 per cent automatic safety cutoffs. When the flame is extinguished these cut-offs automatically cut off the supply of gas.

Most gas heating equipment requires about 54 cubic feet of air to burn and exhaust one cubic foot of low-pressure gas fuel. All sleeping rooms using gas heaters, therefore, must have a constant intake of fresh air. Two manufacturers of gas heaters make equipment that draws their air supply directly from outside the building and exhausts it directly outside. With their equipment no air is taken from the room and no exhaust air from the heater enters the room. These are the only kind that are recommended for motels by the writer. Stewart-Warner and the H. C. Little Company are the manufacturers. Other companies are planning similar equipment for the near future.

With equipment that does not draw fresh from the outside, permanent and unclosable openings for fresh air must be made in the room. The Florida Hotel and Restaurant Commission requires of all Florida motels that the opening be not less than ten square inches and that a minimum of one square inch of opening be made for each one thousand BTU (British Thermal Unit) output by the heaters.

Opening a window by nailing it open or putting permanent blocks under it is not satisfactory. Guests feeling a draft may unwittingly stuff a towel into the opening and endanger themselves.

Where the heater is not designed to exhaust the burned gases directly to the outside, it must be properly vented to discharge the exhaust fumes.

Although the "sealed-in" type of intake and exhaust heater costs more than the old type initially, the cost of venting the old type makes it almost as expensive as the sealed-in type.

Do not tamper with the lives of guests by using equipment that is anything less than entirely safe!

THE SUPERVISOR: KEY TO SAFETY SUCCESS

Safety is largely a matter of training; the supervisor usually is the trainer. He also is largely responsible for identifying and correcting safety hazards. Unless the kitchen manager sets up a regular cleaning schedule of the grease filters in the hood over the ranges and follows through, the filters are not likely to be cleaned and fires result. Unless the dish pantry supervisor is insistent that the floors in the pantry are kept dry, they will be wet and sooner or later someone will fall and injure himself.

The supervisor's interest, attitude and enthusiasm for safety can be transmitted to the employees. A lackadaisical attitude will be reflected just as quickly in employees' attitudes. The supervisor must recognize that safety is an integral part of supervision. Faulty performance which leads to accidents are of the same type as faulty performance that leads to other wastes and to inefficiency generally.

SAFETY COMMITTEES

A number of hotels and restaurants have organized safety committees. This is one area where labor-management committees can receive little criticism. Management has everything to gain and little to lose by arranging for the function of committees representing the various departments in which hazards are greatest. Rotating the membership serves to stimulate the feeling among employees that they are a real part of the organization. It also serves to introduce new ideas and maintain enthusiasm for the safety program. The safety committee may also include fire protection in its program. One large hotel has a safety supervisor who investigates all accidents, keeps accident records, and makes recommendations.

A prominent New York City restaurant has a program in which two safety inspections are made weekly by members of the restaurant staff. The inspection committee sees to it that all belts, pulleys and other moving machinery parts are covered or sheathed. In addition to the staff biweekly inspections, a store mechanic checks freight elevators daily to make certain they are in proper working order. Kitchen and pantry floors are kept free from litter to minimize the danger of falls.

A thorough safety program which functions through a safety committee pays dividends in lower compensation insurance costs and accident figures. In 1947 the Hotel Roosevelt, a 1,000-room hotel in New York City, was able, by instituting a safety committee and appointing departmental safety inspectors, to keep its total number of lost-time accidents to 4. The employees having worked 2,204,688 man hours, the accident frequency rate of 1.81 is striking evidence of the effectiveness of the safety program.

ARE ACCIDENTS ACCIDENTAL?

In raising the question are accidents accidental, we consider the psychology of the accident as well as the physical situation in which an accident may occur. We are immediately faced with a paradox in two apparently contradictory statements often expressed by the same person. The firm conviction that "accidents will happen" is often countered by the equally strong belief that "it can't happen to me." There is also the imputation that it is "manly" to take risks and that somehow it reflects on the person's virility or "ability to take it" to introduce safety measures and devices. The problem of accidents is complex and tied up with many facets of the personality.

By chance alone most of us are likely to have an accident sometime in our lives. Such accidents may be entirely unavoidable. Studies of taxicab drivers, streetcar motormen and other industrial employees seem to show, however, that many accidents are not "accidental." In one study of streetcar motormen a psychologist selected from the group 54 "poor" motormen and 54 "good" motormen. Both groups had the same length of service. The 54 "good" drivers had a total of 57 accidents, while the 54 "bad" drivers had 784 accidents. In other words certain persons have so many more accidents than would be expected by chance alone that it appears the person himself has something to do with the accident. In some studies of industrial concerns it has been found that twenty per cent of the personnel consistently have a higher total of accidents than the other eighty per cent. Such individuals are called accident prone. By use of certain tests many of these individuals can be identified and placed in jobs in which hazards are at a minimum. Oftentimes the accident-prone person has a physical disability.

One of the largest causes of accidents is defective vision. Measured by the standard eye charts such as the Snellen or The American Medical Association Chart, many employees test 20-20 vision. However, when tested by more adequate instruments an individual's vision may be found to be insufficient for certain jobs. One such instrument for measuring total vision is the orthorater, an instrument developed by psychologists from Purdue University working with Bausch and Lomb Optical Company. Besides measuring visual acuity at various distances, the device measures the ability to estimate distance, whether or not the eyes see in parallel planes, and whether or not each eye does its proportionate share of work in seeing. Some clerical work requires good vision at close distances and other visual requirements not measured by the standard eye charts. By research, the visual requirements of every job in the house can be established. It can be predicted within a certain range of error whether or not a person will have an accident on a particular job if his total vision is known. The orthorater is probably too expensive for a single hotel or restaurant to purchase. Associations of employers or chain organizations, however, could well afford such equipment. Oftentimes employees who appear to have excellent vision may be subject to severe headaches and other strains because of poor vision. In one large company in which standard eye measurements were made of all applicants it was found by use of the orthorater that ten per cent of its present employees were in need of ocular attention. Of course it is to the company's advantage to ascertain and correct visual deficiencies.

Other physical disabilities predispose the employee to an undue number of accidents. Partial paralysis, arthritis, defects of the equilibrium sense, or poor muscle coordination may set the stage for accidents. Such disabilities do not disqualify the individual from employment, but should be considered in placing him. Many jobs in the hotel and restaurant are relatively nonhazardous and may be filled by accident-prone employees.

The hotel and restaurant, in addition to having accident problems unique to their industry, have many of the problems of the typical industrial plant. The engineering department personnel are exposed to boiler accidents, repair shop personnel to the hazards of various types of power-driven tools. With the refrigerating system there is the possibility of escape of the refrigerant. Electrical, upholstery, and carpentry shops present fire hazards and the possibility of muscular strains, cuts, and bruises. The laundry department and its machinery, the engineering department, the service department, the steward's department, housekeeping, and the other departments all present special problems.

RESEARCH IN ACCIDENT PREVENTION

As in many other personnel functions, for best results it is necessary to bolster our reasoning with facts and figures. Keeping adequate records of accidents can help in accident control. So that they can be compared, accident rates usually are kept according to a formula. Two rates, the frequency rate and the severity rate, are commonly recorded. The frequency rate equals the number of accidents which result in lost working time per million man hours worked. The severity rate is defined as the number of days lost per thousand man hours.

$$\text{F.R.} = \frac{\text{Lost-time accidents}}{\text{man hours} \div 1,000,000} \qquad \text{S.R.} = \frac{\text{Days lost}}{\text{man hours} \div 1,000}$$

Study of the cause of the accident may suggest ways of eliminating further mishaps.   A standard record of an accident might include the items shown in the following form.

HOTEL HAMILTON

Accident Report Form

Name of injured person _____

Social Security number _____

Any witnesses? _____ If so, list names and addresses _____

_____

_____

Describe nature and severity of accident _____

_____

_____

What type of work was the employee performing at the time of the accident? ____

_____

Was there some observable physical or mechanical cause? _____

_____

If so, name such cause _____

Statement by the injured _____

_____

_____

Statement from the Superior-Department head _____

_____

_____

Was something done to prevent a recurrence of the accident? _____

If so, what? _____ Reported by _____

The National Safety Council publishes an "Accident Analysis Chart" which can be obtained at nominal cost.   The chart appears on the following page.

Since every hotel and restaurant has a more or less unique set of conditions as regards fire protection and accident prevention, the programs developed will vary from one house to another.   Obviously plans and programs must be instituted and changed to meet changing conditions.   However, aids developed by such organizations as the National Safety Council are very worthwhile and will fit any fire protection and accident prevention program.

TABULATION

ACCIDENT ANALYSIS CHART
(list all injuries)

Period _____ to _____

1. Temporary total ____   5. Man hours worked ____
2. Permanent partial ____   6. Freq. rate --
3. Deaths and perm.   (line 4 × 1,000,000
   total ____   Line 5)
4. Total (1, 2 & 3) ____   7. First-aid treatments ___

| Acc. No. | Date of Acc. | Name of Injured | Occ. or Dept. | INJURY | | | Desc. of Acc. (Give exact details) | Corrective Action Taken |
				Nature & Part of	Class (1, 2, 3, 7)	Days Lost		

Fire protection and accident prevention cannot be left to chance. A manager who depends upon luck to prevent fires and safeguard his employees from accidents is guilty of criminal omission. Many disabilities and facilities have been traced directly to management's negligence. Active participation in local and national fire and safety programs can save management time and money and can prevent the possibility of management's being faced with the charge, "You are responsible for this death!"

Following are 30 safety tips which are reminders of value to any hotel or restaurant employee. Use them as points of discussion in safety meetings.

SAFETY TIPS

1. When lifting, keep the back straight and lift with the legs.

2. Don't try to carry too many bags at one time.

3. When carrying any heavy load call for help.

4. Don't stand on the edge of the tub when putting up shower curtains. It's too easy to slip and fall.

5. Never pick up razor blades with your hands. Use a dust pan or a piece of cardboard and wipe the blade on to the container with a dust cloth or rag.

6. Don't pick up broken glass with your hands. Use a damp cloth.

7. Never reach into a waste basket with your hands to empty it. Pick up the basket and pour the trash into the receptacle.

8. When washing glasses inspect them for nicks so that you do not cut your hands. Nicked glasses are harboring spots for bacteria.

9. When turning a mattress, lift it by the side straps, set it on its side, then lower into place.

10. Keep loose articles off the floors where they can be tripped on.

11. Place electrical cords behind the furniture and away from where the people are walking and can trip over them.

12. When opening doors use the doorknobs; grasping the door itself can mean bruised fingers.

13. Don't pull knives toward the body. When not in use store them in racks where they cannot hurt you.

14. If a glass is broken while it is being washed, drain the sink and pick up the pieces with a rag.

15. Don't dry the inside of a glass by forcing a towel inside. The glass may break in your hands.

16. Don't use glasses as an ice scoop. Use a metal scoop which cannot break in your hands.

17. In using step ladders, check them for any defective parts. Don't overreach while on a ladder. Taking a little time may save a lot of time.

18. Note all defects in guest rooms and correct them at once.

19. Before lighting an oven, check for evidence of leaking gas.

20. Stand to one side when lighting an oven and use a taper rather than a match.

21. Use pads for handling hot pots, pans, and other utensils.

22. Wear protective gloves when using steel wool or strong cleaning compounds.

23. Use knee pads for scrubbing bathroom floors or similar areas.

24. Do not crowd elevators above their rated capacities.

25. Permit only authorized personnel to operate elevators.

26. Close elevator car gates at each landing.

27. Do not overload bus trays.

28. Use glass racks for transporting or storing glassware.

29. Place warning tags on all machinery undergoing repairs.

30. Never work on moving machinery.

Whenever you get any kind of cut apply first aid immediately. Avoid infection. Safety is largely a matter of attitude. Think, be careful, be safe.

Wage and Salary Administration

The hotel and restaurant business in common with most service industries experiences a constant press for higher wages and shorter hours; wages are increasing both in amount and as a percentage of the gross income of the business. In hotels, labor cost constitutes about 38 per cent of the gross income; in motels labor costs are considerably less, ranging from about 12 per cent in the smaller operations where part of the work is done by the owner-operator to around 22 per cent in the larger motels that have food services and bars.

In commercial restaurants labor cost varies widely depending upon the menu offered, the efficiency, and amount of sales. In a restaurant serving mostly steaks the labor costs may run as low as 12 per cent of the gross income, while in a luxury restaurant with all of its service, labor cost may go as high as 40 per cent of the gross income. A study conducted in 1963 by the Ahrens Publishing Company showed a wide range of productivity per employee and consequently of labor costs within the restaurant business.

LABOR COSTS IN COMMERCIAL RESTAURANTS

Labor Costs

Under 15%	2.4%
15-19	6.5%
20-24	24.3%
25-29	31.0%
30-34	24.3%
35-39	7.9%
40-44	2.7%
45 and over	0.9%
	100.0%

The chart shows that labor cost varies from below 15 per cent of gross sales to over 45 per cent. The most common labor cost found varied from between 25 per cent and 29 per cent of sales.

The U. S. Census of Business of 1958 compared labor costs in hotels and motels with other selected service industries and produced the chart shown on the following page.

WAGES IN THE INDUSTRY

Generally speaking, wages of hotel and restaurant employees are near the bottom of the wage scale. In 1961, hourly wages of hotel and motel employees averaged $1.15, considerably lower than those found in clothing manufacturing and packing house businesses. The wages for hotels found by the U. S. Bureau of Census do not take into consideration tips and meals which are part of the remuneration for many hotel and restaurant employees.

Around the country there are marked differences in wages paid. For example, state minimum wage laws for restaurant employees call for $1.75 per hour in Alaska, and $1.25 in Washington, D. C., Connecticut, and Massachusetts. Ten other states have a $1.00 an hour rate covering restaurant employees.

About 708,000 restaurant employees come under minimum wage laws or orders, says the U. S. Department of Labor. A remaining 884,000 employees (or 56 per cent) have no minimum wage protection.

HOTELS AND MOTELS: LABOR COST RATIO
IN HOTELS AND MOTELS COMPARED WITH RATIOS
IN OTHER SELECTED SERVICE INDUSTRIES, UNITED STATES, 1958

Industry	: Labor cost ratio : (payroll as a per : cent of receipts)
Hotels	35
Motels	20
Laundry and cleaning services	46
Beauty and barber shops	44
Photo studios, commercial photography	31
Shoe repair, shoe shine, hat cleaning	30
Duplicating, mailing lists, stenographic services	41
Blueprinting, photocopying	32
Services to dwellings	55

Source: U. S. Census of Business, Selected Services, 1958.

In the south, outside of the cities, wages in restaurants are exceedingly low. A U. S. Department of Labor study shows that 75 per cent of the restaurant employees in the south are paid less than $1.00 an hour. Compare this with wages in the west where only 3.3 per cent of the employees received less than the minimum wage in 1961.

It behooves an employee to pick his geographical area for a hotel job. A maid who works in Baltimore, for example, gets less than 60 cents an hour, whereas if she did the same job in San Francisco she would receive close to $1.60 an hour. A waiter in Baltimore receives something less than 30 cents an hour paid by the employer, while the same waiter in San Francisco gets $1.31 from his employer per hour.

In New Orleans, for example, about 79 per cent of the hotel employees were paid less than $1.00 an hour in 1961.

In 1961 the Department of Labor found that about 40 per cent of nonsupervisory hotel employees were covered by a state minimum wage regulations; the others were not.

THE EFFECT OF THE MINIMUM WAGE

The absence of minimum wage regulations inevitably means low wages for hotel and restaurant employees in large sections of the country, especially for Negroes, Puerto Rican, and Mexican employees. The buying public gets a little lower food check, a hotel room for a little less money in these areas. Low wages usually mean less sharp management, less intelligent planning, the use of obsolescent equipment, less system and, in the last analysis, less attractive service for the public. With low wages there is not the push to replace people with equipment to increase efficiency, to get the maximum productivity per employee.

Where minimum wages are in effect and where union negotiation has forced up wages, the extra cost is passed on to the customer.

On the West Coast labor costs in restaurants exceed 36 per cent of gross sales. The customer necessarily receives less for his money. There are no studies to show that there are any fewer people eating out as a result.

Why should the housing and food service industry subsidize the public any more than any other industry. The automobile industry, the coal industry, the shoe industry long ago gave up this notion.

When a minimum wage is introduced into an area all operators are forced to increase their wages together and, consequently, the prices they charge their customers. There is an adjustment in what can be given to a customer and a larger share of the income goes to the employee. In an industry where so many of the employees are less advantaged, it would seem well to welcome minimum wage legislation. As a result the entire industry will gain status because its employees can live in a decent American style.

It is true that a minimum wage forces up the wages of the other employees since a differential between wages is usually maintained. Wages tend to move up together, with differentials remaining about the same. Of course, if wages are forced up too high, the public will change to other forms of entertainment and service, at least to some extent.

DIMINISHING WORK WEEK

The standard work week in large cities in hotels varies from 37 1/2 hours to 48 hours. Most employees in such hotels work a 40-hour week consisting of five 8-hour days. In low-wage areas hotel workers tend to work a 6-day week of 44 to 48 hours a week, offsetting to some degree the lower hourly wage rate. Cities on the Pacific Coast and in the Great Lakes area are high-wage areas by national standards. The opposite is true of Southeast and so-called border states which include Baltimore. It can be expected that the union will press for a lower hourly work week, demanding that time worked in excess of the standard work week be paid at time-and-a-half.

The number of paid holidays has increased since 1954. Most union contracts provide that work on holidays be paid at either 1 1/2 times or 2 times the regular rate of pay. Most contracts specify that to qualify for holiday pay the employee must work the last work day before and the first work day after the holiday. This prevents the employee from converting the holiday into a "short vacation." The New York City contract, for example, states that seven holidays will be paid, and that for holidays worked the employee receives double-time pay.

As the economy continues to improve and as automation reaches the hotel and restaurant business, shorter hours, more paid holidays and higher wages can be expected. The industry need not continue to carry its albatross of long hours and low wages.

WHAT COMPRISES A FAIR WAGE OR SALARY?

The fairness of the wage or salary and the response of the person receiving it is a judgement made by the person based on his attitudes, beliefs, level of aspiration, and the comparative wage or salary being received by those working with him in the hotel or restaurant or on a level commensurate with his in the industry. Of two people with similar abilities, skills and experience, one may consider $2.00 an hour a munificent wage, the other view it as contemptible. The expectations of the individual, his level of ambition, his financial obligations, and his social background are reflected in his attitudes towards the wage or salary. Such attitudes can change rapidly.

About the only constant in the reaction to a particular wage or salary is the emphasis placed by most people on what is being received by others considered to be on the same level. A cook in one restaurant may receive $100 a week and consider himself well paid, since he is the highest paid individual in the kitchen. Across the street another cook may be receiving $200 a week and be dissatisfied because the person he considers to be his equal or less is receiving a higher wage.

A manager of a hotel or restaurant may be quite happy with his present salary until he attends a convention and learns that a former classmate who is doing about the same work is receiving more. Many persons are quite content with a modest salary if they are given stock options or included under a plan by which they will share in the profits or growth in equity of the hotel or restaurant. Usually the more ambitious and energetic, freewheeling type of individual is more eager for a compensation plan under which he may receive a relatively small salary but can share in the prosperity of the enterprise if it goes well.

Some of the newer, more vigorous and expanding hotel and restaurant chains are offering their executives a variety of compensation other than straight salary. Stock options have considerable incentive value for some individuals. Stock options -- rights or options to purchase treasury stock, stock held by the company, at a specified price -- are ordinarily made available only to executive-level personnel. The price is usually stated close to the current market value. For example, if the stock of a company is selling on the open market at $6.00 a share, top-level executives may be offered the option to purchase any number of shares at $6.00 a share any time within a number of years, perhaps ten years. If the company prospers, the value of the stock rises; the executive exercises the option, buys the stock and can either hold it or sell it, pocketing the capital gains which he makes in the transaction.

He must hold such stock for a period of not less than six months from the time he purchases it unless he wishes to return any profits realized to the company. After six months his capital gains are taxable at a maximum of 25 per cent, which is another financial advantage for the executive. Stock options can be immensely profitable and stimulating to executives since the value of the stock of some hotel and restaurant chains has increased tenfold within a period of 10 years. Where the company does not prosper, of course, the stock option has less incentive value, but there is always the hope in the holder's mind that it will prosper, and he realizes that his efforts will, at least in part, benefit not only the company but himself.

Other forms of compensation may have greater appeal to the employee than straight wage or salary, and rightly so. For example, a company-provided automobile may be the equivalent of $500 or more in salary. The compensation is not paid in the form of money, hence the employee pays no tax on it. In other words, he receives the value but is not taxed in the process.

Deferred compensation has special appeals for some employees. Compensation is deferred while the employee is in the higher-tax brackets during his prime of life, and is paid to the employee when he is in a lower bracket. The employee again benefits taxwise. If he is concerned about his future he receives a sense of security which may be important to his work.

Many hotel and restaurant companies are increasing to sizeable amounts the life insurance they make available to company employees. The company pays the premiums -- again the values of insurance protection are given to the employee without the cost passing through his hands and his being taxed in the process. Life insurance can increase the individual's and his family's sense of security, and from the viewpoint of the company help to tie him to the company.

A number of other insurance benefits are currently being offered by some hotel and restaurant companies covering all travel, airplane and automobile, accident insurance, hospitalization, surgical, medical and theft. Some organizations are using what is known as "key man" insurance, which makes the company the beneficiary of the insurance. The company in turn makes a part or all of it available to the executive's estate.

A number of fringe benefits continue to grow: paid memberships in private clubs, trade associations, professional organizations, health examinations, entertainment expense allowances, limited or unlimited bar expenses, housing and maintenance, travel expenses, family vacations and the like. One hotel chain allows its executives $150 a month for entertainment. Some executives are on unlimited expense accounts as long as the expenditures are deemed reasonable by the board of directors.

Most companies should seriously consider executive incentive plans other than those in the form of straight salary increases. Since the hotel and restaurant business is such a dynamic changing business, it should probably avoid wage and salary classification systems of the bureaucratic type in which all employees are granted annual increments.

TO PUBLISH WAGE OR SALARY SCHEDULES?

Most hotel and restaurant owners and top management are not favorable to publishing executive salary schedules, feeling that supervisory and management people are so competitive that, if such rates were published, only those persons receiving the top salaries would be satisfied. There is something to be said for this viewpoint; however, the really ambitious person usually manages to find out, in a general way, the salaries being paid within an organization, published or not.

Establishment of a published wage schedule for hourly employees is usually desirable because it permits the employee to see where he falls on the schedule and what increases are available to him within his bracket. In publishing a wage schedule, the rates paid are reviewed by top management and differentials between jobs made more reasonable than they probably would be if the rates were not published. The wage schedule for hourly employees provides tangible reasons for staying on the job to take advantage of the periodic increments usually a part of the schedule. In many hotels and restaurants the large turnover of employees takes place during the first few days or few months of employment. Wage increases under an established plan encourage stability on the job. The schedule illustrated on the following page is merely an example showing how employees can be placed in various grades, in this case from I through VII, and how within each grade there are five increments. The increments need not be made on the basis of time of employment alone but can be keyed into merit ratings, only those employees receiving a certain rating being granted the increment. In the schedule illustrated the employee receives an increment after three months on the job. The next two increments are given at six month intervals. From then on increments are paid at the end of each year, and the employee reaches the maximum in grade at the end of three years and three months. The wage schedule should be part of the materials provided the employee on his first day on the job. It helps to create the idea of a stable organization and gives him something to look forward to in the future. Because the various grades have been scheduled, the employee knows that he must become more skilled and take on more responsibility, and can prepare himself accordingly.

Too many jobs in the hotel and restaurant business are dead end; the employee starts within a grade and never has an opportunity to change grades. For some employees this is satisfactory; for most, at least some inducement for self-improvement should be part of the personnel program.

THE EUPHORIA CLUB

Rate Schedule

Grade		Minimum	3 Mo.	6 Mo.	6 Mo.	12 Mo.	12 Mo.
I	Bus Boys Dishwashers Pot Washers Night Cleaners Bar Porters	$210	$225	$240	$255	$270	$285
II	Cook's Helper Baker Helper Pantry Helper Locker Room Attendant (Ladies) Club House Maint.	225	240	255	270	285	300
III	Salad Girl Sandwich Man PBX Operator Locker Room Attendant (Men's)	245	260	275	290	310	330
IV	Accounting Clerk Receiving Clerk Kitchen Steward Waitresses	275	290	305	325	350	370
V	Bartenders Host-Hostess Fry Cook Secretary	320	340	360	380	405	430
VI	Maître d' Broiler Cook Butcher & Garde Mgr. Second Cook -- Sauce Second Cook -- Dinner Bookkeeper	370	390	415	440	470	495
VII	Sous Chef Pastry Chef	425	450	475	505	540	575

JOB EVALUATION

A few hotel and restaurant managements have attempted to evaluate jobs in terms of the contribution made by each to the hotel or restaurant. This is known as job evaluation. In such studies the jobs under consideration are rated according to factors chosen so that they are common to all of the jobs under study. Factors such as education, experience, initiative, physical and mental effort are selected and each job is assigned a weight or number of points for each factor.

Job evaluation is difficult to perform in the hotel or restaurant business because of the widespread practice of tipping. It is difficult to reflect tips in a logical system such as job evaluation. The attractive, active waitress can make as much as $40.00 an evening in tips, while the cook who has considerable skill and experience and works under comparatively unfavorable conditions may be paid much less.

Job evaluation makes no attempt to arrive at absolute values; it is concerned only with comparing the relative value of jobs within an establishment. To do otherwise is impossible since payment for jobs is not based upon logic but upon union pressures, tradition, the labor market at the moment, geographical differences, race and other factors. A railroad engineer in the United States may be paid $250 a week -- for the same work in Britain an engineer receives less than $60.00 a week. A registered nurse who must have completed college may receive less than the elevator operator who takes her to her place of work.

It is not likely that job evaluation will be performed widely in the hotel and restaurant field within the next few years.

TENURE OF EMPLOYMENT

Tenure plans are rare in the hotel and restaurant business. Most personnel, including managers, can be dismissed at the discretion of the top management or owner. Some managers who have developed a reputation for promotion or operations can demand a one- to three-year contract and get it. Resort managers should always request a letter stating the terms of the contract including its length. Club managers also are well advised to seek employment contracts, preferably up to three years in length. These contracts can be terminated by mutual agreement, sometimes involving the payment of part or all of the compensation specified in the contract through its duration.

THE EFFECT OF UNIONIZATION ON WAGES

Although some observers see no relationship between collective bargaining in the hotel and restaurant field and the amount of wages paid, it seems apparent that when employees are represented by unions the union officials involved will press for higher wages and other benefits for their members. Exceptions do occur when dishonest union officials arrange "sweetheart contracts" by which they agree to forego pressing for wage increases or unionization in return for money.

Ordinarily where unions are strong, wages are higher. In Seattle, a strong union city, dishwashers receive about $1.92 an hour. In New Orleans, a city where unions are not well entrenched, dishwashers get about 53 cents an hour. Wage rates for hotel and restaurant workers in the South are at least 35 per cent lower than in other sections of the country. Miami is the only city in the South which has been unionized to any extent by the Hotel and Restaurant Employees' Union and wages are higher there than in other southern communities.

The Bureau of Labor Statistics estimates that about 60 per cent of the hotel employees of this country are organized. Probably not more than 30 per cent of the commercial restaurant employees are organized, and most of the organization is among employees in the large cities. The Hotel and Restaurant Employees' and Bartenders' International Union and the Building Service Employees' International Union, both AFL-CIO, are the major unions in the industry. In Puerto Rico the Teamsters' Union has gained a foothold, and no doubt the officials of this union are considering similar moves within the continent.

For a number of years the hotel and restaurant industries were exempted from coverage by the National Labor Relations Act, and there were periods of time when the Hotel and Restaurant Employees' Union did not wish to be covered by it. Today the union favors such inclusion and apparently so does the Department of Labor. The National Labor Relations Act relates to employees engaged in interstate commerce, and the definition of what is interstate commerce varies with the interest of the person defining it. In 1963 the National Labor Relations Board took jurisdiction of a labor dispute involving a hotel employer whose annual gross revenue was in excess of $500,000. In this case 84 per cent of the hotel guests were transients. The hotel purchased liquor supplies in excess of $50,000 annually from outside the state. Jurisdiction in similar disputes between employees and restaurant operators and chain operators of motels and hotels has been taken by the National Labor Relations Board in the last few years.

Where the Board refuses jurisdiction, the dispute goes to the appropriate state agency of the state in which the dispute occurs. Usually the state agencies are more favorable than the Board to the employers.

Statistical Tools Useful in Personnel Management

As indicated throughout this book, research is a prime responsibility of the personnel administrator. Statistics provide a simple language for the development of research. Through statistics it is possible (1) to summarize and interpret vital personnel information conveniently; (2) to make possible comparisons from one company or area to others on such important variables as labor turnover, absenteeism, productivity, and morale; (3) to promote the continued evaluation of policies and practices; and (4) to enhance the general understanding of management functions.

The appendix provides a review of the important statistical concepts with which personnel administrators need to become familiarized.

PERSONNEL STATISTICS

It is not intended in this section to provide information concerning the formulae or computation of statistics. These can be found with "cook book" application in any basic text on statistics. Rather, the intent is to provide some understanding of the basic concepts of statistics used in personnel management functions in order to guide the personnel worker to the most appropriate use of specific statistical techniques.

GRAPHIC PRESENTATION

A valuable statistical tool is the representation of data through graphs and charts. A fundamental principle to remember is that "a picture may be worth ten thousand words" if it is done properly. Personnel analysts constantly are called on to "sell" ideas and facts to management, but ideas and facts that are not understood are not of much value, regardless of their potential importance.

A wide assortment of graphic possibilities are available to the person interested in utilizing them. Examples can be found daily in popular newspapers and magazines of such techniques as bar graphs, pie graphs, line graphs, belt graphs, pictographs, map graphs, histograms, and frequency polygons. The chart below shows just one example of how very complex technical data can be depicted with clarity by means of a simple graphic presentation.

AN EVALUATION OF THE EFFECTIVENESS OF THE FOOD SERVICE TEST BATTERY AS A SELECTION TOOL WITH RESTAURANT X

Of Each 10 Applicants Whose Restaurant Test Battery Total Score Is in the	Will Not Be Accepted by Restaurant	Will Be Accepted and Will Be Rated by His Supervisors after Three Months as			
		A Failure	Just Acceptable	Satisfactory	Outstanding
Highest Quarter ☺☺☺☺☺☺☺☺☺☺		☺	☺☺	☺☺☺☺☺☺	☺☺☺
Second Quarter ☺☺☺☺☺☺☺☺☺☺	☺☺	☺	☺☺	☺☺☺☺☺☺	☺
Third Quarter ☺☺☺☺☺☺☺☺☺☺	☺☺☺	☺☺	☺☺☺	☺☺☺	
Lowest Quarter ☺☺☺☺☺☺☺☺☺☺	☺☺☺☺☺☺☺	☺☺	☺☺	☺	

AVERAGES

The Mean (M): The mean is the most widely used average because it lends itself easily to statistical formulation. It is computed easily by adding the variable -- such as ages, test scores, or hours worked by individuals -- and dividing the sum by the total number of cases. A disadvantage occurs when using the mean with a small number of cases, because a few extreme scores may create a serious distortion.

The Median (Md): The median is the middle person or score in a distribution of persons or scores. In a group of five waitresses standing in the order of their height, the third waitress from either end represents the median of the group. Medians are used as a means of obtaining a quick estimate or when a few extremes might distort the mean.

The Mode (Mo): The mode represents the value that appears most frequently in an array of figures. For example, 100 waitresses may vary in height from five feet to five feet nine inches, but the most common height or mode might be five feet three inches.

Index Numbers: Much of the information used in business -- for example, cost of living, wage rates, production totals -- is expressed in terms of base indexes. The base is selected to express what a representative or normal rate may be and then all further figures are expressed in terms of that base. Research, for example, may establish a base rate for the daily hourly working average of waitresses at seven hours per day during a one-month period. If a waitress averaged eight hours per day during the next month, her relative index of work would be 114.7 or 8/7; if she averaged only six hours per day, her relative index would be 85.9 or 6/7.

MEASURES OF VARIABILITY

It is possible for two groups of workers to have similar (even identical) average values and yet to be quite different. The individual values of one group may be spread much more widely than the values in another group, but there is no way to explain this variability without the proper statistics to tell us how scattered or spread values may be. The following measures are used in personnel to show variability within a group of persons or scores.

Range: The range simply represents the difference between the highest and lowest value in a group. If age were the variable, the range would show the oldest and the youngest person.

Centile (or percentile): This is the value on a scale below which are given any percentage of the cases in a group. For example, the 75th percentile is the point below which are 75 per cent of the cases and the 19th percentile is the point below which are 19 per cent of the cases.

The Standard Deviation: The standard deviation is a widely used statistic which is used to describe the variability of groups for which the means have been determined. Arithmetically, it is equal to the square root of the mean of the squared deviations from the group mean.

One vital function of the standard deviation is in making interpretations from the normal curve. In a normally distributed group, 34.13 per cent of the area lies between the mean and a point that is one standard deviation away from it. One standard deviation above the mean combined with one standard deviation below the mean accounts for about two-thirds of the area, or 68.26 per cent. Thus when we know that the hours Mary worked last month were more than one standard deviation above the mean number of hours worked by all of the other girls, that Mary worked longer hours than did two-thirds of the other girls. (Actually, the comparison can be ascertained even more precisely, as is described in the section following which deals with the normal curve.)

CORRELATION

The most important statistic available to the personnel analyst is the correlation coefficient. There are several types of correlation coefficients and there are special conditions which justify the use of one instead of another. Basically, the correlation simply shows us the degree of relationship between two variables or measures. Thus, if we can ascertain a relationship between education, age, school grades, or a placement test on the one hand with some measure of a person's work performance on the other hand, we may have some information that is vital to us in our future selection.

Another use of the correlation coefficient is as a basis for prediction. For example, we may find that a correlation exists between job success as a cook and scores made in a training course. We then can predict a given individual's chances for success on the job by virtue of his score in the training course.

The most frequent use of a correlation coefficient is to determine statistically whether a relationship or an observation that we discover is a genuinely significant relationship or is due merely to chance. The significance of the correlation coefficient in this latter sense is related to the theoretical normal curve and the laws of probability.

THE NORMAL PROBABILITY CURVE*

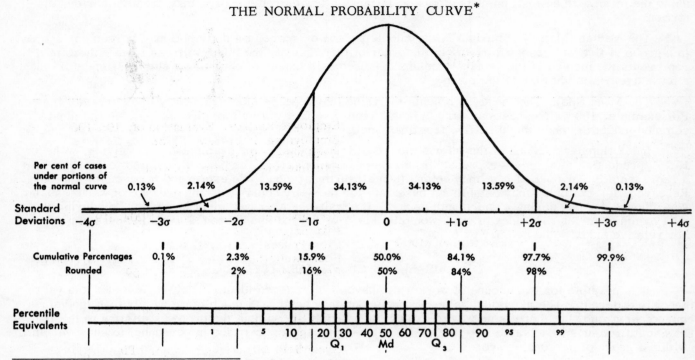

*Reprinted from the Psychological Corporation's Test Service Bulletin No. 48, January, 1955.

The normal curve is a theoretical distribution which follows the laws of chance and represents the approximate range and difference of human variability. Personnel analysts find it useful in three main ways:

1. If it is discovered that large numbers of personnel data approximate a normal distribution, it can be assumed that the personnel data was representative;

2. The curve -- as a distribution of probability -- is used to determine the reliability and significance of many measures of personnel performance. It is thus possible to determine if such measures are the result of certain consistent factors or if they were due merely to chance factors;

3. By following standard laws, the curve is used in a scaling sense in order to compare different units in terms of a standard scale.

Index

229